Black New Jersey

Black New Jersey

~

1664 to the Present Day

G RAHAM R USSELL G AO H ODGES

RUTGERS UNIVERSITY PRESS
NEW BRUNSWICK, CAMDEN, AND NEWARK,
NEW JERSEY, AND LONDON

Library of Congress Cataloging-in-Publication Data

Names: Hodges, Graham Russell, 1946– author.
Title: Black New Jersey : 1664 to the present day / Graham Hodges.
Description: New Brunswick : Rutgers University Press, 2018. | Includes
    bibliographical references and index.
Identifiers: LCCN 2017060310| ISBN 9780813595184 (cloth : alk. paper) |
    ISBN 9780813595177 (pbk. : alk. paper)
Subjects: LCSH: African Americans—New Jersey—History. | New Jersey—Race
    relations—History.
Classification: LCC E185.93.N54 H64 2018 | DDC 305.896/0730749—dc23
LC record available at https://lccn.loc.gov/2017060310

A British Cataloging-in-Publication record for this book is available from the British
Library.

♾ The paper used in this publication meets the requirements of the American National
Standard for Information Sciences—Permanence of Paper for Printed Library Materials,
ANSI Z39.48-1992.

www.rutgersuniversitypress.org

Manufactured in the United States of America

*Dedicated to the memory and achievements
of black New Jersey historians*

Marion Thompson Wright (1905–1962)

Giles R. Wright Jr. (1935–2009)

Clement Alexander Price (1945–2014)

Lawrence Greene (1946–)

Contents

Illustrations

Black New Jersey

Introduction

Black New Jersey covers the complex history of people of African descent in New Jersey, a state that today is among the most diverse, urbanized, and densely populated in the Union. New Jersey is also now one of the five most racially segregated states in America. Accordingly, *Black New Jersey* says much about African American aspirations for freedom and equality and about our nation's legacies of slavery and racism. A slave society from its inception, New Jersey was the last state in the north to initiate gradual emancipation in 1804. Its racial politics have been historically very conservative. Some of its white residents were the most intransigent defenders of slavery and segregation; others were among the sharpest critics. Today, New Jersey is home to some of the most talented and wealthiest African Americans in the United States and boasts a strong, resilient black middle class. Yet many of its black citizens are mired in poverty and burdened by legal problems exacerbated by poor health, housing, and education. Those paradoxes of slavery and freedom run throughout this book. Race may be the predominant means used to interpret New Jersey black society, but increasingly class is also important.

Blacks have been important in New Jersey's population since its origins in the 1660s. People of African descent constituted 40 percent of Bergen County's population in the colonial period. Today New Jersey is the eleventh most populous state in the Union. African Americans make up the third largest group in the state behind whites and Hispanics. The 2010 U.S.

census enumerated 8,791,894 people in New Jersey of which 13.7 percent or about 1.205 million were of African descent, giving the state the fifth largest black population in the nation. New Jersey's location between two major American metropolises make African Americans in the state part of an even more impressive total. Combined with the populations of the Standard Metropolitan Statistical Areas of New York and Philadelphia, two cities with enormous historical and contemporary impact on New Jersey, there are now nearly 30 million people or slightly less than 10 percent of the total population of the United States. People of African descent account for over 4.5 million of this populace, about 10 percent of the national total, all within a straight line distance of less than one hundred miles. Newark is at the exact center of the 600-mile urban area that stretches from Maine to Virginia.[1]

Those numbers are one indication of what *Black New Jersey* can tell us about our nation's history, present, and future. If, as one book has put it, we can search for the meaning of America on the New Jersey Turnpike, the presence in the state of African Americans and their interactions with whites and other ethnicities allow us to grapple with national questions on a state and regional scale. As Marion Thompson Wright, one the state's greatest historians put it, "New Jersey as a state has always reflected the experiences of a nation . . . . Being a pivotal state, New Jersey has had the unique advantage of serving as a proving ground for battles involving opposing ideologies in human relations."[2]

The author and journalist Isabel Wilkerson recently demanded that the North accept its legacy of slavery and racism; New Jersey is a good place to begin that understanding.[3] The themes I address in *Black New Jersey* are not unique to the state and are highly representative of national issues. Among the topics addressed in this book are slavery and its lineages; freedom and racism; black community and acculturation with other ethnicities and nationalities; gender and class; rural, urban, and suburban developments; agrarian, industrial, and service economies; religion; popular culture; and politics.

This book examines African American accomplishments and setbacks from the origins of New Jersey to the present day. Each chapter includes demographic information about black people in New Jersey. As New Jersey law has heavily impacted the history of its black population, the book indicates how state laws affected people of color and how they responded through resistance and accommodation. A second important impact was religion, which made the deepest penetration into the souls of black New Jerseyans. Accordingly, I explain how European and African religions affected people of color during each era. I connect the religious experience with education, and in the second half of the book education intersects with law and politics. New Jersey's black people have contributed mightily to state and national cultures and I trace the creation and development of African American culture. Finally, I use biographical materials about important and lesser-known black New Jerseyans to illustrate these themes.

This study has benefited immensely from several fine general chroniclers of black New Jersey's past. Marion Thompson Wright, one of the nation's first female African American scholars, published a highly influential and unsurpassed study of black education in New Jersey in 1941. She also authored a series of influential articles that laid out many of the themes and evidence used by later historians. I credit her work at moments where she clearly originated the scholarship. Clement Alexander Price's documentary history, and short histories by Giles Wright and Larry Greene have provided sturdy scaffolding for my efforts. Price's collection of documents ranges from the colonial period to the 1980s while Wright's and Greene's concise histories offer excellent demographic and sharp historical commentary about New Jersey's African Americans. My intention is to respect and build on these studies to broaden and deepen our understanding of New Jersey's black past.[4] I have used numerous scholarly works about the Mid-Atlantic and other parts of the United States to inform my arguments about New Jersey.

The enduring legacy of slavery is a dominant them in the American experience. Chattel bondage played a key role in the New Jersey colony's and then the state's development. New Jersey was legally a slave society until nearly the Civil War; it has been argued that slavery affected racial relations and black status in the state up to the Civil War and beyond. Certainly the uneven legal status of blacks within their communities and towns hindered their social and political chances. As with the United States in general, black achievement amid worsening racism marked the Reconstruction and Gilded Ages. Today, even after Barack Obama's remarkable presidency, few would argue that racism does not remain a powerful hindrance to black advancement in New Jersey and the rest of the nation. Two-ness, described by W.E.B. Du Bois as the consciousness of being American and being black, remains, a significant divider, as noted by New Jersey resident and Nobel Prize–winning author Toni Morrison.[5]

Despite the introduction of gradual emancipation in the region in the late eighteenth and early nineteenth centuries, slavery cast a long shadow on black Jerseyans and their neighbors. Pennsylvania ended slavery in 1780, but became afflicted by worsening racism while chattel bondage remained potent in New Jersey and New York long into the nineteenth century, despite the presence and influence of the Society of Friends in all three states. The Quakers, whom Marion Thompson Wright once deemed the "social work-ers" of the eighteenth century, were the first of a series of white religious and reform groups who sympathized and worked to better life for African Americans in New Jersey.[6]

Geography was another factor affecting black life in New Jersey. From its earliest days, the state was widely known as a barrel tapped at both ends, one spout toward New York City and the other toward Philadelphia. New Jersey was a hinterland providing both cities with grain, firewood, and dairy products while consumer products arrived through the ports. From the nineteenth century on, what is now known as the Garden State sold produce locally and to bordering cities. After World War II, the state's suburbs became bedroom communities for commuters to Newark, the state's larg-est city, and neighboring New York City and Philadelphia. Its ports have long served the region and the Jersey Shore and Atlantic City became vaca-tion destinations for people who wanted to escape the cities in the summer months.

New Jersey was a society of slaves from its origins in 1664 to the Civil War. Although the state initiated gradual emancipation in 1804 (the last northern state to do so), slavery's burdensome legacy bore heavily on the state's African Americans until the Civil War and after. New Jersey's white farmers pioneered the practice of reducing free blacks to the status of "cottagers," which was an early form of sharecropping. After the Civil War and passage of the Thirteenth, Fourteenth, and Fifteenth Amendments to the U.S. Constitution, racism hampered the newly earned freedoms of New Jersey blacks. The state and its white residents practiced Jim Crow in nearly all aspects of public life until state laws were enacted in the late 1940s that were bolstered by national laws passed in the 1960s.[7]

There is much to the history of African Americans in New Jersey beyond enslavement. *Black New Jersey* reveals the humanity of those affected by Jersey's history of slavery and racism. African Americans in New Jersey worshipped, played, had families, and worked, while resisting and at times accommodating slavery and racism. Religion was a major means to acculturate Africans into Western society and later to create black communities. Faith and ethnicity are often matched in New Jersey. Early on, New Jersey was a cultural hearth for such major religious denominations as the Society of Friends, the Reformed Dutch Church, Baptists, and Presbyterians.[8] During the colonial period the Church of England regarded New York and New Jersey as prime foci for its designs to anglicize their inhabitants. In the nineteenth century and beyond, black religion, along with fraternal organizations, have centered African American communities across the state. The Society of Friends aimed to eliminate slave owning by the mid-eighteenth century. The church's policy of gradual emancipation mandated black education, although it did not allow blacks into its congregation. More evangelical denominations, particularly Methodists and Baptists, welcomed black parishioners. As Jersey African Americans sought greater autonomy and control from the Methodists and Baptists, tensions arose, leading to a plethora of black dominations of African Methodist Episcopal, African Methodist Zion, and African Union churches in the nineteenth century. A few blacks sustained membership in white denominations but the overwhelming percentage of Jersey African Americans moved into black denominations. After the Civil War, the ministry in black churches became the most reliable avenue to personal success, a pattern that continued into the twentieth century.[9]

Slave culture paralleled and sometimes intersected with religion. Visible through sacred yet bastardized celebrations such as Pinkster, through criminal records and runaway notices, slave culture produced a popular black music and dance out of the tough, tedious work world. As with urban music coming out of the Five Points of New York City, for example, slave culture begat a secular culture in the towns and villages of New Jersey. Later in the nineteenth and twentieth centuries, communities grew from origins in black lodges and fraternal societies, beauty salons, jazz, and athletics. Late in the twentieth century, this erstwhile culture produced popular song groups, disco and funk orchestras, and contemporary hip-hop. Religion and slave culture combine in the tough realist literature of Jersey's ghettos in the works of novelists Lloyd Brown and Nathan Heard and the politicized poetry and plays of Amiri Baraka.

Before the Civil War, blacks in New Jersey prepared to enter politics by holding conventions, petitioning to regain the vote, and individually voting when possible. Politics, religion, and work formed bonds between black New Jersey and the slippery promises of white society. That bond of attachment presumed peaceful change. Earlier, the outright tyranny of slavery sparked a counter tradition of violent black resistance. From self-emancipation, attacks on masters, and occasionally revolutionary actions, blacks in New Jersey sometimes used "any means necessary" to seize freedom. Such practical abolitionism helped enslaved New Jersey blacks to gain anonymous freedom. Allegiance to the Crown during the American Revolution, riots against slave catchers during the antebellum period, and battles against the Confederacy in the Civil War all anticipated the urban riots of the twentieth century. This tradition of violence coexists with the peaceful efforts of black New Jerseyans for opportunity and citizenship.

The fusion of religion and secular pursuits powerfully inflected black political participation. After the American Revolution, black Jerseyans had a brief moment of free suffrage, which lasted until legislative change removed it in 1807. From then until passage of the Fifteenth Amendment in 1870, demand for return of the vote motivated black ministers and, by the 1840s, antislavery activists. Black Jerseyans held their own political conventions and were regular attendees at national conferences. Blacks worked with white sympathizers on the Underground Railroad. Harriet Tubman worked with this coalition during her courageous rescue missions into slave country. These knots on a cord created a parallel political order and an intellectual tradition that prepared blacks to become full citizens after the Civil War. Racism frustrated that potential. After the passage of the Fifteenth Amendment, which created a national standard of citizenship, the number of blacks in political office remained few until the 1960s when black mayors headed New Jersey's major cities. During the first half of the twentieth century, the NAACP and Urban League made New Jersey a chief target for their efforts to integrate society and mitigate racism, and those reform movements turned to political reform. Voter drives and recruitment of talented candidates became priorities. A principal tension lies between black political officials who prioritize local management and interracial cooperation and those with a more nationalist agenda. One recent example contrasts Newark mayors Cory Booker (now a U.S. senator), who espoused a postracial appeal, with the new mayor Ras Baraka, who has emphasized cultural nationalism and community organization. Baraka however has also embraced controversial economic developments such as high-rise buildings.

Black office holders have been scarce in New Jersey. Cory Booker was the first national New Jersey black senator. Newark native Donald M. Payne was the first black New Jersey member of the U.S. House of Representatives, from 1989 until his death in 2012. His son, Donald M. Payne Jr., succeeded him and won a full term in 2014. Joining Payne in Congress in 2014 was Bonnie Watson Coleman, a Democrat from Mercer County who became the first black woman to represent the state in Washington. The situation is somewhat better at the state level, where a number of blacks serve in the legislature and assembly. Sheila Oliver was speaker of the state assembly between 2010 and 2103, and in November 2017 she became the state's first black lieutenant governor. As notable as these achievements are, their very

recent occurrence is testimony to the historically weak political position of
New Jersey blacks.[10]

Ras Baraka, Newark's current mayor, is the son of Amiri Baraka, the
charismatic, politically radical poet and playwright. Baraka is one of several black New Jerseyans whose lives and works are transcendent in American society. The actor, athlete, and singer Paul Robeson was another and
Marion Thompson Wright's works make her arguably the first important
black female historian. In addition to restoring the histories of ordinary
black Jerseyans, this book will highlight such prominent and nationally significant figures.

Black New Jerseyans accomplished much in a racially hostile world.
White belief in black inferiority was intrinsic in the colonial and early
national eras when slavery was the law of the land, and as the state moved
toward gradual emancipation disturbing new attitudes appeared. The
American Colonization Society (ACS) was formed in New Jersey in 1817
with the intent of solving the nation's racial problems by convincing free
blacks that their future laid in Africa, not America. Blacks, reasoned elite
white New Jerseyans who formed the ACS's membership, were so degraded
by slavery and faced such hostility from whites that they could never achieve
full American citizenship. These intellectual positions became key parts of
the emerging American racism of the 1830s. Bolstering them was the psychological resentment former masters felt toward their erstwhile chattel.
Dutch New Jersey slave masters were notorious for telling freedom-bent
bond people that they had a choice: stay and work with the master or walk
out the door and never return. Dismissal of any perceived need for repara-
tions was based upon the master's and mistress's belief that the enslaved
people were family property and displayed ingratitude by choosing a new
life. Many white Jerseyans were convinced that the state's system of slavery
was mild in comparison with southern bondage and eventually developed a
historical amnesia about the historic reality of slavery in New Jersey.[11]

Despite the heroics of almost 3,000 New Jersey black volunteers in the
Union Army during the American Civil War, which finally rid the nation
of legal human bondage, prewar racism and discrimination continued into

the Reconstruction and Gilded Age and well into the twentieth century. Black New Jerseyans responded by creating a web of churches, benevolent and fraternal societies, schools, and homeownership. The clergy became the key avenue for black male success. A tenuous black middle class gradually developed up to the Great Depression of the 1930s.

World War II, the Double V strategy—which aimed to conquer fascism abroad and vanquish racism and segregation at home—and the resulting civil rights movement offered hope in New Jersey. State laws in the late 1940s and a 1947 state constitution forbade public discrimination based on race. Sadly, new social patterns reinforced old racial attitudes. As Kenneth Jackson and Lizbeth Cohen have brilliantly shown, suburbanization in New Jersey created a new form of racism. As African Americans moved into New Jersey's cities, whites fled to suburbs that seemed safer and insulated from racial contacts. Cities became synonymous with crime and disorder. Walter Greason has argued that suburbanization badly damaged the New Jersey civil rights movement. Social distances between black and white increased after the Newark riots of 1967. Drug war policies and mass incarceration led to long jail terms for thousands of young men convicted of minor infractions in the 1980s and beyond. While not as severe as in neighboring New York, these policies cost many young black New Jerseyans their futures.[12]

In the twenty-first century, social and class divisions within the African American population of New Jersey have yawned wider. Some of the wealthiest blacks in America dwell in Alpine, a tiny village perched on the Palisades. Jersey's suburbs are home to a strong black middle class, as is the resurgent city of Newark. Near Liberty International Airport however, thousands of black inmates are imprisoned in maximum security jails, as part of the nationwide epidemic of mass incarceration. Poorer blacks in Camden, Newark, Atlantic City, Trenton, and smaller locales struggle to make a living. This book examines those histories from statistical data, newspaper accounts, and the sizable number of autobiographies and biographies of prominent black Jersey politicians, entertainers, and athletes. In addition, I draw upon interviews and the recollections of ordinary people.

Proximity to New York City meant generations of creative artists flowed back and forth from the metropolis to New Jersey. Talent over and back across the Hudson River included Englewood's jazzmen Dizzy Gillespie and Tyree Glenn, artist Faith Ringgold, and the first star rap group, the Sugar Hill Gang, which formed there in 1973. John Coltrane's *A Love Supreme*, considered one of the world's most important jazz albums, was recorded in the Van Gelder Studio in Englewood Cliffs. Paterson produced internationally known artist Ben F. Jones. Newark and the Oranges produced stride pianist Willie "the Lion" Smith and the poet, playwright, and activist Amiri Baraka and his son and future mayor of Newark, Ras. Also from the Oranges were singers Dionne Warwick and the Houston Family, and rap star/actress Queen Latifah. George Clinton started the Parliaments (later Parliament Funkadelic) in his hometown of Plainfield. Plainfield is also the site of sculptor Melvin Edwards's studio from the 1970s to the present. Princeton's most famous son was Paul Robeson, who, like the others, developed in New Jersey and made it big in New York City and the world.[13]

I have divided this history into eras significant to black New Jersey. Accordingly, I begin with the origins of black settlement in the seventeenth century up to the onset of prerevolutionary activity in 1763. The second chapter discusses the era of emancipation, including the American Revolution, early national efforts to combat and retain slavery, and the Gradual Emancipation Act of 1804. The third chapter takes black New Jersey history through the halting process of gradual emancipation and the emergence of free black religion, education, and politics, the blossoming of the Underground Railroad, up to the Civil War. This chapter addresses the current debate about the effect of slavery upon black New Jersey. There is no doubt that slavery had a long-lasting effect far after the emancipation act in no small part because of the determination of slave owners to extract any value from their human chattel and the indifference of white political leaders to Jersey's black residents. This era also saw the development of a black middle class, which was always under duress but persevered.[14] Chapter 4 discusses black New Jersey during the Civil War, including portraits of blacks who served in the Union Army, and on the politics of national emancipation and

Reconstruction up to the formalization of segregation in 1896. This chapter includes ample material on black clergy, businesspeople, and educators. Chapter 5 examines the Jim Crow racial restrictions in public life in the late nineteenth century, which caused social and economic problems for Jersey blacks. Chapter 6 covers the era of the World War II and suburbanization in the 1950s and black frustrations stemming from racial exclusion that exploded in the riots of the 1960s. Chapter 7 analyses the era of black politics from the election of Kenneth Gibson to the emergence of black political leadership in the late twentieth century, the Black Arts Movement headed by Amiri Baraka, and the emergence of mass incarceration out of the drug war of the 1980s. The chapter continues with analysis of the emergence of a black professional elite in New Jersey and the resulting class split in African American society. Finally, a brief concluding chapter uses black New Jersey's past and present to speculate about the future.

⌒

CHAPTER 1

From Initial Euro-African Settlement to the Pre-Revolution, 1625–1763

A half century before the establishment of the colony of New Jersey, African Americans lived in the region, which was part of Dutch New Netherlands. The Dutch West India Company, proprietor of the struggling colony, invested nearly all of its efforts east of what was called the North and later the Hudson River. A small settlement on the river's west bank included a plantation at Pavonia (Jersey City). An estimated twenty to thirty Creole men and women worked the plantation, many of whom were literate, free Catholics from Cartagena, Colombia. Others had been kidnapped by the Dutch in the West Indies and enslaved. Jacob Stoffelson, who oversaw this gang of laborers, was the first slave master in East Jersey. Stoffelson worked for the Dutch West India Company in New Amsterdam (now Manhattan) and supervised black woodcutters whose other responsibilities in Pavonia included building the "Large House as well as the Guard house, splitting palisades, clearing land, burning lime," and harvesting grain.[1] Later, Stoffelson directed enslaved blacks in resodding the exterior of the fort, constructing a wagon road, and rebuilding fences in New Amsterdam. He directed a work camp of the company slaves around present-day East Fifty-Ninth Street using the same laborers who worked across the river in Pavonia.

Dutch West India Company vessels preyed upon Spanish ports and ships to kidnap free Christian peoples and then force them into labor. Known as

Creoles, these victims of political kidnapping were often skilled cosmopolitan Spanish citizens with dark complexions. Kidnapped people were worked at Pavonia until it was evacuated in 1643 after Algonquian Indians attacked the settlement in retaliation for the massacre of 120 Native women and children in New Amsterdam. After Governor Willem Kieft was recalled to Amsterdam following this disastrous conflict, the administration of Governor Petrus Stuyvesant rebuilt Pavonia in 1653. Stuyvesant then warred with the local Lenni Lenape Indians over Pavonia in the Peach Tree War and concluded this conflict by repurchasing Pavonia in 1658. He purchased Bergen from Native Americans in 1661, thereby opening the Hudson's banks to Dutch settlers and their slaves.[2]

Historian Ira Berlin has identified seventeenth-century American slavery as a "Creole" era during which people of African origins, often kidnapped from seagoing vessels and sold into slavery in North America, survived while learning and adapting to Western laws and religion. Eventually some were able to secure land, rights, and personal freedom before the codification of slave laws. Berlin pointed to New Amsterdam as a key locus for Creoles. To accommodate and enhance their chances for emancipation, enslaved people joined the Reformed Dutch Church, fought for New Netherlands in the Kieft War of the early 1640s, and eventually earned some semblance of freedom. Emancipated Creoles lived and farmed along the Bowery Road in the 1640s and 1650s. By the 1670s, they had moved to northern Jersey or further up the Hudson River. Creoles John De Vries, Sr. and Jr., Frans Van Salee, Nicolas Manuels, Samuel Francisco, and Youngham Antonious Roberts first lived in New Amsterdam and later became very early residents of Bergen County. This group formed the basis for East Jersey's tiny free black society into the next century.[3]

The English conquest of New Netherlands in 1664 affirmed property rights for slave owners even as it recognized the freedoms of emancipated blacks. Creation of the proprietary colony of East Jersey the same year instigated a property scramble. The establishment of the English Royal African Company, formed as a monopoly to supply the colonies with enslaved labor, helped wealthier migrants from Barbados to purchase bondpeople to supplement the enslaved people they brought with them. Other customers of the Royal African Company included Scot-Irish, Dutch, and soon Huguenot farmers who swarmed into East Jersey, intent on establishing freehold properties. Each English immigrant received 150 acres per head of family with an incentive of an additional 150 acres for each manservant, thereby encouraging the introduction of slaves. Wealthier and better-connected Englishmen received more. Lewis Morris Sr. and Thomas Berry from Barbados received substantial grants, reflecting their connections to royal power. Morris Sr. established a forge and mill at Tinton Falls while Berry, William Sandford, and Nathaniel Kingsland developed plantations in Bergen County. All of them employed enslaved labor. Lacking a staple crop, these large manufactories and plantations were not viable in East Jersey, but their owners dominated colonial politics and ensured that slavery was a major girder in the construction of Jersey society. Moreover, as Trevor Burnard has demonstrated, these transplanted Barbadian grandees believed firmly in the benefits of human slavery to propel their economic fortunes and were accustomed to using brutal methods to enforce bondage.[4]

Reasons for the development of slavery in New Jersey varied by ethnicity. Small farmers also sought to buy and use enslaved labor, but official land allocations to Dutch and Huguenot farmers created problems for these non-English settlers. The English authorities discriminated against Dutch and Huguenot farmers who had moved from New York into Bergen and Monmouth Counties. Dutch and Huguenot farmers were allotted smaller grants and were thereby condemned to subsistence agriculture. In addition, Dutch and Huguenot farmers could not practically subdivide their properties to accommodate their children. The Dutch did not practice primogeniture, by which all parental property is bequeathed to the eldest son, so families with several sons faced problems allotting their children land. During the early days of European settlement, Dutch farmers could purchase nearby lands for their sons, giving rise to closely aligned towns. To make their daughters more attractive on the marriage market, Dutch farmers bequeathed enslaved peoples to them. As ordinary Dutch seldom intermarried with the English, such practices promoted closely aligned communities of small farms using slave labor. Eventually, as cultivated land near the rivers or accessible routes to the city became scarcer, Dutch families could not acquire land for sons, who then moved into western counties. Slave ownership often was the most valuable asset these small farmers, male and female, possessed. Owning enslaved people was also common among English Quakers and Congregationalists who arrived in the 1660s from Connecticut and Long Island to establish the towns of Woodbridge, Piscataway, Shrewsbury, Middletown, and later Newark. Whereas established English colonists largely used family labor in New England, young families moving to New Jersey acquired enslaved people to help clear land and create farms. Quakers, Scot-Irish Presbyterians, and Congregationalists moving into New Jersey received larger land grants than did Dutch and Huguenot farmers. Even those groups however secured much larger land holdings than freed black people who subsisted on tiny lots that made long-term capitalization impossible.[5]

Similar conditions existed in West Jersey. The colony of New Sweden (1638–1655) employed at least one enslaved man, Anthony, who was captured and bonded by Swedish privateers operating in the West Indies. Anthony worked on the governor's farm and manned his master's sloop. By 1654 he was apparently free. New Sweden largely existed in present-day Delaware, but Anthony probably worked at Swedish settlements in what is now Salem County, New Jersey. The absentee landlord of Burlington Island, Alexander D'Hinoyosia of Amsterdam, owned enslaved people and later sold them to Maryland farmers. When the English captured Fort Altena and the City of Amsterdam's property at New Amstel, they seized sixty to seventy enslaved blacks. This sizable group of people was likely enslaved in New Amsterdam and sent over to New Amstel to work in the sawmills and brew houses.[6]

Slavery soon became more evident in West Jersey, as Quaker masters in newly settled Pennsylvania who sought a freehold, or in some cases a gentleman's farm, moved into Burlington and Camden counties. Despite the faith's later reputation for abolitionism, members of the Society of Friends initially bought, sold, and used enslaved labor to develop their properties. Daniel Cooper, founder of five generations of ferry masters at Cooper's Point,

conducted slave auctions at his ferry near Camden. Quakers did not dominate New Jersey politics as they did in Pennsylvania, but members of the
Society of Friends did form a sturdy block in the colonial assembly. Whether
or not they owned enslaved people, these Friends allowed the local growth
of slavery and the slave trade. Moreover, as Quaker historian William Frost
has observed, early Friends lacked consensus about slavery and it was not
until 1760 that the church established a "sense of the meeting" in opposition to chattel bondage.[7]

Quakers were not the only early West Jersey settlers to own enslaved
people. Daniel Coxe, an English physician and absentee landlord, specu-
lated in land in the Cape May peninsula and attracted French Huguenot
families to Cape May. Coxe's personal ambitions eventually foundered, but
his prototype of yeoman whalers took hold and his official representative,
George Taylor, introduced slavery to the region. Taylor owned four enslaved
people in 1688.[8] Lenape chieftains also took enslaved people. At the time of
his trial for murder of an Englishman in 1727, the Lenape sachem owned
numerous enslaved people at his farm near Cranbury. Later, the Lenape
stated their opposition to the forced immigration of Africans and use of
Indian slaves, doubtless fearing that they too might be held in bondage.[9]

The earliest census estimates in 1680 for New Jersey counted about 120
enslaved people or 3 percent of a population of about 3,500 souls. In the next
forty years, New Jersey white residents invested heavily in slavery. There
were 1,500 enslaved people in New Jersey by 1715, and 2,581 people of African
descent, nearly all of them enslaved, or 8 percent of the total population of
32,442, lived in the colony by 1726. The number of enslaved people rose to
4,606 by 1745 among a cumulative population of 61,383. Those overall numbers masked heavy investment in slavery in eastern counties. By 1745,
20 percent of the inhabitants of strongly Dutch Bergen County were
enslaved; Middlesex, Monmouth, and Somerset were about 10 percent
enslaved. Males predominated in each of the five East Jersey counties, hampering natural growth and increasing reliance on the slave trade. If, in 1726,
fewer enslaved people lived in the five West Jersey counties, that situation
had substantially changed by 1745. Burlington and Gloucester counties' slave

masters held the most people in bondage. There were fewer enslaved people in Salem and Cape May counties, where whaling families were the predominant master class.[10]

To control this rapidly growing black population, New Jersey magistrates, colony wide and local, constructed and brutally administered slave laws. After a single admonition to slave masters to treat their bond people fairly, the second major legislation concerned slave flight, making it illicit and punishing those who enabled escapees. This law recognized early on that enslaved people would flee from bondage to seek freedom and would find help. The governor and assembly mandated heavy penalties: a fine of five British pounds plus damages and costs to anyone who transported or hid slaves or servants. A century and a half later, such helpers became known as the Underground Railroad. In the seventeenth century, they were early harbingers of an abolition movement.[11]

Laws could not disguise the fierce violence that characterized master-slave relations. Coercing frightened, alienated, and violently angry young black men to become a viable workforce could not be done individually. Masters who needed help in subduing enslaved people looked to their neighbors, local magistrates, and the militia. Resistance was answered viciously, though not extinguished. White masters who killed enslaved people went unpunished. In contrast, Monmouth County officials brutally punished Caesar, who was accused of the murder of Lewis Morris of Passage Point in 1694 after Morris abused an enslaved woman. The officials ordered that Caesar's right hand be cut off before his eyes. He was then hung until dead, after which his body was burned to ashes. Similar torturous executions occurred elsewhere.[12]

The New Jersey government gradually created a punitive slave code. After the law forbidding slave flight, the assembly added injunctions in 1694 against enslaved people carrying guns into the woods for hunting and legitimized the authority for any white man to arrest a suspected escaped slave found more than five miles away from his home. In 1695, the colonial government established special courts to prosecute enslaved people, allowing justices of the peace to convene twelve whites "of the neighborhood" to try blacks accused of theft. Conviction was punishable by whipping. The law also included instructions on capital crimes, allowing any twelve white men to decide the accused's fate and then conduct an execution. Notable in this act was allowance for local prosecution and execution.[13]

Slavery also gained religious sanction. In 1704, the assembly passed a law intended to encourage the efforts of the Society for the Propagation of the Gospel in Foreign Parts by decreeing that baptism did not mandate emancipation. This law, which relegated Christian blacks to second-class status, augmented tougher regulations against slave theft and murder. Capital crimes still mandated immediate execution while stealing now brought forty lashes and branding a "T" on the felon's left cheek. The assembly then wrecked life chances for free blacks by forbidding them from buying or inheriting any land in the province, a denial that effectively removed their civil rights. The assembly nullified a Burlington man's testament in 1693 that willed twenty acres to a young black man when he reached the age of twenty-four. A Gloucester County resident leased land to the "negro Quosh" for 999 years in order to circumvent this terrible injunction.[14]

In 1712, enslaved blacks revolted in New York City, burning homes and killing a number of whites. It was the first slave revolt in the English North American colonies. Brutal suppression followed with many executions involving torture and public display of corpses. Two years later New York Colony passed a complete slave code, which New Jersey quickly copied. The codes were filled with harsh clauses punishing runaways or thieves with whippings and conspirators against their masters with "the pains of Death in such Manner as the Aggravation or Enormity of their Crimes." Anyone harboring escaped slaves could be found liable for financial restitution payable to the master. In a gratuitous slur, the governor and assembly accused free blacks of being an "Idle, slothful people," who "prove very often a Charge to the Place where they be." Although the legislators did not mention any such cases of burdensome charity, it ordered that any master who wished to emancipate slaves had to pay the government £200 for security and grant £20 annually to the free person. Without those payments any "will or testament" freeing a slave was void. Much higher than the amount

required in Pennsylvania, New Jersey's fees aligned with the financial hurdles to freedom enacted in New York. Such laws made emancipation for
New Jersey blacks very difficult and expensive. The slave code meant that
the New Jersey government supported human bondage completely.[15]

Despite the closing vise of slavery, a small free black class persisted in
colonial New Jersey. John De Vries Sr. and Nicolas Manuels, Samuel Francisco, Youngham Antonious Roberts, Jochem Antony, and the Solomon
Peters and Van Donck family, all free blacks from New York, established
farms in Bergen County in the late 1600s. Their descendants maintained
them until after the American Revolution. Other free blacks came from
abroad. Arie Van Guinee immigrated from Surinam in the 1730s to New
York and then to the Raritan Valley in 1714. He established the first Lutheran
Church in the area. He married a daughter of Solomon Peters. Van Guinee's
family remained in New Jersey until the early nineteenth century when
they moved to Michigan and became deeply involved in the Underground
Railroad. In West Jersey, Cyrus Bustill, born in Burlington of an enslaved
black woman and a leading white political figure in 1732, became a baker in
Philadelphia during the Revolutionary War and later was a well-known
abolitionist after the war. His Philadelphia descendants include abolitionists Grace Bustill Douglass and Robert Douglass, a prominent barber and
leading black Presbyterian, their son Robert, a painter known for his early
portrait of antislavery activist William Lloyd Garrison, and their daughter
Sarah Mapps Douglass, a teacher at New York's African Free School and
frequent antislavery essayist. She also attended the Female Medical College
of Pennsylvania and became known for her lectures on female anatomy
and physiology. Part of the Bustill family became prominent in Princeton
and in Philadelphia. Cyrus Bustill was the great-great grandfather of Paul
Robeson.[16]

Despite the high barriers, Elias Mestayer of Shrewsbury, likely a Huguenot, freed two slaves in 1731 dating their freedom five years after his death
and upon payment of one hundred British pounds to his executors. He did
award them the "use of my farm with the utensils, husbandry tools, conveniences and stock of all sorts and the Eastern Room of my house with all

the out houses, barne, garden and orchards." Mestayer awarded freedom to "my Negro girl Nan" as well if she, like the others, paid off her freedom dues at the rate of twenty pounds per year. Similar grants of freedom required a number of years of service or payments. Done long before Quakers initiated freedom grants and many decades before the state enacted the protocols for slowly ending slavery, Mestayer's action shows that gradual emancipation with compensation to the master was the preferred method rather than a simple act of freedom. As discussed in chapter 3, gradual emancipation requirements heavily affected the lives of free and enslaved blacks. Such demands for work and payment became common throughout the northern colonies.[17]

ENSLAVED PEOPLE AT WORK

Members of New Jersey's black class, made up of enslaved people and a small group of free individuals, almost all worked on farms or in the colony's nascent industries. As a "bread" colony, like its neighbors Pennsylvania and New York, New Jersey produced a grain surplus, most of which went to the West Indies to feed enslaved sugar plantation workers and their masters. New Jersey farmers also grew oats, rye, barley, buckwheat, and Indian corn. Farms produced beef, cheese, pork, and lamb. Fish and oysters were harvested from the sea. Enslaved people cut down timber from white cedar trees to make barrel staves and shingles. The abundant forests produced charcoal for copper mines, ironworks, and glass factories.[18]

Enslaved people cleared land, built rough homes, fenced property, and cared for animal stocks. Black laborers planted, tended, and harvested grain crops for their masters. Farm work gave blacks the opportunity to learn more specialized skills including carpentry, blacksmithing, cooperage, butchery, tanning leatherwork, carriage driving, potash cultivation, saw and grist mill operation, cooking, and housework. Some even served as barbers and surgeons. Additionally, enslaved and free blacks toiled at ironworks and mines. Charles Read, a well-known ironmaster in Burlington County, employed numerous enslaved people at his furnaces. The Andover Ironworks in Sussex County employed enslaved artisans who produced superior quality ironware. Enslaved laborers toiled at the lucrative Schuyler family copper mines in Bergen County until immigrant workers from Ireland and Wales replaced them in the 1750s. Enslaved blacks also toiled on ferries and on small vessels in the coastal trade and whaling.[19]

Because of land division problems and personal choices, slavery became the colony's primary form of labor. Unlike neighboring Pennsylvania, New Jersey was not hospitable to indentured servants. During the colonial period, New Jersey was a slave society, differing from southern colonies in that it lacked a staple crop such as tobacco, rice, or indigo, but like them, dependent on enslaved labor for its agricultural economy. New Jersey's economy was more diverse compared with the big market southern colonies, but its rural and small town white residents relied heavily on the toil of enslaved people.

New Jersey's agricultural economy and additional tasks required physically strong workers to perform manual labor. Accordingly, masters preferred to purchase young men. By 1738, every Jersey County was home to more black men than women. Between the censuses of 1726 and 1745, Bergen, Monmouth, Burlington, Gloucester, and Somerset had ratios of 1.4 black males to females. In addition to hampering natural birthrates and destabilizing any unions that did occur, one result was a preponderance of unattached, restless, and frustrated young men, eager to roam the countryside or demanding privileges allowing them to go to nearby cities. There were occasional unions between white males and black females, but known relations between black men and white women were highly uncommon and routinely condemned. Edmund Morgan argued in his classic study of white indentured labor in Virginia that the presence of restless, frustrated young white males created the conditions resulting in Bacon's Rebellion of 1676. In New Jersey, black gender imbalance worsened the already difficult relationships between small masters and their enslaved people.[20]

Although the proximity of enslaved peoples working at adjacent farms allowed some natural increase through disrupted unions, the colony remained dependent on the Atlantic slave trade to meet the burgeoning demand for human chattel. At first, most forced migrants arrived in small parcels of young males from the West Indies. Later newly enslaved people arrived directly from Africa. Although New Jersey was dependent on neighboring New York for most forced imports of enslaved people, a slave port emerged at Perth Amboy. The colony enabled the trade by refusing, except during a brief period from 1714 to 1721, to declare duties on slaves until 1769.[21]

Overall, 75 percent of enslaved people in the colony of Jersey lived in the five eastern counties before the American Revolution. In each of those counties, males predominated, because of the premium on black men as toilers of hard physical labor. Black women were present in East Jersey, allowing for reproduction, but many young black men vainly searched for socially permissible partners. Those facts affected the persistence of slavery among Jersey ethnicities devoted to it, curbed black hopes for freedom, and inspired generations of restless young men prone to acts of violent resistance.[22]

Dutch and Huguenot slave owning farmers, concentrated in Bergen, Somerset, Middlesex, and particular towns in Monmouth, served, in Peter Wacker's words, "to establish a basic population distribution" of people of African heritage. Nearly all people of African descent in Bergen were enslaved during the colonial period, but there was some fusing of cultures. Black residents of Bergen were known for speaking a dialect called Negro Dutch. As noted previously, Dutch and Huguenot farmers struggled to survive on small farms, and often their enslaved people were their most valuable property.[23]

RELIGION AND SLAVERY

In early America, religion was the most common means of acculturating enslaved peoples to the dominant society. However, Dutch towns had trouble attracting clerics to lead Reformed Dutch congregations, so church members often instructed themselves. The home church in the Netherlands allowed masters to teach (or not teach) God's words to enslaved people in the absence of a minister. Such powers instilled a dominant, pietistic personality among Dutch masters and mistresses, giving them the power to explain European theology to their human chattel. Dutch pietism provided a theological underpinning to economic needs for slavery, created fierce defenses for it, and made masters resistant to any reform or talk of emancipation and abolition. At the same time, enslaved people were aware that European traditions supported the emancipation of Christianized slaves. A master or mistress who refused to offer Christianity to an enslaved person created a harsh grievance that could result in violence.[24]

Lacking clerics who could admit enslaved blacks into the congregation, Dutch masters used ritual to perform spiritual baptisms. Pinkster, the Dutch version of Pentecost, was the day when the Holy Spirit descended upon Jesus' apostles and created a Holy Wind that caused servants and handmaidens to speak in tongues and comprehend the Gospel. In addition to its sacred qualities, Pinkster fostered slave culture. One of the few Catholic holidays to survive the Protestant Reformation, Pinkster was a mass celebration that often featured heavy drinking, gambling, prostitution, and much interracial comradeship, all of which was on display at these annual events in New Jersey. One critic described how blacks banged on their drums on Pinkster morning and then directed the writer to a field where he could observe sport, dancing, and music. The narrator found the field covered with booths frequented by whites and blacks together. He listened as enslaved blacks danced "to the hollow sound of a drum," and to the "grating, rattling sound of Pebles, or shells in a small basket." Some blacks played banjos and fiddles while others sang. Many were drunk. Blacks and whites frolicked with prostitutes. There were cockfights and wrestling and boxing matches. The writer drolly concluded "Holidays thus spent could be of very little service if they were not pernicious." The "Spy," as the writer referred to himself, uncovered a rich syncretic culture mixing African and European behavior. Slave masters contented themselves by observing a temporary sacred unity with their enslaved people while at the same time lowering racial barriers to have a good time. These holidays were a pressure release for blacks while granting them a legitimate forum for their African artistic and athletic skills. Pinkster, along with Militia day, the annual occasion when the counties volunteer soldiers mustered, were brief moments of respite during the yearly trudge of hard labor.[25]

Black religious experiences were not uniform and depended on a master's faith. Dutch Jerseyans worshipped in Reformed congregations, French residents attended Huguenot congregations or borrowed Dutch Reformed chapels, and Scot-Irish were Presbyterians. Anglo-Americans were largely Anglican or English spinoffs that included the Society of Friends, Congregationalists, Presbyterians, Baptists, and later Methodists. Enslaved people might remain in a household observing a single faith for their lifetime or move around and experience a variety of Christian theologies. A master's or mistress's denominational beliefs greatly affected their positions on black spirituality, education, and possible manumission. In turn, an enslaved person experienced Western European mores largely through his or her owner's faith.

Because of New Jersey's religious diversity, a black person's interaction with European religion was uneven compared with neighboring New York and Pennsylvania. In New York, the Society for Propagation of the Gospel in Foreign Parts (SPG), the missionary arm of the Church of England, established schools aimed at catechizing enslaved blacks and strongly encouraged owners to send their human chattel to church. Early on, the Church of England and its elite, politically powerful adherents strived to alleviate anxieties about baptism. One result was the 1704 law enacted by the New Jersey Assembly that stated that church baptism did not alter enslavement. Intended to assure masters that the SPG classes for blacks did not threaten their property rights, the law was a major civil rights retreat for enslaved people. It removed a centuries-old avenue to emancipation via membership in a Christian (Protestant) denomination. Generally, only elite New Jersey masters with political connections and aspirations sent their chattel to the Anglican churches.[26]

Somewhat successful in New York City, SPG efforts faltered in rural New Jersey, where Dutch and Huguenot masters, suspicious of Anglican intentions and worried about the emancipatory power of baptism despite the 1704 law, refused to allow their enslaved people to attend catechism classes.

Among Anglo-Jerseyans, the SPG had a bit more success, but even then efforts were spotty and depended heavily on individual missionaries. The first school appeared in Perth Amboy between 1712 and 1715 when clerics and masters collaborated on night classes for sixteen enslaved scholars. Catechism schools appeared in New Brunswick, Newark, Sussex, Elizabethtown, and Burlington. For example, Reverend Thomas Thompson, an esteemed cleric, a graduate, professor, and dean at Cambridge University, came to Monmouth County in 1726 to serve as missionary and clergyman for the Shrewsbury Church of England. Thompson welcomed more than a dozen blacks into the church before his departure for Africa in 1750. His successor, Samuel Cooke, extended Thompson's efforts by baptizing more than three dozen enslaved people belonging to elite whites. Mindful of local white anxieties and holding less power in rural New Jersey than in urban New York, Anglicans did not push evangelizing past the chattel of elite members.[27]

The life of James Ukawsaw Gronniosaw, an enslaved person owned by Reverend Theodorus Jacobus Freylinghuysen of Raritan, Somerset County, illustrates how blacks fared in elite Dutch households. Gronniosaw came to America via the Middle Passage and initially was purchased by a merchant in New York City. Freylinghuysen, a prominent Reformed pastor and a key founder of Queens Colleges (Rutgers), bought Gronniosaw, installed him as a domestic in his Raritan home, and then introduced him to Christianity. Gronniosaw used his faith to survive depressions and downfalls; he became literate and eventually published an autobiography. He served Frelinghuysen's widow and then other descendants before gaining his freedom.[28]

Blacks found crevices of freedom in European faiths. More evangelical denominations embraced black membership. Presbyterians, common in East Jersey, and more radical in the colonial period than later, used mass religious gatherings known as Love Feasts to foster interracial harmony even if they did not ask hard questions about slavery. Evangelical preachers in the first Great Awakening in 1741 and 1742 extended promises of salvation to blacks and whites together and questioned the legitimacy of slavery. Methodism emerged from the Great Awakening as a radical offshoot of the Church of England. Blacks could join the upstart denomination and Methodist churches gave blacks access to sacred rituals including baptism and marriage. Even Anglican masters such as Lord Stirling felt the new enthusiasm and prayed publicly with blacks, undercutting strong legal hierarchies. Baptist masters in Plainfield freed enslaved people, though wills delayed emancipation for years after the planter's death, allegedly to ensure that the free people would not burden local white taxpayers.[29] Outside of European denominational purview, black Jerseyans expressed their own religious convictions. Simon, who escaped from James Leonard of Middlesex County in 1740, "pretended to be a doctor and very religious and says he is a churchman." Mark, who fled from Major Prevost of Bergen County in 1775, was a "preacher, short, black, and well-set." His wife, Jenney was described as "smooth-tongued and very artful."[30]

RELIGION AND THE ORIGINS OF ANTISLAVERY

White criticism of slavery was sporadic in the colonial period and nearly exclusive to the Society of Friends. The denomination began an eighty-year moral discussion about slavery in the 1680s when the Germantown Friends meeting argued that slavery was a sin and contrary the church's sacred goals. In 1715, John Hepburn, a New Jersey tailor and Quaker, combined the moral economy with abolitionism when he condemned slave masters as a vain, ostentatious elite who used "Twisted Hides and Horse-Whips," to rob blacks of their free wills and human rights. Hepburn cited the evils of slavery: forced labor without pay, violence, cruelty and unlawful punishment, separation of man and wife, and the encouragement of adultery, murder, and war. Among other crimes, Hepburn indicted masters for brutality by accusing them of hanging slaves by their thumbs while another slave beat them. Hepburn delineated how slavery broke each of the Ten Commandments. His jeremiad employed a lengthy question and answer format to reject any biblical justification for slavery.[31] The radical abolitionist Pennsylvania Quaker Benjamin Lay frequented New Jersey meetings to shock Friends with his antislavery theatricality and outspoken castigation of slavery and slave owners. In his most famous performance, he confronted the Burlington regional yearly meeting in 1738. He denounced slavery as an act of war and sarcastically mocked Quakers for abandoning their pacifism. To illustrate his point, Lay opened his overcoat to uncover military garb below. He drew a sword, yelled that slavery was murder, and stabbed a Bible in which he had hidden a bladder filled with red pokeberry juice, splattering himself and others with mock blood.[32]

Quaker John Woolman, a Mount Holly tailor, became deeply troubled about slavery as he traveled around the colonies. In his pamphlet, *Some Considerations on the Keeping of Negroes*, published in 1754, Woolman argued against slavery and contended that it unfairly degraded blacks and chastised his fellow Quakers for neglecting racial justice. Philadelphian Anthony Benezet pushed the local meeting further by demanding education for enslaved blacks to prepare them for conversion and freedom. Woolman began to teach black children in his home in 1750 and continued to do so until 1770. Despite Woolman's brave efforts, no Quaker schools for blacks opened in New Jersey during the colonial period.[33]

By 1775, the Philadelphia meeting that encompassed West Jersey and portions of Monmouth County voted to end slavery among Friends, mandated that members manumit their slaves and cease participation in the slave trade. Initially accomplished gradually, proponents of Quaker abolitionism had to confront questions about slave purchases, lengthy slave hires, and variations among meetings over compliance with the new rules. Friends visited their brethren to convince them to cleanse themselves of slavery. The results were substantial in West Jersey, but less so in Monmouth County and other parts of East Jersey that were influenced by the more conservative New York Meeting. Members there profited by requiring sums of money or demanding years of service before granting freedom. Once ending slavery in their meetings, Quakers rarely admitted blacks into their fellowship. However, unlike the Anglican or Dutch Reformed denominations, Quakers did meet the question of slavery head on in the eighteenth century. Their writings also influenced white and black abolitionists. The Seven Years War created a crisis among Quakers, whose pacifism forbade contributing manpower or financial support for war. As Quakers decided to withdraw from governance of Pennsylvania, a colony they had founded and ruled since the 1680s, the church became more intent on cleansing slavery from its membership. It declared that noncompliers would be excommunicated. The church also assisted newly freed blacks. As Marion Thompson Wright pointed out long ago, the Quakers acted as "social workers" by helping blacks to arrange marriages and gain promised freedoms, providing financial aid to worthy blacks, and of course eventually spearheaded the drive for gradual emancipation in New Jersey. Still, the gradual quality of Quaker abolitionism undercuts claims that they were pioneers in creating black freedoms. Credit for that lies with blacks themselves.[34]

Historians have routinely credited the Society of Friends for the earliest phases of abolitionism. This perception ignores the general Quaker acquiescence to slavery in the first half of the eighteenth century, fifty years when slavery became a significant form of labor in New Jersey, especially among members of the Society of Friends. An occasional Quaker radical criticized slavery, but the bulk of Quakers, including most of the Jersey church leadership, invested in slavery. Even after the Friends started to root slavery out of their congregations, actions were slow and discussion could be laborious.[35]

Black Self-Emancipators

By looking beyond literary and theological evidence, there is ample proof that blacks would use flight and any means necessary to gain freedom. As Manisha Sinha's powerful history of abolition argues: "Slave resistance, not bourgeois liberalism, lay at the heart of the abolitionist movement." Sinha includes black self-emancipation and revolt as key methods of black abolition in the colonial period.[36]

Left with few hopes for legal emancipation, enslaved blacks in New Jersey took any measure possible to gain freedom. Flight or self-emancipation was the most common. Enslaved Jersey blacks ran away from their masters and mistresses throughout the colonial period. Destinations included New York City and Philadelphia, New England, Canada and Native People's territories, coastal and deep-sea vessels, iron mines, or the Pine Barrens.

Blacks escaped from slavery singly, in groups, aided by sympathetic free blacks or whites, in all weather and with only the clothes on their backs. They ran away on foot and horseback, in canoes and boats—by any means to distance themselves from their masters.

Early laws reveal the determination for black self-emancipation. To halt runaways, the New Jersey Assembly passed a law as early as 1675 and ordering a ten shilling fine for anyone who harbored a fugitive slave. In 1683 the East Jersey Council asked Native American chiefs not to provide shelter for self-emancipated blacks, signs that fugitive enslaved people were already a significant problem for the colony's masters. These injunctions reappeared in slave laws in 1694 and in the major codification in 1713, which indicates that self-emancipation continued unabated.[37]

New Jersey did not have a regular newspaper until 1775, so masters hoping to retrieve their valuable human property advertised in New York and Philadelphia newspapers. These advertisements provide verbal snapshots of enslaved people and, beyond the biases of the masters, vital information about dress, skills, methods of escape, and even personality. One advertisement that offers a good survey of skills among the enslaved sought the return in October 1763 of "Mr. Low's Cato," from Raritan Landing (now Piscataway). Cato was "an extreme handy fellow at any common work, especially with horses, and carriages of almost any sort, having been bred to it from a little boy, and to the loading and unloading of boats, a good deal used to a farm, can do all kinds of housework and is very fit to wait on a gentleman."[38]

It can be presumed that nearly all the self-emancipated possessed some farming skills and, once they were clear of New Jersey, could earn quick money helping a farmer harvest crops in another colony. Cato was not the only one with multiple skills. Stoffels, who fled from Judith Vincent of Monmouth County, was a house carpenter, a cooper, a wheelwright, and a good butcher. He fled with two others. The most common skill listed about New Jersey's self-emancipated was fiddling. As early as 1730, Clause, who fled from Solomon Bates of Elizabethtown, was described as able to "play upon the fiddle and speaks English and Dutch." A few years later, Isaac ran away from Andrew Reed of Trenton, who described him as able to play upon a fiddle. These songsters, as they were called, could earn cash in taverns, wharfs, or any gathering to sustain their flight.[39]

Literacy became a means to announce, however illicitly, a person's desire for freedom. In the master's unintended irony, self-emancipated people would "pretend to be free." Mando and Tom fled from Samuel Moore and Francis Bloodgood of Woodbridge in 1749. Tom could read and "We hear that he has a sort of indenture with him under the Pretence of being free." Pretenders upon freedom had multiple talents. Cato, alias "Toby," was a "sly, artful fellow and deceives the credulous by pretending to tell fortunes and pretends to be free, speaks English as well as if country-born, and plays upon the fiddle." Some "base person has given him a pass," indicating an early form of Underground Railroad assistance.[40]

Enslaved people would let no impediment block their freedom. Quaco fled in 1761 wearing "an iron collar with two hooks to it round his neck, a pair of handcuffs, with a chain to them, six feet long." A paucity of clothing was no barrier: Jacob of Upper Freehold fled directly from work "at his plough and was without shoe or stocking, and no other clothes but an Oznabrig Shirt and Trowsers, an Old Ragged waistcoat and an old hat." Others took extra clothing with them for protection against the cold or to sell.[41] Enslaved bodies bore witness to the brutality they suffered. James who fled from Thomas Wright of Shrewsbury in 1740 had "his right shoulder out," which was apparent whenever he lifted his arm. York of Middletown had his front teeth kicked out. Others bore psychological pains. Ben talked too much when "elevated with liquor."[42]

In early examples that anticipated the Underground Railroad, enslaved blacks fled together or combined with whites to escape from bondage. Jack of Richmond, Staten Island, fled from his master along with another Jack and Cuff from Bergen County. George Fishman counted thirty-two instances of reported group flight in New Jersey during the first six decades of the eighteenth century. Several, including George, a mulatto slave and shoemaker, fled with "an Irish Lad," probably an indentured servant, in 1745. Nine years later five enslaved men escaped together.[43]

At times, black anger bubbled over. Masters' brutal repression of enslaved people at time had disastrous results. On January 9, 1739, in Rocky Hill, Somerset County, an overseer's wife ordered an enslaved man to bring wood and make a fire. The man apparently had reached a breaking point as he replied in a surly tone that he would make fire enough and pursued her with an axe. The woman hid behind a door but her son was not so lucky. The furious slave struck the boy so that "the whole breadth of the Bitt of the Axe entered the cavity of the body between the shoulders and the Lower Part of the Neck." Next, the attacker burned the barn down, along with over 1,000 bushels of grain. Captured, he was quickly burned at the stake. Two other enslaved men were apprehended, jailed, and executed near Trenton in March 1738 for using arsenic to poison several white people.[44] In 1750 an Amboy enslaved man shot Mrs. Obadiah Ayers dead in her home. He plotted the execution "in conjunction with another New Negroe belonging to one of the neighbors;" the pair planned to steal guns and kill any whites they encountered. They were quickly tried and burned at the stake.[45]

BLACK CONSPIRACY

As did their fellows in New York City, enslaved people in New Jersey plotted to seize their freedoms, at times with messages that spoke to international issues. A white man named Reynolds of Raritan uncovered a plan for a slave rising in Somerset County in 1734 when he encountered a tipsy bondman on the road. The enslaved man informed Reynolds that the "Englishmen were generally a pack of Villains and kept the Negroes as Slaves, contrary to a Positive Order from King George, sent to the G____ [Governor] of New York, to set them free, which they said the G___ intended to do, but was prevented by his C___ [Council] and Assembly." When Reynolds upbraided the bondman, he responded that "he was as good a Man as himself, and that in a little time he should be convinced of it." Reynolds quickly reported the conversation and arrests followed. One slave was hung, others had their ears cut off and a number were whipped. The *New-York Gazette* reported an extensive plot in which "every Negro in each family to rise at midnight,

Cut the Throats of their Masters and Sons, but not to meddle with the women whom they intended to ravish and plunder the next day, and then set all the houses and barns on fire, kill all the draught horses, and secure the best Saddle Horses for their flight toward the Indians in the French Interest." The plotters' meeting places indicated a revolutionary slave culture. Conspirators routinely met at "Colonel Thomas L___ slave quarters," which was dangerously far from his main house. The quarters became a "Rende-vouze for the Negroes . . . and a Pest to the neighborhood by encouraging the Neighbors Negroes to steal from their Masters Beef, Pork, Wheat, Fowles, wherewith they [hold] feasts and junkets." It was at one of these feasts that the plan to revolt was hatched. The chronicler recalled a similar conspiracy in New York in 1712 and more recent risings in St. John and Jamaica as examples of the barbarity of enslaved blacks and the dangers of importing too many of them. Of particular note was the "creative misun-derstanding" of the enslaved people who believed that incoming governors had secret orders to emancipate them, a belief that sparked an insurrection in Virginia in 1730 and that stemmed from continued perception, despite the laws of 1704, that baptizing an enslaved person into Christianity man-dated their freedom. The connection between the conspiracy in New Jersey and similar events in the West Indies and New York was explicit. The con-spirators were another example of restless young men yearning for free-dom. As Manisha Sinha has argued, their conspiracy and rebellion was part of a black abolitionist tradition.[46]

Enslaved New Jerseyans were part of the major conspiracy of the sum-mer of 1741 that shook New York City to its roots. Several blacks were appre-hended following arson that destroyed Fort George in New York City and then were discovered to have been part of a criminal gang that plotted to burn the city and turn it over to the Spanish as part of the war between England and Spain. Once white authorities uncovered the plot they forced confessions from scores of enslaved people, executed more than thirty by horrific means, and sentenced more than 170 to transportation to the West Indies, where the life expectancy of workers in the sugar plantations was but a few years at best. Enslaved conspirators used methods very similar to those employed in Somerset County in 1734 including thefts of food and drink, illicit meetings, this time at taverns, and oaths to kill the whites and over-throw the city to gain freedom. In the aftermath of the conspiracy, enslaved people in Bergen County assaulted their masters with axes, poisoned them, and burned barns. Several blacks, fleeing from the bloodletting in New York City, escaped to Elizabethtown, where they were quickly taken into custody, presumed guilty, and burned at the stake.[47]

Two years later, one horrific incident summed up the bad relations between masters and enslaved people in New Jersey and pointed toward the disruptive qualities of the American Revolution. A powerfully built slave owned by Jacob Van Neste of Somerset County cleft his master's head in an angry dispute involving tobacco. The next day, local whites forced the enslaved black to touch the decapitated head; blood then ran from the nos-trils, proving that he was the murderer. His trial accomplished, execution occurred on the banks of the Raritan River with hundreds of blacks in forced assemblage. Sheriff Abraham Van Doren of Somerset County orches-trated the execution by burning at the stake. As the flames licked up his body, the condemned man shouted to the multitude, "they have taken the root but left the branches." Those branches would soon sprout the fruits of revolution.[48]

As American society roiled over perceived British oppression of its colonies, blacks in New Jersey almost universally suffered in a harsh slave society. Quaker objections to bondage notwithstanding, Jersey African Americans lacked any civil, economic, or social rights. While their white masters pros-pered in New Jersey's rich grain, fishing, and mining economies, blacks lacked control over their labor and possessed no means of improvement. Angry, restless young black men saw nothing to lose as the era of the American Revolution unfolded.

~

CHAPTER 2

From Revolution to Gradual
Emancipation, 1764–1804

The American Revolution birthed the United States and transformed New Jersey, along with its twelve partners, from colony to state. During the forty-one years between the onset of revolutionary turmoil in 1763 and gradual emancipation in New Jersey in 1804, Americans fought against the British, their perceived oppressors, while Jersey Patriots and Loyalists engaged in a bitter civil war. As white Americans continually accused the English government of planning to enslave them, black Americans, the truly oppressed, listened carefully to political rhetoric and waited for their chances. They did not have to be patient long. Lord Dunmore (John Murray), the British governor of Virginia, threatened upstart Patriots that he would free enslaved people willing to offer service to the Crown if the Americans did not back down on their demands for freedom. On November 7, 1775, Dunmore offered freedom to all "indent[ur]ed servants, negroes . . . willing to serve His Majesty's forces to end the present rebellion." His proclamation encouraged innumerable enslaved blacks to flee their masters in hopes of liberty. Dunmore's efforts eventually floundered and he abandoned hundreds of self-emancipated people when he fled Virginia for safety in New York. There, military officers repeated his proclamation. English generals William Howe and Henry Clinton promised freedom to blacks in exchange for military service in 1776 and 1779 in advertisements placed extensively in local newspapers. The effect on New Jersey slaves was potent. The number of free blacks in New Jersey grew exponentially during the conflict, whether by flight, military service, or negotiations with masters. Hundreds of enslaved New Jerseyans fled their Patriot and Loyalist masters during the war to join the British forces in New York. There they united with over 3,000 self-emancipated people from throughout the colonies in the largest burst for freedom before the Civil War. After the American victory and signing of the peace treaty in 1783, about 300 known former New Jersey slaves left for exile in Nova Scotia. Many left in 1791 to Sierra Leone, and those who remained founded black society in Canada's Maritime provinces. Accompanying them were enslaved people who were taken north by Loyalist masters. In both places they strived to establish republican governments even more egalitarian than that of the American Patriots. Enslaved blacks remaining in New Jersey had to face white Patriots who were unwilling to extend revolutionary freedom to them. Still, the black experience in the Revolution, abetted by liberal white agitation for abolition, pushed human bondage in the state toward extinction, even as many whites bitterly defended it. It was twenty years, as slavery expanded and political debate took place, before the state passed legislation for gradual emancipation to negotiate the paradox of the American Revolution, freedom for whites and slavery for blacks. That high-wire tension is the subject of this chapter.[1]

QUAKERS, BLACKS, AND THE COMING
OF THE AMERICAN REVOLUTION

Talk of freedom and the abolition of slavery had been public news in New Jersey ever since the Society of Friends determined to cleanse its faith of slaveholding. Counties nearest Philadelphia were most affected by the famous Quaker Minute decision of 1755, which mandated that members of the Society of Friends should free their enslaved people and no longer take part in the slave trade. At the onset of the American Revolution activists beyond the Society of Friends, stirred by publication of Anthony Benezet's magnum opus *Some Historical Account of Guinea* (1772), initiated a flurry of pamphlets, petitions, and lobbying to end chattel bondage in New Jersey. Defenders of slavery responded sharply, creating a debate that would last until long after the American Revolution. Benezet sought support from Englishman Granville Sharp and other opponents of slavery in the mother country. Their correspondence inspired a Burlington Quaker printer to publish William Dillwyn's 1773 pamphlet *Brief Considerations on Slavery and the Expediency of its Abolition*. Dillwyn argued that slavery contradicted the golden rule and violated natural rights of liberty. A second pamphlet included Granville Sharp's refutation of former Monmouth County Anglican cleric Thomas Thompson's defense of slavery. Recall that Thompson had served as a missionary to blacks in Monmouth County from 1745 to 1751, before moving to Africa.

These pamphlets, argues Jonathan Sassi, undergirded petitions to the colonial legislature calling for revisions of the manumission laws and a ban on slave imports.[2] Most of the signers were Friends, but Baptists and Anglicans were also signatories. Quaker Samuel Allinson from Burlington lobbied the legislature and recruited prominent attorney Elias Boudinot of Elizabethtown to help. Although Allinson and Boudinot secured some discussion of the bill, powerful proslavery advocates coordinated the opposition, citing allegations of "depraved" behavior by free blacks and urging caution before considering such unprecedented measures. A draft bill that emerged in legislative committee allowed for gratis manumissions of enslaved blacks over the age of twenty-one, but raised fees for every year after that. Additional clauses forbade free blacks from entertaining enslaved people and threatened heavy fines. Any free black could be sold into indentured slavery for nonpayment of debts, interracial marriages were punishable by fines of one hundred British pounds, any black who assaulted a white person would be whipped. Free blacks, Mulattos, and Indians were prohibited from voting, holding office, or testifying against whites. Even such oppressive reforms had little chance as the assembly delayed action from year to year. The outbreak of the American Revolution stymied any resolution. At the outset of the war, even though Patriots voiced their opposition to British tyranny, there was little appetite to end genuine chattel bondage.

New Jersey Quakers maintained pressure for abolition with political authorities. Samuel Allinson edited English abolitionist Granville Sharp's pamphlets for publication in America. In 1777, Allinson undertook a lengthy correspondence with Patriot governor William Livingston, arguing that the official should push the assembly harder to enact the abolition of slavery. Livingston responded sympathetically. He promised to use his influence privately against a labor system he considered so "utterly inconsistent with the principles of Christianity and humanity & in America, who have almost idolized liberty, particularly odious and disgraceful." Nonetheless, Livingston had to tell Allinson that the assembly believed the situation too critical to consider abolition during the war. New Jersey Patriots lived in fear of black uprisings and regarded enslaved people and free blacks as dangerous. Livingston, who served as governor until his death in 1790, was unable to transform his ideals into law, although he did free his own enslaved people.[3]

Quakers were not the only white Jersey Christians troubled by the paradox of slavery and freedom in revolutionary debate. Reverend Jacob Green of Hanover, a Presbyterian like Governor Livingston, was mobbed when he sermonized that America, even if it became free of England, would have "inward convulsions, contentions, oppressions, and various calamities," until it cleansed itself of slavery. Green, like many Congregational and Presbyterian ministers before him, had been a slaveholder. He had gone into debt in the 1750s to purchase an enslaved boy, only to have the servant die in 1756. While he shared many Patriots' belief that the English were striving to enslave the colonies, he pushed his analysis further to encompass the true slaves. In his pamphlet *Observations on the Reconciliation of Great-Britain and the Colonies*, Green contended, "What a shocking consideration, that the people who are so strenuously contending for liberty, should at the same time encourage and promote slavery." From the pulpit two years later he asked what Congress meant by the Declaration of Independence. Green thundered that "our Practicing Slavery is the most crying sin in our land," as the mob sacked his church. Despite his radical declarations, Green remained pragmatic in his views about slavery, believing that legislative action was necessary for gradual emancipation, a vision very much in concert with fellow white critics of human bondage. As the war ended in 1783, New Jersey Quaker David Cooper's pamphlet, *A Serious Address to the Ruler*

of America on the Inconsistency of their Conduct Respecting Slavery, declared
the self-evident equality of all men and derided the "pompous declarations"
about liberty for the slaveholders.[4]

Quakers engaged in the most vocal public conversation about slavery.
The more conservative New York Meeting, which included East Jersey, followed the gradualist methods of their Philadelphia brethren and did not
insist upon members' immediate action. Masters delayed manumissions
until they received several years of service. Eventually, however, Quakers
pushed members harder, using personal visits to convince recalcitrant masters. In one evocative instance in late 1775, a delegation from the Shrewsbury Meeting of Monmouth County called upon John Corlies, a Friend
who refused to emancipate his two enslaved people. Corlies's mother, Zilpha,
owned a pair as well. Quakers did not simply drop by, talk briefly, and then
leave. Such conversations could take hours. Corlies had been in trouble
with the Meeting before about his drinking, cursing, and fighting. After
Corlies explained to the Meeting that his enslaved blacks "have no learning
and he is not inclined to give them any," the visitors reluctantly departed,
starting a process that would lead to Corlies's excommunication three years
later.[5]

A third person listened carefully to this conversation. Titus, an enslaved
man belonging to Corlies, was nearing his twenty-first birthday, a time of
perceived manhood. In addition to Quaker admonitions toward his master,
Titus probably had heard rumors floating north of Dunmore's proclamation. Coincidentally or not, Titus fled from Corlies's farm the next day. He
left, as did thousands of other blacks along the Atlantic colonies, to make
the revolution into a war for abolition.[6]

Titus became known as Colonel Tye, leader of gangs of white and black
marauders who attacked and captured Patriot masters and stole their pos-
sessions to sell to the British army. After a first reappearance at the Battle
of Monmouth, Tye terrorized Patriot masters around Shrewsbury in
July 1779 in raids that seized silver, clothing, and cattle. The British army in

THREE POUNDS Reward.

RUN away from the fubfcriber, living in Shrewfbury, in the county of Monmouth, New-Jerfey, a NEGROE man, named TITUS, but may probably change his name; he is about 21 years of age, not very black, near 6 feet high; had on a grey homefpun coat, brown breeches, blue and white ftockings, and took with him a wallet, drawn up at one end with a ftring, in which was a quantity of clothes. Whoever takes up faid Negroe, and fecures him in any goal, or brings him to me, fhall be entitled to the above reward of *Three Pounds* proc. and all reafonable charges, paid by
Nov. 8, 1775. $ JOHN CORLIS.

Pennsylvania Gazette, November 12, 1775. Titus fled south to join Lord Dunmore's Ethiopian Regiment, then returned to New Jersey the following year as Colonel Tye to begin his guerrilla war against the state's slave masters.

Figure 1. Advertisement of the self-emancipation of Titus Corlies (est. 1754–1780), later Colonel Tye. *Pennsylvania Gazette*, November 12, 1775.

New York City badly needed the animals and paid Tye handsomely for them. Equally significant were his human captures. From March to August 1780 Tye's "motley crew" seized Patriot soldiers, including Barnes Smock, the leader of the Monmouth Militia, ransacked his house, spiked his cannon, and spirited him away to prison in New York City. Terrified Patriots beseeched Governor William Livingston to declare martial law in Monmouth to stop Tye and other Loyalists. The banditti's crowning achievement was the capture of Josiah Huddy, a scourge of New Jersey Loyalists, and infamous for summary executions of them. Tye was transporting Huddy and presumably Lucretia Edwards, Huddy's enslaved woman who often fought alongside her master, back to New York across the lower bay when a Patriot gunboat crew attacked them. During the battle Huddy escaped while Tye suffered a wrist wound from a gunshot. Left untreated, the injury soon turned into lockjaw and killed him. Several generations of New Jerseyans remembered

Tye for his fearless raids and wondered if the war might have ended sooner
had the Patriots accepted him as a solider.[7]

Titus was not alone. For several years before the onset of war, young black
men in Monmouth and Somerset had been taking their masters' horses to
attend late night meetings. When confronted, they responded: "they should
not have their masters long." Taking advantage of the absence of whites
serving in the militia, blacks regularly held mass meetings and talked of
their own revolution. The war revealed more black leaders. Major Tom Ward
formed a gang of black woodcutters, foragers, and warriors who controlled
blockhouses at Fort Lee and Bergen Neck and who raided Patriot positions
around East Jersey. These black-controlled forts provided cover for self-
emancipated blacks. As many as thirty self-emancipated blacks in 1779
rolled timber down the hills at Weehawken, tied the wood together, and
floated the raft to freedom in New York City. Talk of black revolt was common. Blacks and British officers planned a thwarted uprising in Elizabethtown in 1779 and frightened Americans began moving enslaved people to
more remote parts of the state, away from the enticements of the English.[8]

If enslaved blacks could not flee, they used the revolutionary tumult to
settle scores with masters. As the British army moved through central New
Jersey in 1776, local masters worried about English soldiers "continually
forming with Numbers of our Negroes," Reverend Alexander McWhorter of
Newark reported that a local master named Thomas Hayes was murdered
by his slave who stabbed him with a sword and then slashed his aged uncle.
As the British retreated to New York City following George Washington's
badly needed victories at Trenton and Princeton, blacks left their masters
throughout New Jersey to join the Crown.[9]

Black uprisings during the Revolution inspired great fear among the
Patriots, who contested British army actions in public displays of anger and
anxiety about rape, destruction, and murder. Describing British soldiers as
barbarians who "play the devil with girls and even old women to satisfy
their libidinous appetites," Patriots argued for a halt in any discussion of
abolition as they believed that such talk would cause economic losses among
slaveholders and inspire potential black revolt.[10]

Formerly enslaved blacks had reasonable fears about Patriots as well. Where British forces did not disrupt it, slavery continued within the Patriot lines. Over 113 blacks were listed for sale between 1776 and 1782, though some were Loyalist property. Ominously, blacks unable to account for themselves were presumed to be fleeing to the British and were held for sale. In 1781, twenty-one blacks seized at sea when Patriots captured the British privateer *Malton* were routinely sold into bondage regardless of their personal claims. Nor were the English above kidnapping. Despite the proclamations of Crown generals, British soldiers stole enslaved people from masters in Monmouth, Bergen, and Burlington counties, likely for use as servants.[11]

During the Revolution, New Jersey blacks responded to British military proclamations to join their forces in exchange for freedom by creating the largest slave escape before the Civil War. During the conflict, thousands of enslaved and some free blacks joined the British army as black Loyalists, many of them escaping to New York City. A list of 3,000 black Loyalists included more than one hundred from Bergen County, six from Middlesex, over thirty from Essex, and twenty-four from Monmouth County. Unlike earlier eras, self-emancipated blacks now included more women and children.[12]

Even as the war neared the American victory, black and white Loyalists refused to go quietly. Ward's gang raided Patriot positions in Hackensack and Closter in the summer of 1781. The following year, forty blacks and forty whites, known as the Armed Boat Company, attacked Patriot homes at Forked River. To proclaim their loyalty, the Black Pioneers at the Fort Lee blockhouse sent New Year's greetings in 1781 to Sir Henry Clinton. In response, Prince William Henry, later King William IV, visited the Fort Lee blockhouse that summer.[13]

During the peace negotiations between Sir Guy Carleton, head of the British forces in North America, and General George Washington, Patriot masters used flags of truce to enter New York City in search of escaped slaves. A Captain Hessius from Totowa Falls traveled to New York City in early July 1782 to seek return of his fugitive slaves. On his way back, Hessius was beset and murdered by more than a dozen of Ward's blacks, who were described as "followers of the army." General Carleton personally reviewed the case and ordered the gang transported as slaves to the West Indies rather than executing them, as was the norm.[14]

Carleton did not always favor black Loyalists. He informed Washington, who was furious about the loss of thousands of blacks he regarded as American property, that only blacks who entered the British lines in 1782 or earlier would be protected under British proclamations. Others would be returned to their masters. For example Thomas Smith claimed that Betty from Aquackanonck, New Jersey, had fled only the previous year, and so regained her after the British officials accepted his argument.[15]

At least 240 former slaves from New Jersey left in 1783 with the English bound primarily for Nova Scotia with others going to England, the West Indies, the West Coast of Africa, and even Australia. Some joined the British army and fought in regiments around the world. They and the others were part of the freedom generation of 1783, as Maya Jasanoff has termed it, choosing democracy and freedom under a constitutional monarchy rather than slavery in a republican state. Black New Jersey Loyalists had fought for the same freedoms as whites, seeking greater political and civil liberties and access to land and opportunity. They did not succeed in ending slavery in New Jersey but they challenged it mightily.[16]

Black New Jerseyans who did not join the British forces found new freedoms in other ways. Colonial laws allowing masters to enlist their bond people continued. Samuel Sutphin of Readington, Somerset County, enlisted in the militia in place of his master, Caspar Berger, who had just purchased him from Guisbert Bogert with that plan in mind. Sutphin fought for four years, saw duty in the Battle of Long Island, and fought against Native Americans in upstate New York. Following the war, the duplicitous Berger, who had promised Sutphin freedom, sold him to a new master named Peter Sutphin. The enslaved man worked out an arrangement with his new master to work for his freedom, years after he had earned it with military service. Prime, who deserted from his Tory master and served as a wagoner in the Patriot army, sued successfully for his freedom after the war with legal aid from sympathetic whites. Others were more fortunate. Oliver Cromwell, an enslaved man from Burlington County, served as a private in the New Jersey Continental Line between 1777 and 1781 and fought in the battles of Trenton, Brandywine, Princeton, Monmouth, and Yorktown. He later received a federal pension. Peter Williams Sr. left his Tory master, John Heard of Woodbridge, and helped the Patriot side. After the war, the state of New Jersey confiscated Heard's property, making Williams a ward of the government. The state legislature credited Williams Sr. for his service and emancipated him. He later became custodian of the John Street Methodist Church in New York City. His son, Peter Jr., became a famous black cleric in New York City. Thomas Fortune was a highly trusted document messenger for General George Washington.

Free blacks also chose the Patriot side with uneven results. Prince Whipple, a "free born native African," crossed the Delaware River with General Washington on December 25–26, 1776, and is pictured in the famous Emanuel Leutze painting of the event. Samuel Charleton worked as a driver for the Americans and saw occasional combat duty. Blacks working along with white indentured servants labored in New Jersey iron furnaces and forges, making cannonballs for the Americans. When the British found enslaved people helping the Americans they were no more merciful than their enemy. Two black women attempting to save cattle from British seizure were killed. After the war, as Judith Van Buskirk has shown, black Patriots who gained their freedom often had to battle for pensions. Samuel Sutphin, for example, had to overcome constant rejections for many years before receiving his first pension payment in 1836 at the age of eighty-nine.[17]

Slavery and Postrevolutionary New Jersey

New Jersey emerged from the American Revolution as part of the new confederation of the United States. As the state recovered from the ravages of the Revolution, its legislators reinstalled colonial laws governing slavery. The loss of over 300 black Loyalists did not curtail slavery's hold on New Jersey's economy and society. In Bergen County, the number of enslaved people grew from 2,301 in 1790 to 2,825 a decade later. Similar increases occurred in Middlesex, Essex, Monmouth, and Somerset Counties. Even in 1810, six years after the Gradual Emancipation Act, Somerset County was the only one in East Jersey with more free blacks than slaves. Newly formed Morris and Sussex Counties used slavery as a principal labor method into the 1820s. West Jersey was different. The impact of Quaker abolitionism and black initiative meant that free blacks outnumbered enslaved people in Burlington, Cumberland, Gloucester and Salem Counties by 1790. Only Cape May County clutched most of its black residents in slavery in 1790, a disparity that did not end until 1810. Cape May whaling families increased their ownership of enslaved people during the war years and its aftermath. The county's whaling families ignored Quaker appeals to emancipate slaves and sought them for the booming whaling business and as woodcutters. By the end of the war, Cape May held the highest percentage of enslaved people in West Jersey. At the same time, the white population of New Jersey increased at a rate six times that of blacks between 1786 and 1800, lessening the need for enslaved labor.[18]

Few white New Jerseyans felt compelled to solve the fundamental contradiction between their own liberty and continuance of human bondage. New Jersey citizens, smarting from the civil war that characterized revolutionary conflict in the state, blamed the Society of Friends for poisoning the minds of blacks about freedom, and argued that talk of emancipation was a Quaker plot to get blacks the vote and control state politics. Others argued that blacks had fought for the British in the American Revolution and did not deserve freedom. At the same time, some white and black New Jerseyans pushed for the abolition of slavery. They joined a petition in 1783 urging the Continental Congress to ban the slave trade and helped boycott itinerant Methodist preachers who owned slaves.[19]

The state played a key role in the formation of the U.S. Constitution in 1787. William Paterson encapsulated the "small states" position in his fears that the proposed Constitution would allow the larger states, including New York and Pennsylvania, to dominate the new government. Paterson's anxieties propelled the successful plan for a bicameral legislature composed of a Senate and House of Representatives and a weaker executive than some originally envisioned. New Jersey's special constitutional convention passed the new Constitution unanimously in 1787, the third state to approve the new government. As New Jersey's political leaders then looked locally, that initial unity gave way to tough ideological battles over the extent of the suffrage for white males, patronage, and party formation. New Jersey was the only state where white, propertied, single females and black males could vote after the Revolution. Amendments to state suffrage removed those unique rights in 1807, when the state was unified on such exclusions. New Jersey politics had a strong two-party government that morphed into general unity by 1815.[20]

One revolutionary dream took a long time to fulfill. For all of the Patriots' demands for liberty and fears of enslavement by the English government, New Jersey's white citizens refused to end slavery in the state after the American Revolution. Indeed, many New Jerseyans were unsympathetic, pairing African Americans with Quakers and Anglicans as groups actively loyal to the Crown. The egalitarian and evangelical sentiment apparent in Virginia and Maryland that led many slave masters to emancipate their chattel was notably absent in New Jersey. One commentator on the subject contended that blacks were property as much as gold and silver, and the state would go bankrupt compensating masters for loss of property. Slaves were described as more degraded than poor whites and therefore were better off in servitude. Another claimed that having been born enslaved, few blacks were discontented, having never known freedom. Enslaved people were too lazy, were addicted to alcohol, and were likely to revolt and created their own kingdom once they were freed.[21]

Other enslaved blacks purchased themselves and their families, even when confronted by masters' duplicity. Emanuel Murray of Gloucester County bought his wife's freedom only to discover that she was legally free at the time of purchase. The old master did not return the money. Peter Upshur fled his master in Maryland in 1787 only to be jailed in New Jersey. A white man paid nineteen dollars for jail costs and kept Upshur in bondage for nine years. The ambitious Upshur took on extra work, became literate, paid back one hundred dollars advanced to him to satisfy the Maryland owner, and eventually bought his wife and two children, paying every penny owed. One white, Joseph Sotwell, advanced money to help twelve enslaved people purchase their freedom.[22]

The Quaker counties in West Jersey, solidly in favor of abolition, had a friend in postwar governor William Livingston. He helped push legislators to pass an act in 1786 to prevent further importation of enslaved blacks into the state from Africa or other American states. The legislature also enabled manumissions by reducing the requirements to obtaining a certificate to be signed by two of the Overseers of the Poor and two Justices of the Peace in a county. Masters imbued with revolutionary egalitarianism acted on their principles by freeing their human chattel. On July 4, 1783, Moses Bloomfield, joined by his fourteen slaves, stood on a platform in Woodbridge, New Jersey. As others celebrated the nation's birthday, Bloomfield asked why "all men are created equal, and why should these, my fellow-citizens, my equals be held in bondage?" Bloomfield then emancipated all fourteen and asked them if they intended to rely on public support, a common belief held by opponents of emancipation. Making a line above the joint of his left-hand fingers, one answered, "Neber, massa, Neber as along as dese fingers are left above dese joints."[23]

Legislative enabling of manumissions had no more effect than in the colonial period. Of the 354 enslaved people mentioned in wills executed in Monmouth County between 1790 and 1809, nearly all were passed on to widows, sons, and daughters. There was but one unconditional grant of freedom and twenty gradual emancipations. Sensing the lure of freedom, white masters and enslaved blacks negotiated private contracts to create legal liberty.[24]

Blacks asserted their freedom even while perceived to be enslaved. Adam from Trenton advertised in the newspaper that one David Cowell had falsely advertised him for sale. Adam stated that Cowell had no right to make such a sale, that he (Adam) was a free man and cautioned any potential buyer that he "expect[ed] that freedom and justice and protection which I am entitled to by the laws of the state, altho' I am a Negro." Over the two decades more blacks took to print to proclaim their freedoms and belief in human equality.[25]

As in New York City, black Jerseyans gained freedom primarily through self-emancipation. The impact of British appeals offering freedom to enslaved people for military service during the American Revolution, the egalitarian and abolitionist beliefs about freedom circulating among whites, and the awareness that some blacks were gaining freedom, made bondage increasingly unacceptable. Not surprisingly, most self-emancipated people, primarily young males, came from East Jersey, the section with the lowest percentage of free people. James Gigantino has argued that the postwar period saw a downturn in the numbers of self-emancipated people, offering more frequent marriages and family formation as reasons for lowered desire to escape slavery. Given the massive numbers of self-emancipated people fleeing to the British lines, peacetime and greater masterly control over bondpeople might produce fewer escapes.[26]

Still, newspaper advertisements announced bursts to freedom. Most escapees from slavery were farmworkers headed for the cities. There were also skilled workers such as blacksmiths, shoemakers, teamsters, dairy workers, carpenters, brick makers, and fiddlers. As in the colonial period, many pretended to be free and forged passes.[27]

Poor relations between masters and enslaved people are apparent in other notices. John High of Scotch Plains in Essex County commented about the flight of his bondman, Jack, in 1802, that the same "fellow ranaway last fall and was taken up in Gloucester County, for which he never showed the least correction, and now he has shewed his gratitude." Barzilla F. Randolph of Piscataway warned that Pomp, who fled in 1801, was "deranged so that he is trouble to people wherever he is." Peter, who escaped from William Chetwood of Elizabethtown in 1805, "when in liquor is impertinent." Rob, according to his master, David Nichols of Newark, was "very much given to intoxication, at which time he is very quarrelsome." Will was a "bold, daring fellow, talks and laughs much and very loud."[28]

The influence of British and American revolutionary actions and stronger Quaker abolitionism abetted black freedom desires. Add to this a general white fear of black revolt stemming from the revolutionary experience and in the 1790s anxieties spurred by the Saint-Domingue Revolt meant finding common ground between intransigent masters in East Jersey, especially Bergen County, and Quakers in West Jersey to end slavery. There were worrisome incidents. After a series of acts of arson and rumors of revolt in Newark, the city magistrates banned slaves from meeting together or leaving their masters' homes after 10:00 P.M. Middlesex County officials executed three slaves after learning of a planned uprising. Bergen County whites fretted after barn burnings, poisonings, and thefts and asked the state for tighter laws.[29]

Fearful of slave revolt and troubled by the contradictions of slavery and freedom, white elites organized to enable black freedom peacefully. The New Jersey Society for the Abolition of Slavery defended the rights of free blacks and helped others successfully sue for their freedom. Encouraged by Pennsylvania's Abolition Society, and founded in 1786 by future governor Joseph Bloomfield and New Jersey Congressman Elias Boudinot, the society provided assistance from the state's elite to blacks seeking freedom. For example, Quamini of Morris County made a pact with his old master, Captain Augustus Bayles of Morris, that he would never be sold if he faithfully served Bayles. After his master's death, his widow remarried and her new husband tried to sell Quamini to one William Leddell. Quamini, with the help of the society, sued Leddell and won his freedom over the broken promise. The society continued to press the state legislature to end slavery in the early 1790s.[30]

Opponents of abolition fought hard against its proponents. Popular racism plagued public discourse as whites derided black achievements and aspirations. After some legislative successes in the 1780s, abolitionists faced new obstacles in the next decade. In 1794, the New Jersey State Assembly, disturbed by court decisions granting blacks freedom, passed legislation making emancipation harder. Three years later, a bill freeing enslaved people once they had worked for twenty-eight years was defeated in the legislature. Defenders of slavery reminded voters of Quaker pacifism during the Revolution and argued that ending slavery and giving blacks the vote would put Quakers in charge, whose tyranny would be worse than the English. Ultimately, the question over emancipation came down to the property rights of the masters and the need to compensate them.[31]

Two developments complicated state discussions about the future of slavery. First, in 1792 enslaved people in Saint-Domingue successfully revolted against their French masters. Thousands of slaveowning refugees fled to the United States with their chattel and more than two hundred headed for the Philadelphia area. Proslavery New Jerseyans raised funds to help them. Enslaved people belonging to exiled masters observed freedom in America and sued to prevent any later return to their home island. Romain, held in bondage by Anthony Salaignac, who had found succor in Trenton, committed suicide to avoid returning to slavery with his master. Salaignac had secured permission from the mayor of Trenton, who had interpreted the 1786 Jersey law barring the slave trade in the master's favor. Helped by abolitionists, Romain's family fled from Salaignac, but after constables brought Romain to Philadelphia for passage to San Domingo, Romain ended his life, thereby raising a furor and accelerating demands for the termination of slavery. Second, the U.S. Congress passed the Fugitive Slave Act of 1793, which required intrastate cooperation over the return of self-emancipated people. Seemingly unremarkable at the time, this law eventually sharpened the divide among whites about the morality of slavery and citizens' roles in upholding state and federal laws. For blacks striving for self-emancipation through flight, the law required increasing savvy about which regions and people among whites could be trusted and who to avoid. Such knowledge was key to the emerging Underground Railroad.[32]

Isaac Hopper, James Forten, Robert Purvis, and other Philadelphia conductors blazed paths on what would become known as the Underground Railroad. Hopper, one of the earliest and most energetic, was born in Deptford Township near Woodbury on December 3, 1771. Hopper's mother was Presbyterian and his father was a Quaker who was disowned for marrying out of the sect. Young Isaac labored on their farm and grew up fearless and fond of pranks. After he moved to Philadelphia and joined the Society of Friends, his predilection for mischief informed his more serious business of helping enslaved people become free of their masters. Hopper's methods took him routinely in and out of New Jersey. In contrast to the more solemn, legalistic vision of his colleagues at the Pennsylvania Abolition Society,

Hopper became adept at finding crevices in the law that suddenly freed bond people to the immense frustration of their masters. Described as a "utility man," for the movement by Richard S. Newman, Hopper, along with Thomas Shipley, Thomas Harrison, and Arnold Bussom, traveled to prisons, gave legal aid to kidnapped free blacks, interviewed deponents for upcoming cases, chased down crucial legal cases, and counseled black families on legal needs. What Hopper initiated in the 1790s would become standard methodology for black and radical white abolitionists by the 1830s and powerfully informed slave rescue cases in the 1850s.[33]

The emergence of black towns in the early nineteenth century in part derived from these early manifestations of the Underground Railroad. Timbuctoo, situated in Westhampton Township, Burlington County, about two miles from Mount Holly, is a good example. Long before abolitionist and wealthy landowner Gerrit Smith established a similarly named settlement in the Adirondack Mountains of New York State, John Woolman, Samuel Aaron, and Joseph Reid formed a syndicate in the late eighteenth century with the express purpose of freeing enslaved blacks. The syndicate's method was unique. The partners traveled to the South and gathered eager blacks to form a company. Then the syndicate paid for their passage to England, where they lived long enough to become British subjects, gained passports stating their citizenship, and then returned to America and on to Timbuctoo. There they labored at a brickyard owned by the syndicate. Each newly emancipated man was given shelter, use of a parcel of land, and a waged job at the brickyard. Timbuctoo became a flourishing settlement of about sixty families with a church, school, and homeowners. It became a key stop on the Underground Railroad.[34]

The slow pace of emancipation politics in New Jersey made free black people from nearby states vulnerable to abuses. Kidnapping of enslaved and free people increased along with fraudulent contracts. In one case in 1798 the Pennsylvania Abolition Society intervened when Doras Jennings, a black master chimney sweep, abandoned his apprentice, a young black named John Allen, in New Brunswick, New Jersey. Allen was soon arrested for vagrancy in a slave state, then sold by the town sheriff at public auction to a doctor who then resold him to another master. The society labored hard for five years to free the lad, but eventually the case disappeared from its record books, which was a troubling indication that he had become a lifetime slave.[35]

Even as the drumbeat for gradual emancipation became louder, New Jersey's legislators passed laws indicating their concerns about unruly enslaved people. A law passed in 1799 provided that disobedient slaves could be committed to a workhouse to serve hard labor or other punishments the justices deemed reasonable. Showing further worries, the legislators enacted a law in 1801 that ordered masters to sell violent and criminal slaves out of the state. Until a sale was achieved, the enslaved person would be jailed at the master's expense.[36]

New Jersey's continued slave status allowed masters to continue to own human chattel even if servitude had ended in their home states. Former Philadelphia Quaker Philemon Dickinson, son of the Patriot leader, John, owned a farm with slaves in Trenton. Asked to free them, he indignantly refused until New Jersey enacted a bill of gradual emancipation.[37]

The Gradual Emancipation Act of 1804 recognized patterns that had emerged since the end of the American Revolution. Most blacks remained enslaved before and after the passage of the act. As in the colonial era, slavery persisted in the five eastern counties, though the numbers of free blacks expanded greatly beyond the earlier miniscule few. The first federal census of 1790 enumerated 192 free people of color in Bergen County, 140 in Middlesex, and 147 in Somerset. Somerset County epitomized slavery's moving frontier. Sparsely settled earlier in the colonial period, Somerset was the focus of Dutch American development in the state. By 1790, nearly 2,000 enslaved blacks lived in Somerset, with only a handful of free people of color. Ten years later, the county's enslaved population had increased. These rises in slavery were most pronounced in Dutch towns. In Dutch-dominated Freehold, Monmouth County, there were but twelve free blacks in 1790 and 627 enslaved people. In the Scot-Irish and Quaker town of Shrewsbury, there were nearly as many free blacks as enslaved people (165 versus 212). In Monmouth County, where Reformed Dutch and Huguenot masters held tightly

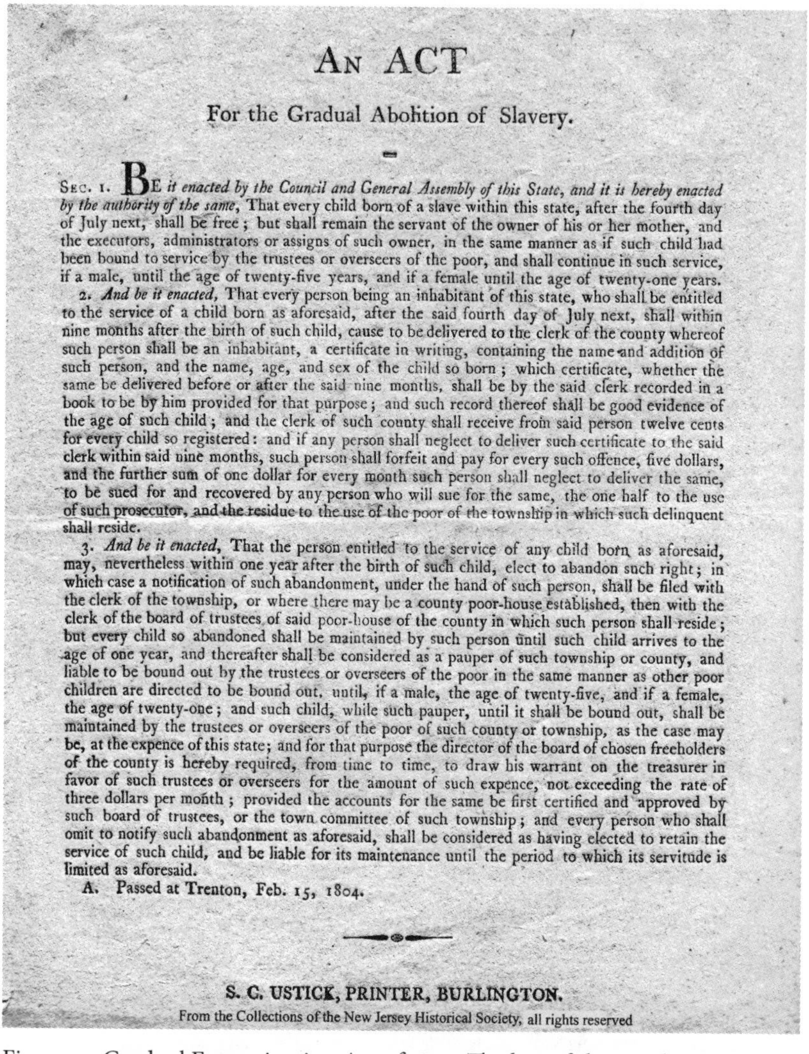

An ACT

For the Gradual Abolition of Slavery.

SEC. 1. BE *it enacted by the Council and General Assembly of this State, and it is hereby enacted by the authority of the same,* That every child born of a slave within this state, after the fourth day of July next, shall be free ; but shall remain the servant of the owner of his or her mother, and the executors, administrators or assigns of such owner, in the same manner as if such child had been bound to service by the trustees or overseers of the poor, and shall continue in such service, if a male, until the age of twenty-five years, and if a female until the age of twenty-one years.

2. *And be it enacted,* That every person being an inhabitant of this state, who shall be entitled to the service of a child born as aforesaid, after the said fourth day of July next, shall within nine months after the birth of such child, cause to be delivered to the clerk of the county whereof such person shall be an inhabitant, a certificate in writing, containing the name and addition of such person, and the name, age, and sex of the child so born ; which certificate, whether the same be delivered before or after the said nine months, shall be by the said clerk recorded in a book to be by him provided for that purpose ; and such record thereof shall be good evidence of the age of such child ; and the clerk of such county shall receive from said person twelve cents for every child so registered: and if any person shall neglect to deliver such certificate to the said clerk within said nine months, such person shall forfeit and pay for every such offence, five dollars, and the further sum of one dollar for every month such person shall neglect to deliver the same, to be sued for and recovered by any person who will sue for the same, the one half to the use of such prosecutor, and the residue to the use of the poor of the township in which such delinquent shall reside.

3. *And be it enacted,* That the person entitled to the service of any child born as aforesaid, may, nevertheless within one year after the birth of such child, elect to abandon such right; in which case a notification of such abandonment, under the hand of such person, shall be filed with the clerk of the township, or where there may be a county poor-house established, then with the clerk of the board of trustees of said poor-house of the county in which such person shall reside; but every child so abandoned shall be maintained by such person until such child arrives to the age of one year, and thereafter shall be considered as a pauper of such township or county, and liable to be bound out by the trustees or overseers of the poor in the same manner as other poor children are directed to be bound out, until, if a male, the age of twenty-five, and if a female, the age of twenty-one ; and such child, while such pauper, until it shall be bound out, shall be maintained by the trustees or overseers of the poor of such county or township, as the case may be, at the expence of this state; and for that purpose the director of the board of chosen freeholders of the county is hereby required, from time to time, to draw his warrant on the treasurer in favor of such trustees or overseers for the amount of such expence, not exceeding the rate of three dollars per month ; provided the accounts for the same be first certified and approved by such board of trustees, or the town committee of such township ; and every person who shall omit to notify such abandonment as aforesaid, shall be considered as having elected to retain the service of such child, and be liable for its maintenance until the period to which its servitude is limited as aforesaid.

A. Passed at Trenton, Feb. 15, 1804.

S. C. USTICK, PRINTER, BURLINGTON.

Figure 2. Gradual Emancipation Act of 1804. The last of the northern, postrevolutionary laws pushing the system of slavery to a slow death. From the Collection of The New Jersey Historical Society, all rights reserved.

to their chattel bondpeople slavery continued to be the main status for people of color.[38]

The 1800 census revealed a sharp divide over slavery between the two sections of the state. In Quaker-dominated West Jersey, the number of enslaved people dropped precipitously. In Gloucester County, for example, sixty-one people remained enslaved, a third of the total a decade earlier. In East Jersey and the newly settled counties, the number of enslaved people actually increased. In Essex County, people held in human bondage increased from 1,171 to 1,521; similar growth occurred in Monmouth and Middlesex Counties. In Bergen, there were 500 more enslaved people in 1800 than ten years before. Morris and Sussex Counties gained more slaves in ten years.[39]

Slave masters in Dutch-dominated counties fiercely defended their right to human property. In addition to the petition to reverse the law of gradual emancipation and maintaining their tight hold on enslaved peoples, Bergen County masters punished petty criminals brutally. Two enslaved men, Ned and Pero, were found guilty of larceny in 1801 and were ordered whipped from place to place throughout the county for a month. In total, the pair each received 400 lashes. Ned died as a result. Blacks responded in kind, assaulting and burning down homes of white men in Bergen on several occasions in the 1790s.[40]

Black Religion

Frustrated economically and socially, whatever their status, black New Jerseyans found succor in religion. Notices of the self-emancipated reveal the desire for religious expression. Cato, who fled from his master in Newark in 1799, "pretends to be religious, calls himself a Methodist," and, "is a great liar." In 1786, Gilbert of Somerset County, "pretends to be religious, and sometimes undertakes to preach."[41] The rise of evangelical denominations such as Baptist and Methodist opened room for blacks to worship in European faiths. Parent bodies of these liberal theologies stymied black aspirations for leadership and full equality for blacks. Occasionally, as in the case of the Methodist church in Snow Hill (Lawnside), congregations were initially interracial, but gradually whites left. As with their counterparts in Philadelphia, New York, and other cities, rural New Jerseyans turned inwards to community worship. Camp meetings and religious itinerancy in the late 1790s and early 1800s fostered black theological talents and made room for black worship. George White and John Jea gave ringing sermons in fields and woods. Initially these were the primary religious experiences in rural New Jersey, but eventually blacks opened their own churches, a key element in community formation. Peter Cuff of Salem attended the founding conference of the African Methodist Episcopal (A.M.E.) Church and later presided over the organization of an A.M.E congregation in Salem. The black Gloucester Methodist Society purchased a lot and built a congregation in 1801 and Trenton blacks boasted their own A.M.E. church by 1807. The A.M.E. connection would become widespread in nineteenth-century New Jersey and was the platform for a highly successful clerical class. The Union Church of Africans (UCA) formed in 1813 in Delaware, and by 1816 it had a congregation in Salem. The UCA stressed local control over congregations, and the only qualified voters were "descendants of the African Race." The UCA developed when black members of white churches split off from parent white denominations to form their own congregations, despite anxieties over alienating landlords and employers. Taking that risk indicated the decline of slavery and accelerated divisions among black Americans.[42]

The first known black female spiritual leader was Jarena Lee (1783–?), born in Cape May. After spending her early adulthood as a servant to a white family, Lee felt called to preach in 1816 by the charismatic African Methodist Episcopal founder and leader Richard Allen. Lee preached in Trenton, Princeton, Burlington, and Salem as well as in Philadelphia and Delaware. She published her life and religious experience in 1836, making her one of the earliest black female writers.[43]

New Jersey invested little in education overall and almost nothing in black schools. The only education provided to blacks in the postrevolutionary era came almost entirely from the Society of Friends and Presbyterians. Friends helped black New Jerseyans attended school more regularly and Gouldtown, a black town in Cumberland County, opened schools in this period, possibly with the assistance of the Presbyterian Church. Unlike their halting efforts of the colonial period, Quakers began to organize regular school committees and conduct regular classes. In 1780, the Evesham Meeting used subscriptions to raise money for black children's schools. Similar efforts occurred in Haddonfield and Burlington during the 1780s. Quakers in Philadelphia organized the Society for the Free Instruction of Orderly Blacks and Free People of Color in 1789 to pay tuition for qualified, impoverished blacks. Soon, the society had branches in Trenton and Burlington, which operated small schools enrolling about fifteen scholars each in night classes. These schools lasted only until 1794, which further indicates the difficulties of relying on religious charity. At the collegiate level, the College of New Jersey (Princeton) enrolled two free blacks from Newport, Rhode Island during the 1780s, Bristol Yamma and John Quamine, to prepare them for missionary work in Africa. Abolitionist Reverend Samuel Hopkins of Rhode Island collaborated with a more conservative critic of slavery, Ezra Stiles, to sponsor the men at Princeton and convinced President John Witherspoon, a proslavery advocate, to be their personal supervisor. Yamma and Quamine were independent abolitionists. They attended meetings conducted by the devout and indigent Sarah Osborn, an abolitionist revivalist. At Osborn's, they heard an interracial message aimed at free blacks and women. Yamma transferred information between Hopkins and another Rhode Island Quaker abolitionist, Moses Brown. Yamma died in 1779 on board a privateer while Quamine lived until 1794 in North Carolina. John Chavis, another free black, attended Princeton briefly during this time.[44]

Such moments of liberality cannot disguise the powerful benefits the College of New Jersey received from the system of slavery. In his pathbreaking book on slavery and American universities, Craig Wilder notes that eight slave masters presided over the College of New Jersey in its first seventy-five years. Principal donors to the school included the Ogden family, which had deep ties to the Atlantic slave trade. Similarly, Queen's College (Rutgers) received significant philanthropy from Dutch Reformed families in the colony, all of whom owned slaves and frequented commerce in human bondage.[45]

Very gradually, free blacks created individual successes. Caesar Brown and his family owned a home in the town of Elsenborough and Harry Tudos of Salem had more than thirty British pounds in property. In Monmouth County, Samuel Lawrence owned one hundred acres and five cattle in 1784. Of the sixteen free black landowners in Monmouth that year, most owned homes and a few owned livestock. Twenty years later, individuals showed greater property holdings. Samuel Mingo, who died in Monmouth in 1802, had an estate worth more than £685 of which £586 was debts owed to him by local free blacks. Mingo was one of the few bankers available for free blacks as wills of white Jerseyans almost never reveal loans to blacks. In West Jersey, there were a few free black artisans. Caesar Murray of Burlington was a skilled shoemaker and operated a vocational school. Peter Hill of Mount Holly was an experienced clockmaker with his own shop. William Boen moved from enslaved person to staunch abolitionist and pioneered the New Jersey free produce movement, which required practitioners to shun products made by enslaved labor.[46]

Free blacks did not always have to rise alone. In a rare instance of cross-racial help, Sampson Adams of Trenton pushed himself up economically during the 1780s but was unable to garner enough cash to build a home and occasionally lapsed into receiving state charity and debt peonage. Sympathetic Quakers pitched in with labor, nails, and lumber to construct Adams's new home. He died in 1792 and willed forty-four pounds to his sister Violet and the rest to the county's poor relief fund.[47]

The Gradual Emancipation Act of 1804

New Jersey became the last northern state to pass an act for gradual emancipation of its enslaved residents. The New-Jersey Society for Promoting the Gradual Abolition of Slavery petitioned the legislature and general assembly in February 1804, stating that there was no continued justification for slavery in a land of freedom and that very few could plead for it on the grounds of defending private property. In deference to such claims, the society argued that future slaves should become free after serving a number of years, with the work toiled during that period considered to be compensation to their masters.

The Act for the Gradual Abolition of Slavery passed on February 15, 1804, with little fanfare. As James Gigantino has observed there was no public celebration marking the act; to many, it would seem that slavery continued unabated. The act set the number of years of service for those enslaved people born after July 4, 1804, at twenty-one years for females and twenty-five for males. The emphasis was on gradualism. No enslaved black was immediately freed and newborn children could expect to serve masters for the majority of their lives.[48] Masters were compensated for the start of gradualism as the act allowed them to abandon infants before their first year of age and then agree to maintain them at the rate of three dollars per month, an inducement that probably put the measure across. Masters also indentured slaves with time owed to artisans in Philadelphia, thereby gaining a profit from their altruism. Initially, there was optimism that the compensation plan would not become burdensome to the state's treasury. One observer countered by noting that the maintenance clause was borrowed from New York State where very few infants were abandoned. "A Citizen" forecast that maintenance charges in New Jersey would not cost taxpayers a penny. By 1807, however, maintenance charges for abandoned slaves had nearly bankrupted the state's coffers. Moreover, aggrieved slave owners in Bergen and other counties petitioned the state in 1807 that the law deprived them of the very property for which they had fought in the American Revolution and asked for immediate revocation of the Gradual Emancipation Act. While that plea was rebuffed, the New Jersey Society for the Promoting of the Abolition of Slavery apparently concluded that it had accomplished its purpose, holding its last meeting in 1809.[49]

The society's demise hardly meant that the struggle for black freedom in New Jersey was complete. As white lawmakers and philanthropists entered into an era of "benign neglect," in which they concentrated on national issues about slavery, free black New Jerseyans created struggling communities centered on church, society, and family and the creation of future politics. For those held in slavery, flight remained the principal manifestation of their abolitionism.

Passage of the Gradual Emancipation Act of 1804 placed the state of New Jersey on a long path to abolition. No one could know that the final demise of slavery locally would occur after the American Civil War and enactment of national amendments that guaranteed black freedom and male suffrage.

In 1804, slavery still flourished in New Jersey with masters retaining the right to buy, sell, hire, and bequeath. At the same time the number of free blacks, unimaginable in 1776, rose to 4,402 in 1800 and 7,843 in 1810. Emancipated blacks had freedom of movement, the ability to organize churches and fraternal organizations, the right to payment, and some political freedoms. For those still held in bondage, the Gradual Emancipation Act increased pressures on their relations with their masters to advance their freedom. In the coming decades, despite the state's political and social conservatism, Jersey blacks pushed the boundaries of freedom wider and wider.

CHAPTER 3

~

Slavery, Freedom, and Struggle, 1804–1860

Achieving freedom and equality was painfully slow for black New Jersey-ans in the decades after the Gradual Emancipation Act of 1804. Chattel bondage remained potent in the state's society and economy. In 1820, more than three-quarters of the state's black population lived in East Jersey and nearly half of them remained enslaved. A quarter century after New Jersey enacted its emancipation act and three years after neighboring New York State permanently ended slavery, human bondage retained a surprisingly strong grip in the Garden State. By 1830, although 90 percent of the state's black inhabitants were free, over 2,000 black men and women remained enslaved, 70 percent (1,596) of whom lived in East Jersey and a third of them suffered in Bergen County. Even as late as 1850, 236 blacks languished in slavery in the state. Some newly freed people were vulnerable. Cape May County opened its almshouse to aged freed people in 1821 because unscru-pulous masters were pushing them from their former homes without any assistance. Cape May masters also freed younger enslaved people very slowly with records showing manumissions as late as 1834. Sensing the lack of opportunity in their home regions, African Americans left as they became free. In 1840, there were 300 fewer free blacks living in Bergen than in 1830; the county did not regain the level of its 1830 black population (1,894 souls) until the beginning of the twentieth century. Overall the state's black popu-lation rose to just 25,000 in 1860 as people of color dropped from 7.7 percent of the entire populace in 1790 to 3.4 percent in 1860.[1]

Poor work conditions, legal inequities, and harsh racial attitudes limited growth in New Jersey's black population. Males continued to concentrate in rural areas and most stayed dependent on their former masters as cottagers. Twenty thousand blacks lived in the state in 1820 and had increased by just 5,000 in 1860 . During this time, the overall population of New Jersey climbed from about 74,000 in 1810 to almost 178,000 at the eve of the Civil War. Black percentages of the whole stayed at about 5 percent in the six decades between 1804 and 1860. That stagnation, exacerbated by white racism, ensured any black economic gains in New Jersey were only incremental.[2]

Enslavement of blacks had supported the state's agricultural economy but New Jersey African Americans did not share in the state's new capitalist economy. New Jersey gradually changed from a rural, agricultural society to one that was urban and industrial. In a move not widely recognized for its immediate impact on black life in New Jersey, and which had long-term repercussions, the Society for Establishing Useful Manufactures (S.U.M.) initiated its plans for a national cotton factory near Acquackanonck. S.U. M. was spearheaded by Secretary of the U.S. Department of Treasury Alexander Hamilton, one of the principal members of the New York Manumission Society, founded by John Jay, the nation's first Chief Justice. Hamilton planned to name the new industrial town Paterson, to flatter the state governor, William Paterson. The S.U.M. at first employed Irish Catholic immigrants from New York City, a move that alienated local Protestants. The mill initially floundered but revived after the Embargo of 1807 and attracted heterogeneous mix of English and Irish immigrants and local Dutch as laborers. Very few African Americans could find work in the mills. One reason was certainly the tight grip with which Bergen County farmers retained enslaved people. Farmers seemed unwilling to hire out their bond people to the new industrial plant. A second, important reason was Hamilton's plan, enunciated in his famous 1791 *Report on Manufactures*, which became the foundational document for American industry. In it, Hamilton called for an industrial plan that would attract immigrant manufacturers and artisans to the new nation, a method Hamilton and associates used in Paterson. Significantly, Hamilton did not include the possibility of employing skilled free blacks, of whom there were many living in New York City and New Jersey. That omission made by an elite political figure anticipated nineteenth-century political indifference to black employment and led to the general exclusion of the skilled black laborers as part of the industrial labor force of the nineteenth century.[3]

Turnpikes, steamboats, canals, and, by the 1830s, railroads accelerated the commercialization of agriculture and trade with New York City and Philadelphia, the nation's two largest cities. New Jersey towns became cities in this era and Jersey City became a suburb of New York City. Newark boasted decent-paying manufacturing jobs primarily for new Irish and German immigrants. Shoes, often manufactured for the cotton-producing slave states in the South, were Newark's primary industry, but Newark's artisans also made hats, saddles, carriages, jewelry, trunks, and harnesses. Young white males concentrated in industrial areas and Newark was the locus of the state's industry by the 1820s. Iron and patent leather factories employed more than 80 percent of the town's population in 1826, canals and turnpikes enhanced the town's delivery of goods to New York City, but blacks rarely found work in the new industries. Artisan republicanism, an ideology that encompassed pride in craft, patriotism, and politics, and a fierce determination to defend wages and control over production, was strong in New Jersey's factories, but working class consciousness did not extend to racial unity.[4]

Employment for blacks in the new industrial order lapsed elsewhere in New Jersey. In Elizabeth, construction of railway lines and factories attracted Irish immigrants, who competed fiercely with black residents for jobs. Black unemployment in the city became so bad that a number of residents left for the British colonies of Trinidad and Guiana. Officials in those colonies paid all moving expenses and welcomed a sizable contingent of former black Elizabeth residents with jobs.[5]

Economic chances were a bit better for African Americans in Camden, where slavery declined much faster than in Newark or Elizabeth. Quaker and black antislavery sentiments made Camden a beacon on the Underground Railroad (UGRR) and a more attractive spot for settlement. Ishmael Locke,

grandfather of Alain Locke, famed Harlem Renaissance writer, was born in
Salem and became a highly regarded school teacher and principal of the
Quaker-founded Philadelphia Institute for Colored Youth. Ishmael Locke
lived in Camden and commuted to work. Richard Fetters, a local businessman, built a planned community that enticed African American buyers to
purchase town lots. Benjamin Wilson, a local black preacher, was among
the first buyers in Fettersville, which soon sported a tavern, mills, grocery,
and garden "for the colored people." Benjamin Vandyke, a black entrepreneur,
created a second black neighborhood nearby. Named Kaighnsville, the
area became a thriving community of stores, churches, and schools. After
a major fire that destroyed much of the settlement in 1854, black residents
quickly rebuilt.

Camden also benefited from clandestine black migration from the slave
South. By the 1850s, Camden's black communities were receptive and safe
harbors for self-emancipated peoples escaping from slavery on the UGRR.
An unknown but significant number of new blacks joined New Jersey society, making it more racially diverse and bringing a new leadership class of
blacks who were unwilling to subject themselves to slavery. This can be seen
in the thick network of black churches, fraternal organizations, and schools
at the time. Similar developments occurred in Trenton, where blacks sustained community via churches and lodges. Most black Trenton residents
worked in menial positions, but some formed a middle class, based upon
education, church membership, and a commitment to antislavery and the
UGRR. Even though self-emancipated blacks seldom settled in the town,
Quakers and blacks provided succor for their flight to freedom. Camden
and Trenton residents lived in largely segregated neighborhoods, but they
fared far better than their counterparts in Elizabeth or Newark.[6]

SLAVERY'S CONTINUED GRIP ON BLACK NEW JERSEY

Slavery persisted in the counties with the largest black populations. Bergen
masters had powerful economic incentive to firmly enslave bondpeople. In
1814, slaveholders in Bergen owned four times as many cattle and three

times as many horses as nonslaveholders. While slave owners made up less than 15 percent of the taxpayers in Hackensack and New Barbados that year, they owned four to five as much improved acreage as those who did not own slaves.[7]

For those still enslaved, life continued much as it had before the American Revolution. The journal of Rachel Van Dyke, a young New Brunswick woman, contains numerous references to lifelong relations with enslaved people. They cleaned her room, prepared her food and clothing, announced visitors, and gossiped with her. She treasured the close relationships and believed that her relatives treated their bondpeople with great love and concern. Continuing a practice from the colonial period, Phoebe Ann Jacobs, born in Morris County, was given to a young woman as her personal slave. Freedom rarely meant social mobility; rather jobs for free people resembled work done as enslaved people. In Cape May County, free blacks clustered at work as laborers or domestics for families or toiled as low-wage workers in the new hotel business. Fugitive slave notices that appeared in New Jersey newspapers even up to the Civil War era attest to the endurance of servitude. Enslaved black women now formed the majority of self-emancipators.[8]

Upward mobility was possible for a few, often through association with elite whites. Betsy Stockton was born enslaved in 1798 in the Stockton family of Princeton. Her mother Celie, or Sealey, belonged to Richard Stockton II; her father was an unknown white man. When "Bet" was about six years of age, Richard Stockton II gave her to his daughter, Betsy Stockton Green, and her husband, Ashbel Green, a Presbyterian minister and the eighth president of Princeton University. In her new household, "Bet" performed such domestic tasks as cooking, cleaning, housekeeping, baking, and sewing. Green recognized her intelligence, provided for her education, and encouraged her Presbyterian faith. He freed Bet when she became twenty years old and subsequently paid her wages. Green recommended Bet for a missionary post to the Sandwich Islands (Hawaii) where, on Maui, Stockton created the first school for ordinary Hawaiians. After her return to Princeton, she founded first a Sabbath school, then two secular programs for children and adults. Princeton University students, seldom noted for their racial generosity, volunteered to teach algebra, Latin, history, and English literature. In 1858, Stockton founded the Witherspoon School for Colored Children, which enrolled students up to the eighth grade. For the next ninety years, the school offered a high quality education and full curriculum for young blacks in the town. Working in a segregated and paternalist environment, Stockton was able to create a memorable social institution.[9]

Early in the nineteenth century in the northern counties, free blacks struggled to survive in New Jersey's rural economy. Jack Earnest was the first resident of Skunk Hollow in Bergen County and was soon joined by thirty other free blacks who combined wage work for nearby white farmers with tending their own tiny plots to create subsistence incomes. Other Bergen County blacks moved from their small freeholds in the Hackensack River Valley to the Ramapo Mountains to the northwest. One reason may have been the Dutch-American tradition of dividing lands evenly among sons rather than practicing entail. These sons and daughters of ancient free black families purchased land and established mountain farms in the Ramapos. By 1830, older black families from New Jersey's earliest days, including the Degroots, Mann, Van Donck, and Sufferns established broad connections as small property owners. By contrast, in Monmouth County, a growing pattern was for free blacks to live as "cottagers" on their old master's property, trading their labor for housing, food, and tools. Working as a cottager was an early form of sharecropping. Gradual emancipation created divisions within families between free and enslaved. A parent might have been free while his or her children were slaves for a term. In Cape May County, only three black families owned taxable estates by 1850.[10]

After passage of the Gradual Emancipation act of 1804, New Jersey's white citizens did not welcome newly freed blacks into full citizenship. Rather, in 1807, they stripped black men, along with single white females, of the vote they had held since 1777. Just as pernicious, New Jersey's white citizens pioneered in the establishment of the American Colonization Society (ACS) in 1816, intended to convince or force free blacks to leave the United States for Africa. The new society, which quickly spread around the nation and gained the support of eminent politicians from Thomas Jefferson to

Abraham Lincoln, argued that slavery had so degraded blacks that they could never exist as equals with whites in society or politics. Additionally, the argument went, white prejudice mandated that blacks leave the nation for their own well-being as discrimination would never allow them to become full citizens. Such thinking, however paternalistically phrased, was a surrender to and intensification of white supremacy. As George Fishman put it, the "raw racist position of the ACS was covered over by hat-tipping to African heritage and exploiting abolitionist phrases for pro-slavery purposes."[11]

One of the ACS's goals was to educate free blacks so that they could evangelize in Africa, which resulted in the first Jersey black segregated schools. The ACS established schools for young blacks as an offshoot of the Presbyterian Sabbath schools. For example, the Sabbath School for Colored People in the Newark Academy taught black females how to read the Bible. The Presbyterian Synod of New York and New Jersey created a small, poorly funded school for black males in Parsippany to train black teachers to instruct Africans in Christianity and science.[12]

Establishing small, segregated schools did not impress New Jersey's free black population, who were quick to reject the ACS's overall mission. Black leaders such as Robert Purvis of Philadelphia recognized that some might want to emigrate, but overall, blacks in the two big cities and throughout New Jersey rejected the ACS message. Blacks also differentiated between their own emigration plans and the designs of the ACS. Defiance of ACS plans became a black rallying cry. The anti-ACS efforts of the African Methodist Episcopal (AME) Church created movements in Philadelphia and throughout New Jersey. Black anticolonization activities occurred in Westfield, Rahway, Elizabeth, Paterson, Newark, Trenton, Princeton, and New Brunswick. Lewis Cork and Abner H. Francis of Trenton spoke for many when they described the ACS as the "most inveterate foe for both the free and slave men of color." Criticism of the ACS became a standard part of the platforms of the so-called convention movement in the 1830s. Black activists and orators in most northern states found little to cheer about in the ACS appeals to leave America for Africa. Samuel Eli Cornish, a distinguished black Presbyterian clergyman was editor of the first black newspaper, *Freedom's Journal*, which was published between 1827 and 1829 in New York City, and the *Colored American*, which appeared in New York between 1837 and 1839 and was a leading opponent of the ACS. After many years battling the relics of slavery in New York City, Cornish moved to Belleville, New Jersey, in June 1838 and then, facing prejudice, moved to Newark to become pastor of the First Presbyterian Church on Plane Street. With Theodore S. Wright, a fellow black minister in New York City, Cornish published in 1840 a sharp attack on the ACS. Cornish and Wright noted that African Americans had long protested the ACS and rejected the image of "degraded blacks" as the fault of slave masters. There was no truth, they argued, that the ACS had promoted education or improved the legal status of American blacks. They called upon whites to allow blacks to improve themselves, a plea consistent with current black ideology and one that would reappear after the Civil War.[13]

New Jersey members of the ACS were aware of criticism of its intentions and blamed free blacks. James S. Green, a prominent member of the state's ACS, argued that although slavery was indefensible, free blacks were a "mass of ignorance, misery and depravity." Green contended that blacks in New Jersey amounted to a "foe in the disguise of slave or servant. . . . one admitted without reserve into the bosom of our families . . . yet one who secretly and cordially hates and despises the hand that feeds them." Education would only indulge them. Adding legal threats to racist comments, the New Jersey Assembly in 1837 voted to require all free blacks to register with the county clerk. Behind this measure were unsubstantiated fears that self-emancipated blacks from the southern states were improperly influencing local African Americans and were responsible for property theft. The state council negated the measure but it clearly indicated white anxieties about black migration and a willingness to introduce discriminatory laws.[14]

As was the case nationally, the ACS had close connections to power and influence. Robert Finley, a graduate of the College of New Jersey (Princeton University), attended the Theological Seminary before becoming a Presbyterian minister. The dean of the seminary, Reverend Samuel Miller, was an aggressive promoter of the ACS and in 1825 pushed his school into support of the ACS. Overall, the Presbyterian Church, once at least critical of slavery, chose to support the ACS. Manufacturers and merchants with southern customer bases upheld ACS ideals. Peter Vroom, later state governor, and Theodore J. Frelinghuysen, a U.S. senator from New Jersey, were colonizationists, or supporters of the plan to convince free blacks to leave America for Africa.[15]

ACS proponents invariably spoke of black inferiority and unsuitability for American citizenship. There was an additional, underlying fear: white colonizationists were anxious about potential rebellion. Samuel Bayard, onetime president of the board of trustees of the College of New Jersey's Theological Seminary, contended that whites were leaving New Jersey because they disliked working with free blacks. In a century, he estimated, free blacks in the state would number over 300,000. As property-owning taxpayers and potentially military veterans, he asked if they would "endure every burden, while they enjoy but few privileges?" Would they be content to have laws, votes, and representation all determined by whites? The answer, he warned, would be in the "din of insurrection." Better to confront that future now by exiling blacks before they revolted against their oppressors.[16]

Such deep-seated fears tinted by prejudice were at the heart of the message the ACS delivered to Americans. The society's strong position was that blacks had no place in American society. Accordingly, a member of the ACS could reason, there was no need to help them after generations of slavery except to provide a minimal education so that exiled blacks could teach Christianity in Africa. Slavery's degradation of blacks sanctioned a new white racism based upon alleged black intellectual inferiority and lack of social potential. Blacks were excluded from political citizenship, including voting, party affiliation, and office holding, and black membership in the ACS was unthinkable. As factories and industrialism appeared in the state, there was no reason, a colonizationist could argue, to hire blacks as skilled workers given their lack of potential and fears of white artisan anger. Moreover, the plethora of antiblack cartoons and open white violence against blacks around the Northeast could comfort the largely elite members of the colonization society with the belief that they were liberals on the race question. Because the ACS's efforts were pointed toward the exile of free blacks, nothing had to be done that would alienate white southern brethren, such as immediate demands to end slavery. New Jersey was perhaps not as dependent as neighboring New York City on the cotton industry, but there were sufficient ties among merchants, manufacturers such as leather dressers and shoe and clothing producers, and educators at the College of New Jersey to build a racial wall against radical abolitionists. Calls for immediate action could result in a race war. Better, members of the ACS concluded, to sacrifice black rights than to provoke racial conflict.[17]

BLACK RELIGION

Despite the rising tide of white racism in the state, New Jersey blacks built their own institutions, an indication that if true racial fraternity was not available, blacks would reluctantly choose separatism. Gaining membership in white congregations could take decades as the Mount Holly black Quaker William Boen learned. His meeting took over seven decades before allowing him a place in the congregation. To counter such extreme gradualism, African Americans built their own churches and nominated their own clerics. As noted, one of the key freedoms gained after 1804 was the right to personal mobility. This means that black itinerant ministers could serve eager black adherents around the state. Building upon his earlier work as an itinerant, George White sought to earn a license as an ordained Methodist minister, a process that took more than twelve years.[18] Richard Allen itinerated in New Jersey for several years before establishing the AME Church in Philadelphia. Their efforts and those of other knights of the saddlebags bore fruit in rapidly developing congregations. Following leads established in New York and Philadelphia, black New Jersey worshippers, tired of racism in white churches, created their own congregations and hired their own preachers. Blacks in Trenton first established a burial ground for blacks and then incorporated in 1811 as the Religious Society of Free Africans of the City of Trenton. Its trustees affiliated with the AME Church in 1816, when now Bishop Richard Allen, founder of the AME Church, came to Trenton and admitted the church into fellowship. Allen also accepted a black congregation in Princeton into the AME Church. In 1822, local blacks joined the AME to found the Clinton AME Church in Newark. Beginning in 1823, black Presbyterians in Elizabeth gathered together under the auspices of the Presbytery of New Jersey. Adherents organized an AME congregation in Mount Holly in 1813, then others in Mount Moriah, Bethlehem, and Mount Zion. The St. James AME Church in Newark, founded in 1842, grew slowly but later became one of the most important black congregations in the state. By the 1850s the AME denomination had spread throughout New Jersey. Ambitious young men barred from most professional work found dignified positions in the clergy. The Bordentown church initially had a female leader. Churches rotated pastors routinely almost on an annual basis. The Burlington chapel for example employed more than twenty pastors, several of them repeaters, between its breakaway from the parent Methodist Church in 1831 and the late 1880s. Church members took leadership positions. In his history of the AME Church in New Jersey, Joseph H. Morgan lists, among the dozens of congregations, clergymen, church trustees, stewards and stewardesses, a local preacher, an exhorter, leaders, a Sunday school superintendent, and Sunday school missionaries.[19]

Religious services were not the only form of black communal life. Often replacing such eighteenth-century gathering moments such as Pinkster and Militia and Training Day, Masonic and other fraternal organizations provided permanent forums for black camaraderie, self-help, and benevolence. The black Masonic movement established branches in New Jersey. By the Civil War the Knights of Pythias had branches throughout the state, anticipating a huge explosion of fraternities and sororities after it. Such fraternal groups were schools for democracy, leadership and organization. Within them black men and women were dignified, equal participants safe from the rough discourse of a racist society.[20]

Black political activism became more organized in the 1830s. As New Jersey blacks realized the intentions and read the rhetoric of the ACS, they, like their counterparts in New York and Philadelphia, rose in opposition to it and created a black politics. The black convention movement of the 1830s strove to rebut ACS views that blacks were incapable of becoming educated citizens, the convention movement aligned itself starting in 1830 with the emerging Immediatist abolition movement. New Jersey delegates John Arnold and Sampson Peters attended the first Convention of the American Society of Free Persons of Color held in Philadelphia in 1830, where they agreed with sentiments supporting a Canadian settlement. Thomas D. Coxsin of Gloucester County helped prepare a report for the 1832 convention that derided the ACS while, in a sign of black ambivalence about a black future in the United States, called for purchase of land in Upper Canada (Ontario), though the overall convention expressed concern that buying land would give credence to the ACS's racist claims. A year later at the next convention, Thomas Banks of New Jersey attacked the ACS, arguing that blacks "feel themselves aggrieved by its very existence and consider it to be devoid of any true sense of benevolence."[21]

Opposition to the ACS and African American dedication to self-uplift spurred black educational efforts. Generally, black self-uplift efforts in New Jersey had collective goals and did not emphasize individual achievement. Bruising racism took its toll on Jersey's tiny black middle class, but there are no indications that they sought respectability to please whites, but rather to serve as examples to their own community. Blacks valued religious belief, education, independence, and fraternity. Such traits are contrary to Patrick Rael's argument about urban middle-class blacks, whom he regarded as stung by white criticism and sensitive about social crudeness of poorer blacks. During this era, Jersey blacks showed solidarity rather than class divisions.[22]

EDUCATION

The Society of Friends initiated the first schools for blacks as part of their mandate to end slavery. After limited efforts in the 1790s, the Society of Friends opened Sunday schools in the decade after the enactment of gradual emancipation. The Episcopalian Church's weak presence in New Jersey meant there would be no counterpart to the famous African Free Schools located in New York City. After formation of the American Colonization Society in 1817, members needed to create schools to educate free blacks to prepare them for self-exile as Christian representatives in Liberia. The Presbyterian Church of New Jersey, a principal backer of the ACS, founded an African school in New Brunswick in 1817 to teach a small cohort of thirty-four men and a dozen women. Black theologian Jeremiah Gloucester of Philadelphia praised the association and beseeched black New Jerseyans to recall how recently they had all been enslaved and to remember the teachings of Woolman and Benezet. He predicted that the school would produce philosophers, mathematicians, and preachers. Funds for the school lapsed however and a plan to use monies from Polish Patriot Thaddeus Kosciuszko's will failed to materialize. The school limped along with just a smattering of students into the 1820s.[23]

White churches enrolled blacks in Sunday schools, the most important of which opened in Newark in 1815, enrolling more than 200 people of both sexes and all ages. Other sizable Sunday schools for blacks started soon after in Hackensack, Elizabethtown, and Aquackanonk. Continuing colonial practices, many of the scholars were enslaved and instruction on obedience to masters and mistresses was an important part of the curriculum.[24]

Black churches created their own schools. In 1826, the AME Church in Newark opened a common school offering curriculum in reading, writing, and ciphering for children and adults. A second Newark school opened in 1827. Poorly funded at first, the school first received donations from sympathetic whites and dedicated black families, then gained tax support in 1836. Short-lived schools appeared in New Brunswick and Bordentown. In 1832 James Still, the famous Doctor of the Pines, studied at a black school in Medford Township. Other black schools opened in the next few years and schools in Mount Holly, Timbuctoo, and Krisson opened in the 1840s. All of these schools were segregated.[25]

While religious philanthropies continued to offer Sunday schools to blacks in the 1840s, public schools became the norm in that decade. The

New Jersey Constitution of 1844 guaranteed everyone admission to public schools. There was some success. By 1860, 369 black children attended school in Burlington County, 343 in Cape May County, 274 in Camden County, and 233 in Essex County. Lagging behind were the older Dutch counties where slavery and its traces remained strong. Even as the county urbanized, only seventy-three black children went to school in Bergen County; similar small totals emerged in Essex, Union, and Middlesex Counties. Importantly, these schools were segregated and black students were not allowed to enroll in schools with white students. The state allowed local option to determine whether schools would be integrated or not. Morris County first established a separate school district for black children with the legal sanction of the state legislature. By 1863, the state school superintendent interpreted state laws on education as providing instruction for blacks in separate schools as long as equal funding was supplied. Equal funding soon lapsed and the black schools in New Jersey, like their counterparts across the northern states, were decidedly inferior. The census of 1860 indicated there were more black adults (3,805) unable to read than there were students attending school (2,741). What these numbers indicate is the drive for segregated schools came largely from the white population. When blacks sought their own schools, such efforts stemmed from their despair and anger over already segregated institutions.[26]

A significant case in Massachusetts in 1849 presaged struggles over black access to public schools. Black activist Benjamin Franklin Roberts filed a suit against the Boston School Committee in an effort to enroll his daughter in a white public school closer to the family home and avoid a lengthy, even dangerous, commute to the nearest black school. Prominent abolitionist Charles Sumner argued Roberts's case, contending that all students had rights under the state constitution and cited the numerous inequalities built into the school board's position. In a unanimous decision written by famed jurist Chief Justice Lemuel Shaw, the court declared that although all persons were equal, the school board still had the right to assign students to schools according to their best judgment and consideration of local conditions. The court thereby sanctioned segregated schools, establishing a precedent for local autonomy over integration after the Civil War and finally reified in the Plessy v. Ferguson decision that gave legal power to a Jim Crow society.[27]

BLACK POPULAR CULTURE

Apart from aims toward self-improvement in education and manners and in the battle for civil rights was a growing black secular sociability. Slave culture transformed into a black popular culture in this era. Sylvia Du Bois, a Somerset County free woman, recalled her nightclub near Hopewell as an interracial spot for dancing, drinking, cockfights, boxing, fox chases, and prostitution. Du Bois remembered the days when she danced: "cross my feet ninety-nine times in a minute and never miss the time, strike heel or toe with equal ease and go through the figures as nimble as a witch." During the long winters, Du Bois said, "we had frolics every week, we hardly get over one frolic when we'd begin to fix for another." Music was constant: "We was sure to have a fiddle and a frolic . . . I could dance all night." Holidays for Du Bois were a must. General Training Day, Pinkster, and horse races were times for drinking, dancing, and loving.[28]

Rural black males used hunting as a bonding experience and as a means to play equally with whites. If New Jersey whites, like their counterparts in the South, used hunting as demonstrations of their prowess, self-control, and mastery, blacks hunted to secure supplementary food sources, items to barter, and a measure of autonomy. Blacks accompanied whites on hunting expeditions into the Pine Barrens. These gaming expeditions might last three to four weeks and shooters would return with deer, rabbit, quail, and barrels of cranberries. Black scouting and hunting skills placed them if temporarily on an equal level of masculinity with whites.[29]

Just as Pinkster had served in the colonial period, religious holidays became moments of rough equality. Old Dick, a household bondman belonging to Andrew Mellick of Bedminister Township, used Christmas to assume center stage while conducting "service of the table," while wearing his finest clothing. If whites tended to mock such airs, clothing and service skills bolstered Old Dick's masculinity. Dick and his wife Nance were careful not to

SILVIA DUBOIS,
BORN MARCH 5th, 1768.

Figure 3. Sylvia Du Bois (1788/1789–1889). Enslaved New Jersey woman, self-emancipated, and survivor of harsh, rural slavery, who dictated her biography in 1883. By permission of the Newark Public Library.

overindulge in alcohol to avoid jeopardizing the good will and respect he had earned. Temperance affirmed their acute sense of survival in a tough world dominated by whites. Unlike the inebriated slave who tipped off whites to the planned rising in Somerville in 1734 or Bood's reputation in the colonial period to surliness when in drink, Dick and Nance were careful to protect their good Christian reputations.[30]

SELF-EMANCIPATION AND THE UNDERGROUND RAILROAD

Troubled by slavery's malignant relics, black and white New Jerseyans combined efforts to help enslaved blacks gain freedom. There were exacerbating elements that spurred action. Kidnappers abounded. They were usually young white men looking for additional income. After the Fugitive Slave Act of 1793 nationalized rendition of the self-emancipated, slave hunters routinely searched New Jersey farms for escaped slaves. Others kidnapped enslaved free people to transport them as slaves for sale in southern states. Slave ships came into New Jersey harbors. One shipmaster purchased several enslaved people in Boston, then transported them in a small sloop toward the south. When the ship came into Egg Harbor for refitting, local magistrates arrested the captain, freed the captives, and allowed them to hire themselves out. There were other abuses within the state. New Jersey state legislators tried to discourage the practice but allowed blacks to "voluntarily" leave for the South. Often kidnappers deceived free blacks. In the summer of 1811, Philadelphia resident T. I. Moses hired a young black man named Peter Reuben Francis Johnson to help him pick cherries in New Jersey. Lured onto a boat to get across the Delaware River, Johnson found himself en route to slavery in Baltimore. There he was sold to another "monster" named J. Roach, a notorious kidnapper. Isaac Hopper, alerted to the case, put it before the Pennsylvania Abolition Society, which enabled Johnson's release and had Moses arrested upon his return from Baltimore. Because of slavery's legality in New Jersey, unscrupulous masters used it to gain profit from newly emancipated blacks elsewhere. One Philadelphia master who failed to register his female slave responded to her potential freedom by quickly selling her to a master in Easttown, New Jersey. Fortunately for the woman, the Pennsylvania Abolition Society learned of her plight, sued, and gained her freedom.[31]

Historical perceptions of the UGRR are undergoing vast changes. Historians are moving beyond dated, hoary arguments of whether blacks or whites worked as conductors and whether the UGRR was real or not. Recent scholarship has revealed a crowded, active escape corridor between Maryland, Virginia, and north to New York City, New England, and Canada. New Jersey was a long connective part of this human highway of self-emancipation. The UGRR encompassed more than helping the self-emancipated secure their freedom. In New Jersey it also meant fighting kidnappers by legal and extralegal actions and challenging the rights of slave masters, in state and out, to sell, hire, and transport enslaved people. More than the numbers of people helped by it, the UGRR in New Jersey created what historian Fergus Bordewich has called the first interracial civil rights movement. In an often proslavery state like New Jersey, such a development sustained hope for aggrieved blacks, and increasingly cast slavery in disfavor in the state.[32]

The UGRR in New Jersey owed much to Isaac Hopper. Working out of Philadelphia, Quaker Isaac Hopper continued his pioneering methods of the 1780s. Many of his activities took him into or placed him in close contact with blacks and whites in New Jersey. During the early nineteenth century, New Jersey was approached cautiously, a safe destination for self-emancipated people from Delaware and the Chesapeake slave states. Hopper several times helped freedom seekers find succor among friendly farmers in New Jersey. On other occasions, he used his impressive legal knowledge to gain freedom and safety for enslaved blacks. In 1809, an East Jersey master, anxious that his slave's sojourn with him to Philadelphia made the bondperson free, had a sheriff attempt to arrest him. The slave then escaped and fled to Hopper's home. The Quaker rebuffed the sheriff and master's attempt to search his house. As Hopper sparred with the law and with a slave catcher, the newly freed person left Philadelphia. In addition to Hopper's legal skills and willingness to directly confront angry and vengeful masters, the incident is noteworthy in that it demonstrates that enslaved blacks knew Hopper's home as a safe harbor.[33]

New Jersey blacks, hearing of Isaac Hopper, fled the state to seek help from him. One woman and her son fled enslavement in East Jersey in 1827 to hide with two free sons in Philadelphia. Their master traveled to the city and, disguised as a Quaker, used subterfuge to learn their whereabouts. As he approached their safe house, the woman recognized him despite his broad-brimmed hat. She and her son fled to a hiding place in the closet of a nearby home. Hopper was summoned and quickly used his contacts to send both out of Philadelphia to freedom. When the master accosted Hopper, the slave owner told the activist that there was no use trying to find escaped slaves in Philadelphia and that the devil himself would be frustrated. Hopper answered the devil could more easily find slave masters because he knew them so well.[34]

Hopper's assistance to area blacks took many forms. He helped one orphan apprentice from Trenton protect his inheritance from an avaricious master by getting top legal talent to secure the money. Hopper was well acquainted with New Jersey farmers who were willing to protect and hire self-emancipated slaves. John Tatum of Woodbury in Gloucester County hired two black men who, "preferring liberty to slavery, had left the service of their master in Maryland."[35]

Hopper was not alone among white sympathizers of imperiled blacks. New Jersey whites raised cash to help self-emancipated people arriving from the South. Sympathetic residents of Newton, Gloucester County, raised $140 to pay for the freedom of Daniel Clark, who escaped from his master in Delaware in 1824.[36]

Self-emancipated blacks in New Jersey lived in considerable danger. An 1826 New Jersey law provided for the return of self-emancipated people who resided or were caught in the state. In 1833 in the case of Johnson v. Tompkins, a New Jersey slave owner reclaimed his bondman from the home of a Quaker, John Kennerdine of Montgomery County, Pennsylvania. During the forced rendition, the slave owner was injured and arrested. In the ensuing trial, the slave master was acquitted on the grounds that he had a right to reclaim his enslaved man.[37] Leonard Black, formerly of Anne Arundel County in Maryland, escaped from his master and made his way to New Brunswick, taking backroads and hiding in the woods. He traveled alone then with other fugitives, one of whom he learned was arrested after they parted. It took Black several weeks to travel by foot through New Jersey to get to New York on his way to freedom in New England.[38]

The capsule biography of Reverend Charles Henry Green of the Burlington AME chapel reveals the routes taken by the self-emancipated. Born in Newark, Delaware, in 1833, Green was sold by the pound at age nine from one master to another to another. Green cited his early conversion to the AME Church as his master's reason to sell him. Upon learning that his most recent owner planned to send him to the south, Green "took leg bail for security," in the early 1840s and left for Canada via the UGRR. Stopping first in Philadelphia, he married city resident Cathrine (sic) Gross. Reverend C. Bias officiated with Charles L. Reason, New York City abolitionist and member of the city's Committee of Vigilance, as best man, whose presence indicated Green's well-planned burst to freedom. Green then traveled to New York, to Albany, and on to Syracuse where Jeremiah Loguen sheltered him for several months before Green moved to final safety in Canada. He remained there until 1859 when he returned to the states to start a highly successful pastoral career in several churches in the AME Episcopal conference.[39]

Hopper was largely alone among Quakers in his antislavery convictions. The abolitionist zeal that had pushed the Society of Friends into the forefront of gradual emancipation in the late eighteenth century had cooled dramatically. Internal conflicts over the true meaning of the church led to conflicts over antislavery activism. William Lloyd Garrison's "immediatist" antislavery position seemed more confrontational than persuasive, more prophetic than healing, and of course less gradual. By 1840 almost all Quaker churches had closed their doors to abolitionist rhetoric and expelled prominent movement figures, including Hopper.[40]

Generally, white New Jersey Protestant denominations joined the Quakers in rejecting antislavery activism. However, there was work to be done.

By the late 1810s, the surging demand for black workers in the cotton fields in the new states of Alabama, Mississippi, Louisiana, and Florida and the desire of New Jersey's slave masters to extract one last profit by selling the enslaved people to southern states created a nasty market in kidnapping. Despite an 1812 state law that forbade "the exportation of slaves or servants of color," and mandated that "slaves for life" and slaves for a term had to agree to emigration, unscrupulous masters stooped to such practices as maintaining that infants had agreed to be sold to the South. Buyers from the south viewed New Jersey blacks as "peculiarly adapted" to the market and "afford the best opportunity for speculation." The invention of the cotton gin and the forcible removal of Native Peoples from the Old Southwest spurred development of the region into slave country. Slave-trading speculators saw acquisition and sale of New Jersey blacks to southern customers as sources of substantial profits. Middlesex County Judge of the Common Pleas Jacob Van Winkle convinced many Jersey masters to sell their enslaved people to his brother-in-law Charles Morgan, a Louisiana plantation owner. Van Winkle adjudicated the law requiring enslaved consent, brokered deals arranged by his son, Nicolas, and routinely lied to blacks about their status in New Jersey and in the South. He went so far as to interpret an infant's cries as assent to be sold. In one instance, Van Winkle's evil chicanery resulted in seventy-five enslaved men, women, and children being smuggled to southern ports for sale. When local Quakers tried to stop the kidnappings, Van Winkle contended that the transported people went with "perfect cheerfulness" and with no dissent. New Jersey slave owners who wished to sell their enslaved workers connived with John Craig Marsh, a failed New York City dry goods merchant, and his partner, William Stone. Marsh bought land in Avery Island, in southern Louisiana, an area becoming rapidly transformed into sugar plantations. Marsh and Stone returned north to assemble a workforce. In addition to enslaved people illicitly sold out of New Jersey, Marsh and Stone signed on impoverished free people desperate enough to risk four years on a sugar plantation in Louisiana. Despite Quaker efforts, Van Winkle escaped indictment.[41]

Many concerned whites who had embraced gradualism flinched at the emerging internal slave trade. Nonetheless the only result was a legislative reform passed in 1818 that required that a slaveholder had to live in New Jersey for five years before he could remove a slave and could not sell one to nonresident masters. Stone got around this by agreeing to use the enslaved persons somewhere else in New Jersey, then smuggling them out through Perth Amboy. New Jersey Senator James Wilson sought a federal ban on the interstate slave trade from those states where slavery was illegal, but his efforts floundered via southern opposition in the House of Representatives and then died in the Senate. As Calvin Schermerhorn has recently demonstrated, deceptive contracts and smuggling tied New Jersey masters directly into the rapidly developing internal slave trade.[42]

During the 1820s, Patty Cannon and her husband, Joseph Johnson, operated an eponymous kidnapping company in taverns near the Nanticoke River on the Maryland-Delaware border. Bribing sheriffs and working with local traders, the Cannon-Johnson Company kidnapped and sold more than 200 blacks in a two-year period in that decade. In a reverse underground railroad, the syndicate worked with black associates, used false documents, and organized a series of "safe" houses to whisk free people into slavery. Albert F. Alberti, a former Philadelphia constable turned slave catcher, was equally notorious. In a forty-year career, Alberti bragged of capturing more than one hundred escaped slaves. Alberti seized Adam Gibson, a New Jersey man, in Philadelphia in one of the first actions following passage of the Fugitive Slave Act of 1850. Alberti caused a huge uproar in 1851 when he kidnapped the two-year-old Joel Thompson, the son of Betsy and William Thompson of Burlington County. Alberti claimed that Betsy Thompson was a fugitive and her son enslaved by birth. Alberti was arrested, convicted, and sentenced to ten years at hard labor for the theft of the child. Pennsylvania Governor William Bigler, who was against personal liberty laws protecting free blacks and escaped slaves, pardoned Alberti in 1852. Even self-emancipated people who succeeded in reaching New York City were vulnerable to kidnappers' clutches. Unscrupulous, proslavery magistrates in New York routinely accepted the words of kidnappers and condemned blacks to transportation from New York to New Jersey and on to sales in the South.[43]

Legislators in New Jersey supported the Fugitive Slave Act of 1850. Senator Jacob Miller of New Jersey extolled it and the institution of slavery. Referring to "the South, where the slave labors contentedly in the cotton-fields for his master," Miller applauded slavery as a key part of the "best system of laws ever devised by man." The Fugitive Slave act ensured that "the rights of property and the rights of citizens are protected and defended by the Constitution and the laws of slavery."[44]

To combat man stealing and help the self-emancipated, sympathetic New Jerseyans expanded the UGRR. Working with Quakers and black activists in Philadelphia and along the Delaware River, UGRR operators created a trunk line from Camden to Burlington, then on to Bordentown. The fullest information on the UGRR in New Jersey comes from an interview conducted by historian Wilbur Siebert in 1895 with Reverend Thomas Clement Oliver, a former state resident who moved to Canada. Oliver indicated several trunk lines. Self-emancipated blacks came across the Delaware Bay to Cape May, Salem, where Quaker Abigail Goodwin often housed survivors, and many smaller towns in between. Once in New Jersey, new free people were given food, shelter, and fresh clothing in the black towns before joining the major routes of the UGRR in the state. Recent students of the UGRR have emphasized the presence of nearby black towns and villages where escaped slaves could find succor. Black towns where fugitives were welcome included Snow Hill (later Lawnside), Guineatown, and Saddlertown in Camden County, Springtown and Gouldtown in Cumberland County, and Colemantown and Timbuctoo in Burlington County. Many self-emancipated people stayed in the black towns. Others, wanting a more secure freedom, moved further north. There were three closely aligned strands up Jersey's western spine to New Brunswick or Perth Amboy or Jersey City. New Brunswick was an especially dangerous spot as spies were stationed there who aided slave catchers. Once past New Brunswick, freedom seekers found shelter at the Raritan Bay Union (later Eagleswood Academy) in Perth Amboy before going into New York City. Abolitionist Rebecca Bussum Spring operated the Union while Theodore Weld and his wife, Angelina Grimke. were stock-holders and active members. Experienced guides met fortunate fugitives at the Hudson ferry crossings on either side of the river before taking them to safe houses in New York City. Arriving in the metropolis was highly dangerous as spies and slave catchers inspected coaches and wagons. Then, self-emancipated people secured passage from the city's vigilance committee and traveled upstate to Albany and Canada or to other routes in Connecticut and Massachusetts by road or sea. New Jersey's black towns were in contact with similar northern locales. John Brown, the famed radical abolitionist, wrote in 1848 to Willis Augustus Hodges, a black man whose radicalism matched Brown's, that he was sending food and tools to Hodges's settlement, Blacksville, in the Adirondacks and to like-minded friends in Timbuctoo.[45]

Slavery and the UGRR affected black New Jersey families. The Still family of Greenwich is an example. Levin Still had purchased himself from a Maryland master. He hoped to free his wife, Charity (first known as Sidney), and their four sons by flight. After a first escape failed, Sidney was able to flee with her husband and two daughters, leaving behind two sons. The couple had many more children in freedom, but the first two sons, Levin and Peter, remained enslaved. Peter, who languished enslaved in the South for decades and was sold several times, eventually purchased himself and was reunited with his family. In an extraordinary act of heroism, a white man, Seth Concklin, volunteered to go to Alabama to retrieve Peter's family. Concklin was beaten and drowned for his efforts. Brother James became a well-known physician. The best-known son was William, born in Burlington County in 1821 and famous for operating the UGRR in Philadelphia in the 1850s and later compiling a vast history that is used to the present.[46]

Gradually New Jersey became enmeshed in the border conflict between the upper south and lower north over fugitive slaves and kidnappers. Black New Jerseyans organized to prevent slave catchers from securing their prey. In August 1836, a black mob estimated at 500 people used minimal force to try to prevent slave catchers from taking fugitive slave Severn Martin on a steamboat to Philadelphia. The Quaker City had by the late 1830s gained a

MRS JARENA LEE.

Preacher of the A. M. E. Church.

Aged 60 years on the 11th day of the 2nd month 1844.

Philᵃ 1844.

Figure 4. Broadside of Jarena Lee, the first female minister ordained by the African Methodist Episcopal Church. By permission of Library Company of Philadelphia.

reputation as a haven for slave catchers and kidnappers. After the Burlington mayor convinced the concerned to demobilize, the slave catchers took Martin aboard and back to slavery. Blacks soon learned not to acquiesce to authority. In December 1836, a slave catcher imprisoned a black family in a tavern near Swedesboro. At 11:00 P.M. forty black men armed with muskets, clubs, and stones attacked the tavern, riddling the building with bullets. This act of physical resistance was not enough to satisfy one black man from Camden, who declared that he was tired of having free territory invaded by these "myrmidons of the south," and expressed hope that soon kidnappers would be rebuffed at the Mason-Dixon Line. Whites were not always sympathetic. One journalist observed that the state legislature should end "these incessant tumultuous assemblages," suggesting that the attack was not the first such example of resistance. Apparently, the state legislature complied. Ten years later sixty or seventy state militiamen prevented a slave rescue near Mount Holly. Yet the New Jersey incidents were part of a festering border war between slave catchers, kidnappers, and angry, sometimes armed blacks.[47]

Protection of self-emancipated blacks in New Jersey increased dramatically in 1836 when Chief Justice Joseph Hornblower ordered the release of Alex Hemsley. Previously, Hemsley, his wife, and his family were apprehended as fugitive slaves. One court issued a certificate of removal for Hemsley but not for his family. In New Jersey v. Sheriff of Burlington, Hornblower freed Hemsley on the grounds that his arrest papers were irregular. Hornblower then denied that Congress had a constitutional warrant to legislate on fugitive slave rendition. He reasoned that under Section 2 (privileges and immunities, fugitives from justice and fugitive slave clause) of Article IV of the Constitution, there was no grant of congressional power on slave renditions although one existed in the first section that governed full faith and credit. Hornblower then noted that while Congress had the right to prescribe the manner, which observed official acts, that was true only where national unity existed, which was not the case with fugitive slave laws. Matters of comity (mutual respect for each state's laws) were up to the states to decide, not Congress.[48]

The UGRR has a mixed history in New Jersey. James J. Gigantino has argued that whatever its successes, the UGRR did not heavily sway white New Jerseyans in support of abolitionism. White New Jerseyans may have been appalled by the Van Winkles and feared the consequences of allowing slave catchers free rein in northern states, but many still regarded self-emancipated blacks as public nuisances and continued to court favor with southern businessmen by supporting the rule of law and therefore helped return the self-emancipated to the south. Still, abolitionists were able to push legislation requiring jury trials for fugitives and encouraged "sectional antagonism" by pointing out how slave catchers disrupted public order and were dangerous. New Jersey, as Gigantino points out, had a long antipathy to black freedom. Still, blacks, sometimes abetted by Quakers and other sympathetic whites, fought back through riots, covert actions, and stealthy organization. Gigantino contends that New Jersey lacked the kind of organized UGRR that existed among New York City blacks, but the degree of black support for the UGRR, the importance of the state for transit from the upper South, and the legal efforts by abolitionist whites gives the New Jersey UGRR a stronger history than he indicates. Yes, the state had many whites who were hostile to the UGRR, but it also had a long history of black and white cooperation and a growing number of black towns that harbored the self-emancipated.[49]

Free blacks and self-emancipated slaves formed townships at Springtown in Cumberland and Cape May Counties. These towns had strong African Methodist Episcopal Zion congregations with ties to Robert Purvis, James Still, Isaac Hopper, and other UGRR conductors in Philadelphia. Itinerant black ministers toured New Jersey and Cape May from the 1810s. The African Society of Methodists initiated church presence there is 1816, later becoming a key UGRR organization. Black women were important members of these churches and the UGRR. Jarena Lee was an early female evangelist working out of Cape May during the 1843 revival and there were Sunday schools teaching black children and adults from the early 1840s. By the 1850s, such resorts as the Banneker House in Cape May and hotels in Tuckertown opened their doors to the black elite of Philadelphia.[50]

Figure 5. Bethel AME Church, Springtown, New Jersey, 2002. Detail of
a photograph by Wendel White displaying the following caption: "The
Bethel A.M.E. Church was established in 1810, most likely at a nearby
location in Greenwich, New Jersey—on the site of the Ambury Hill
cemetery. In both the current and previous locations the church was a
station in the Underground Railroad." By permission of Wendel White.

The memoirs of Mrs. Rebecca Steward of Gouldtown reflect the extraordinary piety of church members in black towns. Born in Gouldtown in
1820, Rebecca Gould married James Steward, a "steady and thrifty mechanic,
having worked nine years in the Cumberland Nail and Iron Works," in 1839.
The couple had six children reared in the AME Church in Gouldtown. Her
son, Reverend T. G. Steward, published a testimonial and memoir of Rebecca
Gould Steward. The volume includes admiring accounts of her faith, penned
after her death in 1877, by leading black clerics, including the president of
Wilberforce University. Steward wrote several essays and poetry on sancti-
fication. Among the many scripturally saturated lines of her essays and
poetry are evidence of her deep despair over sin, her calling to God, and her
belief that if human life was not worthy of perfection, spirituality could

achieve bliss and salvation from her enemies. Steward's life as a parent and homemaker was powerfully augmented by her spiritual labors, giving her a deep community strength.[51]

Gouldtown had a rich family tradition. In their history of the town, William and Reverend Theophilus G. Steward recorded extensive genealogies of white and black families, detailing, for example, five generations of the family of Reverend Rueben Cuff.[52] Black families also had strong ties to enslaved people in Delaware, Maryland, Virginia, and North Carolina. They created the Greenwich Line of the UGRR, which ran up the coast, across the Delaware Bay to Cape May and New York City, to Albany, and beyond. Watermen and ferrymen were critical figures in this connection, taking messages and helping survivors of slavery across the bay to freedom. Trusted farmers helped the self-emancipated en route by hiring them to cut timber and clear forests.

If self-emancipated freedom makers did not want to tarry in New Jersey, they traversed it on the way north to security in New England or Canada. Using trails now several decades old, freedom seekers found help in black and white communities. Thomas Shipley, a Quaker, traveled frantically around New Jersey, Delaware, and Pennsylvania in 1835 to acquire freedom papers for Alexander Hemsley, his wife Nancy, and their three children after slave catchers from Maryland jailed them in Mount Holly in December 1835. Shipley first obtained freedom for Nancy and her children, then rode in wintry weather to Dover, Delaware, to have the state governor authenticate Alexander's freedom papers. Shipley used delaying tactics to stall Hemsley's trial and when even that gesture proved inadequate, Shipley traveled all night to Newark, awakened New Jersey Chief Justice Hornblower, and convinced him to grant a writ of habeas corpus that saved the freeman. Shipley arrived at Mount Holly just as the local judge was awarding Hemsley to the kidnappers. An angry mob outside the courthouse rescued Hemsley, and at a full trial three months later Hemsley was declared exonerated of charges of flight from servitude, thanks to Shipley's extraordinary efforts.[53]

As the abolitionist movement became more politicized nationally, New Jerseyans formed societies to attack slavery and its iniquities. Radical abolitionists Theodore Dwight Weld, his wife, Angelina Grimke Weld (both of whom taught at Raritan Bay Union), and her sister, Sarah M. Grimke, settled in Belleville in the early 1840s. The New Jersey State Anti-Slavery Society, formed in 1841, criticized the General Council of the Methodist Episcopal Church for accepting a secular injunction that removed black testimony against white people "in any state, where they are denied by law." Abolitionists, the society argued, had helped keep Texas out of the Union, had passed resolutions in favor of the abolition of slavery in the District of Columbia, helped rescue hundreds of kidnapped freemen, defended the Amistad captives, helped thousands of self-emancipated slaves in flight to Canada, and "unmasked that greatest of all Humbugs, the Colonization Society." The abolitionists had secured black dignity and rights in American society, settled constitutional and biblical questions about human rights, abolished the "Negro Seat" in churches, and helped black students gain education. The New Jersey Anti-Slavery Society endorsed the spirit and doings of the World Antislavery Convention , which was held in London in 1840. Locally, the society established a newspaper, the *New Jersey Freeman*, which ran from 1844 to 1847. The society supported the Liberty Party in its national ticket in 1844 and 1848 and in 1844 the state party nominated Jonathan Parkhurst as their first candidate for governor, and set up slates for two congressional seats and a number of local offices. The society met monthly in Boonton and hosted such black political luminaries as Henry Highland Garnet and white abolitionists Lewis Tappan and Luther Lee, though Alvan Stewart was clearly the most popular out-of-stater. Similar to the New York State party, the New Jersey branch of the Liberty Party also favored temperance recommended to the state legislature, in that "the colored people of our state, shall have equal privileges in the rights of suffrage, the holding of real estate," and full citizenship in New Jersey. The state legislature rebuffed repeated petitions to gain the suffrage for blacks as well as formally put an end to slavery in the state. By 1847 enthusiasm for the Anti-Slavery Society lapsed and the Liberty Party's successor, the Free Soil Party, received its weakest support in New Jersey of all the northern states.[54]

Organization occurred at the county level as well. An important segment of the state society was the Essex County Anti-Slavery Society. Nominally integrated, the society's leadership included Vice President Samuel E. Cornish, a Bellevue resident and veteran abolitionist. Cornish also worked with fellow radicals Theodore Dwight Weld of Bellevue and Joshua Levitt.[55]

As black politics matured, abolitionists focused on finally ending slavery in the state. By 1840, the number of enslaved people dropped to about 700 hundred in the state, most of whom lived in Bergen County and were over fifty years old. Elderly slaves still had the right to expect their masters' support as long as slavery remained legal. At the same time people were still bought and sold as masters continued to advertise for self-emancipated people. Neighboring states offered clear examples of the need to end human bondage. New York State had officially extinguished slavery in 1827 and Pennsylvania had few slaves, but stalled on any final legislation to end chattel bondage. Jersey abolitionists asked why the New Jersey state constitution could not be amended to allow black suffrage when property requirements had been quickly abolished. Anyone who was otherwise mentally fit or was not a felon, proponents argued, should be allowed to vote, including women and blacks.[56]

In the early 1840s. New Jersey's antislavery activists determined to take a different tack to end slavery by emphasizing equal rights doctrines under the U.S. Constitution. Alvan Stewart, a Utica, New York, lawyer and an abolitionist noted for his eloquent attacks on slavery, argued that slavery was a violation of the Constitution's due process clause. Stewart focused on the close resemblance between New Jersey's constitution and that of Massachusetts, where slavery had ended long before. Opposing attorneys for slave masters argued that natural rights legislation as applied to enslaved people was an abstraction and rhetorical flourish. More important, they contended, were the rights of men to their property. In a compromise intended to settle this dispute, the New Jersey state legislature "officially" ended slavery but limited black freedom by redefining remaining enslaved people as "apprentices," who were legally bound to their masters. By 1860 eighteen slaves remained in the state, who either died in bondage or were liberated by the Thirteenth Amendment.[57]

An editorial appearing in the *New York Weekly Sun* encapsulated opposition to changes. Filled with paternalism and desire for the status quo, the writer praised Jersey blacks and their alleged contentment. He wrote:

> NEW JERSEY NEGROES.—A very interesting motion is being discussed before the Supreme Court of New Jersey in favor of abrogating a remnant of slavery which is still left among the negroes of that state, although actual and positive slavery has long been abolished, but the West India apprenticeship system still exists. The New Jersey negro is far superior in character, attainments and influence to any part of the race in this country or in Africa. During the Revolutionary War few among the "Jersey blues" were more faithful to the cause of liberty than what may be called the "Jersey blacks." Generations live in the same family and its descendants, and although nominally in a state of servitude, they are the most influential persons in the Homestead. No purchase is made of importance in houses, lands, or cattle, furniture, or dress in New Jersey, without consulting David, Nathan or Joshua—for Cato, Ceasar, and Juba are heathenish names—and their opinions are generally sound and discreet. They are well educated, sprightly, intelligent and religious—have a self-pride and self-estimation, are civil and well behaved, and have lost sight altogether of a distinction of colours. No change of policy can better the condition of the negroes in New Jersey, some of whom, particularly the fishermen, are quite rich and hold real estate. Yet the anxiety of the abolitionist is so great that he actually to use a homely proverb "cannot let well alone."[58]

Realizing that only through the ballot box could they secure equity and power, New Jersey blacks focused on removal of voting restrictions and ending the last vestiges of slavery. A convention of free blacks meeting in Trenton in August 1849 argued that "political power is inherent in the people," and appealed to the citizens of New Jersey to recognize the need for justice, patriotism, honesty, and love of liberty, to assist state blacks to

Figure 6. John S. Rock (1825–1866). Early black physician, later Underground
Railroad Operator. Refused passport via Dred Scott decision of 1857. Later
admitted to the U.S. Supreme Court bar and first black to be received on the
floor of the U.S. House of Representatives. Newark Public Library, by permission
of the *Newark Star-Ledger*.

gain the vote. Three black clergymen, Joshua Woodling of Burlington,
W. T. Catto of Trenton, and Ishmael Rock of Camden demanded that the
state live up to the promises of the Declaration of Independence. While the
state legislature rebuffed that petition, blacks continued their efforts as representatives from Gloucester, Cumberland, Mercer, Middlesex, Monmouth,

and Salem Counties sent pro franchise petitions. John S. Rock of Salem, a black dentist and lawyer, eloquently argued in Frederick Douglass's *North Star* in February 1850 that New Jersey blacks were well acquainted with the state's institutions and politics, especially in comparison to newly arrived immigrants. Blacks had fought for the American side in the Revolution and the War of 1812. Blacks were citizens of the United States and should not be required to go to Africa to find prosperity and freedom when they had the right to them in New Jersey. The legislature continued to reject black arguments for the right to vote. After the Democratic Party gained full control of the legislature in 1852, blacks despaired of further petitions for the rest of the decade.[59]

John S. Rock became a leading figure later in the 1850s. Born in Salem, New Jersey, he studied under two white physicians and rose to prominence first in his home state and later in Massachusetts. There he tended to the health needs of self-emancipated slaves in Boston. As a lawyer, he sued to be allowed to appear before the Supreme Court, only to be denied under the infamous Dred Scott decision of 1857, which declared that African Americans had no civil rights. Rock was admitted to the bar in Massachusetts where he and his supporters continued his suit during the Civil War. Rock nearly attained his goal before his death in 1866.[60]

The Underground Railroad in the 1850s

New Jersey's UGRR attracted fiercely committed black conductors. After her self-emancipation in 1849, Harriet Tubman first fled to Philadelphia and then, doubtless directed by the city's vigilance committee, went to work as a maid in Cape May. There she encountered businessman Stephen Smith, known as the wealthiest black man in America and a prominent activist in the UGRR. Smith, Tubman, and local black communities collaborated on at least one of her daring rescue missions into slave country. They were the easternmost point on a thick slab of UGRR actions involving free black townships and Quakers that stretched along New Jersey's harbor boundaries all the way back to Philadelphia.[61]

Figure 7. Harriet Tubman (1822–1913), the famed Underground Railroad operator brought slavery survivors to many
Jersey towns. Courtesy of Swann Auction Galleries.

Tubman entered an established black community in Cape May. About
155 black people, of whom 141 were enslaved, lived there in 1790. They toiled
on farms and in ports, where they worked as fishermen, whalers, and boat
builders. After enactment of New Jersey's Gradual Emancipation Act of
1804, slavery ended quickly in Cape May, with only three enslaved out of

228 black residents in 1830, compared, for example, to Bergen County, where almost 600 people remained in bondage in 1830.

Tubman, like many self-emancipated blacks, found work through the UGRR. Proslavery and antiabolitionist commentators often derided free blacks for being lazy and unemployed, ignoring the massive discrimination in all fields of labor above the level of domestic and laborer. Tubman joined the hundreds of free blacks and slaves who had extricated themselves from slavery and now worked in the resort business run by Quakers from Philadelphia. Emma Marie Trusty's research into the 1850 federal census and New Jersey tax rateables reveals Tubman listed as a cook. Other black occupations included farmers, mariners, hotel workers, hack men, church founders, fishermen, and many watermen.

The year after Tubman arrived in New Jersey, Congress passed the Fugitive Slave Act of 1850, which opened up the North to slave catchers with government backing. For the UGRR black community in Cape May, it was fight or die. They stayed, raising the local population from 443 to 473 between 1850 and 1860. However, the work was now significantly more dangerous.

Harriet Tubman was welcomed and embraced into the Cape May antislavery and UGRR communities. She already knew some of the territory to the south in Maryland. Cape May operators helped her to cross the bay from Smyrna, Dover, or Odessa in Delaware to Springtown near Cape May. There she heard the inspirational preaching of Jarena Lee. Another black town used by Tubman was Marshalltown in Salem County. Family connections enabled the UGRR in Cape May and Edward Turner, a free black landowner and UGRR operative (UGRRO), was related to the Cox, Trusty, Armor, and Taylor families, all of whom were involved in freedom routes. Turner taught Tubman about black towns to the north including Snow Hill and Haddonfield.

From black UGRROs in Salem, Cumberland, and Cape May Counties, Tubman learned about routes in New Jersey along Indian trails and black towns. White antislavery workers helped Tubman, many of whom had cross-bay connections. As is well known about her nineteen rescue missions back into slavery to rescue the enslaved, Harriet worked with Thomas

Garrett of Wilmington, Delaware, who assisted her and hundreds of other UGRR operators and beneficiaries. Several of his relatives were intermarried with UGRROs in Cape May, and Garret's niece, Margaret, married John E. Shepard, a prominent UGRRO, in Greenwich.

Harriet Tubman's first few years of freedom, spent in Philadelphia and southern New Jersey, were critical to her development as a fearless UGRRO. Once she gained her freedom, she joined black communities based upon church and work and dedicated to the UGRR and antislavery activism. Often connected by marriage, black families helped Tubman and hundreds of others. They did so in a remote, seaside resort region run by antislavery Quakers. So, rather than being a sidelight to her career, Tubman's time in the Jersey Shore communities was fundamental to who she was and what she did. She found a world of black radicalism, piety, work, and UGRR activism. Locals helped her devise her routes and provided assistance for the survivors she extricated from slavery. As with Douglass in New York City, Tubman's experience in Cape May was foundational.

Tubman was not the only operative or self-emancipated slave to feel the cold dangers following passage of the Fugitive Slave Act of 1850. It is notable that of those whose escapes were chronicled in William Still's 1872 book *The Underground Railroad*, very few settled in New Jersey. John Spencer and his sons William and John Albert settled in Haddonfield after their escape from bondage on the eastern shore of Maryland in the spring of 1853. The trio worked for several months in Haddonfield until they learned of slave catchers hot on their trail. Quickly, they consulted the local UGRR committee, which procured tickets, disguised them, and "admonished them not to stop short of Canada." Abigail Goodwin of Salem, a prominent UGRR conductor, acknowledged the dangers of recapture in New Jersey, while sending a ten-dollar bill to fund transport to Canada for a seven-year-old boy. Goodwin noted: "There will be no safety for him here."[62]

The Dred Scott decision of 1857 further endangered free blacks and self-emancipated slaves. Emboldened by the Supreme Court decision that no black had a real claim on American citizenship, and that slavery was a normal economy that states should allow to exist everywhere, some whites defended the decision. The *Trenton True American* confidently forecast the end of the antislavery movement: "This puts a quietus on black republican- ism." In contrast, the Republican *Newark Advertiser* worried that the deci- sion put the "thorn of slavery deeper and deeper into the loins of the people of the North."[63]

Slave catchers, now emboldened, sought New Jersey victims. Several months after the March 6, 1857, decision, three men representing some Del- aware masters hunted four black men in Belvidere on the grounds that they used defective papers to uphold their freedom. The slave catchers learned about their quarry from a local white man named John H. Bryan, who "thus sold himself to this nefarious business . . . Judas." The four learned of their pursuit and fled. One was an elderly, respected member of the Methodist Church who had a large family and property and had lived in town for thirty-seven years. In November 1857 two men kidnapped a young black man, Henry Edwards, in Bordentown, tied him into the back of a wagon, and headed south. Edwards was able to attract attention at a river crossing by kicking the side of the wagon. Two bridge men saved Edwards as the kid- nappers whipped their wagon horse into full speed. Edwards then walked home.[64]

Slavery undoubtedly had a severe and negative impact upon black resi- dents of New Jersey in the antebellum period. Families suffered from the mixed status of its members, some free, some enslaved. Predatory kidnap- pers abetted by corrupt magistrates endangered the lives of innocent blacks. Legislative indifference, the pernicious effects of the American Colonization Society, and outright racial animosity made life difficult for Jersey's black middle class. As the United States has recently understood in this era of commemoration of the Second Civil Rights movement of the 1960s, pro- gress can be halting, but it does exist. Black property ownership, education, political involvement, free black churches, and societies all existed in 1860 that would have been unthinkable in 1790. Credit for this goes to the free black society itself, not to well-meaning white congregations and certainly not to white politics. Whatever gains were made were wrenched from an inhospitable and hostile society. Yet there were gains nonetheless.

James J. Gigantino II recently argued that slavery blighted black New Jersey society up to the Civil War. I have argued the same in earlier works on black New Jersey.[65] While undeniably true, slavery was not the only story in antebellum New Jersey. The inexorable rise of a small black middle class of farmers and urban professionals presaged economic gains and political activism after the Civil War.

Before then, New Jersey blacks created a unique black nationalism. Scholars writing on black nationalism have emphasized the roles of intellectuals and the black elite in fashioning an ideology of self-help, devotion to Africa, and demands that the United States live up to its stated ideals. While, as we have seen, there was a small black elite active in New Jersey, the greatest roles in creating a black nationalism came from ordinary free blacks. They, unlike the intellectuals, understood the ferocity of white racism from lived experience. Ordinary blacks in New Jersey supported drives for suffrage and open opportunity but clung to the belief that self-help and a church and fraternal organization-centered society would best protect them from the indifference, or worse: open antagonism of whites. That contained ideology would suffice for decades after the Civil War and remained largely unchallenged until the early twentieth century.[66]

CHAPTER 4

⁓

The Civil War and
Reconstruction to
World War I

The Civil War and its aftermath had deep repercussions for black New Jersey-ans. They faced significant obstacles. New Jersey was home to the highest percentage of black residents of any northern state and white New Jerseyans held powerful sympathies for the southern cause. The state had a potent leg-acy of slavery and an agricultural economy that needed cheap or poorly paid workers. At the same time, the state's black voters, enfranchised by the Fifteenth Amendment, gained more political power than ever before, and determined to use it to battle the smog of segregation blanketing northern states. During the war and after, New Jersey blacks, like their counterparts north and south, sought black male suffrage and equal access to public schools.[1]

The war did not alter racial antipathies. Historians have argued that neighboring New York City was pro-South because of close economic ties. The city's merchants, bankers, industrialists, and insurance companies depended on the South's massive cotton production, which accounted for more than half of the nation's economy in 1860. Southerners were accus-tomed to visiting New York City for shopping, medical care, and relief from the torrid summer months back home. New York's affiliation with the southern states was so close that Mayor Fernando Wood famously argued that New York should become an independent city-state to retain ties with the Confederacy. Philadelphia differed from New York City. While a pro-South contingent existed in the Quaker City, overall the population favored the Union. Philadelphia and its environs hosted large recruitment camps to which Jersey blacks, especially those in the southern counties, could go to enlist in the Union forces. Philadelphia was also the home of many radical black abolitionists and Underground Railroad operators.[2]

If New York's sympathies with the South were economic while Philadelphia citizens held mixed views, what caused much of New Jersey's white leadership to ally with the South before the outbreak of the war? New Jersey's economy fared well during the war and after. Newark's industrial base prospered. In 1861, despite its size, Newark ranked sixth in the nation in the value of manufactured products and was eleventh in population. Most prosperous were the counties nearest New York City, a metropolis flush with wartime profits. Burlington, abutting Philadelphia and Mercer, which included Trenton, also enjoyed good wartime years.[3]

Despite prosperity, much of the state's white population retained the prejudices of the slavery era and expressed open sympathy for the southern cause. Copperheads, as anti-Lincoln men were known, largely identified with the Democratic Party, particularly as the Whig and its immediate descendant, the Republican Party, tilted against slavery. Using Newark resident, former governor, and Democratic senator William Wright as an example, Brad Tuttle argues that pro-South attitudes derived from a mixture of personal economics and political ambition. Wright, a one-time Whig, became a Democrat in the 1850s and was a delegate to the party's national convention in Charleston, South Carolina, in 1860.[4]

White anxieties increased with the prospect of thousands of black migrants from the South, especially after the announcement of President Lincoln's Emancipation Proclamation. This was clear at the local level, despite strong evidence that there was little threat of a black majority. Morris County's black population had dropped from 1,027 persons in 1850 to 687 persons in 1860, making blacks only 2 percent of the county's population on the eve of the war. Nonetheless, Assemblyman Jacob Vanetta of Morris County authored an exclusion bill on March 5, 1863, mandating that any black entering the state would be transported to Liberia. The bill died in the New Jersey Senate.[5]

New Jersey's political conservatism and the lineage of slavery gave state politics an ambivalent cast during the war. Peace Democrats, who opposed the war and sought reconciliation with the Confederacy, were unsympathetic to blacks and argued that emancipation would bring hordes of unskilled blacks into the state to compete for work. David Naar of the *Trenton True American* was particularly antagonistic toward blacks. The military draft allowed exemptions for those who purchased a $400 deferment, creating intense social resentments. Anti-draft riots erupted in Newark in July 1863, emulating the massive rising in New York City.[6]

Blacks could not feel optimistic about national politics. Early in the war, the words of the President Abraham Lincoln did not provide much confidence about a black future in the United States. Lincoln expressed his preference for colonization. In 1861–1862, Congress allocated more than $600,000 to assist expatriation of blacks, especially those freed by the District of Columbia Emancipation Act and the Second Confiscation Act. Black New Jerseyans disagreed. A. P. Smith, a black journalist from Saddle River, penned a letter to President Lincoln that disputed any forced colonization plans. Smith asked the chief executive "is our right to a home in this country less than your own?" Smith pointed out the valiant roles blacks played in settling America and their service to the nation during the American Revolution.[7]

As Eric Foner has argued, Lincoln evolved on the question of race. By 1862, he prepared a dramatic reversal with the preliminary Emancipation Proclamation made final on January 1, 1863, immediately freeing enslaved people living in states controlled by the Confederacy. His words were great news to New Jersey blacks, but not to whites. The Emancipation Proclamation, effective January 1, 1863, epitomized the worst fears of New Jersey's Democrats. After announcement of the preliminary Proclamation, Edward Fuller of the *Newark Daily Journal* thundered that it was "as absurd as it was fanatical," and urged white Americans who "love their country better than the Negro, the Union better than party," should demand that Lincoln's plan be dropped immediately. Opposition to the Proclamation allowed Democrats to easily win the New Jersey legislature in November elections and after it went into effect, William Wright became New Jersey Senator (James W. Wall, an even more virulently racist party member, was a temporary appointment). Wright and other Democrats cheered as Ohio Congressman Clement L. Valandigham spoke in Newark on the need to end the expected draft, expel Lincoln from office, and put an immediate stop to the "miserable crusade against African slavery." The legislature's lack of sympathy was evident when it nearly passed a Banishment Act in 1863 that barred free blacks from entering the state under penalty of forced exile to Liberia. New Jersey's Democratic Party was so opposed to the war effort that it even attempted to bar use of any state funds to pay bounties or employ black troops. This bill was eventually dropped but indicated how deep were the prejudicial attitudes of the ruling party in New Jersey. In his inaugural address that year, Governor Joel Parker declared the Emancipation Proclamation to be unconstitutional and with his support, the legislature introduced a series of resolutions against it. Parker warned against the arrival of southern blacks who would displace white workers. The legislature also supported movements to end the Civil War and respect the property rights of southern slaveholders. Southern sympathies and the state Democratic Party's outright opposition to the Union side continued even after the war began. On the eve of the first Battle of Bull Run, the *Somerset Messenger* opined that colonization was the best means for improving the conditions of black people.[8]

There were occasional whites whose wartime experiences enlarged their views of black people. Private Alfred Bellard of the Fifth New Jersey Regiment found that black mechanics working in government blacksmith and wheelwright shops in Alexandria, Virginia, in 1861 were far more intelligent than he had previously believed.[9]

Black New Jerseyans responded to the Emancipation Proclamation by declaring their willingness to fight to ensure its success. They were able to enlist in the Union Army following General Order Number 1, issued on January 2, 1863, the day after the Emancipation Proclamation became active. Governor Joel Parker and the Democratic Party's opposition meant that black New Jerseyans were not allowed to enlist in state regiments, which did not stop them from enlisting in the regiments of other states. Over two dozen quickly joined the famous Fifty-Fourth Massachusetts Infantry regiment when it began signing up black soldiers from the free states in February 1863; another dozen from New Jersey were in the Fifty-Fifth Massachusetts Infantry. Morris Butler of Mount Holly, a nineteen-year-old laborer, was captured in the battle of Fort Wagner and died in a prisoner-of-war camp. Joseph Perow, a butcher from Burlington and several others were wounded at Fort Wagner. The former occupations of the Jersey members of the Fifty-Fourth regiment reflect the general status of state African Americans. Enlistees were laborers, waiters, farmers, boatman, and coachman. Its extreme measure hurt when New Jersey state officials refused to enlist black troops in their regiments, despite major difficulties meeting quotas of new soldiers by 1863, which resulted in drafts used in several counties and bounties in nearly all. In 1864, a failed resolution in the state senate would have created fines of $500 for recruiting black troops in New Jersey. Under a federal order to enlist them, Union camps in Philadelphia took in black recruits.[10]

Estimates of the number of black soldiers from New Jersey who served in the Union Army range from 2,872 to 3,271. William Wright estimates that 469 died in conflict or from sickness.[11] Among those who served were descendants of the Creole free blacks who migrated from New York to Bergen County in the late seventeenth and early eighteenth centuries. Phillip De Freese and John De Groot served as infantrymen. William De Groat, John Suffern, and William Van Donk died as a result of disease during the war.[12]

According the William J. Jackson's research, most Jersey blacks served in regiments organized at Camp William Penn, a training site on feminist Lucretia Mott's land outside of Philadelphia. Their regimental numbers soon became significant: the Twenty-Second (681); Twenty-Fifth (531); Thirty-Second (319); and Forty-Third (365). The soldiers enlisted outside of New Jersey and many indicated birthplaces in other states so their total numbers are hard to define, but estimates range from 1,185 to 2,872, with the latter figure appearing more accurate. Yet their determination was plain. Charles Haitstock of the Twenty-Second U.S. Colored Troop (USCT) regiment, which included many Jersey blacks, wrote in a letter from Fortress

Monroe in 1863 that, "We can do nothing but fight for the country's cause, and will do that until every one of us perishes by the rebel bullet." Haitstock's dedication was typical. Only 289 blacks deserted after enlistment, in an army troubled by homesick deserters.[13]

A letter one black man wrote to a prominent white businessman indicates the determination felt about fighting for the Union side against slavery. Marcus L. Ward, the Newark philanthropist and later governor (1866–1869) who was known as the "soldier's friend" received a letter from L. D. Sims of Newark that informed Ward of his desire to enlist in the "Color'd Regiment, despite a recent bout with rheumatism." Sims planned to visit the surgeon of the army with a view to enroll in the Invalid Corps and do "effective garrison duty," and then transfer to field service when his health allowed.[14]

Pension records indicate the presence of self-emancipated slaves who served in the Union Army. Several members of the Trusty family who lived in Cape May enrolled in colored regiments. Wallace Trusty of Cape May City enlisted in the Twenty-Second U.S. Colored Troops in Philadelphia in January 1864, but died of measles at Camp William Penn a month later. His family was later awarded a pension of six dollars a month. Another member of the Trusty family, David, received a similar grant for his service and in recognition of the lumbago he contracted during the war. Samuel Trusty of Cape May City served in the Forty-First USCT regiment.[15]

Veteran status rarely guaranteed future prosperity. Poverty was the primary status of New Jersey's black Civil War veterans and their families. Charles H. Harris could not work because of war-related injuries. Henrietta Crawford of Vineland, whose husband James died in service in Texas, was described as "destitute" in her pension application. Mary J. Coy of Woodbridge, the widow of John Coy, was dependent on her daily labor for support. A lump of cartridge lodged in his back caused Charles Finnaman of the Twenty-Second USCT to seek a pension later in life.[16]

After the war, black military service diminished in value. This was especially apparent in segregation statues and extended to stiff hurdles to gaining pensions. Not all black New Jersey veterans received pensions. Those who did not were supported by the state. The files of the New Jersey Home for Disabled Soldiers mention numerous state blacks who suffered their last years in pain and poverty alongside their white counterparts. Samuel Cromwell of Cookstown, a descendant of a distinguished New Jersey family of Patriot blacks, served in the Sixth USCT, only to die alone in a home for disabled soldiers. Henry Amman of Elizabethtown and the Sixth USCT also resided there. Pneumonia from wartime disease killed Primer Jackson of Newark, formerly a soldier in the Twentieth USCT, just twenty years after he mustered out in October 1865. Heart disease and leg injuries put James Huff of Newark, Twentieth USCT, in the grave in 1886. Homes for the disabled soldiers were among the few places in New Jersey that were not segregated; the others were soldiers' plots in state cemeteries, where black veterans' remains "were given permission" for interment.[17]

The close of the war did not create prosperity for New Jersey blacks. Postwar Newark directories list numerous teamsters, laborers, waiters, porters, peddlers, shingle shavers, stablemen, and other semiskilled and poorly paid occupations. Beyond the prominent mention of the city's four black ministers, the few other professionals included were a jeweler, an engineer, and a public school teacher. These trends continued for several decades. The much larger directory for 1886–1887 added the principal of the "colored school," attended by 178 children, a chiropodist, a gold refiner, a physician, two businessmen to supplement the lengthy lists of laborers, waiters, barbers, chimney sweeps, and other low-paid, semiskilled jobs.[18]

While black New Jerseyans showed patriotism by enlisting in the Union Army, like other northern blacks, they were aware that the Emancipation Proclamation depended on continued Republican support. If the Democratic Party regained control of the presidency and Congress, they could repeal the Proclamation and resurrect the 1857 Supreme Court Dred Scott decision that ruled against any African American rights of citizenship. Moreover, northern blacks were aware that the Republican Party might barter away their freedoms in exchange for peace with the South.[19]

Black political efforts built upon prewar black activism and continued into the conflict. Black New Jerseyans renewed their antebellum efforts to regain the vote, lost since 1807. Trenton blacks petitioned in 1863 and 1864 for an amendment to the state constitution to allow for African American suffrage. Blacks from New Jersey attended the 1864 National Convention of Colored Men held in Syracuse, New York. They were anxious about the future and eager to continue the construction of black politics before the war. The convention attracted the best minds and talents among African American men: Frederick Douglass, Henry Highland Garnet, John Rock, John Mercer Langston. New Jerseyans, after meeting to select delegates in Trenton, sent five men: William Howard Day, who served on the convention's Permanent Committee, and Edwin H. Freeman, both of Newark, Thomas G. Gould of Trenton, who was named a vice president, Thomas Cooke of Trenton and D. P. Seaton of Morristown, who sat on the business committee.[20]

The convention declared a long list of historic grievances, including slavery and racism. At the same time, delegates appealed to America's better nature by seeking equal rights in concord with white Americans, especially Republicans, while encouraging black Americans to achieve middle-class values, goals that would guide African Americans for the next decade and beyond. The convention also created the National Equal Rights League to pursue those goals.[21]

New Jersey blacks met in Trenton in July 1865 and Samuel G. Gould was elected president. His first act was to report on the meeting in Syracuse the year before; the convention then created committees and passed resolutions. The 1865 convention sought a census of all state blacks, especially the men who had fought for the Union. Beyond that it focused on restoring "all the rights of Loyal Citizens," who had "in the hour of our peril, when called . . . rallied to the rescue of our nation." Encouraged by the convention, black citizens from Essex, Cumberland, Mercer, Burlington, and Atlantic Counties and the city of Rahway sent memorials to the legislature in 1866 asking that the word "white" be stricken from the state constitution. All these efforts were immediately tabled.[22]

The close of the war did not alleviate New Jersey's legal discrimination against its black citizens. Every Democratic member of the state government voted against the Thirteenth Amendment. Only when the Republican Party

regained control did the measure pass. Public officials were openly antagonistic about the Fourteenth and Fifteenth Amendments. Governor Parker
warned against "mongrel governments" if blacks gained the vote. After the
Republican-controlled legislature passed the Fourteenth Amendment in
1866, when it was already federal law, the new Democratic majority rescinded
that approval in 1867. This scenario was reversed over the Fifteenth Amendment when the Democratic Assembly rejected the new law in 1871, only to
have a Republican majority approve it later.[23]

Black leaders in New Jersey pushed toward getting back the vote after the
war. Members of the Equal Rights League met in Newark in 1866 to raise
cash and institute legal proceedings to force registrars to accept black voters.
Even with assistance from the much larger Pennsylvania group, the New
Jersey League failed to gain its objectives. Money was an issue but more
important was the refusal of the state legislature to settle black suffrage by
popular ballot. In this and other instances, black New Jerseyans found that
the Republican Party could not always be trusted, but the Democratic Party
was useless.[24]

The frustrated hopes of New Jersey blacks were alleviated by passage of
the Fifteenth Amendment. After ratification, hundreds of blacks gathered
on May 26, 1870, in New Brunswick for a massive parade and celebration.
Participants came from Newark, Flemington, Bound Brook, and Elizabeth
to commemorate winning the suffrage. The keynote speaker was William
Whipper, a veteran of the black abolitionist movement and a founder of the
American Moral Reform Society, an organization created to instill Christian morality, thrift, diligence, and temperance among blacks. This time
Whipper did not emphasize those virtues but hammered on the necessity
of race pride and black contributions to American freedom via participation in U.S. wars. Whipper called forth the examples of black revolutionar-
ies, including Denmark Vesey, Nat Turner, David Walker, and the white
radical John Brown. Thomas Peterson Mundy of Perth Amboy became the
state's first black voter since 1807 when he cast a ballot in 1871. His achievement was commemorated with a plaque attached to his grave in 1934.[25]

Figure 8. Thomas Mundy Peterson (1824–1904), from Perth Amboy. Peterson was the first African American to vote under rights gained in the Fifteenth Amendment to the U.S. Constitution in 1870. Newark Public Library, permission of *Newark Star-Ledger*.

Having achieved the vote did not guarantee blacks significant political power in New Jersey politics during the Reconstruction Era. The Democrats had been solidly opposed to the Fifteenth Amendment. The Republican Party, once the amendment passed, was the beneficiary of an estimate of 5,000 to 7,000 new black voters, significant numbers in a state where elections were often closely decided. Black leaders prophesized the 99 percent of the race's voters would be Republicans. While some Democrats continued to employ racist rhetoric, others were more pragmatic and averred a more cautious approach that emphasized the cost of black suffrage to the white working class. One Democrat who moderated his views was Governor Leon Abbett (1884–1887, 1890–1903). A staunch copperhead during the Civil War, Abbett surprised many by pushing for the burial of Samuel Bass, an ex-slave, in an all-white Hackensack cemetery. Abbett later became godfather to a Newark black child who was named after him.

Complicating politics was a strong antiparty movement that criticized both parties' embrace of business measures. Overall the political machines adopted a position that black voters had to fend for themselves now that suffrage had been gained. This posture was similar to the neglect of black freedoms in the early part of the century after gradual emancipation. In sum, the Democrats remained hostile to black interests while the Republicans avoided full support for black needs, a pattern that would continue into the twentieth century and resulted in few patronage achievements for blacks.[26]

Black Jersey voters were further jostled by the election of 1876. They anxiously considered supporting Rutherford B. Hayes, the Republican nominee for the presidency. Hayes had a good track record on civil rights while governor of Ohio and had avidly supported the Fifteenth Amendment. By the early 1870s, like other ambitious white Republican politicians, he began to vacillate on support for black rights and reconciliation with the southern states. He embraced a "let alone" policy that promised to remove northern troops from the southern states and thereby allow the region's whites to determine the fate of their fellow black citizens. John D. Bagwell, chairman of the Colored Republican Committee of New Jersey, which represented

7,000 black state voters, told Hayes in July 1876 that blacks wanted to support him, but could not if he removed federal troops from the South. Hayes did not respond, but Jersey blacks reluctantly supported the Republican nominee anyway. Hayes won the presidency in a decision made by a special electoral commission months after the actual vote. As federal troops left the South, Reconstruction collapsed and over the next few years southern blacks lost their rights as citizens. Hayes ignored terrorism in the South. Segregation triumphed there with significant effect in New Jersey and other northern states.[27]

New Jersey blacks suffered along with their northern counterparts from the weak judicial application to the Fourteenth Amendment that guaranteed equal protection of the law to all citizens, including the right to an education. However, state and federal courts continually found that the principal of equality did not mandate integrated schools.

National events in the 1890s powerfully affected New Jersey blacks. The national press, intellectual class, and government adopted a malignant interpretation of social Darwinism that emphasized perceptions of black inferiority and increasingly accepted a southern interpretation that the Civil War and Reconstruction were colossal errors. Within that context of sharply diminished support for black civil rights, Booker T. Washington's famous 1895 "Atlanta Compromise" speech accepted a racially divided society. In brief, Washington proclaimed that political and civil equality were less important than jobs: "the opportunity of early a dollar in a factory just now is worth infinitely more than the opportunity to spend a dollar in an opera house." Whites wildly cheered Washington's words. The next year in the infamous 1896 Plessy v. Ferguson decision, the U.S. Supreme Court allowed that segregation did not violate the Fourteenth Amendment and even cited several state supreme court decisions to validate its conclusion, one of which was the 1847 Massachusetts ruling that upheld the constitutionality of segregated schools. As Rayford W. Logan brilliantly argued, Washington's speech and the Supreme Court's decision led to the disenfranchisement of blacks in the South and their political weakness in the North. While the speech made Booker T. Washington's career, it consigned blacks throughout the nation to inferior status. Logan aptly describes this era as the nadir of American race relations.[28]

While Washington acknowledged social separation of the races in 1895 and the U.S. Supreme Court affirmed separate schools, separatist policies had existed in New Jersey for over a decade. At times, blacks, hurt by white racism, had accepted segregated schools. In many other walks of life, they resisted staunchly. Washington became a popular figure in New Jersey over the next twenty years, but locals adapted his message to their own purposes and never fully accepted his accommodating stance toward perceived white superiority.[29]

Demographic Change

Black political efforts and goals occurred within massive internal demographic changes. Population growth dramatically affected black life in postwar New Jersey. Black New Jersey's population tripled between 1870 and 1910 via the wave of the first black migration. The number of blacks living in New Jersey but born out of state was 43 percent in 1870 and 58 percent in 1910. Blacks in New Jersey migrated to urban centers. Camden, Newark, and Atlantic City experienced massive influxes of African Americans in the late nineteenth century. Atlantic City's black population soared from 763 black residents to nearly 7,000 in 1900 as African Americans flocked into the emerging resort industry. New Jersey's black population grew steadily in the first decades of the twentieth century. In 1900 blacks made up 3.2 percent of the state's populace; thirty years later that fraction climbed to 5.2 percent, or 209,000 souls.[30]

New Jersey, like other northern states, benefited from postwar black migration from the southern states. Determined to find better lives and to escape postwar terrorism wreaked by the Ku Klux Klan and other groups, New Jersey's population of blacks born in the South increased from 5,166 in 1870 to 7,401 in 1900. Though not as hefty as the 6,000-plus jumps in black population in New York, the New Jersey increase was significant.[31]

New Jersey blacks began their move into its cities. Newark's black population rose from 7,000 in 1900 to 9,500 in 1910. Jersey City's black population jumped in ten years from 3,704 to 6,000 in 1910.[32] During the 1870s the black population of Camden grew steadily, although the city remained predominately white. Part of this increase came from urban consolidation. Fettersville became the South Ward, home to nearly 90 percent of Camden's black residents. The long established black community of Kaighnsville was also absorbed into Camden. While blacks in these communities lived among whites, there was a substantial amount of segregation within each ward. City realignment in 1871 created eight wards out of the original three. Blacks lived in all wards, but primarily in the wards stemming from Fettersville and Kaighnsville. Within these wards, blacks clustered along certain streets, living near but usually not adjacent to white residents. The Seventh and Eighth wards were the hearts of Camden's black community with major African Methodist Episcopal, African Union, and Methodist Episcopal Churches, significant black fraternal organizations, and residences of such prominent blacks as real estate broker Dempsey Butler and magistrate Phillip Colding. The majority of blacks were working class or unskilled laborers. By 1920, 8,500 blacks lived in Camden or about 7.3 percent of the city's total population.[33]

For those who wished to escape society's general racism, black towns provided succor. Gouldtown was the home for five generations of the Gould family along with the Pierces, a mixed-race family. Eventually urban life beckoned. By 1907 all but fifty families remained as the rest had moved to New York and other big cities. Springtown in Greenwich Township was the landing place for many self-emancipated people from Delaware and Maryland, but by 1900 only forty families remained. Whitesboro was the place of refuge for blacks fleeing the 1898 racial riots in Wilmington, Delaware. Even as the enticement of urban work lured young people away from the black towns, they attained group integrity. Segregation in white schools created opportunities for black teachers in black communities. There were numerous social and mutual aid societies. That community solidarity in a hostile world led some blacks to opposed plans for integration.[34]

Some areas showed limited growth. Elizabeth did not experience large-scale influxes of African Americans in the decades after the Civil War. The city's black population was 301 in 1860, a mere 2.6 percent of the city's total populace. Sixty years later, that percentage was even lower at 2.1 percent, reflecting a small boost in the black population to 1870. Elizabethtown blacks lived, as they had done in antebellum years, in close proximity to whites, either native-born employers or recently arrived immigrants. The small size of Elizabethtown's black population and the residential legacies of slavery slowed the pace of segregation throughout the late nineteenth century.[35]

Southern blacks began migrating into lower New Jersey in the 1870s. Cape May attracted domestic and hotel workers. Initially, such workers received favorable comments. A writer in the *Christian Recorder* noted that "the class of men who go are mostly young men, many of them are highly intelligent, some of them have trades, and not a few of them are members of Church. Prejudice, keeping them out of other business, forces them to engage in this kind of employment to so great an extent." Cape May boasted a series of black hotels beginning with Banneker's in the 1850s and extending to the Dale Hotel into the 1910s. Overall, however, Cape May's economy could not sustain sufficient work after the Civil War and black workers looked elsewhere for wages.[36]

The answer lay up the coast. Atlantic City's resort economy began to boom and employed numerous blacks as waiters and cooks. As Atlantic City became "America's Playground," blacks flocked to the city to work in service jobs. By 1900 hotel staffs had become 95 percent black. Young black men were attracted by wages of eight to twenty-five dollars per month, depending on the size of the hotel plus supplements for room and board and expectations of sizable gratuities. Initially, blacks lived among whites without any discrimination. By 1915 only 20 percent of blacks had white neighbors. Housing restrictions jacked up rents and forced more blacks to take in boarders and increased the likelihood of childhood infectious diseases. By 1910, nearly a quarter of black children died before the age of one compared to about 8 percent of whites. By 1915, blacks accounted for more than one of four residents of Atlantic City, making it the greatest concentration of blacks in New Jersey. Atlantic City boasted several prosperous black churches, YMCAs and YWCAs, along with a leadership class led by lawyer Morris Cain. Black voters in Atlantic City were closely tied to the corrupt yet protective leadership of hotelier Louis "the Commodore" Kuehnle. In contrast to the openly racist Democratic Party, Kuehnle prompted black hotel workers to vote with fixed ballots in exchange for two dollars. Jim Crow crept into Atlantic City during the 1890s but even the Boardwalk was not fully segregated. September became the most common time for blacks to use the beaches without incident, though big spenders such as the Black Elks were welcome anytime.[37]

More southern black migrants arrived in New Jersey in the 1880s to work in one of the state's massive farms. Jersey's agricultural economy mechanized and consolidated in this era to battle competition from midwestern farms. Rather than general farming, landowners specialized in potatoes, cranberries, tomatoes, and strawberries. Using modern plows and fertilizer, New Jersey truck farms could now feed the burgeoning cities. Humans were still necessary to pick the crops. At first, the padrone system supplied large numbers of Italian workers, but urban industry attracted Italians. Southern blacks migrated to New Jersey as part of an agricultural proletariat laboring whenever and wherever crops demanded their skills. Replacing the padrones were crew leaders who organized black farm laborers in New Jersey. During times of scarcity, such as World War I, the state government ordered black workers to the fields, disregarding their wage demands. At the same time, southern blacks increasingly remained in New Jersey, transforming the population.[38]

The program commemorating Booker T. Washington's 1914 state tour provided detailed information on New Jersey's rising black middle class before World War I. Washington made a lengthy tour of the state in 1914, just as he had visited a number of southern states previously. Louis Harlan, Washington's biographer, contends that one tour was like all the others, a triumphal march. During the New Jersey visit, the "Wizard of Tuskegee" first traveled from New York City to Morristown, where, using a formula repeated across the state, local choirs opened with spirituals, followed by prayers by area ministers and Washington's address. From Morristown, Washington traveled by automobile to Montclair, where his address preceded a parade, an industrial exhibit, and a banquet. The next day, after a brief visit to Paterson, Washington was feted in a huge ceremony at Bethany Baptist Church in Newark with numerous spirituals, prayers, comments, and a banquet. Over the next day, Washington moved quickly across the state, going to Princeton and Burlington in one day. He visited the black towns of Gouldtown and Cape May City on the third day, then spent the evening in Salem before departing to Philadelphia. At every stop, black clerics dominated the speakers, as befit their roles as social and religious leaders.[39]

The program for Washington's tour highlighted the black populations of the towns he visited. These brief portraits offer telling details of smaller New Jersey black communities. Morristown, for example, a prosperous town known for its American Revolutionary importance, had nearly 1,000 black residents among its 12,500 residents in 1910. About a quarter of Morristown's black population were of voting age and owned taxable property worth $748,000. Local blacks worshipped at either a Methodist or Baptist church. Blacks in Morristown included a staunch middle class with careers and jobs as doctors, barbers, ice and coal dealers, a silversmith, music teacher, real estate agents, and four taxicab owners. The town had a black YMCA and a troop of Boy Scouts.[40]

Montclair also boasted a black middle class with about 3,500 people, four churches, a black newspaper, the *Eastern Observer*, black operated branches of the YMCA and YWCA, Boy Scouts and Campfire Girls, and most important, integrated public schools. Prominent black ministers headed an array of occupations including hairdressers, druggists, contractors, photographers, a watchmaker and jeweler, nine dressmakers, an undertaker, and two taxicab companies. In his address to Montclair's black citizens, Washington congratulated them on their prosperity and self-help, saying that their accomplishments belied critics of black people.[41]

Princeton's black population of about 1,100, in a town of 5,500 souls, featured the Witherspoon Presbyterian Institutional Church, headed by wealthy whites, which also supervised the local "colored YMCA" and other philanthropic agencies. Most black residents of Princeton worked as waiters, cooks, and domestic servants, though the town had a coterie of black professionals as grocers, ministers, carpenters, furniture dealers, and restaurant owners. William Moore supplied the clothing for Princeton University students. Princeton blacks had local branches of numerous fraternities and sororities including the Masons, Odd Fellows, Pythians, Elks, Eastern Star, and Household of Ruth. In an early sign of the segregationist policies he would implement as president, Princeton's chief executive Woodrow Wilson fired all of the school's black dining hall service employees and replaced them with Greek immigrants. The discharged blacks were forced to leave town to find work elsewhere.[42]

Paterson's black population was much smaller than its overall population, with but 1,500 African Americans in a populace of 125,000 in 1910. Paterson's black population suffered badly from its exclusion from the silk and other manufactories. Only a tool handle factory, reputed to be the finest in the world, employed blacks. Among Paterson's black professionals were a doctor, barbers and hairdressers, and ministers at four churches. Showing black weakness in politics, only one man worked for the municipal government as a policeman. Washington also visited New Jersey's black towns in the southern counties. The program highlighted the Hotel Cape May where Washington stayed as well as the ornithology work of G. R. Jefferson of Cape May who experimented with flightless pigeons.[43]

Black Churches

As before, black churches were the mainstays of African American community. Churches provided status and mild prosperity to male New Jersey African Americans in the late nineteenth century. William J. Simmons, born in slavery in Charleston, South Carolina, escaped with his mother and brother from slavery in Charleston, eventually settling in Bordentown. He later attended Madison Institute (Colgate University) before becoming a minister and compiling his mammoth book, *Men of Mark*, a biographical dictionary of eminent black men. Reverend J. W. Stephenson was the presiding elder of the eastern district of the state's African Methodist Episcopal (AME) Church and a practicing physician. Stephenson, born in Baltimore, Maryland, in 1836, spent time in Trinidad, West Indies, returned to the United States and served as an apprentice to a stove dealer and barber, and eventually studied at the Pennsylvania University of Medicine. After appointments in Pennsylvania, he became a physician and pastor of an AME Zion Church in Freehold. He moved around the state to Trenton and Burlington before his appointment as presiding elder. He supervised ministers in twelve large towns including Jersey City, New Brunswick, Elizabeth, Newark, and Princeton. Stephenson was adept at fundraising and church construction. Another clergyman, Reverend B. F. Lee, was born in Gouldtown in 1841. Orphaned at ten, he was sent into service and excelled in school. He studied at Wilberforce University and later preached in Kentucky and Ohio before becoming editor of the *Christian Recorder*, the official organ of the African Methodist Church. The nationally known violinist Professor Walter F. Craig was born in Princeton in 1854.[44]

The black middle class founded new churches. Peter Wycoff, a broom maker in Plainfield, was a sponsoring founder in 1870 of the Mount Olive Baptist Church. Mount Olive grew rapidly, built a parish, operated missionary units, and helped other charities. The AME Zion Church held its annual conference in Jersey City in 1908. Pullman porters held balls at Columbia Hall in Jersey City.[45]

Church renovations were big news. Parishioners announced with pride the expensive remodeling to the Bethany Baptist Church in Newark, promising that it would be one of the handsomest religious edifices in the state. The church would have stained glass windows, harmonized frescoed walls and ceilings, would be heated by gas or electricity, and would possess a powerful new organ. Black newspapers routinely published lengthy paeans to prominent ministers, providing several pages to the teachings of Rever-

end G. H. Eggleston of Jersey City one week and a full account of the sermons of Reverend Dr. H. P. Lymon Wheaton of St. James AME Church in
Ridgefield on another. Prophet Jones promised during a four-week revival
to shake New Jersey and New York like an earthquake. Promotions of
important black ministers received adulatory stories. Ministers took their
roles as leaders of the race very seriously, advising that only good men should
undertake the job and that the careless and unconcerned should get out.[46]

Ministers were still the top figures in black New Jersey society. Annual
religious conferences were significant events. AME Episcopal members met
in Long Branch; the Zion AME met in Jersey City.[47] Newspapers reported
their rotation and their deaths inspired solemn eulogies by their peers who
gathered from all over the state. When Reverend Owen Lee Simmons of the
Bank Street Baptist Church of Paterson died in 1906, no less than five fellow
pastors eulogized him. The service included singing of the deceased's favorite hymns, resolutions, a poem composed for the occasion augmented by the
presence of the Past Grand Master's Pride lodge of Newark, which Simmons
had founded twelve years before, twenty more preachers, and more than 800
other parishioners.[48] Revivals were chronicled and a two-week service at
St. Mark's AME Zion attracted hundreds.[49]

While the overwhelming bulk of black ministers were male, women
preached as itinerants in New Jersey and in surrounding states. Amanda
Smith began preaching in churches and at Holiness camp meetings in New
York and New Jersey, becoming a popular speaker to both black and white
audiences during the 1870s before embarking on a religious mission that
extended to many parts of the world. Other women concentrated their missionary efforts in New Jersey. C. Christmas, Ann Anderson, and Josephine
Smith headed the Women's Division of the New Jersey Conference Branch
of the AME Church between 1900 and 1916.[50]

Other women constructed their own agencies. Reverend Florence Randolph moved from Charleston, South Carolina, in the 1890s to Jersey City,
where she was licensed to preach in the AME Zion Church. For fourteen
years Randolph served as a voluntary, unsalaried missionary. Later she pastored several churches in New Jersey and southern New York State and spent

time traveling and preaching in England, Scotland, and France. Her ministries extended to temperance groups and prisons. She was the founder and
first president of the New Jersey State Federation of Women's Clubs, and of
the state suffrage association and made substantial efforts in foreign missions. Her career and devotion mirrored her male counterparts. While her
sisters in the ministry were few, Randolph was part of a significant black
women's movement in the late-nineteenth and early-twentieth centuries
that espoused a politics of civic righteousness. Randolph and counterparts
such as Violet Jackson organized working class women in their congregations to battle legal and social discrimination. Operating out of Summit,
New Jersey, Randolph, Jackson, and their membership from the class of
domestic workers called for civil rights, blasted segregation in schools and
the workplace, and called for black self-uplift, on their own terms.[51]

Divisions in churches made the news. The Newark Presbyterians fired
their minister in 1906 and then decided to go without a leader. In 1900, black
members of the First Presbyterian Church withdrew from the congregation
to set up their own parish, known as Lafayette Presbyterian. In its early
years, three pastors and a leading layman and physician, George Cannon,
led the congregation. Within ten years the church had attracted over one
hundred members. Still, it struggled financially and depended on First Presbyterian to pay the pastors' salaries. In 1907, with Cannon's prodding,
Lafayette Presbyterian hired Charles H. Trusty, a New Jersey native and, like
Cannon, a graduate of Lincoln College. Trusty had ministered to a number
of Presbyterian parishes in the South. At Lafayette, Trusty successfully
appealed to the Jersey City Presbytery for $200 from the Barbes Fund of the
national Board of Home Missions. Trusty's application to get $6,700 to pur-
chase a Universalist Church was endorsed by the Board of Church Erection.
Trusty did not fare as well with his congregation, however, and was soon
forced out amid allegations of fiscal mismanagement. Even after Trusty's
departure, Lafayette churchmen pursued the allegations. Trusty had moved
on to the famed Grace Memorial Church in Pittsburgh, once led by Henry
Highland Garnet. After a substantial career at Grace Memorial that lasted
until 1925 and included expansion of its membership, creation of satellite

congregations, and rebuilding the physical plant of Grace, Trusty moved, after a dispute over his salary, to Omaha, Nebraska. His final assignment was back in New Jersey at the Siloam Presbyterian Church in Elizabeth. Like other black congregations, Siloam was in tough shape financially because of the Depression. Nonetheless, Trusty was able to use his fundraising skills to extract sizable sums from the state Presbytery. He pastored at Siloam until his retirement at age 70 in 1938. He then returned to Jersey City and participated in the annual Lafayette Church council meetings.[52] In an ironic twist, several years later he married George Cannon's widow, Genevieve Wilkinson Cannon. The couple lived at the Cannon residence at 354 Pacific Avenue in Jersey City.[53] Dennis Dickerson has ably described Trusty as a hard-working though not inspiring pastor, whose organizational skills helped spread black congregations throughout the North and West.

Ministers, who made up a prominent portion of the black middle class, faced racial limits. The Reverend William Paul Robeson had escaped in 1858 via the Underground Railroad from servitude in eastern North Carolina to freedom in Pennsylvania. Robeson joined a Union Army labor battalion during the Civil War and later received his bachelor's and master's degrees from Lincoln University. During his years of study, Robeson met and married Maria Louisa Bustill, whose family descended from Cyrus Bustill. Born a slave in Burlington, Cyrus later bought his freedom, served as a baker for the Patriots in the Revolutionary War, and was a founder of the Free African Society in Philadelphia. Though they were not social equals to the Bustills, the Robesons prospered. Reverend Robeson became pastor of the Witherspoon Street Presbyterian Church in Princeton, a black congregation funded and controlled by local wealthy white Presbyterians. Robeson shaped the congregation into a center of civic and social activity. He defended the community interest and earned universal respect. The couple had seven children (two died in infancy), one of whom, Paul (born 1898), became world famous for his singing, acting, and political activism.

Despite the family's central place in Princeton society, Robeson Sr. could not place his eldest son, William, at the local college, Princeton University. After his son was rebuffed in 1900, Reverend Robeson appealed in person to

Woodrow Wilson, then president of the university. Wilson refused to help and, after the minister beseeched him several times, angrily retorted that the school would not accept "colored" students. Wilson doubtless did not care, but his crass, vicious rejection of William Drew Robeson smudged the memory of generations of prominent free blacks in New Jersey and Philadelphia. The student traced his family history through his mother's ancestry to Cyrus Bustill and via marriage to fabled black Philadelphia families such as those of James Forten, Robert Purvis, the artist Sarah Mapps Douglass, and journalist Gertrude Bustill Mossell. Other young blacks got the message about Wilson's racism. Future Harlem Renaissance literary giant Alain Locke chose Pennsylvania over New Jersey for his home state, despite his mother's longterm residence, in the Rhodes Scholarship competition, knowing that Wilson would have a powerful say in the state's nomination for the prize.[54]

Reverend Robeson was also involved in a local protest over the national horror of lynching blacks. Robeson and his close friend, Abraham P. Denney, superintendent of the Witherspoon School for Colored Children, organized an antilynching meeting at the Witherspoon Church. The meeting created a resolution aimed at President William McKinley Jr. The resolution was peaceful and simply asked for laws to prevent the monstrous violence. For their efforts, Witherspoon and Denney soon lost their jobs. Using a pretext, the church fired Robeson although he tried for several years to gain reinstatement. More troubles loomed. His wife, Maria Louisa Bustill Robeson, died tragically in 1904, leaving the family motherless. Robeson Sr. strived to raise his family in a hostile world. Robeson moved the family to take a smaller parish at the AME Zion Church in Westfield. The minister literally built a church from the ground up. Paul helped his father lay bricks. The family lived in an attic over a grocery. Within a year, William Drew Robeson had achieved the near-miraculous construction of a new church. No doubt embittered by his Princeton experience, he advised the young Paul: "Climb up if you can ... but always show that you are grateful ... Above all, do nothing to give them cause to fear you." While that advice may have been practical in segregated New Jersey, Paul rejected it soundly as a famous adult.

During his childhood, Paul Robeson had to learn to ignore racist taunts and physical abuse in local schools. While he made many white friends, he experienced open racism in the school. The principal of the school was overtly hostile. The school's singing instructor objected vehemently to Paul's participation, even though his extraordinary talents were already obvious. William Drew Robeson emphasized education but Paul excelled in sports. Opponents piled on him in football games hoping to hurt him. Undeterred, Paul Robeson became the third black student to enroll at Rutgers College. The football team threatened to strike if a black player tried to integrate "their" team. Fortunately, the coach, Foster "Sandy" Sanford, recognized Paul's potential and encouraged him. Sanford had to accept obstacles as other universities threatened to cancel games if Robeson played. Often the Rutgers administration acquiesced. Very gradually, Robeson won the respect of his teammates and, by his junior year, was recognized as an All-American ball player. His grades improved and Robeson was elected to the national Phi Beta Kappa honor society as a junior. Paul Robeson attended Rutgers during the World War I and learned to speak and act in patriotic ways. In private discussions however he defended the radical teachings of W.E.B. Du Bois against the conservative stances of Booker T. Washington, whose acceptance of separate but equal lives dominated white-black relations in this era.[55]

Personal loss accompanied Paul Robeson's achievements. His father died alone in May 1918. A month later Paul graduated as an acclaimed athlete with fourteen varsity letters. Winner of the Rutgers debating team's prize for oratorical prose, a member of Phi Beta Kappa, he was selected as one of the four seniors who represented the ideals of Rutgers. His graduation speech, vetted by the school president, called for creation of a "national unity . . . to provide full opportunities for the development of everyone, both as a living person and as a member of a community upon which social responsibilities devolve." He quoted Abraham Lincoln in a reference to the

Figure 9. Paul Robeson (1898–1976) as Rutgers University student, on the cusp of the greatest life of any New Jersey native. By permission of Rutgers Special Collection and University Archives.

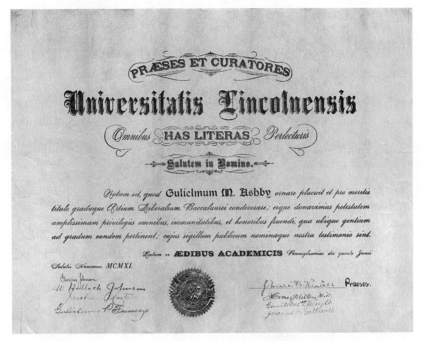

Figure 10. Lincoln College Diploma of William Ashby (1890–1991). The proud bachelor's diploma for several generations of black New Jersey men. Newark Public Library.

human sacrifices of the Civil War, at a moment when racial prejudice cast a negative perception of the accomplishments of the war, that its "dead must not have died in vain." That speech, drawn from Robeson's reading of the memory of the Civil War and the Jim Crow society that stymied his talents and ambitions, but using the unceasing support and power of the AME Zion Church, became Robeson's valedictory from the Bustill family, from Rutgers, and New Jersey. He moved to New York City, entered Columbia Law School, and then found opportunity on the stage.[56] Still, his formative years were spent in New Jersey and he remains, in the estimation of this writer, the most important person ever to emerge from the state.

Robeson's admission to Rutgers was unusual. White colleges and universities occasionally admitted ambitious young blacks, but the numbers on any campus were few. More often, blacks found the university gates closed to them; the rear gate of Princeton University, near the black community, was always bolted shut, just as were the school's classrooms to students of color. Smart young Jersey blacks found an alternative home at Lincoln University, just eighty-five miles from Trenton in Chester County, Pennsylvania.

The school was founded in 1854 as the Ashmun Institute, the nation's first college dedicated to the education of blacks. Its name was changed in 1866 in honor of the slain president and emancipator. Six men graduated in the first baccalaureate class in 1866. The Presbyterian Church dominated the school's vision, which included matching the colors and mascots of Princeton University.

Francis J. and Archibald Grimke were among the first graduates. They were blood nephews of the famous white abolitionists the Grimke sisters, who lived in Belleville. Their parents were Henry Grimke, who died in 1850, and an enslaved woman, Nancy Weston. All were emancipated via Henry's will, but a vicious half-brother attempted to block the new freedoms and enslave mother and son. Archibald ran off and served as valet to a Confederate officer during the Civil War. Later, helped by a kind white woman, the young men were sent North, first to Massachusetts and then on to Lincoln. Both brothers, despite their accomplishments, often met discrimination from society. The success of the Grimkes and others like them made Lincoln a favored choice for higher education for Jersey blacks. In addition to those already named, William Ashby, New Jersey's first black social worker and a founder of the state's first chapter of the Urban League, graduated from Lincoln University in 1911.[57]

New Jersey black achievement was individual rather than collective. At times blacks had to descend to minstrelsy to prosper. In the early decades after the Civil War, most towns featured members of the picaresque proletariat, who scraped by using eccentric talents. In Trenton Old Black Hester, a rag picker, lived in poverty but frightened abusers with maledictions. Harris, the blind beggar, accompanied by his wife, entertained onlookers with hymns and slave songs while shaking his tin cup. Archibald Campbell Seruby, aka "Spader the peanut man," patrolled the streets and parades shouting, "Get your hot, roasted double jointed peanuts here." He exclaimed "just 5 cents a bag," to which young boys would respond "yeah five in a bag." His retort was "strong as a rail and never stale." Spader dressed in an old double-breasted satin-lapelled Chesterfield coat and sang classical songs in a strong baritone voice. Levi "Pigeon" Jackson sold buckets of water and played music to accompany spelling bees. John H. Richardson, "Sweet Lamb, the Cider Man," sold the drink, was a staunch member of St. Paul's A.M.E. Church, and lit gas lamps at night. Mary, Princess of Savoy, claimed to have royal lineage, demanded to speak with President William McKinley on the telephone, and was arrested numerous times for strange behavior. Such characters eked out an existence, yet their personas reflected a demand for equality in a world that increasingly sought subservience.[58]

Other blacks adopted racial stereotypes to amuse. A woman dressed as Aunt Jemima regaled an audience at the Newark Colored Home for the Aged. Dressed in her usual costume befitting the log cabin world of the South, the ersatz Aunt Jemima reportedly kept her audience in stitches during her performance.[59] Blacks had to endure insults via exploitation of members of their race. For years William Henry Johnson, known as Zip, had been exhibited at P. T. Barnum's Museum as an African "freak," with an elongated face, bulbous nose, and topknot. Zip was reputed to be over one hundred years old and born in Africa. His real birthdate was in 1857, in Bound Brook, but his parents "sold" him to Barnum when he was four. For nearly two decades he was made up as a freak and exhibited. He reported that he feared the crowd and despised their giggles. Only when he died in 1926 in Bound Brook was the truth revealed that his physiognomy was quite ordinary and that he had normal hair, not the wig of massive woolly hair that had later replaced the topknot. He was never feebleminded, as his racist keepers claimed.[60]

Soon, however, more stable fortunes appeared. This was the era of the self-made person. John H. Miller owned several elegant cafes, a game parlor featuring pool tables that was the pinochle headquarters of northern New Jersey. Miller was also a prominent member of a number of black fraternal societies. Thomas Cheatham, a long-standing member of the Salem Baptist Church and an officer in the Masons, was a major dealer in coal and ice, selling to blacks and whites. E. W. Reeves owned a piano and furniture moving company. A horse lover, he owned some of the finest stock in the state. Mrs. Mary Crummell moved north from Augusta, Georgia, to Jersey City. She opened the Southern Kitchen, which soon had the largest patronage of any restaurant in the city.[61]

One of America's most famous jockeys in the 1890s was Willie Sims of Asbury Park. Starting as a stable boy, he gathered the attention of wealthy white patrons because of his uncanny ability to stay in the saddle. He won several Dwyer Stakes, an important race of the time, gaining enough earnings to build magnificent homes for his mother in Asbury Park and Augusta. Sims also won the Kentucky Derby twice (1896 and 1898) and the Belmont Stakes, winning over $300,000 in his career.[62]

Herbert White of Jersey City was born in Albemarle County, Virginia, the descendant of enslaved people owned by Thomas Jefferson. White was injured in a train accident while working for the Chesapeake and Ohio Railroads. He then moved to New Jersey where a lawyer helped him file a successful grievance against the railroad. Using the cash gained from a settlement, White bought a horse and cart. Though unschooled and unlettered, he partnered with his brother-in-law to secure contracts to collect garbage and trash from Montclair and Bloomfield homes. White expanded his business alone in the 1910s buying a truck and hauling freight between New York City and Philadelphia. Gradually White purchased more trucks and extended his business down to the Carolinas and up to New England. When the Interstate Commerce Commission began regulating the trucking business, White secured a franchise covering New York State, New Jersey, eastern Pennsylvania and Connecticut, the only black man with such a federal trucking commission in the United States.[63] Blacks moved into emerging technologies. Camden entertainment impresarios planned a black-only motion picture theater along the lines of the Lafayette Theatre in New York City.[64]

Prosperous black Jerseyans created cooperatives. The New Brunswick Cooperative Stock Company formed in 1900, five years later the twenty-four members held stock worth $5,000, owned six lots in New Brunswick, and held twenty shares in the New York Mercantile and Realty Company of

New York. The Colored Branch of the YMCA held open meetings for black businessmen.[65]

George Cannon epitomized the achievements of the black New Jersey middle class in this era. Cannon combined professional work, religious and educational devotion, and politics that characterized the highly successful black male New Jerseyan in the early twentieth century. His career demonstrates movement from the accomodationism of Booker T. Washington to the more forceful, challenging politics of W.E.B. Du Bois. Cannon's achievements just a few decades after Emancipation show the remarkable upward striving of the black middle class.

Cannon was born on July 7, 1869, in Fishdam (later Carlisle), South Carolina, the son of Barnett G. Cannon, a farmer, and Mary Tucker Cannon, the daughter of an English plantation owner and his Malagasy housekeeper. The couple had twelve children. Early on, George Cannon joined the Presbyterian Church and attended the faith's Brainerd Institute. Cannon's principal biographer, Dennis Clark Dickerson, argues that Presbyterianism gave Cannon an upward boost.[66]

Inspired by the oratory of Joseph Charles Price, a prominent minister, educator, and graduate of Lincoln University, Cannon determined to attend the school, which produced many successful graduates who peopled the professional ranks of the northern black middle class. Cannon worked for two years to afford Lincoln's tuition, continued employment as a Pullman porter, and was assigned to the private car of a wealthy, white grain importer. Cannon grew into a deeply moral, religious, and principled adult, who eschewed tobacco and alcohol, never cursed, and always attended chapel. At Lincoln, he excelled in sports and was sufficiently popular to be elected as president of the class of 1893. Cannon used his office to campaign against hazing, which led to his class being remembered as the Reform Class. Dickerson interprets these years as indicating Cannon's receptivity to white paternalism, but I view his accomplishments as evidence of extraordinary personal drive and morality.[67]

Lincoln powerfully impressed Cannon and he later led fundraising for a memorial arch at the entrance of the school. Cannon then moved to Jersey

City and earned his medical degree at the New York Homeopathic Medical College (New York Medical College) in 1900. He married Genevieve Wilkinson of Washington, DC, and the couple set up household in Jersey City where Cannon established his practice. Jersey City's black population in 1900 was only 3,701 souls, barely 1.8 percent of the city's population, but Cannon rapidly developed a prosperous medical career, served in important posts in his field's national organizations, and became a part of the respectable elite who saw the race question as a constant challenge. Cannon was good at creating institutions. He was a founder of the black Lafayette Presbyterian Church in Jersey City and was adept at securing funds from the parent white church. He insisted that the church's clergy not be eloquent but show example in the "consecrated life he leads." When a pastor ran afoul of Cannon's perception of morality, as did Charles H. Trusty in 1911 on charges of embezzlement, Cannon did not hesitate to have the cleric discharged. Cannon was so devout that he always suspended his Sunday patient hours between 11:00 A.M. and 1:00 P.M. so that he could attend church.[68]

Cannon expanded his career into other ventures. During World War I, he founded the Frederick Douglass Film Company to counteract negative, cinematic portrayals of blacks. On July 14, 1916, the Majestic Theater in Jersey City hosted Cannon's film *The Colored American Winning His Suit* to an interracial audience of more than 800. The movie related the story of a young African American attorney. The film company, named for the prominent African American freedman, hoped to counteract the negativity toward blacks found in the film *The Birth of a Nation*, as well as the stereotypical image of black entertainers in comedic roles. The company made only three more films, including *The Heroic Negro Soldier of the World War* in 1919.

White filmmakers and distributors effectively squelched the company by threatening to withdraw product from black-owned theaters that screened Douglass Company films. Cannon also memorialized John Brown by heading a building and loan association in the name of the martyr. The society later merged with a New York counterpart in 1925.[69] Cannon was an Exalted Ruler of the Elks and the Jersey City chapter is named after him.[70]

During World War I, the U. S. War Department did a poor job of recruiting black medical officers, despite the avowed desire of black doctors to help the war effort and their anxiety over treatment of the thousands of black troops by white doctors. The War Department refused to consider assigning black physicians to black units, an act that George Cannon described in an article for the *Journal of National Medical Association,* as one of race prejudice. Cannon tried to enlist U.S. Senator David Baird (R-New Jersey) to help but too little avail. Emmett Scott, the secretary of war's special liaison to the black population, also failed to extract any concessions from the War Department.[71]

In 1917, Cannon organized a peaceful procession of 10,000 black men, women, and children through the streets of Newark to protest rising murderous Jim Crow. Similar to a march in New York City, the participants demanded the tearing down of "destructive walls of prejudice," warned against repetitions of "Waco, Memphis, and East St. Louis," where Jim Crow murderers were active. Men dressed in black, while women and children were adorned in white, declared it was a "crime to be silent in the face of such barbaric acts." They marched to show they were "thoroughly opposed to Jim Crow cars, Segregation, Discrimination, Disenfranchisement, LYNCHING, and the host of evils that are forced upon us."[72]

Cannon emphasized the importance of local protest. Jersey City, where a black community had long shown a proud presence, also suffered from the onset of Jim Crow. After news of some disorderly blacks in late 1920, the chief of police ordered a 9:00 P.M. curfew for all blacks in the city. George Cannon protested the order as "an affront to the race." Cannon operated politically in a city controlled by the legendary political boss Frank Hague, a Democrat.[73]

As more and more blacks began to feel the sharp pinch of Jim Crow, Cannon led a group of black businessmen who supported a bill before the Assembly that guaranteed everyone equal rights in restaurants and other public places. Cannon complained that he had been in Newark late at night because of his work and had been denied service "in one restaurant after another." He argued that the "spirit of intolerance" was not so bad in Jersey

City but in Essex County it was deplorable. The group contended that in a civilized country like the United States, "the respectable colored man" should be accorded decent treatment.[74]

Cannon believed that politics would best increase his reputation and influence. A lifetime Republican, Cannon grew to resent the paternalism of the party. He led a delegation of black leaders to the White House to protest lynching to President Warren G. Harding, whose election had created false hopes for blacks. Cannon later blasted Harding's indifference to the murder of blacks and the Republican Party's lily-white methods in the South. Harding's successor Calvin Coolidge did little better. Even so, the National Colored Republican Conference, with Cannon as president, backed Coolidge's reelection in 1924, but opposed congressmen whose race records were poor. Locally, Cannon led an effort to defeat Republican incumbent Walter Edge, favoring Hamilton Kean. Though that effort failed, Cannon displayed, along with other Jersey blacks, a growing disaffection to the party of Abraham Lincoln. Cannon was not yet ready to jettison the Republican Party. He was nominated as a delegate to the party convention in 1924 and had the honor of seconding the nomination of Calvin Coolidge for reelection. Cannon was castigated in the black press for his inability to press for reforms within the party despite his influential position.[75]

Cannon secured a major success in 1923 when he led a movement of black Republicans from eighteen states to form a national movement to push the Republican Party to accept all interested blacks as members and to support nationally the Dyer Anti-Lynching Bill. Cannon was elected president of the new movement. Four years later, Cannon again worked to defeat Governor Walter Edge, putting his support behind Joseph S. Frelinghuysen, who was credited for his work supporting the Bordentown School and for favoring an anti-lynching bill. Cannon and Assemblyman Walter Alexander supported Frelinghuysen because of his support for the bill.[76]

George Cannon was fatally injured in a bus accident in Jersey City as he was returning home from a trip to Philadelphia. After reaching his destination, Cannon attempted to step off the city bus when the driver suddenly accelerated, throwing Cannon into the gutter. The doctor suffered broken ribs and a severe concussion and died ten days later. His wife and children were grief stricken. Coverage of his death circulated in black newspapers and in white establishment media such as the *New York Times*. Jersey City blacks held a massive memorial service for Cannon. Among those sending tributes were W.E.B. Du Bois and President Calvin Coolidge.[77]

Dickerson's evaluation of Cannon emphasizes that Cannon's social status and influence emanated from his ability to gain acceptance from key, paternalistic whites in the Presbyterian Church and in New Jersey's Republican Party, which was very common.[78] In my perception, Cannon was a major transitional figure from the accomodationism of Booker T. Washington into the integrationist educational and professional aspirations of the black bourgeoisie of the twentieth century. Cannon combined racial pride, professional status, and associational connections with strong nationalism and vital political effort to become the most important black New Jerseyan of the first quarter of the twentieth century. His son, George D. Cannon, an important radiologist in Harlem, constantly battled for better medical conditions for blacks and advanced to high leadership in the NAACP. George D. Cannon was a close friend of Paul Robeson and defended him during political attacks in the 1940s and 1950s.[79]

Black women in New Jersey joined forces with their white sisters in the battle for female suffrage. Black women from the AME Conference passed a resolution in 1915 endorsing female suffrage. The New Jersey State Federation of Colored Women's Clubs affiliated with the New Jersey State Federation of Women's Clubs in 1917 and two women of color joined the state board of the latter organization. The Federation of Colored Women's Clubs had formed in 1915 to bring together thirty black societies engaged in the temperance movement. The federation had a strong New Jersey contingent. Reverend Florence Randolph of Summit was the president. The vice president was Violet Johnson from Summit, who worked as a domestic for the family of white printer John Eggers. While working for the Eggers, Johnson served as president of the Young Women's Uplift league and the Girls Patriotic League and was vice president of the Colored Women's Clubs from 1926 to 1931. Later she created the Girls Industrial Home in Washington, D.C.[80]

The Federation was part of the National Association of Colored Women, founded in 1896, with a national membership of over 50,000 women from 1,000 clubs spread across twenty-eight states. The Federation derived from the black women's club movement, part of the self-help drive from before the Civil War. Generally, these women supported the Republican Party.[81]

WORK

Even as New Jersey blacks created a sturdy middle class, hardship faced most. Migrants coming north found jobs that paid far more than agricultural or industrial work in the South. Yet they made less than whites. A 1903 wage survey found that while black workers at eighty-three manufacturing establishments were paid equally with whites when in the same position, African Americans were concentrated in the lowest-paying jobs. Labor union hostility and the general white angry prejudice toward blacks made the latter amenable to "scab" positions designed to undercut union work actions such as strikes. Only six of twenty-two statewide labor organizations opened doors to blacks. Employers also feared disruptions in the workplace if whites and blacks were grouped together. This combination of white worker antagonism and employer fears restricted black workers' mobility.[82]

Segregation accompanied the congealing of white racism in postbellum America. As blacks migrated from South to North, labor competition caused friction with white workers and skilled black workers lost their employment. Use of newly arrived blacks as strike breakers worsened acrimony. Discrimination in public accommodations became frequent. New Jersey's prosecutors became reluctant to charge hotels and restaurants with violations of the Fourteenth Amendment, knowing that white jurors would refuse to convict. When suits were successful, the resulting restitution rarely even covered court costs. White neighborhoods closed against would-be black real estate purchasers. When not rebuffed by bankers who refused loans, blacks faced vigilante justice and restrictive covenants.[83]

Black workers went on strike for higher wages. The washerwomen of Newark walked out in 1906 demanding $1.25 for a daily "ordinary wash," a slight raise from the one dollar a day they were earning.[84] When accepted, black men were eager to join unions. Black waiters in Atlantic City applied to join the union. Atlantic City hired a number of black teachers for its adult night schools. Trenton barbers sought a union monopoly to shave corpses and asked coach drivers not to pull hearses unless a union man had done the shaving. Red Caps or railroad station attendants working at Pennsylvania Station won the right to unionize as the Brotherhood of Railway Station Attendants; the movement would inexorably move into New Jersey. In another major victory in 1918, the American Federation of Labor declared that all unions would be admitted on the same basis in favor of wiping out the color line in organized labor.[85]

World War 1 increased the employment of blacks in industrial work, though usually in menial positions. As New Jersey blacks moved into industrial work, they left domestic and personal service jobs. By 1920, factory work in Newark had replaced some domestic and service positions. However, the latter jobs were always important sectors of the black economy. The state placement office featured work for black women as servants, cooks, children's nurses, waitresses, and steam pressers. Black businesses such as barber shops and restaurants expanded because there was no direct competition with white shops or workers.[86]

Blacks in New Jersey realized that segregation at work impoverished all and sought different ways to combat the ferocious terror of Jim Crow. A forum in Newark in 1905 heard Royal L. Melody, general secretary of the Newark Settlement Association, recommend that black professionals (such as himself) should take young black women into their families and teach them the tenets of race-based social work. The young women, once educated, would work in a new institute in the city's poor districts and teach domestic economy, industry, and gymnastics. White employers would be asked to employ graduates of the institute, though Melody recommended that whites should not be allowed in the building. Almost simultaneously, thirty young black men met in Newark to form a league to promote intellectual, moral, and social advancement. The two organizations vowed to collaborate. Soon, however, the New York Age sadly reported that the social house movement had collapsed when black members realized that whites who supported it were only interested in canvassing for votes.[87]

Sports

Black New Jerseyans embraced baseball as a performance and spectator sport. Newark, Atlantic City, Jersey City and Trenton supported teams, though players' locations and league affiliations changed almost every year. The first black baseball stars were New Jerseysans George Stovey and Fleetwood Walker. Stovey led his Newark club in 1887 with a pitching record of thirty-three wins and fourteen losses. Walker starred as an infielder for white and black teams.[88]

Stovey, Walker, and other black Jersey ball players found themselves excluded from white baseball when Cap Anson of the Chicago White Stockings of the International League refused to play against them in a game in Newark. White organized baseball accepted Anson's prejudicial behavior and barred black ballplayers, a ban that held until Jackie Robinson integrated the game while playing for the Montreal Royals against the Jersey City Giants on April 18, 1946. During the sixty-year exile, state African Americans built teams in towns and cities that formed parts of the Negro Leagues.

Boxing was another aspirational sport for young blacks. Joe Jeanette of Union City had a successful career as a heavyweight boxer between 1904 and 1919. He was considered one of the most dangerous foes because of his "inside style," in which he battered his opponents with short, hard punches. Jeannette fought future champion Jack Johnson equally seven times in two years, with two losses, two victories, and three no decisions. Because white heavyweights refused to match with black fighters, Jeannette often battled the same foes over and over again. After Johnson won the heavyweight championship, he refused to fight Jeannette, who regarded such behavior as racial treason. As a result, Jeannette never secured a heavyweight championship fight. He did have a memorable forty-nine-round battle with Sam McVey in Paris, winning when McVey could not stand for the last round.

Jeanette was given the title of World Colored Boxing Champion after this bout. When his boxing days ended, the thrifty Jeanette operated a successful livery stable, a taxi fleet, and an Esso oil station replete with an active gymnasium where he trained young boxers, including future champion James Braddock. Jeanette remained a constant part of the boxing world in the eastern United States.[89]

BLACK SOCIAL ORGANIZATIONS

Blacks throughout the state established social organizations including black lodges of the Masons, Odd Fellows, Elks, Knights of Pythias, American Woodmen, Sons and Daughters of Africa, Order of Moses, Good Samaritans, Eastern Star, Queen Esther Court of Calanthe, and the Household of Ruth.[90] These organizations created leadership training and community and social activism within a black world. They offered voluntarism and civic services. Blacks established glee clubs, literary societies, and race-defined versions of the Boys and Girl Scouts.[91]

The career of one black minister, labeled as a rising star among black Jersey clerics, illustrates the confluence of church and fraternal organizations and their mutual assistance for black mobility. Reverend H. P. Anderson of New Jersey worked with his mother and sister to support their family after his father's early death. His talents and diligence earned him a spot at Wilberforce University in Ohio, America's oldest black university. After completing his education, Anderson returned to New Jersey and spent five successful years as the pastor of the AME Church in Morristown. He was then transferred to the pastorate of St. James Church in Atlantic City, one of the most important Jersey parishes of the denomination. He became a general leader of the AME conference while attaining the position as grand chancellor of the Knights of Pythias of New Jersey.[92]

Jim Crow, which occurred sporadically during the 1890s, lessened at New Jersey's resorts. The Black Elks met in Atlantic City in 1904, drawing thousands of members from Baltimore, Philadelphia, and New York City. To serve the throngs of blacks seeking respite in Atlantic City, black restaurateurs, hoteliers, and cottage operators welcomed individuals and conventioneers. Big plans were announced in 1910 for hotels and centers that could accommodate the conventions and church meetings of blacks and whites. The Black Elks continued their annual gatherings in Atlantic City during the second decade of the century. The 1915 meeting, for example, was widely attended; the biggest controversy of the session was whether to increase the salary of the Grand Secretary.[93]

The *Afro-American Ledger*, which maintained an office in Atlantic City, frequently celebrated the arrival of noted blacks in the resort town. Ex-Congressman Thomas E. Miller of South Carolina stopped by in November 1910. The newspaper celebrated the 100,000-strong visitors who came in September 24, 1910, to commemorate the Grand Army of the Republic, including "our own heroes of Fort Pillow [scene of an infamous massacre of black troops] and other bloody fields." Black veterans held a campfire at the Asbury Methodist Episcopalian Church with a speech by Reverend M. C. B. Mason, one of the secretaries of the Freedman's Aid Society.[94]

Battling Jim Crow

Jersey blacks might differ among themselves about the efficacy of segregated education, but none accepted the push for a segregated society emerging in the state and elsewhere. The "bathing question," became the focal point of discrimination in Atlantic City. White and black residents understood the free market rights to public space, but as white customers complained to hoteliers and amusement spots about the presence of blacks, they often couched their irritation in terms of etiquette, anxieties over perceived black vice zones, and sanitation. Even as middle-class blacks pointed out their worthiness, whites pushed hard for segregated facilities, forcing blacks into less desirable and distant beaches. David Goldberg has cogently argued that white efforts were uneven but direly successful by the 1920s, forcing blacks to construct their own leisure, housing, and eating facilities.[95] In 1893, the *Philadelphia Inquirer* complained about black men and women overrunning the Atlantic City Boardwalk and swimming areas. Blacks dominated the service positions, lamented the *Inquirer.* Similar complaints in Cape May County led to newspaper campaigns to evict blacks from the community. Not everyone accepted these exclusions passively. Henry Brown of Cape May sued the city of Cape May for $10,000 after police forcibly evicted him from a concert. Brown refused to sit in the blacks-only area and insisted on occupying a seat in the visitors' section. By 1896 amusement operators in Atlantic City barred blacks from their rides, even forcibly ejecting George Clinton, a delegate to the Republican National Convention. By 1904 police-men ordered blacks not to attempt to use carousels or to bathe in front of the hotels, in deference to white southern customers. Blacks experienced a severe blow when, upon the complaint of southern whites, black, maids, bellboys, and waiters were banned from the beaches in front of the major hotels. Hotel management explained that without southerners spending money their businesses would be unable to pay their black employees.

Annual black excursions occurring in September came under vitriolic attack from newspapers. Housing became segregated and blacks were forced to live in poverty during the off-season. Schools, restaurants, and dance halls now catered to separate races. Despite the presence of middle-class blacks visiting from Philadelphia and beyond, newspapers increasingly characterized blacks as criminals. Any black advance met harsh white criti-cism. When retiring Mayor Harry Bacharach appointed James Bourne, a black druggist, and Sidney Rosenbaum, who was Jewish, to the Board of Education, white members strongly objected. The State Supreme Court later approved the appointments. Yet even after restrictions became laws, blacks still strolled down the Boardwalk. The *Afro-American Ledger* described the gorgeous yellow bonnets worn by black women on the Boardwalk one Easter.[96] The *Afro-American Ledger* saw many prominent blacks from New Jersey and the southern states along the Boardwalk in late July 1910. The newspaper reported that the visiting blacks crowded the city's hotels.[97]

Black resistance to Jim Crow was evident everywhere. Deeply concerned that the "doors of factories, department stores, and positions in city and county governments are more or less closed to competent member of the race," a large gathering of men invited by Attorney Alfred B. Cosey sought to protect the civil and political rights of Afro-Americans in Essex County. They decried the "serious and menacing conditions" that inhibited blacks. Cosey then offered a bill to the legislature that mandated a $1,000 fine on school boards that tried to segregate New Jersey schools. Opponents questioned its constitutionality and then offered a compromise that would allow segregating low-intelligence students. Black citizens angrily denounced the compromise contending that it was another form of segregation and that no white student had ever been categorized as having low intelligence.[98]

Camden blacks showed political muscle when they convinced the local mayor in 1909 not to allow a play entitled "The Clansman," a paean to the Ku Klux Klan, to be licensed and performed on the city's stages. Sixteen years later, a black policeman halted a Klan rally outside Camden before the group could light crosses afire.[99]

Blacks strived to gain equal representation in city offices. Competing fire companies battled along racial lines in Asbury Park. White firemen, with the backing of the new local Democratic administration, vociferously condemned the black company. Previous administrations in Asbury Park had funded the black firefighters, remodeling their engine house and equipping the company until early 1912. In 1916, the city administration devised a plan that allowed for an entirely black fire company with their own building.[100]

Ministers spoke out against Jim Crow. When New Jersey legislators took up a bill that would outlaw marriages between black and white people, Reverend Eggleston, pastor of the Thirteenth Avenue Presbyterian Church in Trenton, called it a "snake bill," that was against "the law of mankind." He and others argued the bill was simply a wedge toward more Jim Crow legislation. Their protests worked. The bill died in committee the following month; one reason had to be that Republicans were anxious they might be blamed for the noxious law, at a time when Democrats were making some inroads among black New Jersey voters.[101]

Others took to the courts to combat Jim Crow. Two ministers filed suit against the Olympic park in Newark because blacks were denied access to the park. On several occasions, hired agents of the park blocked the preachers' paths as they tried to enter because of their color. Judge Scotland, a political leader among Newark blacks, attempted to purchase ten-cent tickets for amusements, but was told each cost one dollar. After that exorbitant sum was produced, the price was raised to ten dollars, as the agents used insulting and intimidating language. The black men sued the park for violating the amended act of 1894 that "no persons of good character" should be denied admission to any places of amusement, under penalty of fine of $500 and costs of imprisonment. Usually fines were less. Harry J. Simms received $50 and an apology from a Vineland restaurant in May 1923 after refusal of service.[102]

Sea bathing was not the only attraction in Atlantic City. The black community there built a sturdy religious presence. The St. James AME Church raised money for a Sea Shore Home and Sanitarium for tubercular blacks in Atlantic City. The church was so popular that during one prayer service, the floor gave way under the weight of 500 congregants. As the Easter rush to Atlantic City began in 1910, black visitors gained access for the first time to the YMCA hall where they watched a documentary movie about Tuskegee.[103]

Asbury Park was a second favored vacation spot, especially for blacks from Baltimore. According to the *Afro-American Ledger*, thousands of blacks found a warm welcome and cooling sea breezes there. The large New Jersey contingent of the Knights of Pythias enjoyed conferences there. Long Branch was a third spot where blacks could rent summer homes And Wildwood attracted blacks during the 1910s.[104]

Sour incidents of Jim Crow brought official condemnation. The mayor of Trenton blasted jitney drivers who refused to transport an aged black woman to Fort Dix where her son was quartered. After being refused for two hours, the woman found an officer who attempted to intercede for her; his efforts met with harsh refusal from the drivers who feared objections from their white passengers. The mayor, hearing of the incident, threatened to fire any driver who repeated such refusal of service.[105]

EDUCATION

Urbanism and the rise of the industrial economy sharply increased black Jerseyans' needs for improved education. The legacies of slavery and racism hampered black efforts in New Jersey to improve and integrate public schools after the war. New Jersey's history is paradoxical in regard to black education. Generally, most of the schools in the southern part of the state were segregated. Schools in Northern New Jersey, where blacks held power within the Republican Party, were often integrated. Sizable numbers of blacks moved into the southern counties after the Civil War and were not welcomed by the white population. Greater ethnic diversity and creation of cities in the north allowed for racially mixed schools.[106]

In 1881 the New Jersey state legislature passed the toughest antisegregation law in the Union. In addition to outlawing segregated schools, the measure guaranteed equal access to public facilities and barred discrimination in jury selection. While a number of townships had already integrated their schools, the law seemed to settle any doubts about racial equality in the state's public schools. The law used strong words but lacked power. Localities routinely ignored the sweeping law, and New Jersey over the next few decades proved to be one of the worst states for black education with highly segregated schools and public discrimination.[107]

As Davison M. Douglas, the most informed of recent scholars on racism in northern schools in this era, has pointed out, New Jersey blacks filed only two suits against violations of the 1881 legislation. There were several reasons for this dearth of legal actions. Suits required expensive appeals to appellate courts, bearing costs beyond the means of most New Jersey black families. Fair Haven, the town in which the poor conditions of the black schools initiated the lawsuit that led to the 1881 decision to integrate schools, built a separate school for blacks, which satisfied the local black community. Fair Haven's schools remained segregated far into the twentieth century. Even fundraisers were unsuccessful in fulfilling the financial demands of a case. There were no organizations such as the NAACP to help pay such costs. There were only three black lawyers in the entire state in 1890, although, as in the antebellum period, sympathetic white lawyers did occasionally step in. Moreover, integration was not universally popular. Black residents of Camden, New Brunswick, and Trenton filed suit to retain black schools and opposed integrated education. Black teachers, fearful of losing their jobs, were behind such efforts. This was a reasonable concern because no New Jersey school appeared ready to allow a black teacher to instruct white students. In other states, integration meant the loss of black teachers. Parents wanted black teachers for their children and believed that a white teacher could not properly instruct them or would be abusive. In addition, parents feared a return of insults and mistreatment suffered by blacks in white schools before the war. Impoverished parents worried their children would be subjected to abuse because of their cheap clothing. Moreover activists who pushed against the tide of segregation often experienced retaliation and violence. School authorities often ignored their demands or felt secure that, lawful though appeals were, they were unlikely to be punished in the courts.[108]

Such was the case of a landmark decision in 1884 when Reverend Jeremiah H. Pierce petitioned the New Jersey Supreme Court to force admission of his four children into segregated white schools in Burlington City. Pierce based his argument on New Jersey's 1881 antisegregation law and the 1844 constitution. The law forbade discrimination at all public accommodations, including inns, transport, theaters and places of public amusement, and cemeteries, and outlawed segregation on juries, with fines payable to the victims. This landmark legislation guaranteed equal access to all public accommodations. There were ample provisions for fines and fees for damages to the victims of discrimination. In practice, however, the law was seldom observed and often flouted. In the key area of education, the court agreed that Pierce was correct, yet the impact of the decision was negligible as local school boards simply ignored it.[109]

New Jersey blacks employed boycotts against segregation in public schools with limited success. One of the first school walkouts occurred in Englewood in 1879. Racism among public officials and the judiciary proved insurmountable. Englewood's school superintendent commented that black parents threatened to boycott public schools but, failing to gain any redress in the courts for their "supposed wrongs," were willing to make an amicable settlement that accepted segregation. Black parents threatened to boycott public schools and sue to ensure full integration of public schools in

East Orange at the end of the nineteenth century. They had ample white sympathizers for a time including a state Supreme Court justice. The parents labored hard to reverse the plan for separate schools, but in time, as white support declined and eventually disappeared, the boycott failed and East Orange's schools segregated.[110]

Residents of Orange continued their struggle in the early twentieth century. Dr. William Hayes Ward, editor of the *Independent*, wrote a scathing editorial in 1905 expressing consternation that the East Orange Board of Education was creating separate schools for blacks and whites. Ward recalled a recent conversation he had had with three aged blacks from New Jersey, who remembered the whipping post used for disobedient slaves. Ward stated that he thought slavery was a thing of the past, but that the board's actions seemed akin to the whipping post. Thousands of readers endorsed Ward's argument. T. Thomas Fortune, editor of the *Age* and a resident of Red Bank, firmly adopted Ward's jeremiad.[111]

Whites enforced segregation. New Jersey schoolteachers were ill equipped to instruct the new arrivals from the South, many of whom suffered from poor education in southern schools. Instead of utilizing patience and kindness, teachers and administrators often considered these students to be of low intelligence who should be segregated from their white peers. Open racism characterized Jersey educators' response to their new charges. An Atlantic City administrator called black students "animals," and claimed there was "no civilization in their homes." Intelligence tests allegedly bolstered such views. Curriculums were designed to give more vocational training to blacks, particularly for poorly paid, menial tasks. White teachers refused to allow black students in their classes. Too often white parents opposed any move toward integration; a second popular view was that white parents would not accept a black teacher. New Jersey cities with more black students were more likely to employ African American teachers.[112]

In some instances, blacks accepted segregation. Fair Haven blacks allowed segregated schools, partly based on the influence of Civil War General Clinton B. Fisk, after whom the famous university is named, to accept segregation. In 1917, state legislators amended the 1884 law banning segregated amusement parks by extending punishment to those who were "aid-ing and inciting denial." Amended again in 1921 and in 1935, these laws were on the books, but public experience showed that they were rarely observed.[113]

The Fair Haven decision prompted black self-help schools. A coalition of black religious figures, educators, and families founded the New Jersey Industrial and Manual Training School for Colored Youth, commonly referred to as the Bordentown School. The AME Church, led by the Rever-end Walter A. Rice, was instrumental in the founding of the school, which seemed an adequate agreement between black leaders and white adminis-trators. The state legislature chartered the school in 1884, established it in 1886, and legalized the church's right to sell and convey real estate to sup-port the parent organization, the Colored Industrial Educational Associa-tion of New Jersey. Designed to provide both industrial and academic instruction in a segregated setting to young black boys and girls in a board-ing school, its success prompted the State of New Jersey to adopt it as a public school with funding in 1896 with a budget of $5,000. Constructed on the estate of a former commodore, the Ironside School, as it was also known, provided manual training and a literary course for 196 boys and 317 girls in 1896. By 1902 attendance dropped to 55 males and 70 females, taught by 11 teachers. Rebuilt after a fire in 1907, the school began to offer regular high school diplomas in 1928 and became nationally known for vocational training. Shortly after World War II, Governor Alfred Driscoll ordered the term "colored" dropped from the school's name. While it sur-vived the Depression, the end followed the U.S. Supreme Court's decision in Brown v. Board of Education, which outlawed segregated schools in 1954.[114]

Bordentown also showed how white leaders in Jersey supported the ideas of Booker T. Washington. The state budgeted $95,000 to support the school in 1914 and the state board of education was so impressed by the results at Bordentown that it allotted $35,000 in 1902 to establish a second industrial school in Cranbury, this time based entirely on the teachings and methods of Booker T. Washington. The board even sent a contingent to Tuskegee to learn closely from Washington. Visiting ministers extolled the virtues of all-black colleges in the South and suggested strongly that New Jersey should open one.[115]

Controversy hit Bordentown after the ministers made their report. Professor James M. Gregory, who had been the principal of the school for eighteen years, abruptly resigned in February 1915. He had been instrumental in persuading the State of New Jersey to take over control of the school in 1897. That act ultimately proved his undoing. While Gregory had been in poor health for some time, the principal reason for his resignation was his refusal to submit a recommendation to the state school board to convert Bordentown's curriculum entirely into industrial education. Critics argued that the school had been drifting for a number of years and new blood was necessary to revive it. Succeeding Gregory was William E. Valentine, a Harvard graduate and native of Montclair. After the transfer of leadership and adoption of an industrial curriculum, the state board of education allocated $123,000 to make Bordentown the best school for blacks in the state.[116]

Bordentown served a small number of New Jersey blacks. There was no room for them in the state's colleges and universities. Segregation extended into higher education and was most apparent at Princeton University. Four black students attended Princeton's Theological Seminary in 1876. All went well until one of the students attempted to enroll in a psychology course on the main campus. White southerners attempted to boycott classes and even left campus in protest against the presence of the black student. The university refused to expel the black student and the southerners had to petition to return to campus. Princeton became segregated when future U.S. president Woodrow Wilson headed the school from 1902 to 1910. The new university president set the tone at his inauguration. Prominent black leader Booker T. Washington was invited to join the procession to the installation and was given a spot at the luncheon. However he was the only honored guest forced to seek local housing when the faculty, which opened the doors of their homes to other dignitaries, refused to admit him. Wilson further insulted Washington by not inviting him to the dinners during the events. Once in office, Wilson rebuffed a black applicant to the theology school and famously refused to even consider acceptance of the eldest son of Witherspoon Street Presbyterian Church minister Reverend William Drew Robeson, father of Paul.[117] Princeton University employed one black professor at the time. Alexander Dumar Atkins was hired in 1895 as a tutor in histology (cell anatomy) and later advanced to become an assistant in the biology department before his early death at the age of fifty-one.[118]

Generally, New Jersey's black leaders accepted Booker T. Washington's influential philosophy, which emphasized hard work, thrift, and personal uplift while eschewing overt protest against political disenfranchisement and segregation. Washington's ideology prevailed for many decades in New Jersey. There were important variations. James Still of Burlington County, the older brother of the famed abolitionist, William Still, encouraged diligence among blacks and avoidance of laziness and fast living. He disliked urban mores. At the same time, Still rejected any acceptance of racial segregation in education. Reverend Junius C. Ayler of Princeton, who published *The Trumpet*, a small black newspaper, followed Washington's mottos of "educate, educate, make money, make money," but contended that the state's legacy of slavery and black impoverishment were the root causes of prejudice. A. P. Miller, pastor of Jersey City's St. Mark's AME Zion Church denounced racial indolence and, like Washington, extolled the virtues of hard work. He differed from Washington by arguing for academic rather than vocational education and rejected black subservience to the indifferent Republican Party. Miller's ideas, as with other black Jersey leaders, fused Washington's conservative approach to race relations with the newer, more militant ideas of W.E.B. Du Bois. In a nod to antebellum black nationalism, Bishop R. H. Cain of the New Jersey Conference of the AME Church encouraged consideration of African roots, Christianizing Africa, and the possibility of future generations returning there.[119]

Overall, schools became the center of the nation's change into a segregated society. Rebuffed from white public schools and unable to force politicians to live up to the promises of the 1881 laws, black Jerseyans developed their own institutions with their own staff and funding. This method, born of desperation, could maintain quality for a while, but was doomed by

economic and political forces. As blacks became poorer and deprived of
political rights, schools became underfunded and underequipped.

COMMEMORATING BLACK HISTORY

The anniversary of the Emancipation Proclamation in 1913 served as a
bulwark against contemporary ills. While whites held their own celebrations
and conscientiously excluded blacks as an act of reconciliation between
Union and Confederate soldiers, blacks held their own anniversaries.
Initially, the annual celebrations were sleepy affairs. The 1905 memorial
of William Lloyd Garrison drew a tiny audience at the YMCA in Newark.[120] The fiftieth anniversary was a much bigger affair. The State of
New Jersey announced a commemoration of freedom at the Exposition
Hall in Atlantic City for October 1913. Organizers focused on parades
involving numerous trades such as dressmaking, millinery, real estate,
and teaching. All of the major black religious denominations became
involved as did the mechanical schools. Exhibits came from the various
mixed-race schools in Jersey City, Bayonne, Paterson, Montclair, and
Morristown and from all of the "colored schools" in the state. Aged, former slaves talked about their lives. Booker T. Washington gave the keynote address in which he emphasized racial uplift in the home. Exhibits,
as Mabel O. Wilson notes, included a log cabin attended by a mammy
preparing hoecakes, followed by a small whitewashed shanty, and concluding with a modern home, windows adorned by lace curtains and
electric push buttons demonstrating all the latest household conveniences. As with its Philadelphia counterpart, the Atlantic City convention attracted little national notice.[121]

Localities held their own remembrances. Montclair celebrated the fiftieth
anniversary of the Emancipation Proclamation with a pageant, singing, and
featured speakers. Jersey City blacks heard a speech from Oswald Garrison
Villard, the editor of the *New York Post* and grandson of William Lloyd
Garrison, one of the greatest abolitionists. Interspersed with the accounts

of the black communities around the state were historical reminiscences that featured black New Jersey's contributions to state and national histories. Chief among them were soldiers. Colonel Tye was mentioned as was Revolutionary War Patriot Oliver Cromwell. Tadeuz Kosciuszko, whose famed will gave Thomas Jefferson a chance to free his slaves, joined the American forces in Morristown. Captain Theophilis G. Steward, the chaplain of the Twenty-Fifth Black Regiment of the Civil War was among the most famous New Jersey black veterans. According to the souvenir program, black veterans from the Civil War marched in formation at many state Independence Day celebrations.[122]

New Jersey's black teachers organized and held meetings with more than 200 people. Starting in 1915, the group met annually with symposiums and speeches by educational leaders including Charles H. Wesley, head of the history department at Howard University. Negro History Week became an annual celebration of black achievement. Black businesses evoked past heroes. The Frederick Douglass Building and Loan Association incorporated in Camden in 1918.[123]

Commemoration of important past figures continued to be a feature of black organizations. The Lincoln-Douglass Celebration Society of Newark held its fifth annual event in 1924 with speakers representing the two heroes reading from their works. Held at the historic St. James AME Church, the event culminated in a parade with a brass band leading 500 white and black Boy Scouts from Newark and adjoining cities, marching from St. James to the white First Presbyterian Church and then on to the courthouse.[124] The *Baltimore Afro-American*, a nationally known black newspaper with strong distribution in New Jersey, even marked the exact 300th anniversary of the arrival of the first enslaved people in Virginia.[125]

Gradually, black historical commemoration transformed into recognition of contributions. An outgrowth of the popular series initiated by Carter Woodson on black contributors, speakers at Atlantic City churches in 1925 hailed the laboring people of the city who had constructed the beachfront; their efforts contradicted the prejudices against blacks.[126]

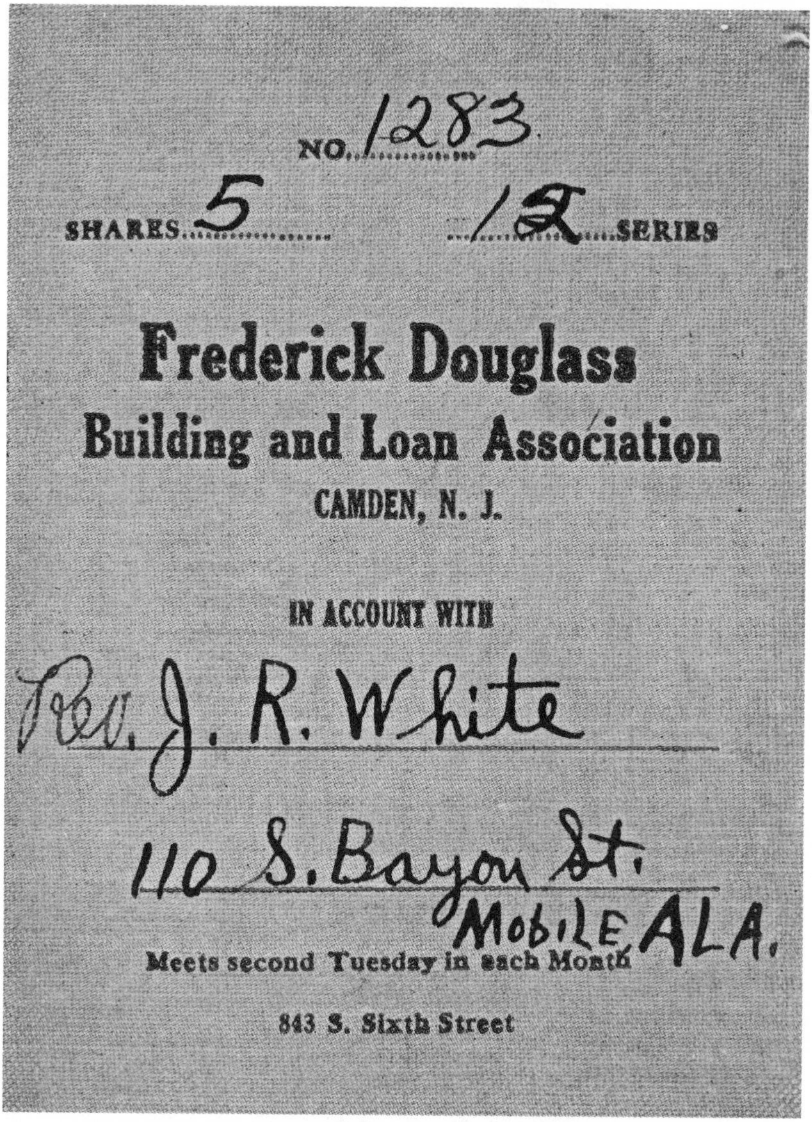

NO. 1283.

SHARES 5 / 12 SERIES

Frederick Douglass
Building and Loan Association
CAMDEN, N. J.

IN ACCOUNT WITH

Rev. J. R. White

110 S. Bayou St.
Mobile ALA.

Meets second Tuesday in each Month

843 S. Sixth Street

Figure 11. Frederick Douglass Building and Loan passbook, one of the multiple demonstrations of how black history permeated the lives of New Jersey blacks. Author's collection.

BLACK POLITICS IN THE NEW CENTURY

New Jersey blacks generally supported the Republican Party. Loyalty was evident in the most powerful social organizations. Three thousand delegates of the Grand United Order of Odd Fellows met at Young's Pier in Atlantic City in 1908, declaring their support for William Howard Taft for president. New Jersey blacks again supported Taft, a strong supporter of Booker T. Washington, in 1911. At a Christian Endeavour Convention held in Atlantic City, both men spoke. Taft lauded Washington, describing him as "one of the men of four or five generations, a man who has contributed to the welfare of another race . . . whose power for usefulness in the future cannot be exaggerated.[127]

Booker T. Washington, the champion of black industrial and segregated schools and the foremost black educator of his time, was deeply popular among black Jerseyans. In 1908 he spoke to a mixed-race group of several thousand on the pier in Atlantic City and then a smaller group, again integrated, of businessmen. He returned in 1911 to Atlantic City to be feted at a giant banquet sponsored by the Negro Business League of Atlantic City and specifically by the leading "colored headwaiters" of the city. During his speech Washington advised the waiters to hone their skills to be able to compete with their white counterparts. Skill, rather than requests for sympathy, would create demand for their services. He also advised the black professionals of New Jersey not to isolate themselves from the "masses," for they were the people on whom they depended for a livelihood. Professionals and skilled workers, he urged, should work hand in hand. The waiters, based upon their hearty applause, strongly agreed.[128]

Yet there were alternative voices and politics and education often mixed. T. Thomas Fortune, editor of the *New York Age* and a New Jersey resident, lectured before the students and faculty of the Bordentown School. Fortune, who was a key ally of Booker T. Washington, assured the audience that the highest form of education "fits a man to render the highest and most efficient service to society and to himself." Referring to W.E.B. Du Bois's devastating critique of industrial education, Fortune argued that the number of years of learning made no difference, but rather the amount of specialized skill attained. Alluding to local controversies over schools, Fortune contended that New Jersey ranked the average intelligence of its citizens above average, due to the wise and generous provisions of primary, secondary, and higher education. If there was a failure in New Jersey education, it was a lack of more agricultural, manual, and industrial education in the state. Subsequently, Fortune argued that graduates of Bordentown should be granted admission to the State Normal School at Trenton (now the College of New Jersey), a plan that did not gain favor. Fortune was deeply concerned about segregation in the North as well as the South and made eradication of northern racism a key part of his National Afro-American League goals. This organization attracted much support in the North and was a counterbalance to Booker T. Washington's more accommodating style. Anxious to improve conditions at Bordentown, the state board of education, concerned about the school's financial woes, called upon Booker T. Washington to lend his connections to garner greater financial support.[129]

At this time, Jersey black voters became restless about relations with the Republican Party. East Orange's black parents threatened to leave the dominant Republican Party and join the Democrats after the local school board sanctioned school segregation. Resisting racism, East Orange blacks united in common cause to battle against Jim Crow and to strive for the benefits of a prosperous society. Significantly, the new association declared that political affiliation was secondary. White and black citizens of Orange heard Booker T. Washington speak on a cold night in February 1914. The packed house listened as he advised mutuality among the races and that anger never solved any racial disputes. The black population of the Oranges, he argued, needed to lift themselves above menial positions by their own hard work and determination. Disputing tales that the Tuskegee Institute did not favor higher education, Washington informed the audience that the institute employed more black college graduates, male and female, than any other institution in the world.[130]

How much New Jersey's black ministers upheld Booker T. Washington's self-uplift philosophy may be gleaned from the speech in 1910 by Bishop G. W.

GEORGE E. CANNON, M. D., LL. D.

Figure 12. George E. Cannon (1869–1925). Jersey City physician, political leader, and important transitional figure from racial accommodation to a more militant, political black nationalism. From Clement Richardson, *National Cyclopedia of the Colored Race.*

Clinton, the incoming head of the New Jersey Conference of the AME Zion Church. Clinton thundered "I have no faith in any man who will sit around and complain in an active, busy world, instead of doing something for himself . . . my race must climb by industry, honesty, and thrift. Take up the essentials of life. Manhood is represented by push and energy."[131] Similarly, the keynote speaker, Bishop P. A. Wallace, at the fifty-fifth Zion conference in Camden argued that the sole mission of the church was to save lives, not change society.[132]

Washington's ally, T. Thomas Fortune, linked black aspirations with the party of Abraham Lincoln. Fortune produced a major speech on Abraham Lincoln's legacy at the Union Baptist Church in Newark under the auspices of the Literary Union. In addition to reviewing Lincoln's career and major achievements, Fortune harped upon Lincoln's rustic and impoverished beginnings. Lincoln, Fortune contended, was a great example of what a young black man could do with grit, determination, and skills.[133]

New Jersey blacks and whites joined the nation in mourning Booker T. Washington's death on November 14, 1915, at the age of fifty-nine. Newspapers in New Jersey ran extensive obituaries. The state Colored Educational Conference, chaired by Dr. George E. Cannon, requested that black people fly their flags at half-mast during the hours of Washington's funeral. Cannon, a local resident, undoubtedly urged local schools to eulogize the fallen leader. Churches followed suit, including small ones such as the Mount Zion African Methodist Church in Bridgeton. Edward M. Ludlow, a renowned white clergyman, prepared a eulogy for Washington at the East Orange First Presbyterian Church.[134]

THE RISE OF THE NAACP

Despite Washington's massive influence in New Jersey, there were signs of change. Serious concerns about Washington's methods were raised at the Fifth Annual Meeting of the Niagara Movement in Sea Island City in 1909. Organized by W.E.B. Du Bois, the conference demanded that black people not apologize for who they were and demand their rights as citizens and workers. The conference blasted "our enemies [who] seek to scare and vilify us while they despoil us." The conference speakers argued that there were fewer black criminals than whites, "yet we are daily pictured as thugs and murderers and lynched without trial."[135] Openly contesting the message of Booker T. Washington, Du Bois told a General Convention of Friends (Quakers) in Ocean Grove that southern schools were worse than they had been ten years before and that New Jersey should avoid emulating them. Similarly, the National Independent Political League, headed by W. Monroe Trotter, an ambitious opponent of Booker T. Washington, met in Atlantic City and declared non-allegiance to either major political party. They contended that members would only support candidates who opposed disenfranchisement and peonage, favored an antilynching law, opposed Jim Crow transportation, and sought the restoration to rights of the Brownsville soldiers, who had been unfairly blamed for a racial incident in Texas and dishonorably discharged, costing them their pensions. They were reinstated only in the 1970s.

Founded in 1909, the National Association for the Advancement of Colored People (NAACP) gave New Jersey and other American blacks hope that they were not alone in their battle against Jim Crow. The NAACP was founded in a series of meetings among elite white liberals appalled by the Springfield, Illinois, race riots in which two people were lynched, another six killed by other means, fifty people wounded, and over 2,000 blacks forced to flee white mobs. The meetings led by Oswald Garrison Villard, president of the *New York Evening Post* and grandson of William Lloyd Garrison, eventually fused with similar meetings of African American intellectuals disillusioned and frustrated by the policies of Booker T. Washington. Over the next few years, further meetings determined that black suffrage and nonindustrial black education were primary aims; the movement coalesced around the name of The National Association for the Advancement of Colored People. W.E.B. Du Bois was hired to publish a high-quality magazine, *The Crisis*. Du Bois was perhaps the most influential American social scientist of the twentieth century.

Rejecting Booker T. Washington's conservative leadership, philosophy of racial uplift, and accommodation to white supremacy, the NAACP sought

legal methods to confront Jim Crow and racial terrorism. The NAACP concentrated its efforts in the American southern states to fight against lynching,
beatings, mob rule, economic and political oppression, and almost universal
Jim Crow social behavior from bathrooms to schools to politics. While New
Jersey did not have a tradition of lynching, the state's black residents suffered from many of the ugly aspects of Jim Crow. Black New Jerseyans were
quick to join the NAACP and the organization spent considerable time,
attention, and resources battling social ills over the next decades. Blacks in
Newark formed the first chapter in the state in 1913, making it the second
oldest in the national and the largest in New Jersey, a status it enjoys to the
present. Other branches quickly formed in Camden, Asbury Park, and
Trenton. The initial membership of Trenton's branch of the NAACP indicates
black New Jersey's middle-class support. The first membership included
numerous ministers, teachers, dentists, doctors, businessmen, artisans, and
city employees. As a biracial organization, the NAACP also could tap into
the financial and legal resources of whites.[136]

As Jim Crow seeped further into American life, New Jersey blacks tried
to remain optimistic in the face of declining opportunities. One of the first
actions of the New York branch, called the vigilance committee, was to force
integration of Palisades Park near Fort Lee. The committee's usual method
was to send a black person accompanied by a white to purchase tickets. Once
the black had been rebuffed, the white person would buy a ticket, thus
demonstrating inequality. In this case a black family had been refused
entrance. The Palisades Park company agreed to integrate, avoiding a court
decree. As the company had accepted the principle, the NAACP encouraged the family to take $300 and season tickets to the park as a settlement.[137]

The Wilson Administration and Jim Crow

Black New Jerseyans followed with horror the spread of Jim Crow in Washington D.C. Placing their faith in newly elected President Woodrow Wilson,
formerly head of Princeton University and governor of New Jersey, they
believed the new chief executive would not condone segregation. Rather

they blamed a radical element in the Democratic Party for the closing of jobs to blacks. The first department to go Jim Crow was the Bureau of Printing and Engraving. Other departments shunted blacks into separate parts of their buildings. Sadly, the *New York Age* noted, there was not a single organization in the capitol that intended to protect black jobs. Wilson proved to be cold and indifferent to blacks.[138]

As Eric Yellin recently explained, African Americans who gained jobs through Republican Party patronage over several administrations had created a black capitol. Ambitious young black men found work as clerks and inspectors with good annual salaries and plans for upward mobility. All that changed with Wilson's ascension to the presidency. Despite complaints from the NAACP and after a heated exchange with Monroe Trotter, a commanding black activist, Wilson, argues Yellin, sought to proletarianize blacks by removing them from federal positions. Wilson, an avowed white supremacist, gave federal approval to Jim Crow behavior in the states. Jim Crow had certainly existed before, but now blacks lost any influence in the executive branch, upon which they had relied for support and work.[139]

The message from the Wilson administration affirmed segregation. Soon, Trenton blacks had to battle against ice skating rink owners who wanted to bar blacks.[140] Elsewhere, blacks experienced trouble buying homes. White residents complained bitterly in 1915 when George S. Mills, a prosperous black man, bought a home in an exclusive residential section in Leonia, New Jersey, for which he paid $6,500. Rumors quickly circulated that other blacks wanted to buy homes near Mills's new home.[141]

Where money talked, segregation was more limited. Integrated Easter celebrations in Atlantic City continued even as debates over segregation raged in the rest of the state. Not all professions and organizations adopted Jim Crow. The New Jersey State Dental Society elected John. D. Ballard, a black dentist from Orange, to membership in 1907. The Eclectic Club, a national fraternity of whites invited Booker T. Washington to their annual meeting in Jersey City. When he was unavailable, the group selected as their speaker Fred T. Moore, the editor of the *New York Age* and the *Colored American Magazine*. The New Jersey Central Railroad ordered Jim Crow seats removed from the dining car after complaints by leading blacks. The railroad admitted that the practice had been in place for about ten years.[142]

The Elks continued to hold meetings in Atlantic City without Jim Crow. The 1917 conference was well attended "by all shades," but noteworthy was the absence of black visitors from Baltimore, a group that had been a mainstay of Atlantic City's Easters.[143] One method to solve the contradiction between Jim Crow laws and Atlantic City's immense popularity among New Jersey blacks was to create a "Negro Day." The first Thursday of each September saw an influx of thousands of blacks from all over the Mid-Atlantic states to invade the city's shops, restaurants, and amusement places before departing late in the evening.[144]

THE WORLD WAR I EXPERIENCE

New Jersey blacks served bravely for the United States in World War I. Trenton native Needham Roberts was the first American soldier to receive the French Croix de Guerre for his brave service in the 369th Infantry. He later received two purses of money from grateful white and black Trenton residents. Dr. Arthur Thomas, a Trenton dentist attached to the Fourth Regiment, and Vincent Harvey, Trenton's first black policeman (appointed December 3, 1917), served in the 349th Division along with Mitchell Davis, a promising young lawyer killed in action. The black Newark branch of the American Legion was named after Emmet Guyton, a Newark native killed during the conflict. With more than 150 members, Guyton-Callahan American Legion Post 152 is the oldest black American Legion post in the state and had auxiliaries for women and a Boy Scout troop.[145]

Overall the U.S. government scarcely bothered pretending to give black soldiers and sailors equal treatment. Enlisted men had to obey curfews not extended to whites and they routinely received inferior equipment. The black officer class was tiny, shunned by white counterparts and barred from officers' clubs. White officers made it plain they regarded black soldiers as primarily fit for manual labor, rather than combat.[146]

World War I brought a more public Jim Crow presence. Black draftees serving in the U.S. Army at Fort Dix experienced color discrimination, many for the first time in their lives. Attendees at a baseball game at Fort Dix between white and black teams were offended by whites-only sections in the stands. On the walls of Cafeteria #2, which was often used as a mustering station, suddenly appeared a sign that said "For White Men" only. Racial epithets were tossed around frequently. All the officers of black regiments were white, which was a new development in the military. Previously, black captains and lieutenants were common. Now the army argued that black soldiers were not accustomed to taking orders from their own people, a fallacy the *New York Age* refuted by reference to the remarkable showing by the 367th, 368th, and other distinguished units with black officers. An additional acerbation came from visiting soldiers. At the bequest of Jersey City citizens, the War Department promised to punish all rowdy soldiers who molested "colored citizens." Apparently there were incidents of misconduct on trolley trains in which white southern soldiers objected to the presence of black riders. A *New York Age* editorial claimed that "radical southern customs," previously found only in the South, were now "religiously observed" at Fort Dix. Emmett J. Scott, special assistant to the Secretary of War, was asked to use his influence to halt racial abuses at Fort Dix.[147]

Support for the federal anti-lynching bill divided blacks and whites in New Jersey. The NAACP vigorously supported it while few whites were courageous enough to do so. One who did was Reverend Dr. Fred G. Boughton of the Central Baptist Church in Woodbury, who proclaimed that blacks had made enormous progress since the Civil War and that "race prejudice is largely due to selfishness and ignorance."[148]

New Jersey's black citizens showed a growing unease about segregation's creep during Woodrow Wilson's presidency. The Negro American Alliance declared in Atlantic City in March 1918 that the "American Negro needs to exercise extreme caution lest he be swept always on a wave of false optimism." While America was at war with Austria, its prisoners of war held by the United States had more privileges than American blacks. Floyd Francis warned that "democracy is being made a farce of and mockery" right in the United States.[149]

By 1919, the Alliance, feeling the dangerous effects of Jim Crow, wrote to President Woodrow Wilson, appealing to him to take action against mob violence and ensure that black people had the same rights and privileges due their fellow white American citizens. They cited the recent uprising in Washington D.C. as evidence that black people were willing to protect themselves, even to making the supreme sacrifice. The letter also reminded Wilson that "at your command," black soldiers fought and died that other races and nations might be free." George Cannon, its leader, admonished Wilson that "we will not submit or return to the quasi-slavery, lynching, and burning we endured before the world war," Cannon and his group pleaded with Wilson to "make ours a land of real democracy."

In his masterpiece of American literature, *The Souls of Black Folk*, W. E. B. Du Bois described the black American as living a life of "twoness," one as an American and a second existence behind the veil of race. New Jersey blacks were caught in this conundrum. Between the Civil War and World War I, black New Jerseyans experienced the exhilaration of civil freedom and the nasty frustrations of Jim Crow. Across their society, blacks organized churches and fraternal societies, engaged in politics, and used community efforts to battle discrimination. Individuals such as George Cannon sustained sophisticated, remarkable lives. The social composition of black New Jersey changed dramatically as older residents urbanized and were replaced in rural areas by migrants from the South. Black New Jerseyans enjoyed, behind the veil, a lively society marked by communal events, sports, and music. They, said Du Bois, wished "to make it possible for a man to be both a Negro and an American without being cursed and spit upon by his fellows, without having the doors of Opportunity closed roughly in his face."[150] They did so at the nadir of race relations in America. Jim Crow behavior belied American ideals by creating nasty racial barriers to ordinary life and to human progress for blacks. Crushing disappointments were common and further triumphs and frustrations lay ahead.

~

CHAPTER 5

Black New Jersey Battles
Jim Crow, 1918–1940

New Jersey blacks had not faced the violent terrorism suffered by their people in the South. Nonetheless they could feel with icy chill of segregation on their lives. Sadly, in the aftermath of World War I, race relations in New Jersey turned meaner. Atlantic City became the model of increased segregation with sizable restrictions on housing, education, job opportunities, and political power. Segregation could be uneven in application, but the overall thrust was toward diminished black rights. African Americans in Atlantic City and elsewhere responded with staunch opposition and took cases of Jim Crow to court whenever possible. Ultimately, blacks responded to Republican Party failures by moving toward the Democratic Party. This process happened intermittently over the next three decades until a permanent switch in the 1960s.

Demographic Change

New Jersey's black population grew steadily in the interwar period. New Jersey proved to be attractive to southern black migrants eager to leave white terrorism and lack of opportunity in the southern states. Along with better known destinations such as Detroit, Chicago, and New York, black migrants found succor in New Jersey's extant black cities and communities and churches. Between 1910 and 1930 the black population in New Jersey grew from 89,760 to 208,828, an increase of 132 percent. By 1940, New Jersey's state

black population rose to more than 226,000. Several examples illustrate the
hardships of migrants who built success for their progeny. Coyt Jones, father
of famed poet and civil rights activist Leroy Jones (Amiri Baraka), moved at
the age of ten from South Carolina to Newark. He found work unloading
vegetables at a local grocery store and shined shoes at a barbershop. Jessie
Jackson, an educated professional woman, moved north to escape an abusive husband. She tried several states before settling in New Jersey. Although
better than conditions in the south, she and her family were often homeless
at first and had trouble finding work, let alone something to match her skills.
A local church took her family in and sheltered them until she found menial
work. The mother of future mayor Sharpe James migrated north and, after
hard times, successfully opened a restaurant.[1]

Newark's black population jumped from 9,400 in 1915 to 38, 880 in 1940
or about 9 percent of the city's total population. The first big increase
occurred between 1910 and 1920, when the city's black population rose to
nearly 17,000 during the first Great Migration. Arriving blacks faced daunt-
ing hurdles in industrial employment, and as of 1930 more than two dozen
Newark trade unions officially barred blacks from their membership. No
one could join the union without passing an apprenticeship course and
African Americans were not permitted to take it. The union customarily followed a "last hired first fired" policy, so black men and women who had
been able to gain employment in the overheated job market of World War I
lost those positions soon after. During the Depression, the number of black
Newark residents rose by 7,000, but, as Brad Tuttle has detailed, the number of employed black males dropped from 13,308 to 7,990. Black males often
lost skilled positions and were forced to take any work available, no matter
how poorly paid or demeaning. Newark, pointed out Clement Price, also
suffered from a dire shortage in housing. World War I brought fuller employment to Newark. Not everyone benefitted. Housing prices soared. The city
government had to construct a tent colony for those evicted from their
dwellings or who were already homeless. Newark's bonded debt pushed tax
rates higher as the price of running the government soared in the 1920s.[2]

Segregated housing became the norm in the early 1920s. Whereas blacks had been dispersed throughout Newark before 1920, they now became restricted to older, working class wards. Between 1920 and 1930 over two-thirds of black Newark residents lived in the densely packed Third Ward. As the Third Ward was designated as a commercial zone, residential construction was effectively blocked and fewer than ten new homes were built there in the 1920s. Because of the crowding, the Third Ward became known for high death rates from tuberculosis, influenza, and other highly contagious diseases. Worsening the problem was that segregation prevented blacks from visiting many hospitals and medical offices. Segregated housing conditions condemned blacks to living in dilapidated homes with inadequate kitchens, lavatories, and heating. Whites increasingly gave up on the inner wards and escaped to the suburbs.[3]

Problems were similar in smaller cities. Ira Reid's highly detailed report on Elizabeth's black population, though much smaller than Newark's, demonstrated the demographic changes stemming from the Great Migration. Elizabeth's black population doubled between 1900 and 1920. By 1930, Reid learned nearly 2,000 blacks lived in Elizabeth. His report, prepared for the Elizabeth Interracial Committee, found that 55 percent of blacks in the town had arrived since 1920. Georgia, South Carolina, and Virginia arrivals outnumbered locally born blacks. The survey indicated that migrating blacks, came in families of four to seven people, seeking "better conditions" and work. What they found was more poverty. Over two-thirds of their new homes had neither baths nor indoor toilets and sharing privies with other families was common. Kitchens were inadequate, leaky roofs were a constant problem, and landlords consistently refused to make repairs. While blacks often lived in integrated neighborhoods with Jewish, Spanish, Polish, Portuguese, and Eastern Europeans, their homes were always the most dilapidated on the block. As a result, blacks often moved every year.[4]

Black employment in Elizabeth was often in poorly paid, unskilled jobs with no chance of promotion. The black population often had to commute to jobs with such employers as the Central Railroad of New Jersey, Standard

Oil Company's Linden plant, and in foundries, warehouses, shirt and blouse manufacturers, trucking companies, and coal yards. Reports indicated that blacks were diligent and reliable workers, but were held back by illiteracy. Males earned more than females, with a sizable number earning twenty-five to thirty dollars per week. Most women lagged behind at five to ten dollars per week. Many families received relief funds or took in lodgers. Black unemployment levels in 1930 were about 27 percent for men and 17 percent for women. Overwhelmingly, black men worked as laborers and women as domestics. Independent businessmen in Elizabeth were rare, and included six barbers, several auto mechanics, and a handful of pool hall operators, restaurateurs, and grocers. T. J. Taylor, an Elizabeth native, owned an ice cream factory.[5]

Black social conditions in Elizabeth varied. Death rates nearly equaled birth rates throughout the 1920s and mortality from epidemic and infectious diseases was common. At the same time, Elizabeth's health facilities were open to all. Elizabeth recreational centers welcomed blacks only on two evenings a week during the winter. Still, young blacks attended in large numbers, but the city refused to extend hours or days. Movie going was the most popular recreation, followed by attending church, visiting the sick, going to dances and church socials, and reading, all of which indicate respectable, positive activities. There were two boy scout troops but none for girls. Young literate blacks frequented the public library, reading books by W.E.B. Du Bois, Carter Woodson, Alain Locke, Langston Hughes, and many other black authors.[6]

Even such positive attributes did not keep young blacks safe. Despite their small percentage of the population, blacks accounted for one of six police arrests in 1930. Reid's report indicated that almost 70 percent of those arrested came from southern states, with the overwhelming numbers laboring men in their twenties. The most common offenses were low-level crime including disorderly conduct, motor vehicle violations, "suspicion," gambling, and drunkenness. Very few arrests were made for serious crimes such as assault and battery or home invasion. Social agencies helped somewhat with ameliorating poverty but had limited funds.[7]

Elizabeth's schools were integrated, though educators felt that young blacks had difficulty adjusting after arriving practically illiterate from southern states. There was only one black teacher in the entire Elizabeth school system. Private schools were segregated save the Elizabeth Music School, which enrolled two black students. The center of the black community was, as in past eras, the church. Most of Elizabeth's churches served southern parishioners, but only the First Black Institutional Church offered social and recreational programs. First Baptist housed a bowling alley and pool tables, meeting space for boy scouts, who met there regularly, and a free medical clinic three days a week for an hour each day.[8]

POLITICS

Blacks could not find reliable help even from the Republican Party. After black voters were strong supporters of Governor Walter Evans Edge's successful candidacy in 1916, he betrayed their hopes for a law forbidding color discrimination in public accommodations. After making many promises to sign the bill to place a $500 damage payment to victims of discrimination and possible jail time against offenders, Edge changed the legislation to pay any damages recovered to the local poorhouse. The Federation of Colored Organizations charged the governor with a breach of faith. The bill was finally signed in 1922, well after Edge had become a U.S. senator.[9]

Walter Alexander, along with George E. Cannon, led the New Jersey black political scene. A graduate of Lincoln University and a successful physician, Alexander was a leader in the New Jersey Medical Association. Both Cannon and Alexander were active in the National Medical Association, the largest and oldest national organization representing African American physicians in the United States. Alexander entered electoral politics in 1911 in Essex County, ascending to the Republican Assembly ticket in 1919 and winning a seat in 1920, the first black New Jerseyan to do so.

Assemblyman Alexander designed a state civil rights bill in 1921 that was modeled after New York's legislation, the Levy Civil Rights Bill. Alexander presided over the assembly for an hour, the first of his race to hold such an honor.[10] Alexander's bill forbade mobbing and beatings, the favorite tactics of the Klan. Shortly after the law was enacted, it was applied in the case of Samuel Barnett, a black man from New York City. Barnett had entered an ice cream parlor in Hackensack and requested some soda water. The attendants refused to serve him. Barnett returned later and was sold the soda water but at an exorbitant price. He sued with the support of the Colored Voters Association. The jury returned a guilty judgment and fined the store $100. In a second case a few years later, another Hackensack man won a $300 judgment against a movie theater for refusing to sell him a ticket.[11]

Despite the bill's passage, blacks learned that white politicians often took for granted the perceived captive black vote. Republican Walter Edge was indicative of such disinterest. Edge served as governor of New Jersey twice, from 1917 to 1919 and again from 1944 to 1947. Edge also served as a U.S. senator representing New Jersey from 1919 to 1929. Despite his strong political power in the state, black political figures had sufficient reservations about Edge that they considered throwing their support behind Hamilton Fish Kean for Senate in the Republican Party's primary elections in 1924. Kean advised black Republicans that he disavowed the Klan and respected black rights and Chairman Isaac Nutter of the black Republicans endorsed Kean. Black Republicans questioned whether Edge had done anything for them beyond the token appointments of an elevator operator and one assistant attorney. Nonetheless, Edge was reelected.[12]

Walter Alexander was among those opposed to Edge. He was a delegate to the National Republican Convention in 1928 in Kansas City, where Edge was rumored to be nominated as Herbert Hoover's running mate. Alexander and other New Jersey blacks had stated their opposition to Edge and named Mrs. Bessie B. Mention, president of the Colored Republican Women's Conference in New Jersey, as an alternative to Edge as the Vice Presidential candidate. Ratification of the Nineteenth Amendment to the United States Constitution in 1920 empowered black women in New Jersey as never before. Florence Randolph and Violet Johnson continued their organizational work. Under their leadership the State Federation of Women grew to forty-nine clubs by 1917 and reached eighty-five the next year. The number of individual organizations peaked at twenty-one in 1920.[13]

Earlier, Alexander's popularity had been weak. In 1922, some black Republicans moved to replace him with another candidate solely on the grounds that Alexander's skin was too light.[14] Alexander kept his seat and campaigned against discrimination, firing off an angry letter to Metropolitan Life Insurance Company that accused the corporation of diverting black clients from Orange to Newark, where it maintained a Jim Crow office. He received an evasive reply. The company then reversed its policy as bad publicity rose and other, black-oriented insurance companies began to move in. Upper-echelon officials at Met Life declared that local policies discriminating against blacks were illegal and must be stopped.[15] Quick to fill the void, Northeastern Life Insurance, a black company, became licensed in New Jersey. Northeastern established a significant portion of the black business in the state, but later merged with other companies, much to the dismay of the stockholders. The Southern Aid Society of Virginia, the nation's oldest black insurance company, received a license to operate in New Jersey.[16]

With deepening concerns about national commitment to black rights, the Federation of Colored Organizations continued to meet and lobby the Republican Party to act on their behalf. The 1928 meeting indicates the mixture of progressivism and more hesitant ventures. The keynote address by Mrs. A. H. Douglas, president of the New Jersey State Federation of Colored Women, was considered a masterpiece of forward thinking about the unity of the male and female political efforts. At the same time, Major Lester B. Granger of the Bordentown School received a standing vote of thanks for his splendid address about a school whose mission reflected the older politics of Booker T. Washington.[17]

Whatever misgivings black New Jerseyans had about the Republican Party, it rightly regarded the Democrats with far more hostility. When the *Pittsburgh Courier* revealed that the Democratic Party had established a segregated office for blacks in New York City, New Jerseyans joined their support of the rising protest. Blacks also criticized the Democratic New Jersey governor, A. Harry Moore, for refusing to consider appointing blacks to government posts. Subsequently, black Republicans assured the national party that all their votes would go toward presidential candidate Herbert Hoover.[18]

There were occasional signs that the Republicans appreciated black support. In the summer of 1924, the National Association for the Advancement of Colored People (NAACP) held its fifteenth annual convention in Philadelphia and took a weekend excursion to Atlantic City where the Black Elks, boy and girl scouts, and several citizen committees welcomed them, escorted them to Asbury M. E. Church where they left their luggage and walked to the beach and took a stroll along the Boardwalk. While in Philadelphia, the NAACP received a personal greeting from President Calvin Coolidge.[19]

On a local level, Atlantic City blacks showed political muscle in helping mayoral candidate Edward L. Bader defeat the now "Ku Kluxed" former mayor Harry Bacharach in 1924. Over three-quarters of black voters favored Bader. Observers believed that the total would have been higher had not two former black leaders, attorneys Isaac Nutter and James A. Lightfoot, attempted to convince the black electorate that the Klan was no danger. This endorsement came despite a massive Klan rally on the Steel Pier and in every white church in town.[20]

Black Republican political pressure began to reap rewards. Data from Camden indicated that black teachers were paid less and the board of education adjusted their salaries upward to equal pay for white teachers. Atlantic City, Plainfield, and Jersey City governments agreed to hire black policemen. The Urban League worked with Jersey City's Department of Safety to find more qualified black officers.[21] In 1926, the Hudson County Republican Committee Association nominated P. Sample for county assembly. Sample was a graduate of the University of Michigan, president of the local NAACP, and worked as a social worker for the Pullman Company.[22]

Assembly elections became more heated as blacks in both major parties demanded candidates of their race. The Pittsburgh Courier reported in 1929 that "the colored voters on both sides are mobilizing their forces to strike en masse to land their candidates in office."[23] C. Bion James was nominated and did creditably well, placing fourth in the state in votes. He lost his hope for a post, but showed that a black person could draw substantial ballots.

Walter Alexander was also very critical of his profession. In 1930, he warned that medical schools were shutting blacks out and thereby creating a crisis in the future of medicine. Unless blacks were allowed to enter medical schools and become doctors, black and white hospitals would suffer from a lack of trained physicians. White hospitals would become more segregated and would fail to serve the entire population.[24] Health issues were always a problem in a segregated society. Newark did not have a hospital dedicated to patients of color until 1927. Founded by Dr. J. A. Kenney, who had been the chief health officer at Tuskegee for more than twenty years and a personal physician to Booker T. Washington, the new medical complex could accommodate thirty-five patients. It had an outpatient facility, surgical suites, and a full staff. Well-wishers from all over the eastern seaboard crowded into the hospital to give Kenney and his team a positive sendoff. Kenney struggled for three years but finally was able to gain the right to practice surgery at the Beth-Israel Hospital, the largest in Newark. Kenney also led a struggle to force the American Medical Association to drop the term "colored" as an identifier in its directory of physicians.[25] New Jersey's paucity of black doctors attracted talented physicians from other states to fill the void in black neighborhoods and hospitals.[26]

In 1931 significant splits occurred within the New Jersey black Republican ranks. Much of it had to do with clashing personal ambitions, and the selection of longtime Republican stalwart and Atlantic City lawyer Isaac Nutter as head of the state's black Republicans was marred by Oliver Randolph's accusations of shady deals and backroom negotiations with Democrats. More than two hours of wrangling occurred before Nutter was selected.[27]

Republican inactivity toward state blacks during the Depression caused many New Jersey black party members to jump to the Democratic Party. George Bates, chairman of the Essex County Republican Association, warned that President Hoover's indifference toward blacks made Democrats

out of aggrieved blacks. All the major black newspapers were going Democratic. Republicans realized that something had to be done to preserve black
support because "Negro votes" would decide the elections in New Jersey.
Republican efforts to retain black loyalties were damaged when David Baird,
a former U.S. senator seeking election as governor of the state, defended his
vote to place Judge John Parker on the U.S. Supreme Court despite condemnation of the racist juror by the state NAACP. Later, Baird, desperate for
black Republican votes, apologized for his support of Parker, calling it a
mistake. His belated words did not help as Baird went down to a crushing
defeat in the race for governor against Democrat A. Harry Moore, to whom,
in a significant political switch, black Jersey voters gave their support. The
NAACP threw all its powers against Baird, a warning shot for Republicans
across the nation who supported racist jurors. W.E.B. Du Bois chimed in
with a speech in Atlantic City denouncing Baird.[28]

New Jersey blacks did not hesitate to complain about mistreatment.
Margaret Holly, executive secretary of the Charity Organization Society of
Plainfield, rejected a number of black applicants for relief in 1931, saying
that "all the colored people should be run out of town." The NAACP immediately took up the case, seeking her dismissal.[29] Relief efforts often became
political footballs. Local people complained that commissioners, most of
them black, who were appointed to investigate poverty among blacks, were
eating away sizable sums of the money allocated to the commission. The
commissioners denied accusations that they were working for David
Baird.[30]

Notwithstanding black Jersey Republicans' misgivings about the party,
religious leaders remained loyal in the presidential election of 1932.
Bishop E.W.D. Jones of the AME Zion church in Paterson declared that he
would vote for Herbert Hoover. Jones opined that Hoover was no race man
and that blacks could not expect much of him. By contrast, Jones warned
that Democratic Party candidate Franklin D. Roosevelt's running partner,
John Nance Garner from Texas, was terrifying. An advocate of the poll tax
and a firm upholder of segregation, Garner , Jones argued, was dedicated to
destroying black aspirations.[31]

Despite Garner's presence, by 1936 blacks across the country had moved away from Republicans to the Democratic Party and its popular president, Franklin D. Roosevelt. This may have been because the president and his vice president had drifted far apart. New Jersey black Republicans did not quickly become Democrats. In the election of 1940, almost half of the state's black voters supported Republican Wendell Willkie for president.[32]

Black Democrats in New Jersey had little to show for their new allegiance. Once in power, Jersey Democrats allocated tiny bits of patronage to state blacks. Helen Myers, daughter of a leading figure in the Democratic Party, was appointed as postmaster for Lawnside. There were rumors that Camden County might run a black for the state legislature.[33] The federal government did however begin to make positive inroads in housing. The U.S. Housing Administration earmarked $2.5 million for the construction of homes for blacks in Camden to alleviate the slum conditions that existed in the city.[34]

SEGREGATION

As Atlantic City developed into a nationally known vacation and leisure destination in the early decades of the twentieth century, African Americans found themselves restricted to work pushing large rolling chairs along the famous Boardwalk. Although there was some leniency on the beaches before 1920 blacks were eventually barred from swimming with whites. Similar injunctions, always made to avoid alienating white customers, meant that theaters, amusement parks, restaurants, guesthouses, and hotels were all off-limits to blacks. Even as Louis Armstrong and Duke Ellington performed at the Steel Pier, black residents were barred from attending. Atlantic City political and economic leaders strictly enforced dress codes for rolling car pushers on the Boardwalk. Atlantic City's cabarets came under fierce criticism in 1923 after reports of white women dancing "a la Eve," or naked, before mixed race audiences. Members of the local Civic Affairs Committee, a watchdog group, criticized police laxity over the dancers and for allowing the city to become a "paradise for bootleggers, gamblers, prostitutes, pimps, panderers and confidence men." A raid on a "black and tan," or mixed race, nightclub in 1924 revealed illegal drinking and young black men "dressed up as women." The police reported that black and tan taverns were doing a big business in the back parts of the city with entertainers doing "off-color stuff." Policemen arrested a number of white women who attempted to enter black clubs. Making an example of one, the court sentenced her to a $200 fine or ninety days in jail. Seven more white girls were arrested on charges of being "disorderly persons," a catchall term to punish ordinary human behavior.[35]

State lawmakers seemed to equate mixed race love with illicit sex. Jersey officials busily poked into people's private lives. An assemblyman from Monmouth County introduced a bill that would outlaw mixed race marriages. Fighting the odious proposal were Assemblymen J. Leroy Baxter, the sole black member of the assembly, attorney Isaac Nutter, and a delegation from the NAACP.[36]

As Jim Crow segregation spread across New Jersey, blacks were increasingly barred from public facilities. In Atlantic City and Camden, the YMCA and YWCA had separate branches for whites and blacks. The Boy and Girl Scouts, Salvation Army, and movie theaters became segregated. School segregation hardened into an unofficial but rigid policy.[37] Towns took different approaches to creating service institutions, such as Englewood's construction of a YMCA for blacks, which was developed using personal donations. Jersey City by contrast opened a regular branch of the YWCA for use by blacks and whites. Black Ys formed an association, which met quarterly at Princeton and Bordentown. The Princeton Y was a source of community pride among local blacks.[38]

Elsewhere blacks were forced into second-class status. Trenton, the state capital, had a fairly small black community until mid-century. Before then, blacks could take any seat available on city buses, but they were not allowed to dine freely at the city's restaurants or hotel dining rooms. Black theatregoers were restricted to the balcony. Hotel hiring became segregated. Trenton's black waiters at the famed Stacy-Trent Hotel lost their jobs when, in 1924, the hotel's management replaced all of them with young white women. Later, when guests complained of bad service by the inexperienced women, rumors abounded that the veteran black waiters would be recalled, but that never occurred. Downtown Trenton saw few black faces except behind brooms and dust mops.[39]

More racial discrimination occurred at the Asbury Park Casino Arcade in 1934. Catherine Harris, wife of Lorenzo Harris, the sculptor and artist, took her daughter to the merry-go-round at the amusement park. After she placed her daughter on a wooden horse, the manager told her that blacks were not welcome and pulled the girl off the ride. Mrs. Harris then grabbed the manager by his tie and choked him. A passing police officer declined to press assault charges against the lady and ordered the manager to let the girl complete her ride. When Mrs. Harris sued the company, she was induced to drop her complaint after the ride operators published an apology claiming that discrimination would not be tolerated. That apology did not work for long. By 1938, Asbury Park restaurants were accused of serving "negro dishes," while theaters forced black patrons into a separate section. Blacks using Asbury Park beaches self-segregated to avoid problems with whites.[40]

In an event that belied staunch, unyielding segregation, the Stacy-Trent Hotel, which had earlier fired its black employees, hosted a massive interracial meeting of churchwomen in 1929 with ancillary forums at the Bordentown School. Women from New York and New Jersey listened to lectures on "What It Means to Be a Negro in New Jersey" and "Negro Working Women in New Jersey." Dr. George Haynes, a leading black intellectual and head of the Federal Council of Churches in New York, spoke at Bordentown. The following year the group met again, and Walter White, the acting secretary of the NAACP, was the prime speaker.[41]

The pastor of Plainfield's St. Mark's Episcopal Church achieved a singular honor in 1933. Reverend Edgerton E. Hall became the third person at Rutgers University to earn a PhD in education. He was the first black in the nation to receive such a doctorate. Reverend Hall was from the West Indies and had previously received an undergraduate degree from the University of London, a theological bachelor's degree from Payne Theological Seminary, and a master of arts degree from Rutgers.[42]

Social behavior became increasingly segregated. Even visiting professionals suffered Jim Crow tactics, such as the *Pittsburgh Courier*'s theatrical correspondent who was refused service at the Long Branch boardwalk restaurant. At another restaurant he was handed a Negro menu with prices four times the cost for white customers.[43] The NAACP went after theaters that discriminated. The Bayonne branch sued the newest and most modern cinema in the city for instituting a policy of sending blacks to balcony seats. Numerous respectable blacks were told that orchestra seats were already sold out, when they could see many unoccupied seats during the performance. The theater claimed that it had set a policy based upon proper attire and suggested that some of his employees had been too officious in their treatment of patrons. After the NAACP met with the manager, there was no further discrimination.[44]

Clothing stores refused to let blacks try on garments before buying them. To store owners the idea that blacks could work at their stores was unthinkable.[45] The Klan frowned upon interracial coalitions. In 1938, it plastered stickers on the cars of members of the Cosmopolitan Club, a mixed-race group, and burned a cross on the front lawn of the president of the organization.

Access to the state's beaches was contentious. Long Branch attempted to segregate its beaches by requiring a three-dollar-a-day beach fee for nonresidents. They provided no facilities for changing clothes and outlawed walking on the boardwalk clad in just a swimsuit. The NAACP objected and convinced the Long Branch city council to build a bathhouse. They agreed, but charged an exorbitant fee for its use. Black residents also complained that no permits for the beach had been issued to people of their race.[46] One enterprising woman found a way around the ban. Virginia Flowers, who could pass for white, purchased a long string of tickets and handed them out freely to would-be black beach patrons. Flowers became a star witness during the suit against the regulators. Her heroics earned her a flurry of marriage proposals, which she declined because, at only seventeen years old, she wanted to pursue her education while remaining "a shining light among the exclusive younger set" of blacks in New York and New Jersey.[47]

EDUCATION

As was the case in the decades after the Civil War, black efforts on desegregation focused on education. Parents now had several decades of experience with segregated classrooms and understood the hazards. The more racism prevailed in New Jersey, as in other northern states, the more abuse black students suffered. Principals often used racial epithets and threatened to send students "back to the jungle." Teachers and guidance counselors routinely discouraged black students from applying to colleges or even taking college preparatory courses.[48]

Sensing harsh criticism of separate but equal schools, members of the state's Department of Rural Education issued a report in 1921 boasting of gains in school funding, especially teacher salaries. Somewhat defensively, the board noted that its work did not receive as much attention as lynching. Using private donors and state funds and cooperating with local school boards, the department announced plans to lift teacher salaries higher and to construct better buildings. Above all the department commended black families and communities for their hard work, diligence, and sacrifice.[49]

Attitudes among black intellectuals differed about the benefits and detriments of black-only schools. Proponents argued that black schools had higher graduation rates. William Valentine, the head of the all-black Bordentown School, supported segregated schools. The previously mentioned 1925 study concluded that black youngsters in segregated schools in the southern counties were far more likely to graduate from high school than their integrated counterparts. Another study, done in 1937, contended that black parents, many recently arrived from the Jim Crow South, were more likely to accept segregated education. In contrast, most northern blacks, and particularly the black media, upheld principles of integration.[50]

Further hampering black students' progress were antiquated and even dangerous schools. In 1923, an elementary school in Atlantic City was regarded as a firetrap. Administrators in Newark schools in the 1930s routinely assigned the bulk of funds to white schools, leaving the black schools in poorer neighborhoods in inferior physical condition. Such conditions spurred black intellectuals, journalists, and activists to demand integrated schools as the best means to ensure equal opportunity for black and white students. Trenton blacks angrily denounced a 1924 plan to segregate students by forcing black pupils to attend a segregated Lincoln school.[51]

White parents and children were capable of mean-spirited racial discrimination. School officials, parents, and schoolchildren at Pennsgrove caused an uproar in 1923 when a black youth was named class orator by the principal because of his academic achievements. Parents and classmates objected to the appointment because they did not want a black student to speak before a white audience.[52]

New Jersey's schools again considered separate schools for black children in 1925 when the Hopewell Township Board of Education discussed segregated education. Black children had been attending school with white children, but there was renewed pressure to resegregate.[53] By the 1920s, parents angered by segregated conditions no longer had to suffer alone. The NAACP started to hold rallies in New Jersey in the early 1920s and pushed hard for passage of the antilynching bill introduced by Leonidas Dyer of Missouri. The effort received a setback in 1922 when Republicans nominated an opponent of the Dyer Bill for Congress in the Ninth District, which included Newark. The bill passed the state assembly in 1923 and Governor George Silzer signed it into law shortly after.[54]

The NAACP mounted significant campaigns in Toms River and Atlantic City in 1927 and 1928. In Toms River, parents aided by the NAACP demanded the ouster of supervising principal of local schools, Edgar M. Fink, who had related lessons he had learned from a recent trip to Texas. Fink remarked that had attempts in New Jersey to integrate schools occurred in Texas, or any other southern schools, "they'd have been lynched." In Texas, blacks would be glad to go to any school whites told them to attend. Toms River had recently constructed a new school building yet sent black students to attend classes in a one-room church. The NAACP, headed by author and activist James Weldon Johnson, used its national power and organized all fifteen of its New Jersey branches to protest Fink's remarks and actions to the governor.[55]

The NAACP pressed the school board in Atlantic City hard over desegregation. In State of New Jersey v. Mary F. Willey, Carrie Simpkins, a widow
and mother of four school-aged children, applied to enroll them in a nearby
public school, and Willey, the school principal, refused to admit them.
Although the Pennsylvania Avenue School was two blocks from the Simpkins's
home and other white-only schools were also close by, Willey directed the
children to travel to segregated schools much further away. As a result,
the children were not attending any school. Willey denied all the charges
and stated that the children were welcome at the Pennsylvania Avenue
School but had not attended. She did describe the children as incorrigible
and claimed that Simpkins was a "disorderly person." Despite Willey's dis-
paraging comments, the Supreme Court of New Jersey ordered the students
admitted to the Pennsylvania Avenue School.[56]

The famed intellectual W.E.B. Du Bois argued fiercely for integrated
schools, citing poor physical conditions and extra costs for a dual system
resulting in less money allocated to black schools. There were also psychological ramifications. Dual systems implanted prejudice and attitudes of
racial superiority in white students and defensive, fearful attitudes toward
whites among blacks. Du Bois argued that without cultural exchange, the
mission of public schools to promote democracy would fail. Yet, by 1934, Du
Bois had changed his mind, pushing instead for the development of black
institutions, including schools, as well as economic enterprises and political power (New Jersey blacks had very little). Du Bois broke ranks with the
NAACP over legal action to end segregation. The organization, of which Du
Bois was a founding member, responded with harsh criticism of Du Bois's
views, attacks that led him to abandon his post as editor of the Crisis, the
leading black intellectual magazine of the time. In turn, the NAACP force-
fully initiated legal actions to end segregated schools. The split between Du
Bois and the NAACP characterized the dilemmas of New Jersey African
Americans. Should black leaders, especially educators and clergymen, push
for integration, knowing that such designs might cost black jobs and be
fruitless, or should they accept the occluding fog of racism and segregation,
understanding that it would mean inferior education, no political power,

meaner and shorter lives, and frequent public insult. As in slavery days, Jim
Crow New Jersey offered very little or no opportunity for racial advancement. For a number of black thinkers, huddling together seemed the best
way to survive, provide jobs for black teachers, and have some, if impoverished, control over education.[57]

Black families continued in the 1930s to demand integration into better-
funded, more academically challenging schools attended by whites. In 1933
and 1934, black residents of Montclair demanded better schools to replace a
shabby outdated school where young African Americans were forced to
learn while their white counterparts studied in modern well-equipped classrooms. Black Montclair residents complained that the local superintendent
was trying to bar blacks from attending public schools. The school superintendent retorted that blacks in the South were content with whatever crumbs
they received and that local blacks should learn to do the same. A similar
boycott occurred in East Orange in 1936. The NAACP forced out the principal of the Lincoln School in Trenton for using highly arbitrary hiring and
firing methods. By the end of the 1930s, the NAACP had begun to organize
statewide protests, armed with a Teachers' College study of inequality in
New Jersey. The NAACP demanded the hiring of more black teachers and
improved conditions in schools with large percentages of black students.
The NAACP also pushed the state government to enforce its antidiscrimination laws.[58]

The Bordentown School

Now an established institution, the Bordentown School (The New Jersey
Manual Training and Industrial School for Colored Youth) flourished
during the era of Jim Crow. The school reported in the mid-1920s that it was
opening a new dormitory to accommodate boys and girls seeking admission. The school reported full enrollment in 1928 and added a dormitory
for one hundred girls. Bordentown School boasted that 68 percent of the
young blacks who had enrolled since 1915 were employed. Female graduates
became dressmakers and domestic workers, while males became employed
as auto mechanics, painters, carpenters, plumbers, and electricians. Most

worked in New Jersey, though better openings had attracted some to go to New York and Philadelphia. About 20 percent of graduates sought a college education.[59]

The school boasted in 1926 of their superior 300-acre farm located on the banks of Delaware River. It was replete with apple orchards and produced a variety of summer vegetables. Annually it harvested over 2,000 bushels of corn, or 200 tons of corn silage. The farm possessed a huge flock of black giant chickens, which produced over fifty eggs each day; overall, chickens laid more than 160 eggs a day. The cattle herd generated sixty gallons of milk a day and the school planned to expand its operation to cultivate even larger crops and produce. Doing so would educate students in the finest methods of agriculture, an occupation held in high respect across the nation. The school advocated farm work as the best prospect for black youth.[60] Despite this rosy picture, the school's instructors were dissatisfied. Bordentown's teachers organized in 1924 to achieve pay equality with their white counterparts in the state educational system.[61]

As was the case earlier, its attractive location made Bordentown a favored place for annual black meetings and retreats. The Laymen's Council of the YMCA met there in 1931 to hear speeches by K. E. Vergese of Bombay on Indian political unrest and by Max Yergan, the Y's secretary in South Africa on conditions there. The New Jersey Federation of Colored Women's Clubs held their annual meeting at the school in 1934 with Walter White, secretary of the NAACP, as the speaker.[62] Bordentown also attracted major black speakers. W.E.B. Du Bois, a critic of industrial education, spoke at the school in 1922 on the topic of "The Choice of a Vocation," emphasizing the individual nature of life's course.[63]

CRIME

Urbanization and the rise of Jim Crow produced dangerous tensions. In a Jim Crow society, any crime committed by a black against a white merited the most brutal reactions. After Johnny Carroll, a white boxer, was stabbed to death by a black man in 1926 in Carteret, 700 furious whites marched into the black district, burned homes, torched the black First Baptist Church, and randomly beat individual blacks wherever they were encountered. Reverend George H. Reed was starting his Sunday evening service when the mob burst in. He attempted to reason with them but was beaten. The church was destroyed, with damages amounting to $3,000. After a policeman ordered the mob to disperse, the crowd bullied its way to the Liebig Chemical Company where it beat more blacks. Two weeks later a second mob burned down the Fairhaven Public School, which housed forty black students. Local blacks were upset that their children were forced to attend the racially divided school.[64]

The murder of a white policeman who was breaking up a card game in Newark in 1930 prompted mob attacks on innocent black residents. Even though a black policeman had been part of the squad that disrupted the gamblers, a white mob took the killing of the other policeman as a racial incident and roamed the streets accosting and beating blacks. A second incident involved the police and members of a black teenage gang that had stolen a car. When stopped, a white policeman investigating the theft was shot and killed. Immediately a posse of 200 cops from Jersey City, Hudson County, Kearney, Harrison, and East Newark formed and scoured the meadowlands searching for the black youths. The gunman was apprehended not by the police but by a black truck driver. One teenager quickly confessed as he and his partners were held without bail. Both incidents demonstrate that white reaction to the killing of a policeman inspired massive mob manhunts.[65]

In 1925, a "race riot," or a fight between whites and blacks, broke out in Beverly, though injuries were limited to black eyes and bruised knuckles.[66] Black and white youths battled with guns and fists at a carnival in Newark in the summer of 1925.[67] White millworkers battled with black strike breakers in Lodi in 1926.[68]

Black newspapers dutifully reported crimes committed by race members. William Battles of Orange confessed to the murder of Mrs. Charles M. Brigham of the same town in early 1923. The jury in the murder trial of bricklayer Theal Robertson was unmoved by the tearful plea of his attorney and convicted him.[69]

Black and white prisoners at the New Jersey State Reformatory in Morristown rioted against each other. The warden had to call in the state troopers to quell the fighting, which fortunately left only one young man slightly injured. More battles occurred in the prison over the next few years.[70]

A white police officer tried to arrest dice players at a massive picnic near Pittman in 1925. After disarming him, the furious players nearly lynched the officer who took refuge in the camp ranger's office, where he was saved by two black officers.[71] As an indication of the criminalization of black persons, the Newark police department first banned former heavyweight boxing champion Jack Johnson for holding a fight, then barred him from making a speech. Apparently, two weeks earlier, Johnson had spoken out in a public forum in Newark and declared that someday black people would have equal rights and the same opportunities as whites, notions that the police deemed unacceptable.[72]

Segregated Churches

New Jersey blacks had to battle efforts by white congregations to segregate churches. Bishop Thomas B. Neely and others spoke out against resolutions before the New Jersey Methodist Episcopal Churches in 1917 that would exclude the 325,000 black members of the northern portion, including New Jersey, from the denomination. I. Garland Penn, the noted author and one of two black members of the church's Denominational Committee, argued that exclusion would go against everything the Methodists stood for. Penn noted that the northern portion had spent more than $200,000 yearly on black education while the southern part had expended only $15,000 each year. Penn regretted that fifty years after emancipation, he (and other blacks) had become "an innocent problem."[73] A few years later, Bishop Edwin Holt of Chicago spoke in Atlantic City and scathingly denounced the Ku Klux Klan before a mixed gathering of Methodist clergy. There were low murmurs of protest from a few of the clergy, but Holt warned that if "we keep up with our silly movement, "there will be race wars.[74] In 1926, white thugs ransacked the recently renovated St. James M. E. Church in Newark, turning the pulpit upside down, trashing hymnbooks, wrecking a valuable piano, and smashing the stained glass windows.[75] Such incidents radicalized Black Jersey ministers, as indicated in the case of sixty-five-year-old Newark cleric Dozier Graham, a pastor who was identified as the Communist Party candidate for the U.S. Senator from the state. He and two white party members were convicted on charges of sedition along with the assault indictment.[76]

THE IMPROVED BENEVOLENT AND PROTECTIVE ORDER
OF ELKS OF THE WORLD

The Improved Benevolent and Protective Order of Elks of the World (IBPOEW) was among the most important black societies during the golden age of fraternity from the 1880s to the 1930s. The IBPOEW and its female ancillary the Daughters of the IBPOEW held the largest membership of any black fraternal organization. The IBPOEW created solidarity among African Americans, wielded significant political and economic power, supported the NAACP, offered scholarships, and provided many other community benefits. Founded in Cincinnati in 1898 the order was incorporated in Jersey City in 1906. Lawsuits between the white Elks and the IBPOEW over use of the name and insignia occurred throughout the early decades of the century. The white Elks invariably prevailed in these actions but had little power or ability to squelch the black brotherhood, which generally ignored the injunctions.[77]

New Jersey blacks were significant actors in the IBPOEW. In addition to the initial incorporation in Jersey City, the state boasted forty-five chapters with memberships ranging from a handful of people to fourteen chapters with more than 1,000 brothers. The state hosted national conferences in Atlantic City (1904, 1913, 1919, 1929, 1932, 1941, and 1952) and Newark (1922) and members flocked to other meetings in nearby New York City and Philadelphia. Holding the annual national conference in Atlantic City was of particular importance because the events occurred during the rise and triumph of Jim Crow and ugly friction over black use of the Boardwalk, the piers, and the beach. Visits by well over 2,000 IBPOEW members, Daughters of the IBPOEW, and their families and friends, all dressed in Elk regalia, parading, partying, and spending lots of money pushed hard against segregation edicts and practices. New Jersey members were important officers, with George Bates of Newark serving as general secretary of the national organization between 1911 and 1928. The IBPOEW often intervened and supported antiracist and anti-segregation laws in New Jersey. Black Elks' significance in numbers and influence during an era known as the nadir of race relations indicates their social capital. At a time of noxious Jim Crow behavior throughout white society, the Black Elks were a major faction of the vast array of fraternal organizations that anchored communities, battled segregation, fought for civil rights, and shaped overall American society.[78]

Black Elks had to battle even against presumed brethren. A conference between the white and Black Elks produced an agreement to ignore suits against the presence of the Elks of color. The following year, ruffians threatened the Black Elks with beatings if they tried to hold their annual ball on the pier in Atlantic City. Soldiers and other white men planned to gather by the hundreds and drive the Black Elks into the ocean if they appeared.[79] The national Black Elks convention took a more militant stance in 1921 when it met in Boston. Dr. M. A. Shaw, pastor of the Twelfth Baptist Church, roared at the Elks in attendance that no one was fooled by the inactivity of the Harding administration in defending the rights of black people to the vote and other civil rights and demanded that lynching become a federal offense. In fact, Shaw, like other black leaders such as W.E.B. Du Bois and James Weldon Johnson, found the Harding administration's actions to be disappointing. Doubtless relieved that the Republicans had taken over the presidency from the openly racist Wilson administration by defeating his successor, James M. Cox, blacks generally found little satisfaction in Harding. He continued the Wilson policies of segregating federal employment, did nothing about a lynching law, despite some supportive comments about a law in his candidacy speech, and appeared abysmally ignorant of the American invasion of Haiti when questioned by black leaders in a private meeting. In one important speech Harding seemed to endorse segregated schools in the South, a position that would apply to other states as well. Harding's stance also meant that he would do little to stop increasing Jim Crow actions.[80]

JIM CROW AND THE KU KLUX KLAN

Jim Crow economic and political behavior often spilled over into Ku Klux Klan activity. The revival of the Klan in the early 1920s premised a "true Americanness," that excluded Catholics, Jews, and most of all sought to police the color line by intimidation of blacks. Strongest in the southern states, where the Klan wreaked savage violence and murder of blacks on the slightest pretexts, the organization was publicly evident in the north as well. The Klan established a headquarters in West Hoboken and met regularly at the First Reformed Church. Other Klaverns opened in Paterson and Elizabeth. Over 2,000 businessmen and other local men established a large Klavern in Newark at the Grace Methodist-Episcopal Church. The Klan was also strong in Asbury Park, Long Branch, Lakewood, Neptune City, and throughout Monmouth County. In Camden, the Klan was so potent that members patrolled the highways wearing U.S. Army uniforms adorned with organizational badges. Yet the Klan suffered from intra organizational squabbling and, importantly, heavily attended anti-Klan demonstrations. In Perth Amboy in 1923 a large mob, unrestrained by the police, attacked a Klan meeting at an Odd Fellows home with bricks and stones. Despite such counter protests, the Klan remained a significant nuisance throughout the next two decades.[81]

Despite the Klan's and other hooligans' threats, spring 1921 saw thousands of visitors including blacks mingling easily along the Boardwalk. African Americans used the famous rolling chairs, pulled by fellow blacks, and had no difficulty entering movie theaters and photography parlors "like anyone else."[82] Two years later, Kappa Alpha Psi, one of the largest black fraternities in the nation, held a stag party for a well-known Chicago physician and then listened to Ford Dabney's Jazz Band, fresh from a lengthy engagement at New York City's New Amsterdam Theater. In spring 1924, the Howard University singers entertained a mixed race audience at Young's Million Dollar Pier and the following year the Lincoln University Quintet sang on the pier before "some of the most prominent people of both races at the resort." The Atlantic City Field Club, an exclusive club of black gunners, showed remarkable ability in shooting clay pigeons in a public exhibition the same years. Black visitors also found new restrooms and shelter waiting for them. The most popular traffic cop in Atlantic City was Officer E. Eggleston Jr., a Newark native and son of a prominent minister. Eggleston won a popularity contest in early 1925 with more than 3,000 votes. The Black Elks female auxiliary, the Sunshine Charity Club, held annual teas in Atlantic City. Overall, blacks were still enjoying the nation's playground.[83]

Resident and visiting blacks in Atlantic City possessed sufficient muscle to convince the mayor of the city to refuse to show Thomas Dixon's inflammatory and racially objectionable film, *The Birth of a Nation*, in a local theater. A group of local ministers, the theater owner, and the film's distributor agreed to censor portions of the film that held blacks up to ridicule and humiliation. Battling distribution of the infamous film had been a priority of the NAACP since its release in 1915. Widely hailed by white Americans (President Wilson called it history written on lightning), the film angered blacks with depictions of their people as rapists, ignorant fools, venal politicians, and faithful but doddering idiots. Initially the film was enormously successful and NAACP members bickered over censorship and freedom of speech, allowing the picture widespread and easy distribution. Racist real estate agents handed out flyers for segregated housing units to the film's patrons. A white man shot a young black man after seeing the film. The film was revived numerous times and when future presentations were announced, NAACP branches moved into action. When theater managers in Camden attempted to show it in 1923, the local NAACP succeeded in having it barred. The film was also banned in Montclair and Newark. The Jersey City NAACP also succeeded in having *Birth of a Nation* barred from local theaters in 1931.

Seven years later, a theater owner in Orange was jailed for showing *Birth of a Nation* on the grounds that it was a pro-Nazi film. The manager then sued for damages, alleging false arrest. Montclair residents also charged that a local cinema was forcing blacks to sit in segregated seats and town officials charged the cinema with violations of the civil rights bill. New Jersey blacks maintained vigilance about demeaning films. In 1930, the Trenton branch of the NAACP sent an angry note to the town board of commissioners protesting the screening of a fictional portrait of Africa that included scenes in which African tribes purportedly offered women to gorillas as concubines. Protests also occurred in 1936 in Jersey City against the films *Prisoner of Shark Island*, *Frisco Kid*, and *The Barbary Coast*, which portrayed blacks as inferior or glorified lynching.[84]

As Jim Crow spread throughout New Jersey life in the 1920s, courage was required just to celebrate fraternal membership. The Knights of Pythias defied a local Ku Klux Klan warning not to parade through the streets of Trenton under threat of disruption and removal from the city. The Knights asked the state police for protection and the parade proceeded without incident. An Elizabeth minister publicly repudiated the Klan in 1921 and the Klan received another rebuff when Mayor Edward L. Bader refused to grant a permit for them to march in Atlantic City in late 1923. Undeterred, the Klan burned crosses outside of Atlantic City.[85]

The Ku Klux Klan convened in Newark in 1921 to warn against the scheduled appearance of pugilist Jack Johnson at a large assembly. They organized a branch in Atlantic City in 1922 and inducted seventy-five more members in Newark in December of that year.[86] Several years later the Klan burned a cross on the lawn of a building to warn black and white residents not to live together.[87]

Racial threats worsened in 1924. The Klan issued a warning to Reverend Crosby Wilson, pastor of the Galilee Baptist Church in East Trenton, and Police Commissioner George B. LaBarre told his officers in Trenton to "shoot to kill" in any racial disturbance. This order was denounced by the local NAACP. The Klan warned out several black families in Lawnside that summer.[88]

The Klan attempted to demonstrate racial amity by showing a benevo-lent side. Klan members helped the congregation at the Mt. Pisgah AME Church in Washington, New Jersey, to pay off the last of its mortgage. The pastor suddenly fell ill when he learned of the intended gift. A church stew-ard conducted the service, preached the sermon, and received the gift. On another, even more bizarre occasion, Klan members invaded the black Jethro Presbyterian Church in Atlantic City on a Sunday morning to inform congregants that they should expect to see eight crosses burned that night, but not by Klan members. In Pleasantville, 200 Klansmen accepted an invitation to attend services at a newly organized black church. Black congregants and hooded Klansmen sat in the pews as the new minister, Reverend Alfred Johnson, and the Klan leader prayed for the church's success.[89]

In 1926, white residents of Palisades Park protested when a black mail clerk attempted to buy a home in their town. Nearby neighbors of William P. Adams evinced no concern, but others in the town were vociferously angry. The mayor at first supported Adams, then changed his mind when confronted by angry white citizens.[90] In Kearney, the Ku Klux Klan burned a ten-foot cross to show its displeasure when a black man obtained a permit to build a new house in the community. Cravenly, the town council revoked the permit.[91]

The Klan objected to an early appearance by Paul Robeson at the Ocean Grove Opera House in 1925. The venue engaged Robeson in a series that had included Caruso and other noted singers. By coincidence, Robeson's con-cert immediately preceded a Klan rally. The Klan had no objection until the hooded ones learned of Robeson's race. Even as acoustic tests were made for the concert, other workmen constructed huge signs bearing the Klan's hate-ful messages. Despite the Klan's objections, all tickets for Robeson's perfor-mance rapidly sold out.[92]

BATTLING JIM CROW

The rise of racism, the need for community, and the recognition that the makeup of New Jersey's black population was changing prompted black

leaders to call for a New Jersey Colored State Fair to be held for the first time
in the first week of September 1929 in Belleville. Seeking to recognize the
progress Jersey blacks had made, plans were made for achievement exhibits
in addition to sporting events and other popular amusements. Oscar
DePriest, a Republican congressman from Illinois and the first black member of the House of Representatives elected outside of the South, was the
keynote speaker at the fair. DePriest lauded Jersey black achievement and
declared that "Negro leadership put me in Congress; nothing else did it."[93]
DePriest argued that if a grocer ran a store in a neighborhood that was
50 percent black, then half of his employees should be black. DePriest called
for full support of the Fourteenth Amendment to coincide with the Eighteenth Amendment. He was given a handsome brown felt hat made by the
Marvo Hat Shop in East Orange, which was owned by blacks and had all
black employees.

In the late 1920s, the mayor of Asbury Park ordered police officers to force
black sunbathers off the main beach to other parts "down where the colored
people belong." The NAACP sent a strong letter of protest to the city government, noting that blacks in Asbury Park paid more taxes than any other
seaside resort, Atlantic City excluded, and that the beach was public property just like the streets or library. One company did not get the message.
Local justice of the peace Amos Williamson, a black man, was walking
along the beach when guards employed by Edward T. Mitchell, a white millionaire, assaulted him, threw him into deep water, and attempted to drown
him because the rich man had given orders that "no Negro be allowed upon
that section of the beach." Supported by the NAACP, Williamson filed suit
for damages of one million dollars against Mitchell's Asbury Bathing Company, though there is no record of his success.[94]

The battle against Jim Crow was constant. Black fraternities and societies fought a bill in 1933 that would criminalize groups that took a name
close to that of another registered organization. Black organizations feared
that the new legislation would outlaw them, despite decades of history. At
their annual meeting, the New Jersey NAACP stated its opposition to the
bill. The NAACP also pronounced its disfavor of a Negro Migrant Commis-

sion and agreed to push for more black teachers in mixed schools in the state, an end to segregation in cinemas and theaters, and more jobs for blacks in public works projects. The fraternal groups won an amendment to the proposed legislation that allowed any group extant for three months before the bill's passage to be exempt from exclusion.[95]

THE DEPRESSION

Job loss in the Great Depression years hit New Jersey blacks hard. A 1932 survey estimated that over 30 percent of employable blacks could not find any type of work. Labor unions continued to deny membership to black workers, further hampering work possibilities. A vicious cycle existed for unskilled workers, in that blacks could not get jobs because they lacked skills and training yet they could not gain skills or training because they were barred from jobs. Only six of twenty-two unions canvassed by the state's Bureau of Statistics of Labor and Industries were open to blacks. Teachers also found opportunities limited. The city of Newark did not grant a single new job to a black teaches during these years.[96]

As the Depression worsened, Jim Crow grew stronger. Helen Jackson Lee, a widow with several children, tried to find work in the late 1930s to augment her dreams of becoming a writer. While her children were in class she "went into insurance, real estate and finance offices, banks, and department and five-and-dime stores. What did I see? A sea of hostile white faces." Whites, learned Jackson, controlled the typewriters and cash machines while "all my dark-skinned brothers and sisters were pushing the brooms, washing the windows, carrying out the trash . . . and attending public washrooms." Living in Trenton, the state capital, she never encountered a black clerk to take her insurance premium or a teller receiving her money at the bank. "And curiously enough, I had never seen a black garbage collector or street cleaner in Trenton."[97]

Relief efforts failed to reach the bulk of Jersey's black population. Few state blacks belonged to unions, which had the strongest lobbying abilities. Local blacks often worked in agriculture or, in the case of women, as domestics.

Federal programs for unemployment insurance excluded both types of
work. Protecting those who already had some buffer against poverty, unemployment insurance for example structurally excluded many Jersey blacks.[98]

The 1932 survey revealed variations in the effects of the Depression. Housing, unemployment, and black health were particularly bad in Asbury Park, a
town with a lengthy tradition of segregation. Plainfield, Bloomfield, Atlantic
City, and New Brunswick by contrast fared better with low illiteracy rates,
had steady professional classes, lower unemployment, integrated swimming pools, and active black political organizations. Black towns in
Cumberland and Gloucester Counties, with large influxes of recently
arrived blacks from southern states, suffered from high rates of unemployment. Overall, despite the human ravages of the Depression, churches and
YMCAs sustained communities and violent crime was low among blacks
throughout the state.[99]

Blacks accounted for nearly a quarter of the unfortunate on the relief
roles, despite being only 5 percent of the population. The Salvation Army
and Goodwill ministries barred blacks from lodging in Newark. Overall the
city had little or no housing for destitute blacks as none of the charitable
organizations had sufficient funds or facilities to help. They were also hampered by a general belief that generous assistance would attract massive
migration from the southern states, although most of black arrivals occurred
before 1932 and transients were from northern states, including New
Jersey.[100]

Segregation at charities was uneven. The American Legion Convalescent
Home on the north side of Atlantic City welcomed black veterans including
those disabled by gas poisoning in World War I.[101] At the same time, female
wards at the Long Branch Memorial Hospital were segregated even while
the men's wards were not.[102] The Salvation Army and Goodwill refused shelter to blacks, but segregation could be costly for these institutions. A wealthy
benefactor canceled his hefty donation to a Newark hospital after one of his
longtime black employees was refused care for tuberculosis.[103]

Blacks pushed for more jobs in relief organizations. Arthur Hays, a World
War I veteran and doctoral candidate at Columbia University argued in a

speech at a meeting of the Veterans of Foreign Wars at the Union Baptist Church in Orange that blacks were entitled to more spots in the Civilian Conservation Camps based upon the number of black veterans from the war.[104]

During the Depression, some Atlantic City blacks secured jobs with the Works Progress Administration (WPA). Blacks performed skilled and unskilled labor on a project resurfacing Baltic Avenue. More than 120 men of color worked on the project, which they finished ahead of schedule. Their success inspired a celebration attended by the mayor and other dignitaries.[105]

Generally, government relief did little for black children. Newark charities with government funds sponsored an educational camp for the daughters of unemployed black women. Nine instructors strived to raise the young women's moral and physical standards and to send them back to their communities with a "realistic attitude toward possible types of employment." Forty-give girls attended the first session of the camp and received simple instruction in English, basic economics, public health, and domestic science, a strong indicator of what the job training was about.[106]

Black churches strived to help victims of the Depression. African American denominations now made up as much as 11 percent of all churches in the state, and tried in vain to make up for government failures. Father Divine, the self-appointed God and leader of the Kingdom of Peace Movement, established three missions and two large hotels in Newark to provide inexpensive lodgings and meals for the poor.[107]

As the Depression deepened, the question of what black churches were doing for impoverished parishioners became contentious. Reverend Adam Clayton Powell of the Abyssinian Baptist Church, one of New York City's most noted congregations, in a public letter to Newark Jersey black Baptist clergy, castigated them because their efforts for economic sufferers were insufficient. The ministers took their time answering Powell. Their eventual response did not deny his sincerity but contended that his words had done them irremediable harm, saying that had they not seen Powell's name at the bottom of the missive, they would have thought it the "ranting of some restless Red, or some arch-enemy of the church." The ministers blandly asked

for more verbal charity and informed Powell that more people were suffering from gloom than from hunger. Despite these harsh criticisms, black
churches remained the mainstay of their communities. By 1938, there were
over four hundred black churches in New Jersey with total memberships of
more than seventy thousand people.[108]

The *Pittsburgh Courier* complained that white "overseers" of the poor
treated needy blacks according to their whims. One overseer kept a vicious
police dog in his yard to discourage applicants. Black supervisors also came
under harsh criticism. Speakers at a conference called E. D. Jones, black
adviser to the state WPA, a hindrance to black people who had allowed RCA
Victor and Campbell's Soup factories in Camden to discharge black workers and replace them with whites. Such losses were individual and also cost
the black community hundreds of thousands of dollars.[109] Blacks were out-
raged when the *Newark Evening News* sponsored a plan to convince a third
of New Jersey's black residents to return to the South by giving away railroad tickets.[110]

Camden survived the Depression. Known as the "city that works," Camden benefited from large factories including Campbell's Soup, New York
Shipbuilding, and RCA Victor Records, as well as a plethora of smaller businesses and professionals. European immigrants created self-contained
communities with churches and synagogues, social organizations, schools,
and housing. Eastern European Jews, Italians, and Poles all benefited from
Camden's prosperity. Blacks, who had been a presence in Camden since its
beginnings, were not allowed access to good jobs and better homes. Camden was, as Howard Gillette Jr., put it, as segregated as any southern town.
Campbell's Soup offered blacks only temporary employment, usually on a
seasonal basis, in lower paying jobs. In contrast, Ulysses Wiggins, a local
black doctor and head of Camden's NAACP for over a quarter of a century,
was able to convince RCA Victor to hire African Americans above the level
of custodian.[111]

As the Depression began to affect New Jerseyans, black churches stepped
up their universal charity. In early March 1930, the black Asbury M. E.
Church began to distribute food to unemployed black and white workers.

Cooperating with local butchers, grocers, and bakers, the church served substantial meals to those who had lost their jobs.[112]

Overall discrimination by government relief agencies and the scattershot abilities of private charity measures recreated the meaning of race in New Jersey and America. Because the Social Security Administration recognized two kinds of workers—skilled, unionized, white versus agricultural, domestic, black—and restricted aid to the first, African American victims of the Depression in New Jersey as elsewhere became identified as an underclass. This had occurred before of course, but now government relief programs reified the notion and anticipated such notions in the 1960s.[113]

Life was tenuous for blacks in New Jersey. A 1932 report found that about five African Americans died from tuberculosis for every white person who met the same fate in the state. Only three southern states had worse rates according to 1927 data. Children and women of color were especially vulnerable with death rates many times those of their white counterparts. This scourge was worst in Newark where 37 percent of tuberculosis deaths occurred among blacks who made up only 19 percent of the population. There were only two "Negro clinics" in Hudson County, which were used by the white and black population.[114]

Having lost their jobs and homes, black men in New Jersey joined the transient proletariat. Of the slightly over 10,000 persons applying for care in early 1934 at the state's transient bureaus, about 14 percent were black; six months later more than 20 percent were African American. In July 1934 about 16 percent came from Pennsylvania and New York. Other transient poor arrived from Ohio and South Carolina. Over 90 percent of transient blacks, the vast majority of whom were unskilled, blamed unemployment as the chief reason for their situation.[115]

Employers exploited transient labor. Big Jersey farms focused on single crops such as potatoes and cranberries. Black laborers moved up and down the Atlantic coast in search of work. Crew leaders gathered workers by truck and employers contracted with the crew leader, giving him all responsibility for housing, feeding, supervising, and even directly paying their proletarian laborers. Big farmers could contract an entire harvest to the crew leader. Wages were abysmally low at about seven to eight cents for a one-hundred-pound bag of potatoes, of which the crew leader took two or three cents. Congressional committees learned in 1939 that of twenty dollars paid for 250 bags of potatoes, the crew leader took eleven dollars and the rest was split among a gang of five men. These wages did not include hours of idle time when the sun was too hot to expose the potatoes. Not surprisingly, such depressed wages undercut any local workers' hope for work. Most New Jerseyans blamed these conditions not on the growers but on the migrants themselves. By casting guilt on the migrant workers, New Jersey citizens copied southern arguments that black farm workers were willing to labor cheaply and so caused low wages. Housing conditions were poor because black people did not understand or want modern conveniences. Soon, white New Jerseyans extended southern logic by attacking and torturing five migrant workers while they slept. Night riders, who turned out to be local college students, attacked black migrant workers in Cranbury, swearing to drive them out of Mercer, Middlesex, and Monmouth Counties. A local minister was fired after being implicated in the attack. Local blacks called for control of migrant workers, saying that they undercut their wages. The local NAACP called for the arrest of the whites who beat the migrants.[116]

Grassroots organizers attempted to unionize migrant agricultural workers. Strikers walked out at the giant Seabrook farms, located outside of Bridgeton, in 1934, just as black and white cannery workers faced off against police in Camden and Campbell's Soup prepared to arm its strike breakers. Black and Italian workers formed a union and elected a black farmhand, Jerry Brown, as president. The new union demanded improved wages above the subsistence level of $1.75 for a ten-hour day. When Seabrook fired Brown, more than 300 black and Italian workers struck, to the company's surprise. Seabrook settled quickly and Brown was replaced by professional organizers, both of them communists. During the summer, Seabrook lowered wages again, When workers struck, the company used goons and tear gas to battle strikers. State police strived to beat down and expel the organizers. Eventually, with federal mediation, the company recognized grievances but not the workers. There were few if any tangible gains for the strikers. At the same time, the strike showed that black and white workers could act together.[117]

The Black Middle Class

New Jersey blacks were able to eke out a middle class existence in the face of ferocious national and statewide racism. Walter Greason's study of the Russell, Ham, and Brown families through an able examination of family photos indicates the continued importance of church, societies, athletics, and, increasingly, professional work and military service to bolster black middle class status.[118] Moving into integrated society was hard and living in Princeton, for example, was difficult for blacks. Being admitted to the school was nearly impossible, but future judge Bruce Wright applied and was admitted with a full scholarship in 1939. Overjoyed, particularly because his family was poor, Wright arrived at the school and prepared to register. The university was apparently unaware of his skin color. An upperclassman spotted Wright, asked his name, and then told him that the dean of admissions wished to speak with him. Wright's admission was quickly revoked. He received a letter explaining that while his qualifications were fine, the dean "could not in good conscience" put him in an environment that would likely be hostile, especially because of the many southern students who had a "feeling that is quite different" from New England. Wright had sent a picture to Notre Dame, which rejected him immediately. Wright eventually was admitted to Lincoln University in Pennsylvania, which was "where all the black guys refused at Princeton enrolled." Deep into his distinguished judicial career, Wright indicated that he had never forgiven Princeton for its treatment of him.[119]

Despite the possibility of such mean-spirited rejections, blacks clearly saw education as the avenue to success. Famed baseball pitcher Joe Black recalled his father's insistence on the importance of excellence at school and did his homework on a table where his father prepared his own work. Black Sr. always attended PTA meetings and paid close attention to his son's progress. His mother was just as adamant. When the local high school placed Joe in technical courses "to better prepare him for work, as he probably would not go to college," Martha Black stormed into the school and successfully ensured that Joe was in the same classes as the wealthy white children. Despite their poverty, Joe Black's parents were determined that their son would receive a quality education.[120]

Other blacks used ties to paternalist whites to gain prosperity. Newark's black businessmen thrived in part because whites and blacks shopped on the same streets. Aided by white support, C. M. "Chicken" Brown operated a popular poultry stand at the city's Center Market. White firemen and policemen favored Mary and Frank Anderson's restaurant and hotel. Black caterers had customers across the color line, as did black carters, movers, and storage businesses. Mrs. Leah Lasher of Spring Lake near Asbury Park was able to overcome prejudice to establish a thriving laundry business. Upset over being derided as a "colored washerwoman," Mrs. Lasher and her husband Preston purchased a small home with their savings in Spring Lake, despite the protests of local whites. Well-to-do residents began calling at the Lasher home to get their laundry done. Her connections helped Lasher get better plumbing and acquire gas for the block. Soon she developed a sizable laundry business serving the largest hotels in Spring Lake and most of the prominent families. At peak season around Labor Day, the Lasher Laundry took in "heavy wash," and established such a positive reputation that one client sent her laundry from Europe.[121]

Women found opportunities for work in the beauty business. Black cosmetician Christine Moore Howell, born and raised in Princeton, operated a famous beauty salon there and was for many years an appointed board member of the New Jersey State Board of Beauty Culture Control. She published the book *Beauty Culture and Care of the Hair* in 1936. Doris Burrell operated a beauty salon in Princeton for fifty-six years after her graduation from the Simplex Beauty College in Newark.[122] Olivia Brown, a graduate of Newark schools and the Poro Institute of St. Louis, opened a beautician's shop in Newark in 1937. Several husband and wife teams owned laundries. Mrs. Viola Berry Dixon partnered with her husband, L. R. Dixon of Orange, to operate one of New Jersey's largest cleaning and dyeing plants owned solely by blacks. Mr. and Mrs. Joseph D. Herbert owned the East Orange Laundry Company and employed thirty people servicing several thousand customers of whom 98 percent were white. In a related company Helen Rowles Duncan owned a venetian blind business in East Orange. Other male and female Newark and Orange entrepreneurs included a candy retailer, a typist, postal clerks, an undertaker, and a chiropodist. Workers in the arts and education were rare.[123]

Black professionals gained prosperity despite the dismal shadow of Jim Crow. J. W. Rodman built a prosperous grocery business in Trenton. Dumar Watkins prepared slides for scientific instruction and research at Princeton University. William Jones of Newark was said to be the only African American jeweler in the world; however, exaggerated that claim, it still speaks to the respect he received. Mrs. Birdie Toney Davis of Jersey City was a widely known elocutionist and Jack Dabney became New Jersey's first black to pass the state embalming examination while starting his famous funeral home in Newark. Sara Spencer Washington of Atlantic City built a substantial black-owned business of nationally distributed black hair care products. Started in 1919, Washington's business, Apex Beauty Products, eventually operated eleven beauty culture schools that graduated more than 4,000 students annually. Apex employed more than 200 professionals and 4,500 salespeople. Washington staunchly resisted segregation especially in Atlantic City and built up a sizable empire of profitable real estate. Her hotel, Apex Rest in Atlantic City, included tennis courts, a dancing pavilion, and a croquet field. Washington opened a golf course and huge spa just outside Atlantic City.

Segregation had an unintended effect with the growth of black hotels. New Jersey had the third highest number of black-owned and operated hotels in the nation in the late 1930s. Washington bought other hotels to ensure lodging for black tourists and supported black political candidates. While hair styling had been considered frivolous in earlier eras, Washington promoted her products as empowering for black women. She accentuated the scientific quality of her work, argued that hairdressing promoted respectability and self-uplift, financial independence, and race pride. At her

death in 1953, Washington's estate was worth more than $1 million. She was
at the top of a network on black female beauticians. As much as the beauticians
admired Washington, their ultimate heroine was Madame C. J. Walker,
the famed cosmetics entrepreneur, first black female millionaire, and major
philanthropist, whom they honored annually with a walk to her grave.[124]

Very occasionally examples occurred of the rewards of faithful service.
A lucky domestic might find a lifetime payoff. Such was the case for Amelia
Stewart, a Trenton domestic who was bequeathed $50,000 in 1925 by her
employer, a woman named Woodward. Amelia's mother had worked for
Woodward and brought Amelia into the household when she was an infant.
Amelia worked there for thirty years, before receiving the legacy. Beating
back counterclaims by Woodward's sister, the newly wealthy Stewart soon
married a dental student at Temple University who was also a graduate of
Bordentown.[125]

Professional study brought middle class status to Jersey blacks. After several decades in which there were but one or two black doctors in northern
New Jersey, their numbers and prominence increased in the 1920s. By 1927,
sixty black dentists were registered in New Jersey.[126] Dr. A. A. Phillips, a
graduate of Howard University Medical School became a district physician
in Newark in 1933 at a salary of $1,000 per year. Ulysses Wiggins, a migrant
from Georgia, graduate of Lincoln University and University of Michigan
Medical School, became a prominent physician in Camden.[127] Other middle
class blacks worked in nonprofit organizations or cultural affairs bureaus.
Joseph W. Bowers, an experienced YMCA director, became the director of
the first black YMCA in the Oranges in 1917 and served in that post for more
than twenty years.[128]

New Jersey's black middle class spawned several talented female historians. Dorothy Burnett Porter (1905–1995) was a child of middle class parents
in Montclair. Porter went on to have a distinguished career as a librarian
and historian of abolitionism.[129] New Jersey's first great black female historian was Marion Thompson Wright (1905–1962). She was born in East
Orange, the fourth child of Minnie Holmes Thompson, a housekeeper, and
Moses R. Thompson; her parents separated when she was very young. She

had two stepfathers. Despite her troubled upbringing, Marion Thompson graduated at the head of her class from Barringer High School in Newark, one of the city's best schools.

Thompson nearly failed to graduate from Barringer. While in high school, she married William Moss and had two children, Thelma and James. Her mother disliked Moss and encouraged her to divorce him. Marion left the two children with Moss, finished high school, and enrolled at Howard University. Howard, like many white coeducational colleges, restricted its student class to never-married women. Marion disguised her status, abandoned her children, who were then raised by her mother, and was constantly fearful that her early family would be discovered and her career destroyed. She received her BA and MA degrees from Howard. After her graduation and eventual employment, Wright had a second short-lived marriage to Arthur M. Wright, a postal worker, though she retained his name after their divorce. The imbalance in their status was reflected in her findings on black education in New Jersey. While working during the Depression for the New Jersey Emergency Relief Organization, Wright participated in a massive study of 10,000 people that demonstrated the greater opportunity in the state for black woman and men. It also confirmed the huge disparities of opportunity between white and black wages, the prevalence of black teachers at black schools, and the growing problem of "delinquency" among young black males.[130]

Although she spent most of her academic career at Howard, New Jersey remained the focus of Wright's research. Her foremost work was her doctoral dissertation, *The Education of Negroes in New Jersey*, which detailed black education in the state from the colonial period to the early twentieth century. Wright earned her PhD at Columbia University and was the first black woman to receive a doctoral degree in the United States. Gunnar Myrdal cited her work in his massive study, *An American Dilemma: The Negro Problem and Modern Democracy*, and it was prominent in the briefs for the major 1954 Supreme Court case Brown v. Board of Education, which dismantled the rationale for segregated schools. Wright was highly critical of the Bordentown School, which had served as the model school for young

Figure 13. Marion Thompson Wright (1905–1962), an East Orange native who became the first African American woman to earn a PhD in history. Wright was a prolific author on black New Jersey history and a key advisor for the 1954 Brown v. Board of Education decision that ordered national school desegregation. Courtesy of the Moorland-Spingarn Research Center, Howard University Archives.

Jersey blacks for several generations. Her scholarship was thorough and well respected, receiving numerous favorable reviews in contemporary black journals. She also published many articles on New Jersey history and served as a professor at Howard University from 1929 to 1962.

Wright suffered from lifelong depression and eventually committed suicide. Her principal biographers contend that Wright was the victim of unfair criticism of her life choices and scholarly devotion, which caused her to neglect her children. Hers was the dilemma of the black female intellectual for generations to come. Her legacy inspired future black historians of New Jersey, including Clement Price, Giles Wright, and Lawrence Greene, who composed a Marion Wright Club to bring together black historians of New Jersey. Today, the annual Marion Thompson Wright lectureship at Rutgers University–New Brunswick is a highly prestigious event.

Childhood racism embittered even the most successful. The Morrows of Hackensack were high achievers. The grandfather, Reverend John Samuel Morrow of North Carolina, was a prominent educator. His son, John Eugene, moved to Hackensack and became a prominent minister. The eldest daughter, Nelly, earned a state teaching certificate and began teaching white students. The Klan organized a petition of 1,500 parental signatures protesting Morrow's placement and she was transferred to the lowest level classes.[131] The first son, John, won an honors scholarship to Rutgers on his way to becoming a diplomat and ambassador. When he graduated magna cum laude in 1931 with a degree in French, he was compared favorably with Paul Robeson, who also had shown that color was no barrier to success. The second son, E. Frederic Morrow, also achieved important positions in his lifetime. He addressed the Young New Jersey Republicans as a high school student and later graduated from Bowdoin College, worked for the NAACP in New Jersey, served in the U.S. Army in World War II, and was discharged as major of artillery in 1946. Despite his success and his closely knit family, E. Frederic Morrow's autobiography of his childhood years chronicled the meanness of petty racism, limitations that local schools placed upon Morrow and his talented siblings, and the "iron ring of defeatism," that pervaded the lives of young black residents of Hackensack. Morrow recalled that such an atmosphere made him "a disgruntled, defensive child," who regarded his teachers as personifying "the cruel plot to keep him in embarrassed and abysmal ignorance." Only his family's strength and determination, which set them apart and kept young Frederic socially ostracized, sustained his future. Morrow took little stock in black religious or secular culture. In an argument that resonated across the decades, Morrow despised the white Republican political candidates who would speak before black voters, invoke the memory of Abraham Lincoln, and then leave with no promises of benefits. Despite these misgivings, Morrow remained a Republican Party member and later became much more visible.[132]

Political support of the Republican Party spawned no real jobs for local blacks. In the 1920s, there was one lone black Assemblyman from Essex County. Oliver N. Randolph, holder of the post, left the assembly in 1923 after his appointment as a special assistant federal attorney, "the first race man in the state to hold a high Federal position." Beyond that, party favors created only jobs as janitors and elevator operators. Attempts to create black policemen, firemen, and sanitation workers failed.[133]

Middle class blacks created private refuges. In 1921, the Progressive Realty Company of Westfield purchased a formerly segregated golf course, renamed it the Shady Rest Country Club and Golf Course, and made it a home for black golfers. Shady Rest became the finest black retreat in the state and among the best in the nation. From the beginning, there were no social boundaries as businessmen and porters were equal members; their wives enjoyed conversation on the wide verandas as children chased fireflies. Club president B. C. Gordon noted that Shady Rest created "an atmosphere among refined ladies and gentlemen." Shady Rest overcame a power struggle in 1925, with one contingent making off with the club treasury. William Willis Jr., a successful black taxicab company owner, rescued Shady Rest from insolvency. Shady Rest then rose to become a haven for top black golfers. In 1932 John Shippen, considered the best black golfer of his era, became the club professional and superintendent. Tennis was also a key sport among Jersey's black elite. Throughout the 1920s, the New Jersey Tennis Association conducted tournaments, ranked players statewide and nationally, and held classes for children. Its work was also done on the local level.

Shady Rest was one of several major venues for black social and political events. Ten thousand blacks gathered at Shady Rest in May 1923 to hear a speech by W.E.B. Du Bois. Du Bois routinely spoke at events in New Jersey, appearing at conclaves of black teachers in Asbury Park, the Bordentown YMCA, the State Federation of Colored Women's Clubs, the state Normal School at Trenton, and at the Plainfield Forum in the 1920s. Du Bois was the keynote speaker at the Monmouth County Emancipation Celebration in 1931, an event sponsored by the local Elks.[134] Other nationally known blacks came to speak in New Jersey, including A. Philip Randolph, head of the Union of Sleeping Car Porters, who spoke at a Youth Conference in Newark in 1930. The Montclair YWCA was a significant attraction and featured appearances by Du Bois, Langston Hughes, and jazz composer Noble Sissle.[135]

There were also lovely artistic events. To cite just one of many terrific concerts held within the black community, Charlotte Wallace Murray, a noted mezzo-soprano gave a lecture-recital at the Fort Heel High School on the place of the "Negro Spiritual in American History," discussing the Fisk, Tuskegee, and Hampton Choirs and singing arrangements by such renowned composers as H. T. Burleigh and R. Nathaniel Dett.[136]

SPORT AND MUSIC

The Atlantic City Bacharach Giants were the finest black New Jersey team in the early twentieth century. Named after Harry Bacharach, the mayor of Atlantic City (and father of the famous composer Burt Bacharach), the team enjoyed heated rivalries with top squads from New York, Philadelphia, and Chicago. A Newark team formed in 1924. After creation of the National Negro League, the team played in the Negro World Series and boasted such stars as Dick Lundy and Orville "Ghost" Marcelle before the league broke up in 1931, a victim of the Depression.[137]

Two years later the league was reincarnated as the Negro National League. The most famous team was the Newark Eagles, first known as the

Dodgers and operated by the legendary Manley family. Abe Manley emerged from Newark's gambling world. His wife, Effa Manley, the beautiful, hard-nosed co-owner of the Newark Eagles, was also prominent in the city's NAACP and helped organize boycotts of local businesses that refused to serve blacks. Effa Manley worked hard to ensure that opening day crowds were packed with celebrities and had leading white politicians throw out the first ball. The Eagles were among the best national black teams from 1935 to 1948. Known for underpaying her players, Manley demanded compensation from major league baseball when her most talented players, including a number from New Jersey, such as Monte Irvin, Don Newcombe, Larry Doby, Joe Black, Ray Dandridge, and John Henry "Pop" Lloyd, joined the majors. As in the case of other forms of entertainment, baseball provided young black New Jersey males with pathways to careers.[138]

Black Jerseyans found some opportunity and enjoyment in jazz. In the 1920s, Newark became a hotspot for touring musicians including Florence Mills, Buck and Bubbles, and Bessie Smith, who played at Miner's, the Orpheum, or at movie theaters. In the 1930s, Newark was a maze of theaters, clubs, and after-hours joints for sporting people. Stride pianists Willie "the Lion" Smith and Donald Lambert were Newark-raised musicians who became immensely popular locally and across the Hudson River in New York. Newark's jazz scene later produced female vocalists Miss Rhapsody and the immensely popular and influential Sarah Vaughan.

Resort towns fostered black musical talent. Growing up in poverty in Red Bank, bandleader and composer Count Basie was inspired by traveling carnivals and early motion pictures to bolster his dreams. Filling in one day as a piano player at the local film theater, Basie mastered the instrument. He was also an adept drummer. Soon he was featured at vaudeville shows around Red Bank and later graduated to larger venues in Asbury Park and then on to New York City and international fame.[139]

Jim Crow extended to the arts. Entertainers performing in Newark, then known as a mecca for jazz in the 1930s, were required to stay in rooming houses or with friends until the opening of the black-owned Coleman Hotel. Fans wishing to see and hear such traveling stars as Ella Fitzgerald, Duke

Ellington, or Sarah Vaughan were banished to the upper balconies of down-town theaters.[140]

By 1933, the effects of the Depression had ravaged the New Jersey middle class. Seven banks in Atlantic City failed in February 1933, taking away the savings of Sarah Spencer Washington of the Apex Hair Company ($30,000), the Ocean Temple of the Daughter Elks ($15,000), noted figures including attorney Isaac Nutter, churches, taxi companies, undertakers, and the YMCA. Atlantic City schoolteachers had not been paid in four months. Mayor Harry Bacharach announced his government would issue script to meet the back pay of 412 instructors.[141]

In addition to battling economic woes, Jersey blacks had to battle Jim Crow constantly. The state Supreme Court determined in 1933 that segregating children by race in school swimming pools was "unlawful discrimination." Chester Patterson, father of Thaddeus Patterson, a junior at Hackensack High School, instituted the suit after his son was barred from using the pool with his white classmates. At the same time, the NAACP found that Newark schools allowed blacks to use their swimming pools on Fridays, then the pools were "drained, cleaned and refilled" for use by white students on Monday.[142]

The New Jersey State government continued to issue laws barring discrimination in the 1930s. In the summer of 1933, Governor A. Harry Moore signed legislation that barred contractors doing state work from discriminating against workers because of race, creed, or color. The bill had previously passed unanimously through the house and the assembly. Moore credited the NAACP for pushing forth the legislation and noted that the bill used language supplied by its national office. The immediate sponsor of the bill was Assemblyman J. Mercer Burrell of Newark, the only black member of that body. New Jersey joined Indiana as the only states in the union with such a law.[143] Blacks continued to make modest political gains in 1931. Kanelon D. H. Boyd was elected county magistrate in Passaic County. At thirty-two years of age, Boyd was the youngest black magistrate in the nation.[144]

Segregation happened during leisure time at the Atlantic Ocean. Atlantic City beaches were increasingly segregated. A 1930 *Pittsburgh Courier* report indicated that blacks who sunbathed and swam in front of major hotels were increasingly pushed out. At one point white hoteliers constructed a stone wall to keep out black bathers; swimmers simply moved around it. The NAACP investigated attempted beach segregation. Walter White, Secretary of the NAACP, informed local Congressman Isaac Bacharach, brother of Mayor Harry Bacharach, that there was no legal basis for the discrimination. The brothers replied that no one had complained about the police clearing the beaches of black bathers. White noted that many blacks were employed at the hotels and were reluctant to speak out, and that the police were effectively silencing others. Meanwhile blacks were still finding rooms at the hotels for holidays, but were unable to swim in the ocean. In 1938, the Atlantic City council announced an ordinance designed to avoid congestion on the beaches that allowed for badges, insignias, and other forms of identification for the beaches. Black activists quickly denounced the ordinance arguing that its purpose was discriminatory and that suits would follow any violations of civil rights. In the summer of 1938, the *Pittsburgh Courier* announced, a wave of Jim Crow behavior swept New Jersey as swimming pools advertised signs for "colored" and "white" days. Elizabeth authorities ordered local pools closed after young black men who used it found their street clothing soaking wet and tied in knots. It noted that several young fellows had drowned in the nearby bay because they were not allowed into the public pool. Restaurants and taverns up and down the highways displayed signs stating that they were open only to white patrons. One explanation was that the use of segregated schools taught everyone that discrimination was normal social behavior. A few weeks later the pool was reopened with mandatory access to all. In an ugly incident, whites hurled tomatoes as four young black males tried to enter the pool.[145] Beaches were not the only site of contention. Several black couples filed suit against the

Atlantic City police in 1932, charging that the cops had beaten them without provocation right in front of their homes.[146]

Advocates of discrimination kept up their hateful efforts. State Senator A. Crozier Reeves of Mercer County introduced a bill that would effectively ban black fraternities and associations from public display of the regalia, emblems, pins and buttons without first registering for approval from the secretary of state. Prominent blacks including Counselor Nutter, grand treasurer of the Elks, and other fraternal officers called on Reeves to ask him to reconsider the bill.[147] The NAACP even had to correct discrimination against dead people. It was successful in convincing a cemetery owner to remove "colored" and "white" signs from graves. The owner had claimed that he was just trying to help identify the race of the interred, but agreed to take down the signs.[148]

When a white policeman beat a black man in his cell in Red Bank in 1930, the International Labor Defense Council rallied hundreds of black workers to assail the policeman's brutality. The black man, John Wilson, had been arrested in error for assault; when the cop entered the cell to whip him with a black jack, he snarled that if they had been in the South, he would have lynched him. The New Jersey State Troopers were little better. Trying to get a confession out of a suspected robber in Salem, troopers took Earl Giles, a teenager, to a morgue, lifted him into a coffin, and clamped the lid down. In a hearing about police brutality, other blacks complained that they had been beaten without warrants in their homes because they would not give evidence about robberies. The troopers were arrested. After the NAACP's investigation, the troopers were charged with assault and battery. The organization charged that the beating of Giles was just one of many such assaults as the state police conducted a reign of terror against young blacks. As a result of the troopers' brutality, membership in the NAACP soared. The director of public safety in Newark suspended a policeman for slapping a respectable black woman.[149]

The NAACP was willing to intervene in the most racially charged cases. In 1936, a young black woman, Willa Hempfield, was going home by car from a social affair in Princeton with two friends when a car driven by white men crashed into them. An argument ensued in which Edward Thompson, a young black man, was beaten senseless, Hempfield was kidnapped and raped. The NAACP sought full charges against the white men.[150]

Jim Crow attacks on young black women inspired increasing public ire. In late 1937, Laura Almond, described as an attractive and cultured young black woman, took at seat along with another woman, Mrs. Audrey Tilden, in the whites-only section of movie theater in Atlantic City. The usher called the manager of the theater to move the ladies. After threatening and verbally abusing the women, the manager pulled Almond violently out of her seat, dislocating her shoulder. After Almond filed assault charges, a grand jury refused to indict the manager, infuriating the black community. Thousands of flyers blanketed the city denouncing the decision not to indict. The NAACP and other groups quickly intervened. Almond appealed to the district court. Almond and Tilden inspired young blacks. Edith Savage-Jennings, just thirteen years old in 1937, initiated a long and distinguished career as a civil rights activist by refusing to sit in the segregated balcony at a Trenton movie theater.[151]

Even the wealthy experienced increased discrimination. A prosperous dentist who failed to reveal his race on a real estate application found his purchase of a mansion in East Orange canceled by a Chancery court. The dentist decided not to appeal the decision as he had multiple offers from other locations not blighted by Jim Crow.[152] The NAACP pursued even the most trivial discrimination. A Paterson tavern owner was told she could not display Jim Crow signs that informed patrons that one type of glass was for whites and another for blacks.[153]

Jersey blacks fought back individually and in groups. Black World War I veterans uttered bitter words as segregation spread in 1930s New Jersey. Needham Roberts killed twenty-four Germans in one day in November 1918 and received a Croix de Guerre from the French government. Now with prejudice widespread, Needham contended that whites were insufficiently grateful to blacks who had fought to defend the country. In support of Roberts, white war vets refused to use a Jim Crow park for their Flag Day festivities. Dean William Pickens of the NAACP attacked the Daughters of the Revolution for their scandalous refusal to rent a recital hall to famed singer Marian Anderson by recalling the blacks that fought for the British against the slave owning Yanks in the American Revolution.[154]

To combat racism a civil rights group used a creative "sit-in" approach in 1937 to Jim Crow seating arrangements at Atlantic City theaters. As planned, whites sat in large groups in the "colored section," while an equal number of blacks did the opposite. Their efforts were successful as several theaters dropped policies pushing blacks into the balcony. Unimpressed, the leaders of the Atlantic City Civil Rights Enforcement League planned more actions for the autumn.[155]

Chappy Gardner, a reporter for the *Pittsburgh Courier*, claimed that money, not color prejudice caused white businessmen to call for segregated beaches. He reported that one black couple, Mr. and Mrs. R. A. Walker, took out a half million dollar lease on a restaurant and bath building right on the Boardwalk and enjoyed patronage from whites and blacks. Continuing his investigations, Gardner found that local theaters were Jim Crowed. Blacks sat in the gallery rather than the main floor even for performances by Cab Calloway and Duke Ellington. The management explained the segregated policy as a means of preventing blacks from hurting others when fights occurred.[156]

Some individuals took very particular approaches to the color line. William E. Jackson of Montclair, a prosperous carpenter, refused his fiancée's plea to state that he was white on their marriage license, after the Ku Klux Klan burned a cross on his front law after learning of the prospective union. Jackson, a graduate of Lincoln and Columbia University was seven-eighths Irish and one-eighth black, and was considered black. He had previously married a black woman and had two children with her before obtaining a divorce in 1922. His prospective wife, a twenty-year-old white women and a telephone operator, pleaded with him to designate himself as white. When the couple appeared before the county clerk that wrote "colored" on the license, the young lady then decided to postpone the wedding. W.E.B. Du Bois, hearing of the case, poked fun at the clerk and asked if he was one-eighth Jewish, would he be considered a Hebrew. Despite her parents' opposition, the woman declared she would marry Jackson anyway, stating "I am tired of going around with cake-eaters and sheiks. He is a fine man, gentlemanly and courteous, and he thinks of worthwhile things."[157]

White parents objected publicly to prospective marriages between their daughters and black men. Lillian Pristop's parents kidnapped her when she declared her love for John Stoke Jr. Lillian announced that "all the other white girls wanted Johnny," because he has a "snappy car and makes $125 a week." If "I don't marry him, some other white girl will." Unimpressed, her parents threatened to shoot the young man if he followed through with his promise to take Lillian to New York City for a marriage license. To thwart such plans the parents spirited Lillian away to an undisclosed location up the Hudson River. The couple's courage was particularly evident in a state where the Ku Klux Klan attempted to police any mixed-race unions. In 1923, the state Grand Dragon claimed without any proof that "87,000 white girls were living with negroes and members of the yellow race," practices he decried as attacks on civilization. The Klan was sufficiently anxious about female sexuality that it held a "Mother's Day" tribute in an Ocean Grove auditorium in 1925.[158]

Young women at elite levels could push aside racial barriers. Vivian de Maurice Opydyke was of French-Canadian ancestry and was adopted by a wealthy black Newark couple, the Charles Ruffins. Vivian spent her early life traveling in elite Jersey black society. She became one of the most popular members Girl Friends Society, an upper-class club for black girls. In 1935, Vivian suddenly left the Ruffin home because she had fallen in love with a wealthy young white man, Charles Opydyke. After their marriage, Vivian hosted a party for the Girl Friends at her new home, demonstrating her skills at navigating racial borders. Three years later she and her parents reconciled and held a large party for the Girl Friends at their home. Vivian's husband did not attend.[159]

Another instance demonstrated the extreme isolation a black person could feel in a largely white, even Ku Kluxed, environment. John W. Underhill, the only black man in Mays Landing, was a poor, candy store operator.

When he died at the age of eighty, he bequeathed $100,000 to white churches in the town, but only $500 to his two sisters. To show their appreciation, the entire town of 2,800 whites turned out for his funeral, which was conducted by several white pastors. Underhill was lauded as an intellectual who had studied the subject of evolution thoroughly. Rather than inter Underhill's remains in the black section of the cemetery, he was buried in the white section under a tall, specially designed monument.[160]

In the midst of the hardening racial lines and rise of Jim Crow in New Jersey, blacks could take some comfort in the friendship of a world genius. Albert Einstein, the brilliant physicist, fled Nazi Germany and settled in Princeton, New Jersey, at the Institute for Advanced Studies. Einstein observed the sharp prejudice against blacks in Princeton and likened it to anti-Semitism in Germany. Unwilling to accept such attitudes, Einstein struck up friendships with local blacks, both prosperous and poor. He was frequently seen walking the streets with them and bicycling to their homes. He became especially close to Alice Satterfield, who worked in the kitchen at the Institute for Advanced Studies. Children recalled his kind behavior. Shirley Satterfield, Alice's daughter, recalled with delight sitting in the genius's lap and loving his wild hair, shaggy sweaters, and that he never wore socks. Einstein was liberal with candy and small coins to other local black children. He honored the great as well. Paul Robeson and Einstein met after the singer gave a homecoming concert at McCarter Theatre Center at Princeton. The scientist warmly shook Robeson's hand and told him how honored he was to meet him. Later they discussed their mutual hatred of fascism. When Marian Anderson was refused lodging at a local hotel, Einstein invited her to stay at his home, which she did frequently. Einstein promoted Paul Robeson's return concert at local theatres helping staunch the wounds suffered by the Robeson family decades before. And Einstein was willing to sign any petition the NAACP presented to him to battle discrimination.[161]

During the interwar period, New Jersey blacks faced increasing virulent racism in all walks of life. Rather than adjust to racism, New Jersey blacks fought back, employing the tools of social activism via the NAACP and women's organizations and pushed the Republican Party to expand benefits and rights. When the party dithered, male and female state African Americans shifted to the Democratic Party of Franklin D. Roosevelt. Given black people's enduring loyalty to the Republican Party and the Democratic Party's embrace of racial supremacy and Jim Crow, this shift was nearly revolutionary. Blacks did not cut all ties with the Republicans, but rather learned to be more adept in their political choices. Neither political party helped much during the Great Depression and state blacks were forced to endure and find solace in their own institutions. At the same time, African Americans maintained a robust culture behind the veil. From that they gained strength for battles, both military and political, during World War II and beyond.

CHAPTER 6

World War II and Its
Aftermath, 1940–1960

The U.S. entrance to World War II in 1941 offered a renewed opportunity for African Americans in New Jersey and elsewhere to demonstrate their patriotism and at the same time demand equity and overcome the potent Jim Crow policies that had been put in place over the previous two decades. Given that the draft gave blacks little choice about military service, leaders crafted a double V strategy: victory in the world and victory at home. Triumph in America meant ending discrimination broadly and enabling blacks to gain equality. This was clear nationally. White leaders were more sympathetic than they had been in years. President Franklin D. Roosevelt issued an executive order in 1941 barring racial discrimination in defense employment.

Black leaders were not satisfied with the slow pace of progress, A. Philip Randolph, head of the Brotherhood of Sleeping Car Porters, which had a number of New Jersey members, organized a march on Washington, D.C., in 1943 to protest racial injustices. While the plurality of black Americans vowed patriotism through military or civilian service, leading activists (including W.E.B. Du Bois) expressed grave reservations about war against Japan, which he perceived as a nonwhite nation. Du Bois infuriated the Nationalist Chinese, who were key allies against Japan, by minimizing the 1937 Nanjing Massacre and arguing that Japanese domination of China was preferable to Euro-American colonialism. Black drives for equality benefited from improved social attitudes. It was hard for American politicians to maintain support for Jim Crow during a war against Fascism. Whites generally became more receptive to black demands. As President Roosevelt acknowledged, discrimination undercut the war effort. After the conflict ended, racial discrimination damaged American claims of superiority over communism. As a result, racial liberalism became more legitimate. The most significant event was President Harry S. Truman's 1948 order banning bias in the armed forces and in federal jobs.[1]

Black New Jersey's patriotism was evident. Almost 25,000 New Jersey black men served in the U.S. armed forces during World War II. More than 20,000 enlisted in the army, 3,697 served in the navy, and 481 joined the marines. The coast guard had only one black New Jersey serviceman. The Women's Army Corps enrolled eighty-nine New Jersey women. Many Jersey blacks served with distinction, earning Bronze Stars, Purple Hearts, Legion of Merit awards, and the Oak Leaf Cluster. Many came from state national guard units while others were from black state militia units organized after World War I. On the home front, nearly 2,800 black volunteers served as nurses' aides and drivers and in blood donor programs. About 6,000 Jersey blacks took part in the state's Office of Civilian Defense activities.[2]

Even as American blacks demonstrated their patriotism by enlisting in the armed forces, racial problems persisted at military bases. Many of the nation's soldiers mustered at Fort Dix, which was sixteen miles southeast of Trenton. Troubles soon arose between military police, often southerners intent on maintaining Jim Crow methods, and black soldiers, who refused to accept old ways while at the same time fighting for their country. Riots occurred and soldiers were killed.[3] Racism at war camps discouraged blacks. To support his family, writer James Baldwin worked in 1943 to help construct the Army Quartermaster depot at Belle Meade, New Jersey. Working and living with southerners, white and black, at the depot traumatized Baldwin. He recalled that what happened at defense plants and camps marked for him, as for many blacks, a turning point: "To put it briefly, and somewhat too simply, a certain hope died, a certain respect for white Americans faded."[4]

Population Changes

Major demographic shifts occurred in New Jersey during the war and afterward. Migrants from the southern states increased the state's black population by 40 percent, from 226,973 to 318,565. The second major trend was continuation of the vast shift to urban living. New Jersey blacks made a net migration of 112,084 between 1940 to 1950. By 1960, the state's black population was 73 percent urban, the exact opposite of the state's black makeup in 1910. Most of this occurred in northern cities in the state. Overall, the number of blacks in New Jersey surged from 226,000 in 1940 to 770,000 thirty years later. As the number of blacks increased in urban New Jersey, so did their demands for political power.[5]

New Jersey in the aftermath of World War II underwent nearly revolutionary changes: booming suburbanization and creation of shopping centers occurred as cities suffered sharp demographic declines and impoverishment. New Jersey's cities, especially Newark, suffered because wealthy and middle-class whites moved to suburbs that were now increasingly accessible via express roads, built to support the new developments. Reflecting rapid demographic changes, Weequahic High School, one of the cultural hearths of New Jersey's Jewish population (Philip Roth made it the setting of numerous novels) transformed rapidly in the 1960s to a nearly all black student body. Cities also lost major industries. Newark, for example, lost companies that produced scissors, meat products, thread, metalwork, and crafts. Newark's population dropped dramatically after 1950 and, according to Robert Curvin, was now run by Italians. The city experienced long-term corruption and a powerful criminal underworld along with ethnic strife. Despite these problems, Newark was a small city with big dreams.[6]

The State and Segregation

State reform started just before World War II. Assemblyman Frank Hargraves introduced a bill in 1938 to establish a commission to investigate the state of black New Jersey and to uncover patterns of discrimination. His bill called for the appointment of a fifteen-person committee of blacks and whites. The New Jersey Assembly voted to fund $30,000 to create a seven-man commission. There was opposition including a senator from Salem County who stated that as New Jersey had funded more than a million dollars for the Bordentown School, it had "done enough for the Negro." Even proponents found the bill lacking, noting that there were funds for clerical work but nothing for executive or investigative staff. Governor A. Harry Moore vetoed the bill arguing that there were already state agencies to do such a job and that the allotted money would be a "gift to the Negro." Then for some reason, the governor changed his mind and accepted the bill. Hargraves, who had recently been defeated in his bid for reelection, was named chairman of the commission. Lester Granger, a long-time associate of the Bordentown School, was named director at a salary of $300 per month. Granger announced that he planned to quiz industrialists over their hiring patterns, with an aim of getting more jobs for blacks in private and government work. A scramble for jobs quickly emerged at the commission itself.[7] One of the first findings of the new commission was that the 1932 report was inadequate and had covered up terrible conditions in black New Jersey life.[8]

Blacks advanced in local political power during the war years. By 1945, the bulk of Democratic district leaders in Newark were African American. James Curtis, a black Republican, won election to the Assembly in 1947, followed by another black Republican, Edward T. Bowser, Sr., who captured a suburban assembly seat in 1951. Reverend Raphaeus P. Means became the first black elected to the Essex County Board of Freeholders in 1954. Madeline Rogers, an NAACP leader from East Orange and a Democrat, was elected to the assembly in 1957. Several blacks served on the Newark Board of Education in the 1950s and others held positions such as chairman of the Newark Housing Authority and Felix Fund housing projects. Despite these gains and others on the municipal level, large problems in housing and employment plagued black life.[9]

Proponents of desegregation and civil rights benefited from the new national mood by linking segregation with fascism during and after the war. New Jersey's Urban Colored Population Commission asked in 1943 if a dual educational system did not prove the rightness of Hitler's rants about racial superiority by "raising a new generation of little Fascists."[10] To battle fascism among the young, black and white children willing to grapple with racial issues found summer homes at the Brotherhood Camps (despite the name, girls joined boys in attendance) sponsored by the National Conference of Christians and Jews. One large camp was located near Newark. The head of the camp, Walter Chambers, a Newark native, had attended segregated schools in the 1940s, then worked on the Mayor's Commission on Group Relations when local schools desegregated in the next decade. As a black man, Chambers sought to change the image of African Americans into something more than a "statistic and a problem," by inspiring young people to use their intellects and emotions to care about solving the nation's massive racial problems. James Horton, a Newark teenager, argued that camp members were nice people who needed to learn that racial issues were very real and permeated discussions of God's intentions for people: "did God intend us to be separate from each other?" Horton asked his campmates.[11] Horton felt a sense of destiny after his father explained to him the immense possibilities of the 1954 Supreme Court decision, Brown v. Board of Education.

Initially, reform resembled individual efforts of earlier eras. There were, as in previous eras, "firsts" and individual achievers. Bamberger's, the preeminent Newark department store, begin employing more blacks, albeit as elevator operators and washroom attendants. Bamberger's had started hiring blacks in 1909 but stepped up the numbers during World War II. However, the store hired no black sales or administrative personnel.[12] Newark's Bill Cook became the first black disc jockey in the New York region and subsequently launched his own television show, *Stairway to Stardom*. Later, investors established the first black radio station. On the first anniversary of Cook's show, Billy Eckstein, Sammy Davis Jr., and other stars turned out to celebrate.[13]

To gain civil rights, New Jersey blacks took matters into their own hands, aided by the NAACP and eventually the state government. New Jersey black parents were quick to seize the opportunity and demand better schooling for their children. Black parents in Pleasantville protested exclusion of their children from a nearby school; the children were directed to walk six blocks along the railroad tracks to a segregated school.[14] Black parents, frustrated with the poor quality of segregated schools, began to boycott them. They began with a major protest in Hillburn, New York, on the northern border of New Jersey. Hillburn was the residence of many established black families such as the van Dunks, de Groats, and other descendants of Creole blacks from the seventeenth century. Hillburn had long had separate but unequal schools, a system that black teachers and local patriarchs defended. The NAACP, led by attorney and future Supreme Court Justice Thurgood Marshall, organized boycotts that lasted months. These efforts spread to other towns in the north and particularly in New Jersey. Organized mostly by mothers, boycotts in East Orange, Montclair, Toms River, Long Branch, Fair Haven, and Mount Holly were grassroots efforts. They demonstrated the splits within northern black communities over black separatism and integration and, as argued by Thomas J. Sugrue, foreshadowed the major battles in northern metropolises in the 1970s.[15]

The NAACP's broad reach across a sizable New Jersey membership helped focus and energize the movements against Jim Crow and toward equality during the war. The NAACP announced that it would "fight to the bitter end" against restrictive racial covenants planned for future housing developments in Nutley. Under pressure from the NAACP, the town of Livingston ended its restrictive covenant. In 1941, the NAACP and the *New Jersey Herald News* initiated a powerful challenge to segregation when they attacked the adequacy of the curriculum at the Bordentown School. The NAACP also published a general study of the state's segregated school system that year. Dorland Henderson, head of the New Jersey Conference of the State Branches of the NAACP, initiated a vast program to end Jim Crow education in the state. The NAACP convinced the Federal Workers Union to end bias in 1944 and the NAACP worked closely with the state attorney general to create a civil liberties division tasked with enforcing desegregation.[16]

Two cases filed by aggrieved parents in 1943 set the stage for integration of New Jersey's schools and were precursors to the famed Brown v. Board of Education, which established the right to integrated schools across the United States. In Hedgepeth and Williams v. the Board of Education of the City of Trenton, Berline Williams's son, Leon, had attended six grades as the only black student in his school. After promotion to junior high, he was directed to attend a black school sixteen blocks away from his home rather than a school for whites just three blocks away. The board of education informed Williams by letter that no black students had ever been allowed at the closer school, which also boasted a college-oriented curriculum. The school further away was substandard, offered no foreign language instruction, and was badly overcrowded. Another Trenton student, Janet Hedgepeth, had experienced similar discrimination and joined the case. In 1944, the New Jersey Supreme Court ruled in the students' favor, stating that the Trenton Board of Education was guilty of discrimination and ordered the students admitted to the better school. The case established precedent and was cited in the Brown v. Board of Education decision. Today, a junior high school in Trenton is named after Williams and Hedgepeth. In New Jersey the case underlay the decision to create a fair-employment commission the following year and set the stage for the 1947 constitution, which forbade racial discrimination in public schools around the state.[17]

Grassroots politics drove civil rights actions during the war and after. Ernie Thompson, born in Maryland, began work as a construction worker helping to build the Holland Tunnel to New York City. Nearly killed in a workplace accident, he moved to the American Radiator Company, where he organized fellow black workers seeking job security and better pay. Although his initial foray into organization failed, he successfully aligned his workers with the United Electrical, Radio, and Machine Workers of America (UE). In 1943 Thompson became the first black organizer for the UE, a post that lasted until red-baiting destroyed the union in 1953. Disenchanted with the Congress of Industrial Organizations (CIO), which had created a rival union to the UE, Thompson was a charter member of the

National Trade Union Conference for Negro Rights. One of his family friends, Paul Robeson, helped Thompson attract worker-members. The National Trade Union Conference led to the formation of the National Negro Labor Council (NNLC), of which Thompson became director of organizations until it was disbanded under right-wing pressure in 1956. Thompson and his wife, Maggie, a white woman from Ohio, moved into Orange to battle against racial gerrymandering that kept local schools segregated. His New Day program demanded an end to discrimination in the schools, recreational programs, pushes for fuller employment for blacks, and assistance to all families displaced by the new highway system. Aided frequently by Robeson, Thompson worked tirelessly for years to achieve these goals.[18]

Thompson's work with the IUE and the National Negro Labor Council expanded its compass to help female black workers. During World War II, the IUE won pay increases for women workers in General Electric factories and ended pay discrimination in a number of other local plants. Thompson identified the GE tactic of hiring black women only for the night shift to keep them apart from white women working during the days, a method that promoted disunity. He helped Thelma Jones file a complaint to the New Jersey Department of Labor, Wage and Hour Bureau, against Westinghouse Lamp plant in Trenton. Jones claimed successfully that her job as matron had the same responsibilities and tasks as higher-paid, male janitors.[19]

Returning black New Jersey veterans insisted upon equal treatment. Having risked their lives in the military, few vets were willing to accede to segregation. One four-year veteran from Montclair reasoned his support for an end to segregated public facilities, declaring that "I'm tired of being kept out of places where any bum, prostitute or criminal can go without questioning, but not a Negro. If that's democracy, then I don't want any part of it." Black newspapers decried segregation at home as similar to the oppression of Fascism and Nazism. A second black New Jersey newspaper published a "Jim Crow Guide" to the United States and compared the nation's race relations to those of Hitler's Germany. Indeed, there were few tangible benefits for blacks remaining in the military; the most significant was President Harry S. Truman's Executive Order 9981 mandating desegregation of the armed forces. Military leadership procrastinated even then, but later wars in Korea and Vietnam showed that delay was inefficient, making way for true integration.[20]

Black New Jerseyans honored their veterans. There were frequent stories about the activities of local black soldiers and occasional profiles, including some who were career soldiers. One such article covered the life of Major William J. Jackson. The officer had first enlisted as a "doughboy rifleman" (infantry) in a regiment of the New Jersey National Guard in 1936. He was called to active service in 1941 at Fort Dix and enrolled in the Army Officer Training Corps. He later fought in the battle of Pusan during the Korean War, achieving the rank of Third Battalion Commander, Sixtieth Infantry, in 1951. He studied at Rutgers and was married with three children.[21]

Building on the heroism of black military men, New Jersey civil rights organizations pushed all levels of government to integrate and dismantle discrimination throughout society. A committee drawn from many organizations and headed by A. Philip Randolph, a prominent activist, met in Butler to demand that President Harry Truman end segregation in the armed forces.[22]

On April 16, 1945, Governor Walter E. Edge, now in his second stint in office, signed a bill sponsored by Dr. James O. Hill, enacting the New Jersey Law Against Discrimination and creating the Division Against Discrimination (now known as the Division on Civil Rights). Hill, a state assemblyman from Newark, drafted the law to prevent discrimination on account of race, creed, color, and national origin or ancestry.[23]

Despite the legal gains, New Jersey's blacks were often unable to share in the generous government grants that enabled their white peers to move rapidly up the social ladder. Stymied by racism in government agencies, more likely to be burdened by a dishonorable discharge than whites, blacks were generally unable to profit from the G. I. Bill, which funded college educations, faced discrimination and were channeled into low-level jobs by the Veterans Administration, and found themselves "redlined" from getting government-supported housing loans. Private housing covenants excluding black homebuyers were common and inequality extended to education. Burdened by New Jersey's localized property tax support for schools, young urban blacks faced inadequate school facilities and poorer futures than their white, suburban peers. Even though black majorities in Newark paid more per capita in housing taxes than nearby Montclair and Bloomfield, the net worth of their property was less. Accordingly, the percentage of black home-owners in Newark in 1960 was 27.2 percent, far less than the near 45 percent in Bloomfield, 61 percent in Montclair, or 73.2 percent in nearly all-white Milburn. Newark's median family income was almost one-third of Mil-burn's and only 31 percent of Newark's employed persons worked at white-collar jobs compared with 75 percent in Milburn.[24]

New Jersey's children showed militancy. Newark High School students turned down an opportunity to participate in a contest sponsored by the Daughters of the American Revolution (DAR) in protest of the organ-ization's refusal to permit singer Hazel Scott to perform in its Constitution Hall in Washington, D.C. The state's branch of the Congress of Industrial Organzations (CIO) recognized the group's courage with an award, but the issue did not end there. The New Jersey branch of the Daughters of the American Revolution (DAR) tried to mediate with the organization's national office to remove the "whites only" clause from the guidelines for use of its Constitution Hall. All this occurred of course seven years after the DAR's refusal to let Marian Anderson sing in the hall had shocked and appalled the nation. The New Jersey delegation strived to liberalize the DAR to little avail. Shortly afterward, black New Jersey women initiated a new organization known as the Improved DAR that would accept all races, espe-cially those who were "descendants of slaves."[25]

Blacks protested restrictive public ordinances and customary discrimi-nation. Allie Bullock of Long Branch sued successfully to bathe at any of the town's beaches, rather than be shunted to one reserved for blacks. Randolph Wilhemsteen of Newark sued a barbershop in 1944 for refusing service because of his race. The suit was later dismissed because barbershops were not specifically listed in state antidiscrimination laws.[26]

The NAACP helped aggrieved New Jersey blacks in personal ways. It filed a successful injunction against Georgia authorities' attempt to extradite Sam Buchanan of Newark, who had served fourteen years on a chain gang for allegedly stealing two packs of cigarettes. He had escaped and then was picked up on charges of vagrancy in Newark. The local branch fought the extradition and Buchanan was freed. Later the NAACP petitioned Governor Alfred Driscoll to fight the extradition of Jasper Lark (aka Anderson Salter), who had escaped from an Alabama prison where he had been incarcerated after a conviction of the rape of a white woman. Lark, who had settled in New Jersey, married, and fathered a son, insisted that he had been framed.[27]

The NAACP was prepared to utilize the new liberalism in New Jersey government. Some of the organization's staff had personal backgrounds in the state. Robert L. Carter joined the NAACP in 1944 after a stint in the army. A graduate of Lincoln University and Howard University Law School, Carter had grown up in East Orange and was the first to integrate the town's high school swimming pool. That experience plus the hazardous racism in the army made him commit to change. Carter served as Thurgood Marshall's top assistant for over a decade.[28]

Jersey blacks benefitted from the government's new opposition to open prejudice. The Klan marched in Jersey City in 1939 after a series of unexplained arson cases. The Klan "strutted" through Wanaque and Butler in February 1940, and were greeted with boos. They burned crosses in Demarest in late 1946 and in Wall in 1948. In response the state government revoked the Klan's charter to operate in the state. Governor Walter Edge declared that "there is no place for the Klan in New Jersey." In October 1946, the state attorney general outlawed the Klan for violating the U.S. Constitution and for advocating and fomenting racial violence.[29]

Churches and fraternal organizations helped the cause. The Methodists and Baptists met at conventions in Atlantic City and East Orange advocating integration and better economic opportunity for blacks. Ministers continued to be significant contributors to New Jersey's black population. Cleric

Milton A. Galamison preached radical sermons between 1947 and 1949 at Witherspoon Presbyterian Church in Princeton, where Paul Robeson's father once preached. In his sermons, Galamison attacked racism and anti-Semitism, and, in a brave message following World War II, militarism. Galamison regarded Christianity as a revolutionary ideology and identified Jesus and Paul as social radicals who stood up for the poor and oppressed. Christian practices and following the scripture, he contended, were the best pathways to economic and social justice. Although Galamison's tenure at Witherspoon was brief before he departed to become the minister at the distinguished congregation of Siloam Presbyterian Church in Brooklyn, New York, he personified the socially conscious younger postwar black New Jersey clerics.[30]

New Jersey black political power at the national level remained limited. Hampering efforts was the malignant power of the Federal Bureau of Investigation (FBI), which regarded all integrationist efforts as communist and closely tracked Paul Robeson and others it suspected of radicalism. The FBI kept close tabs on black organizations in New Jersey during the war years and beyond. In addition to its sizable surveillance of New Jersey native Paul Robeson, the FBI maintained a field office in Newark and hired informants in Atlantic City, Jersey City, Trenton, and Paterson to keep tabs on state NAACP, CORE, and Urban League activities. The FBI kept a close eye on the Moorish temples and on fringe groups that espoused anti-Japanese war attitudes. Always interested in what it perceived as communist allegiances and actions, the FBI reports uncovered very few communist sympathizers in New Jersey: confidential sources indicated that there were only 370 black communist party members in a state population of about a quarter million African Americans. The report argued that the numbers showed general black skepticism toward the Communist Party. Overall, black dissatisfaction had more to do with incidents of racism.[31]

The push for black civil rights and integrated schools accelerated in the postwar years. The state NAACP released a study that told of inequalities across New Jersey. Black students in Berlin attended a two-room "colored school in bad condition." In West Cape May, black students studied in an annex to the white school. White students were bused past the black school to their own building. In Mount Laurel, the white and black schools were one block apart. The Moorestown school did not offer Latin, French, or algebra, all of which were required college preparatory classes. Sixty communities in New Jersey had at least one "colored school." Teachers at the schools for blacks had instructional loads three times their white counterparts.[32]

The NAACP's concerted drive and the strong protests by black parents convinced the state to create a Division Against Discrimination and to amend its constitution barring segregation on grounds of race, creed, or color. Historian Thomas J. Sugrue has hailed this law as one of the great civil rights successes of the postwar period. In late 1946, the state employment service stated that it would no longer refer candidates to any employer who discriminated based upon race. The state department of education started investigating and enforcing its rules in 1948 and issuing cease and desist rules in 1949. There was much to be done. One potent rule outlawed the practice of dismissing black teachers because of their race. As a result, the number of black teachers soared by almost 75 percent between 1943 and 1954, despite the closing of a number of black-only schools. Successful integration efforts occurred in Mount Holly, Princeton, Toms River, Camden, Atlantic City, and Asbury Park. The Trenton School Board announced that it would abolish its Jim Crow school practices in 1946. In Camden, the school board resisted demands for integration, arguing that black parents had not requested transfers for the children into white schools. The NAACP then advertised the opportunity to black parents and ensured payment for the costs of any legal actions. Sugrue argues that New Jersey's integration efforts typified the limitations of efforts made in the North. For all the victories schools often remained segregated de facto because housing was racially homogeneous. In 1947 an NAACP study found that over fifty school districts, mostly in the southern counties, used explicitly segregated schools. A state study, done a year later, concluded the same and led to withdrawal of state funds from recalcitrant districts. This method proved effective and soon integration was achieved in many, but not all districts. Some schools flatly refused or gerrymandered their catchment to exclude blacks. What the

Figure 14. Harold Lett (1908–1989). Principal black activist for the Union
League and New Jersey state government. Newark Public Library by permission
of *Newark Star-Ledger*.

drive did mean is that the NAACP was forcing the state to live up to its own
laws. Guided by New Jersey's example, Pennsylvania's educational system
conducted a similar survey with concurrent findings and actions.[33]

 After a decade of leaning toward the Democratic Party, New Jersey blacks
returned to the Republican Party with the election of the racially liberal

Governor Alfred Driscoll, in 1947. After 1945, the NAACP gained support from the New Jersey state government. Dorland Henderson worked closely with Joseph Bustard, an experienced state school administrator who was named the newly created Director of the Division against Discrimination (DAD). His assistant director was Harold Lett, a long-time officer of the Urban League, and the educational director was Myra Blacklee, head of the New Jersey Goodwill Commission. The DAD held many public hearings to persuade and conciliate contending parties, a method that developed skills for negotiations, as the division studied and acted upon inequities in the school system.[34]

Using his position to push reform, Bustard studied the constitutions of other states to determine methods of protecting the civil rights of minorities in preparation for New Jersey's constitutional convention, scheduled for 1947 and the first in over a century. The DAD recommended borrowing from New York's charter that mandated equal protection for all citizens regardless of race, color, creed, or religion by any firm, corporation, or by the state and any of its agencies. After some modification, New Jersey became the first state in the union to outlaw segregation in public schools or in its militia. By banning segregation, the state undercut older methods of justifying separate but equal schools. Having sustained this major accomplishment, the state, with the strong assistance of the NAACP, moved to end segregation in schools.

In April 1947 the NAACP released a comprehensive survey of schools in fifty-two communities in eighteen counties around the state. Marion Thompson Wright contributed substantial research to the project. The survey indicated the degree of segregation and inferior facilities in towns in southern New Jersey, Monmouth and Essex Counties, and in the Newark area. Initially local school officials informed the NAACP investigators that segregated schools were necessary as they were the only means by which black teachers could be hired and that local blacks requested racially defined schools. The NAACP referred back to the 1884 opening of the Brook Street School in Long Branch on a segregated basis. The NAACP concluded in its report that the teaching load in black-only schools was three times that of

white-only schools, that most black parents did not know they had a right
to send their children to integrated schools, and that custom and entrenched
racism belied New Jersey laws against separate but equal schools.[35]

The survey found overcrowding in black Cape May schools that were
located just fifty feet away from less-crowded white schools. Black teachers
across the state were often fired during budget crunches. The white Mount
Holly school had a lunchroom while the black-only school did not. White
students in Moorestown took Latin, French, and elementary algebra in
junior high school while black schools lacked these subjects. One-room
schoolhouses abounded in black communities. Buses were not available to
black students in Penns Grove and Berlin, in Camden County, had a two-
room "colored school in bad physical condition," with outdoor toilets and
an outside pump. Further north, schools were integrated but black teachers
were classed as "permanent substitutes." There were no black teachers in
Perth Amboy, Metuchen, or Middlesex, while Trenton, Jersey City, and
Asbury Park had black teachers in mixed schools. Toms River, the focus of
much NAACP work in the 1920s, used a crude elementary school located
"out in the woods." Overall, while there were a few towns with mixed schools
and that employed black teachers, the bulk of New Jersey schools were segregated and used deficient facilities for black students. Shortly after publication of the report, one NAACP official contended that New Jersey's school
were more Jim Crow than any other state north of the Mason-Dixon line.[36]

Further legitimacy occurred in the New Jersey's revised constitution in
1947. Only the third in the state's history after 1776 and 1844, the new constitution mandated school desegregation and pushed for economic equality,
particularly from directives made in state supreme court decisions. Governor
Alfred E. Driscoll ordered that all schools be immediately integrated, a
motion that most towns chose to ignore or obeyed grudgingly. One immediate change was the removal of the word "colored" from the state-supported
training school at Bordentown. As a sign of black gratitude, the Black Elks
awarded Driscoll their Elijah Lovejoy Award in recognition of his distinguished public service in the area of civil rights.[37]

Blacks sued successfully for integrated schools in Trenton. The state supreme court mandated reassignment of white and black students to ensure integrated schools. The following year the Asbury Park Board of Education ordered the integration of its elementary school, though numerous white students withdrew to enroll in a parochial school. In a move that historian Marion Thompson Wright called "a dramatic historical event," Governor Driscoll received a constitutional draft that outlawed racial discrimination in civil and military rights, public schools, or religious principles. Spurring Driscoll were the efforts of Congressman Emanuel Celler (D-NY), who announced plans for a series of new congressional laws outlawing segregation. Wright enthusiastically noted that the draft was the first occasion in which a state put language into its basic charter banning segregation in public schools and the militia. She credited Oliver Randolph, a lawyer with a degree from Howard University, with pushing through this charter reform and directly linked his struggle with free blacks of the antebellum period who sought unsuccessfully to ensure the vote and ban discrimination. Written largely by Deputy Attorney General Oliver Randolph, the only black delegate of the constitutional convention, the law toughened the state's drive against Jim Crow. Wright then commenced a series of articles detailing black New Jerseyans' historic struggle for legal equality up to the Civil War. Joining her optimism was Joseph L. Bustard, the state's Assistant Commissioner of Education, who also hailed these events as proof that New Jersey was leading the nation in integration of its schools and public facilities. In November 1947, New Jersey's voters ratified the new constitution.[38]

Desegregation made some Jersey African Americans uneasy. Blacks in Princeton were concerned about their children's safety. They perceived Witherspoon High School, integrated since 1916, as providing the best education available. However, black students graduating from the school did not receive diplomas but rather certificates of achievement. Princeton schools formally integrated in 1948 to little fanfare. All children in grades one through five from the borough would go to the previously all-white Nassau Street School. All students in sixth through eighth grade attended the

Witherspoon School, formerly the famed Witherspoon School for Colored Children, but now integrated. Immediately black students had better books and supplies.[39]

However, combining schools was only part of the battle. In 1996, graduates of the segregated Witherspoon School recalled that the all-black school had built character including pride of race, the importance of hard work and seizing opportunity, respect for women, and reverence for black history. In an integrated school, black students faced hostile and prejudiced teachers who did not hesitate to use racial slurs in class. Social clubs disappeared. Black students were tracked into nonacademic curriculums and often never had an opportunity to see a guidance counselor. Black students had customarily gone to historically black colleges and continued in doctoral and professional programs in medicine, engineering, theology, and law. In the years after desegregation, the number of Princeton black students enrolling in colleges after high school dropped dramatically, curtailing the employment prospects of a generation.[40]

The NAACP scored a significant victory in 1948 when Camden agreed to drop housing requirements that barred black students from attending integrated schools. Even so, the NAACP admitted the victory was incomplete because the Camden Board of Education refused to hire black teachers and maintained separate primary and junior high schools. The NAACP continued the pressure on Camden and pushed harder on schools in Long Branch. Future U.S. Supreme Court Justice Thurgood Marshall wrote a number of the comments and recommendations on actions in Long Branch, including notes about threatened Ku Klux Klan activities. By 1947, the NAACP forced the local board to integrate its schools. In 1952 Stanley Lucas of Atlantic City became the first black to head an educational system in the United States. By 1952, 425 black teachers taught in secondary and elementary schools in nine counties in southern Jersey.[41]

Governor Alfred Driscoll, whom the *Pittsburgh Courier* called a "man of destiny," made a large step toward desegregation in early 1948 by eliminating Jim Crow practices in the state militia. Within weeks, new divisions organized on nonracial basis, as black World War II veterans flooded into the ranks. At the same time army units in New Jersey remained segregated.[42]

Private organizations began to desegregate. The YWCA adopted a thirty-five point program to end discrimination in early 1946 and the YMCA desegregated months later.[43] When private businesses continued to practice Jim Crow, activists quickly confronted them. The United Public Workers, CIO, blasted an Atlantic City restaurant for refusing to serve blacks; similar grievances were stated against a Chinese restaurant in Newark. The NAACP pushed hard to prod the street and bus companies in Atlantic City to hire black drivers and mechanics. The CIO had better luck integrating the Trenton Westinghouse electrical plant in 1946 and used New Jersey as the site to announce its national ambitions to end poll taxes and job slavery in southern states. Overall, the national CIO hesitantly embraced desegregation, refusing to write antibias clauses into its constitution, while offering young New Jersey blacks scholarships to Fisk.[44]

Desegregation efforts moved into the arts. The Montclair Museum worked with the Harmon Foundation to create a special exhibition by black artists Palmer Hayden, William Ellsworth Artis, and Ellis Wilson as a means to "proceed toward racial understanding." At the same time, black artists had to turn to race-defined organizations for exposure; for example, black opera singers worked through the American Negro Opera Guild for auditions. White organizations such as the Rotary Club provided scholarships for talented young black artists to attend college. The NAACP moved to censor racially denigrating films, convincing Universal Studios to drop a demeaning cartoon short called "Scrub Me Mama."[45]

Blacks fought in 1947 to integrate the swimming pools at Palisades Park in Fort Lee, a white-only working class resort. The park's owner, Irving Rosenthal, used a typical excuse to exclude blacks by announcing that the resort was a private club. The Congress for Racial Equality (CORE) and the Modern Trend Progressive Youth Group organized nonviolent stand-ins, in which young blacks lined up near the pool's ticket booths and chanted: "Don't get cool at Palisades Pool, get your relaxation where's there's no discrimination." They succeeded in closing down the pool in the first week of

July. Then, Palisades Park security guards, many of them off-duty police-men, manhandled the protestors. The local police chief announced that blacks were not allowed in the pool but could use the park, if they behaved themselves. Beatings of protestors continued. Unknown to them, the Mafia controlled the police force, a fact revealed in state testimony several years later. The *New York Age* deplored the crackdown and compared the Park's owners with southern racists. CORE denounced the violence against the protestors and filed successful civil rights suits against Palisades Park, which continued to discriminate on the basis that it was a private business, and thereby beyond federal regulation. That argument did not convince the U.S. Court of Appeals that decided that the sale of tickets to the park constituted a contract in which blacks had equal protection with whites under federal law. In the case of State v. Rosecliff Realty, the New Jersey Supreme Court ruled that racial exclusion at swimming pools was prohibited by the 1935 state civil rights act. In 1949 the State of New Jersey outlawed discrimina-tion at swimming pools. Nonetheless, the park owners resisted change and claimed that the protestors were communists who would not be admitted into the pool. In 1953, a black woman dancing poolside with a white man was evicted because her pedal-pusher pants did not meet pool dress codes, despite the fact that such attire was routinely fashionable. When asked if she was a communist, the woman, Minnie France, an editor and journalist, replied that she was a Catholic. CORE continued to push integration at the pool but the long effort to bar blacks had created a hostile and tense atmo-sphere, thereby discouraging them from using it. As Martha Biondi has argued, the incident demonstrated the distinctions in the pre-Civil Rights Era between de jure discrimination in the South and de facto segregation in the North. At the same time, the protestors' efforts did result in changes for open access in New Jersey law.[46]

In 1949, New Jersey African Americans gained a major victory when the Freeman Bill unanimously passed the state legislature and Governor Driscoll signed it into law a few weeks later.[47] While black civil rights had been guaranteed since the nineteenth century, the new law guaranteed equal access to schools, restaurants, stores, hotels, public transport, theaters, and beaches. Violations were punishable by fines and jail terms. The bill also created slots for many additional black teachers. Yet the NAACP had to continue the fight to end local discrimination. For example, the city of Orange declared that the new law did not apply to segregated veterans' housing. The NAACP successfully sued to end discrimination there and in Newark. The *New York Age* blasted the army for maintaining segregated barracks at Fort Dix, a problem that continued into the early 1950s. One commentator wrote in the *Pittsburgh Courier* after the war that southern white officers could be very nasty especially under the influence of alcohol. The anonymous writer complained of cliques among the black officers and described many of them as "Uncle Toms" who followed illegal orders without question.[48]

The new law did not however apply to housing. Discrimination in housing did not become illegal until 1957 when Governor Richard Hughes vowed to pass amendments to the 1947 constitution that barred discrimination in house and apartment rentals, motels, trailer camps, and resorts. Hughes claimed that the new Democratic majority could overrule Republicans who had blocked the bills for years.[49]

Housing discrimination remained rampant. The NAACP represented black residents of Perth Amboy when they protested local government's refusal to allow "qualified Negro families" access to the newly constructed low-cost William Dunlap housing project. The government told black applicants they would be giving spots in a segregated project to be "built sometime." Similar attempts to exclude occurred in Trenton. In 1944, the city of Orange attempted to block the purchase of homes by educated black professionals. A few years later white neighbors in Newark attempted to bar Amy Spencer, a black veteran, from entering a home she had purchased on the spurious claim they were holding the home for another veteran. In 1949, a superior court judge ruled that the city of East Orange could not discriminate in housing, especially against a group of nine veterans who had initiated the suit. Judge Alfred A. Stein stated that the plaintiffs had lived up to their responsibilities as citizens, had made dangerous sacrifices for their country, and that common sense dictated that if there was no racial segregation on the battlefield, there could not be any in Orange's housing.

He rejected the defense's argument that similar housing would be available on a racially exclusive basis in the future.[50]

New Jersey African Americans did not accept housing inequality passively. Newark Civil Rights activist Harold Lett complained bitterly that the real estate market was rigged to favor whites and that blacks had to pay more to get less. Even those blacks who earned sufficient income to buy homes in the suburbs faced opposition, as segregation affected those with incomes of $50,000 incomes as much as those who were much poorer.[51]

Even well-known athletes experienced problems buying homes. Larry Doby was raised in Paterson before he became a famous baseball player for the Cleveland Indians. He and his wife were rebuffed in their attempts to purchase a large home near Paterson. Doby declared his anger about the situation and argued that if he could not get a home in New Jersey, his family would move to Cleveland, where "the people have been especially nice to me." After the New York Age publicized their anger, multiple offers appeared to keep the Dobys from moving out of the state.[52]

Buying a home was not the only problem. For the next decade, black activists challenged discrimination on private property. At the same time, the development of malls and suburban towns helped real estate agents, retailers, and consumers create new kinds of segregation. Equally pernicious was the negative effect of malls and shopping centers on black employment, which existed largely in the downtown urban districts. The NAACP, Urban League, and CORE pushed such major retailers as Macy's and Bloomingdale's to hire more black clerks, rather than restrict them to low-level positions as elevator operators, porters, custodians, and wrappers. These drives to integrate the workforce were largely successful until shopping malls created a new environment for suburban, middle-class consumers with automobiles. In the years after World War II, as economist Robert Gordon has shown, American automobiles improved in convenience, power, and affordability as consumers traveled easily between home and work on improved government highways. Airline travel became inexpensive, less noisy, and safer. All this occurred on a racial basis as whites benefited and blacks generally fell behind. One major example was the decline of New Jersey's downtowns. As blacks moved into

Jersey's cities, they did not benefit from the improving economy. Between 1963 and 1992 every major department store in Newark closed, leaving gaping holes in the downtown landscape and marooning urban blacks who did not own cars. Newer malls and office buildings were constructed like forts, with lobbies on the second floor and retail spaces in atriums and courts. Prosperity gained visual and psychological exposure in cinema and television with their entirely white casts and settings.[53]

The Police and Jersey Blacks

New Jersey's police used harsh tactics with young black men. In early signs of a future plague, police initiated arrests of young blacks for selling heroin. The state government cooperated with southern states that wanted black felons returned. Police arrested a youth named William Henry Harris in Newark in October 1946 on charges of escaping from a chain gang in South Carolina, where he was serving four years for his part in an armed robbery. To ensure Harris's return, the police used a device known as an "Oregon," by which heavy chains connected a ring around his neck and a u-bar around his ankles.[54]

The case of the Trenton Six indicates just how deeply racism was ingrained in the justice system of New Jersey. On January 27, 1948, the *Trenton Evening Times* reported sensationally the murder of a white, elderly used-furniture storekeeper named William Horner and blamed the death on several young black "thugs." Police, using limited evidence, soon rounded up six young black men and charged them with murder. Their trial, before an all-white jury, and replete with numerous procedural errors, resulted in convictions and automatic death sentences. Few showed any interest except for Bessie Mitchell, the sister of one of the condemned men. She could not convince the NAACP or the American Civil Liberties Union to intervene, but succeeded in attracting the support of a leftist, New York City organization, the Civil Rights Congress. Together Mitchell and the committee garnered public outcry by naming the case "Scottsboro North," in reference to a notorious miscarriage of justice fifteen years earlier. Their appeal attracted the intervention of Paul Robeson, Thurgood Marshall, Eleanor

Roosevelt, Josephine Baker, Pete Seeger, and Albert Einstein. Even Klan cross-burnings did not deter them. America's black newspapers gave the case ample coverage. Mitchell's brave crusade resulted in reversals by the New Jersey Supreme Court; subsequent retrials found one man guilty and acquitted the others. Collis English died in prison before the trial.[55]

POLITICAL FRUSTRATIONS

The Republican Party in New Jersey may have been helpful, but the national organization downplayed civil rights from 1946 to 1954, when the Brown v. Board of Education decision forced its attention. Paternalism ruled Republican responses, just as it had in earlier eras. Consider the case of E. Frederick Morrow. After establishing himself in New Jersey and following a tour working on Dwight D. Eisenhower's successful 1952 presidential campaign, Morrow rose to become administrative assistant to the chief executive, the first black man to hold such an elevated post. He later became vice president of Bank of America's international division. The election of Eisenhower to the presidency in 1952 saw a national plunge in black party affiliation as the Republican Party dropped to less than 14 percent, coming mostly from the middle classes in the northern states. Morrow was aware of the frustrations and complexity of his position. He regarded himself as responsible for explaining the attitudes of black people to the administration while conveying to his race the administration's frequent equivocation over civil rights. Morrow worked behind the scenes, but often to no avail. Despite his constant prodding, Morrow could not convince Eisenhower to condemn the vicious murder of Emmett Till in Mississippi in 1955, despite an admonition that the nation was on the brink of racial war. Morrow was dismayed when an Eisenhower administration cabinet member denounced blacks as insufficiently grateful for civil rights advances. His position did not carry over past Eisenhower's election. Despite Morrow's pleas, no job opened until the 1956 election when the president decided that he needed a stronger presence among African Americans. Morrow then became the first black presidential special assistant, though the job largely concerned allocation

Figure 15. Cover, *Black Man in the White House* by E. Frederic Morrow (1906–1994). After a distinguished career with the New Jersey Union League and the NAACP, Morrow was appointed special assistant to President Dwight D. Eisenhower, a post Morrow found deeply frustrating. Author's collection.

of parking spaces. Morrow experienced sharp racism in Eisenhower's office and in the segregated capitol. Yet, he, a lifelong Republican, also made more than 300 speeches defending Eisenhower's slow-moving civil rights policies to black Americans. In one sad instance he persuaded baseball hero Jackie Robinson not to participate in a Youth March on Washington, citing communist infiltration. Morrow worked hard to get Eisenhower to abide by the Brown v. Board of Education decision and achieved a meeting between the president and civil rights leaders, an occasion that had little significance outside of its occurrence. Richard Nixon was one of the few in the administration who befriended Morrow, though often with condescension. When Morrow eventually left the administration in frustration, Eisenhower did little to help him get a job in the private sector. When Morrow prepared a book for publication detailing his experiences, an angry Eisenhower threatened publishers with a personal boycott if they printed his former aides' memoir.[56]

Morrow campaigned quietly and persistently to convince Eisenhower to meet with important black activists, including Roy Wilkins, Lester Granger, A. Philip Randolph, and Reverend Martin Luther King Jr., a group Morrow and the black press dubbed the "Negro Big Four." After that event, Morrow hoped for big things, but the indifference of the Republican Party cost strong black support and led to major party losses in the midterm elections of 1958. Morrow anguished in public stating that until the Republican Party accepted blacks as equals, they could never count on their firm support. Morrow continued to work hard for the Republican Party, believing in and campaigning for Richard Nixon for the presidency in 1960. By now, he was increasingly alone and embittered. For our purposes, it is telling that Morrow was the last significant New Jersey black that Leah Wright Rigueur or Joshua Farrington mention in their deeply researched studies of black Republicans.[57]

Morrow achieved minor success when Helen Edmonds, a black history professor from North Carolina State, was selected to deliver Eisenhower's seconding speech for his reelection, the first time a black person received that honor since George Cannon in 1924. That small step paid dividends as southern blacks voted strongly for Eisenhower, helping his reelection. Given that Morrow was close to Reverend Martin Luther King Jr., Eisenhower's indifference stalled historical change.[58]

Morrow was increasingly a vestige of the past. Despite the efforts of New Jersey Republicans, especially the much-revered Governor Driscoll, black New Jerseyans had shifted away from the Republican Party, a long-term transition dating back to the 1910s. Republican appeals were further hampered by the revelations of a "rat fink" conservative wing of the party that routinely used anti-Semitic and anti-black slurs. Newspapers exposed several of the "rat finks" who sang vulgar racist songs at party meetings.[59]

New Jersey blacks advanced in state political office, however gradually. Oliver Randolph became the state's Deputy Attorney General. The state Republican Party selected Dr. E. Gaylord Howell of New Brunswick, a graduate of Yale University and the Howard University Medical School, as its first black presidential elector in 1944. On a more local level, Robert Burk Johnson was appointed assistant prosecutor of Camden County. The major problem was the lack of a mass of political figures who could achieve more collaboratively than could token appointments. And once in a job, blacks experienced a glass ceiling. James O. Hill was the sole black member of the state assembly in the mid-1940s until Madaline A. Williams was elected to the assembly in 1957, the first African American woman to do so. Williams was born in Georgia in 1894 and after attending all-black schools, attended Atlanta University for one year. Her family moved north in 1917 to Trenton where she attended the State Normal School (now the College of New Jersey) and later taught in the Trenton system. Married to Samuel A. Williams, a Newark postal worker, with whom she had a son, the family moved to East Orange. The parents were active in the state NAACP and Samuel Williams was a national board member and New Jersey state president. Madaline Williams became involved in electoral politics through the Migrant Labor Board and League of Women Voters. After serving in the state assembly, she was elected Essex County registrar in 1960 and won reelection in 1964. In 1961, Williams was involved in a highly publicized racial exclusion, when, as a member of the centennial of the Fort Sumter attack, she was refused admission to the Francis Marion Hotel in Charleston. President John F.

Kennedy intervened and the proceedings were moved to a navy hospital. She was an alternate delegate to the national Democratic convention in 1960 and Vice Chair of the Delegation to the 1964 Convention in Atlantic City. Williams died in 1968.[60]

A housing case in the late 1950s showed increasing black power in the courts. In 1958, the Levitt Corporation announced plans for a Levittown, New Jersey, to be located in Willingboro Township in Burlington County. Levittowns were famous for their uniform, neat, inexpensive suburban homes; they were notorious for their whites-only sales and residential policies. These noxious qualities lasted even though the company violated federal and in this case, state laws. The Levittowns were receiving Federal Mortgage Insurance, for example. W. R. James, a black army officer stationed at nearby Fort Dix, attempted to buy a home in 1958. After being refused, he sued. James won his litigation in the New Jersey Supreme Court, which forced the Levitts to integrate the town. James became a minister and a leader in the local NAACP. The company hired veteran activist Howard Lett to create a plan to integrate the town. Lett created a list of "live prospects," that included a counselor at Bordentown and his wife, a dental technician, and their baby girl. After the family moved in, over time more black families purchased homes. Plans to limit the percentage of black owners were declared illegal and today the town, now renamed as Willingboro, is three-quarters black.[61]

WORK

Wartime cities began to open jobs for African Americans. Factories began to employ blacks in skilled and semiskilled positions. The Forstman and Botany woolen mills integrated early in the war. The demand was so great that one manpower recruiter decoyed black workers illicitly from Georgia. The Farm Security Administration forced farms to offer sanitary living facilities to migrant labor. Seabrook Farms in Bridgeton granted union organization, but, even with the arrival of black college students from the South sent to improve conditions, the company soon squeezed out African American workers in favor of immigrant and prisoner-of-war labor.[62]

Many black men remained mired in manual or low-level work, despite educational achievement, innate intelligence, and diligence. In the town of Princeton, employment in the kitchens, building and grounds crew or as caddies was reserved for blacks. Some were able to ascend to restaurant work, shop keeping, or carpentry. Music and sports offered very narrow access into greater financial success and fame.[63]

Black New Jersey women often combined business, personal, and political leadership. The obituary for Cordelia Green Johnson of Jersey City informed that she had led the National Beauty Culturalist League of America, was founder and president of the New Jersey Beauticians Association and head of the Jersey City NAACP. Jack and Jill, a prominent black social club, held dinners and dances to support the NAACP.[64]

Dr. Marie Metoyer of Jersey City was appointed as an intern at the Newark City hospital, the first black woman physician at the hospital in over fifty years. She had recently received a medical degree from Cornell University Medical College. Dr. E. Mae McCarroll became a doctor of proctology at the Newark City hospital in 1946, the first black to hold that position. In 1948, two Newark residents became the first black women to pass the New Jersey Bar Association exam. Reverend Thomas Campbell Jones became the state's first black Roman Catholic priest in 1945. Wilbur Parker celebrated another milestone when he became New Jersey's first black Certified Public Accountant in 1954. Too often, however, these "firsts" also meant "the only." Along with these individual accomplishments, the state of New Jersey added to black historical memory by establishing in 1949 a day recognizing Crispus Attucks, a black man who was the first Patriot martyred in the run up to the American Revolution.[65]

Popular Culture

Even during the war, black New Jerseyans found comfort in popular pleasures. Boxing and baseball were the favored sports of black New Jerseyans. Throughout the war years, fans enjoyed watching the Newark Eagles baseball team battle against such foes as the New York Black Yankees at Ruppert

Stadium. Boxers Sugar Ray Robinson, Pennsauken's Jersey Joe Walcott, Joe Louis, Henry Armstrong, and others routinely trained for big fights at New Jersey gyms. The state's blacks were thrilled when Walcott became the heavyweight champion in 1951 and mourned when he lost the crown to Rocky Marciano a year later.

Labeled a children's game for grownups, baseball was inherently political. Jackie Robinson's integration of baseball paved the way for New Jersey ballplayers to move from the Negro Leagues to the Major League Brooklyn Dodgers. The Black Elks gave Branch Rickey, the general manager of the Dodgers, the Elijah Lovejoy Award to recognize Rickey's role in integrating baseball. New Jerseyan Larry Doby became the first black player in the American League when he joined the Cleveland Indians in 1948. Two years later, East Orange native Monte Irvin starred for the New York Giants. Don Newcombe of Elizabeth was a pitching ace for the Brooklyn Dodgers and in 1949 was the first black hurler to start a World Series game[66]

Black sportsmen had trouble transferring their public fame into private business. The wildly popular boxing champion Joe Louis, who frequently trained in New Jersey and whose matches and every move were constantly featured in black newspapers, started the Brown Bomber Baking Company in 1939 and at its peak owned 24 trucks, had 92 employees and a distribution base of over 1,200 groceries and 900 restaurants in New York and New Jersey. Unfortunately, as Louis's boxing career declined, his business faded as well. Similar fates affected the efforts to merchandise the name of Jersey Joe Walcott.[67] Former baseball players had better luck. Joe Black retired from baseball after the Washington Senators released him in 1957. Black then got a job teaching in the Plainfield Elementary School. Later he became an executive at the Greyhound Bus Company.[68]

Gradually more blacks appeared in college sports. Melvin Murchison, freshly discharged from the U.S. Navy, became the first black to enter Princeton University as an undergraduate and to play for its football team. Integrated teams were fine in the North, but travel to the southern states brought trouble. When Rutgers football, track, and basketball star William "Bucky" Hatchett went to Baltimore with his basketball teammates, he was refused hotel lodging based upon his race. Rutgers angrily stated that its teams would no longer play in the southern states if such discrimination continued. Hatchett had the last word, scoring 28 of the team's 71 points as Rutgers beat Johns Hopkins by 31 points.[69]

Sports enabled Princeton University to desegregate very gradually. During World War II, four blacks, John Henry Howard, Arthur Jewell Wilson, James Everett Ward, and Melvin Murchison were admitted to the school as part of the U.S. Navy's officer-training program, a highly selective program to prepare commissioned officers. Howard graduated in 1947 and Wilson was a top basketball player. Several Witherspoon High School graduates were admitted in the late 1940s including Robert Rivers and brothers Joseph Ralph and Simeon Moss. The latter received a master's degree from Princeton in 1949 and a year later wrote a scholarly article on African Americans in New Jersey for the *Journal of Negro History* that was one of the first to note how long slavery lasted in New Jersey. Throughout the 1950s, only one or two black students were admitted per year. In 1955, Charles T. Davis joined the English department at Princeton, becoming the school's first black professor. In 1959 Princeton University awarded an honorary degree to Marian Anderson and one the following year to Reverend Martin Luther King Jr. Still in 1960 only two black students were enrolled in a student population of 809. Students paraded confederate flags from their windows and were known to throw away silverware after a black student had used it.[70]

Popular music captivated black New Jerseyans. Curious enthusiasts consulted *Trend Magazine, After Hours,* or *Gospel News,* Newark magazines published by Carl J. (Tiny Prince) Brinson, who was also an indefatigable promoter of local businesses, many of which advertised in his weeklies. Later, Brinson became a minority business and affirmative action officer for the City of Newark. Readers could learn that Delores Collins Benjamin had formed a glee club featuring local black men that lasted over a half century.[71] *Trend* and *After Hours* detailed the numerous theaters and clubs where top and local groups performed. The Ink Spots entertained happy fans at Newark's Apollo Theater. Blacks could gather to hear top singers and groups at the Paradise Club and Club Harlem in Atlantic City. Local favorite and

Figure 16. Sarah Vaughan (1924–1990), "I come from Newark," Sarah Vaughan often stated after she became a world-famous jazz and pop singer. Publicity image from 1948. By permission of the Newark Public Library.

bandleader Count Basie was a frequent performer at Club Harlem. Others who thrilled audiences at the club included Billie Holiday, Newark native Sarah Vaughan, Dinah Washington, Sam Cooke, James Brown, Ray Charles, B. B. King, and Aretha Franklin. Sammy Davis Jr., grew up in the club where his father and uncle routinely performed as part of the Will Mastin Trio while his mother worked as a barmaid across the street at Grace's Little Belmont. Comedian Slappy White convulsed patrons with laughter. The house band was Chris Columbo and his Swing Crew. Club Harlem was a gathering point for afterhours sessions for white entertainers Frank Sinatra, Milton Berle, Dean Martin, and Jerry Lewis. The Six A. M. show was especially popular. Club Harlem routinely attracted white patrons.[72]

Newark and surrounding towns enjoyed more local musical celebrities.[73] Black popular culture influenced the youth of one of New Jersey's most important cultural and political figures. Poet, playwright, and critic Amiri Baraka (LeRoi Jones) grew up in postwar Newark. The son of a postal worker father and office worker mother, Baraka's childhood home was "one secure reality," where adults were Lincoln Republicans. Political affiliation helped during the hard times. After his grocery business failed in the Depression, Baraka's father gained a patronage job as a watchman in the election machine warehouse for Essex County in Newark. Baraka recalls taking his father's dinner to him, accompanied by his grandmother in her "slow rocking style of walking." Baraka's grandfather was president of the Sunday School and a trustee at the black Bethany Baptist Church before becoming disabled after a street lamp fell on him. Tom Russ, the grandfather, fell from parish dignity to a silent paralytic. Although Baraka's home life was intensely religious, he found time for favorite cowboy shows on television and reading Charles Dickens, H. Rider Haggard, Rudyard Kipling, and Arthur Conan Doyle's Sherlock Holmes. Gang life and sports dominated Baraka's teenage years. Future historian James Oliver Horton never fully forgave Baraka for taking his treasured bicycle. Baraka went to films made by Mantan Moreland and followed Amos and Andy on the radio and then television. Butterfly McQueen, Hattie McDaniel, and Louise Beavers were other favorites. His father took him to Newark Eagles games to watch Leon Day, Monte Irvin, and Larry Doby, local boys who became stars.[74]

Black women found careers in popular song. Sarah Vaughan became a nationally famous chanteuse. Her parents raised her to sing and play organ in the Mount Zion Baptist Church in the Ironbound District of Newark. By her mid-teens, Vaughan regularly sneaked in to sing briefly at Alcazar, known as "the Zoo," the Piccadilly, the Hydeaway, and others of the city's thousand odd nightclubs. Her parents relented as long as she continued in the church choir. After dropping out of high school around 1941, and after becoming a regular in Newark jazz circles, Vaughan made a risky but highly successful appearance at an amateur night at the Apollo theater in Harlem. Vaughan left Newark in 1942 to join Earl Hines's band and returning for a triumphal performance with Illinois Jacquet in a week-long engagement at the Adams Theater in November 1947. By 1949 she was commanding $4,500 a week at the Adams. In 1957, the mayor of Newark named February 23, 1957, "Sara Vaughan Day" and gave her numerous testimonials including a gala dinner at the Military Park Hotel that raised $3,500 for local philanthropies.[75]

Vaughan's mother, adopted sister, and twelve-year-old daughter lived in Newark until 1974 when the singer bought a large expensive home for all in a gated community in Hidden Hills in California's San Fernando Valley. But Vaughan always told listeners "I come from Newark." After her death on April 4, 1990, Newark's City Hall was draped in purple bunting. On Sunday, April 8, the New Jersey Symphonic Orchestra presented a farewell concert in her honor. Her funeral took place at the Mount Zion Baptist Church on Monday, then thousands watched as a horse-drawn carriage carried Vaughan through the streets one last time to her interment at Glendale Cemetery in Bloomfield.[76]

Black organizations remained prominent in this era. Eleanor Roosevelt, the nation's first lady, spoke at Bordentown before the State Federation of Women's Clubs. She later appeared and accepted an award from the American Federation of Negro College Students in Newark. Atlantic City became the preferred spot for black societies and organizations. The Madame Walker Pilgrimage became an annual conference. Father Divine opened a new chapel/hotel in

Atlantic City and thousands of members attended large black church groups that convened in the town. The American Nurses Association, a black organization, held annual meetings in Atlantic City. The parent nurses organization moved in 1946 to end discrimination in its New Jersey chapters. Black fraternal and sorority societies met regularly around New Jersey.[77] The Alpha Phi Alphas, one of the leading black fraternities, held annual conventions in Atlantic City.[78] Crossing racial lines in college organizations proved harder. There was resistance to change. Upsala University roiled in 1947 when a sorority rejected a black pledge even though she was friendly with many of the sisters. Dissenting members then formed their own bias-free sorority.[79]

As a sign of the easing of Jim Crow, Atlantic City attracted numerous black conventions and entertainers. The National Association of Real Estate Brokers met there frequently and lobbied against restrictive covenants. When the National Black Elks held their annual meeting in Atlantic City in 1952, they invited presidential candidates Dwight Eisenhower and Adlai Stevenson to speak to its 50,000 delegates. Black leaders Mary McLeod Bethune and *Courier* publisher Robert Vann spoke to the group. Jersey Joe Walcott joined the Elks march each year. Leadership battles in the Elks often proved contentious, particularly because the top posts were well paid at $8,000 per year. Members packed Atlantic City hotels, big and small. The Elks awarded annual scholarships of $1,000 dollars. Less affluent Elks slept in their cars and lived off sandwiches. Everyone had to be on the lookout for pickpockets who worked the crowds. At night, members headed off to popular nightclubs such as the Harlem to hear vaudeville and singing acts. As the New Jersey civil rights movement gained steam in the late 1940s, calls to ban segregated groups became louder. There were threats to evict the annual convention of the American Bowling Congress, a whites-only group, from Atlantic City. The bowlers agreed to discuss ways of ending discrimination.[80]

The Black Elks continued to have a strong presence in New Jersey. The national annual meeting was held in Atlantic City in 1955 for the first time in over twenty years. Sixty thousand people lined up to watch Elkdom's most impressive parade in years. More than 200 marching units, 35 bands, and 10,000 marchers participated in the parade. The Pride of Newark's Elk branch won the award for largest drum and bugle corps. In a mark of integration, a young white man from Arizona won the Elks' National Oratorical Contest.[81]

Not all was cheery at the Elks convention. E. Frederic Morrow, special assistant to President Eisenhower, gave a blistering speech in which he warned listeners about the dangers of integration. Morrow had recently become the third New Jersey black to gain an appointment in the Eisenhower administration. As in earlier decades, the appointments were fairly low level. The other two were Joseph A. Clarke of Montclair who had been named as assistant to the assistant postmaster general and Dr. Francis H. Hammond of Orange who became minorities affairs advisor in the U.S. Information Agency. Black businesses were closing, black teachers were losing their jobs, Morrow warned, as wealthy blacks spent millions on alcohol, cars, fur coats, and cosmetics while the NAACP and Urban League had to beg for donations. Morrow defended the Eisenhower administration for its commitment to civil rights, but demanded that prosperous blacks had to bear the responsibilities of citizenship, show selflessness, and develop strong leadership.[82]

Barriers stayed down in the 1950s. The NAACP made plans to celebrate the triumphal 1954 Brown v. Board of Education decision, which outlawed separate but equal schools. There was an early dispute in which Atlantic City hoteliers indicated they did not want the NAACP in the seaside city. The Chamber of Commerce argued that a lack of rooms, not race, was the problem, as the hotels had welcomed the black Shriners and the youth division of the National Baptist Church in white-owned venues. Eventually, the NAACP overcame the problems and held a giant conference.[83]

The theme of the conference stressed freedom. Whites and blacks mingled freely in restaurants, on the Boardwalk, and at the convention site. Thurgood Marshall claimed that the Supreme Court had done all that it could about integrating schools. After Vice President Richard Nixon spoke at the conference, newly elected Executive Secretary Roy Wilkins bitterly denounced politicians, groups, and individuals who sought to keep America segregated. He outlined the nation's history since Plessy v. Ferguson in 1896 and condemned Congressman Carl Vinson and President Eisenhower for trying to circumvent the ruling and the Fourteenth Amendment. At the same time, Wilkins rejected communism as a means to secure more black rights. Despite this, the convention showed the much greater militancy blacks in the nation and in New Jersey felt since the days of Booker T. Washington.[84]

There was a major tribute to the retiring national organization head Walter White, but the NAACP convention barely mentioned its erstwhile leader W.E.B. Du Bois. One speaker lamented that Du Bois was a forgotten man because, she said, he had so much to offer. Du Bois had major problems with the U.S. government, which had labeled him a communist and clawed back his passport. Yet he remained a popular figure in New Jersey. In addition to speaking at left-wing conferences in the state on peace, trade, and jobs, Du Bois gave the keynote speech on "Colonial Imperialism in Africa" at the New Jersey State Federation of Colored Women's Clubs' annual meeting at the Bordentown Manual Training School in 1952.[85]

Not everyone in New Jersey welcomed the historic Supreme Court decision. Police Chief George Kane of New Brunswick attempted to intimidate NAACP members who tried to circulate 100,000 flyers announcing the decision. Kane called Nathan Gumbs, the local NAACP head, into the police station and told him not to distribute the flyers or else, telling Gumbs that New Brunswick did not want to have problems with blacks and civil protest like what was happening in the southern states. After the NAACP threatened to sue the police, the chief backed down.[86]

Similarly, Theodore Griffin, head of the Asbury Park NAACP post, was suspended from his job as a civilian employee of the U.S. Air Force for alleged association with communists. After the NAACP questioned the suspension, the Air Force's Security Review Board concluded that Griffin's only contact with communists was through his work with the NAACP and that he had moved to limit communists' involvement with the organization. The suspension was then lifted.[87]

Even after the Brown v. Board of Education decision, the NAACP had to labor hard to end segregated schools in New Jersey. Mary Walker of Englewood, supported by the NAACP, successfully sued the township for drawing lines to create a separate junior high for blacks. The state commissioner ordered the Englewood Board of Education to close the Lincoln school for blacks and integrate the students into its regular schools. The Englewood method was denounced as part of a pattern to maintain segregated schools.[88]

Jersey blacks showed their support for the Montgomery, Alabama, bus boycott in 1955. The Jersey City Board of Education considered allowing children to leave school an hour early to join a protest prayer in support of the arrested leaders of the boycott.[89] Reverend Russell Roberts of Atlantic City went on a fast for eleven days to support the protest.[90]

The NAACP was vigilant about shutting down demeaning cultural events. It forced the Pleasantville Board of Education to cancel a planned minstrel show in 1955 In which white students would perform in black face and use racial epithets freely.[91] The organization continued to help citizens aggrieved by racism. The NAACP helped William Wayne file an antidiscrimination suit against Camp Happiness in Monmouth County, which attempted to bar the blind man because of his race.

Postwar American politics veered between hard right and global liberalism. Concerned about its international image, the U.S. government initiated important actions to desegregate its society. The New Jersey State government was well ahead of these efforts and passed a new constitution prohibiting school segregation. The state government also made some effort to improve housing integration. The NAACP and Urban League were welcome in the state capital and many of their leaders shuttled between government and social movements. Marion Thompson Wright's historical research on school segregation in New Jersey found adherents in state and national policies.[92]

At the same time, major social developments undercut decades of integration efforts. Postwar housing booms were restricted largely to whites and only after years of efforts could a few blacks gain access to suburban housing developments. As blacks moved to New Jersey cities, white residents and major industries and businesses moved out to the suburbs, which were often inaccessible and unfriendly to African Americans. New Jersey's cities became impoverished as a result of unfair tax structures. Blacks were unable to attack these problems because they had few if any political representatives. These forces of advance and decline would collide in the next decade.

CHAPTER 7

The 1960s–2014

New Jersey blacks shared the nation's general optimism at the beginning of the 1960s. John F. Kennedy, a more liberal president, took office in 1961 with a mission to expedite school integration. Though constrained by his narrow electoral victory and beholden to racially conservative white Democratic legislators, Kennedy seemed determined to succeed, at least in the American South. He appointed far more blacks to posts in his new administration. In New Jersey, the NAACP continued its legal efforts to ensure the civil rights of blacks. After the assassination of Kennedy in 1963, his successor Lyndon Baines Johnson embarked on a massive antipoverty campaign and an overly optimistic determination to end racism in American society. Johnson was renominated at a massive convention in Atlantic City in 1964, an event that featured the debut of the Mississippi Freedom Party, led by Fannie Lou Hamer. Hamer daily walked along the boardwalk with the family of Michael Schwerner, a recently assassinated civil rights worker, and worked closely with local blacks.[1]

Still, there were warning signs. White flight rapidly shifted New Jersey's urban population. In 1950, 17 percent of Newark's populace was African American or Puerto Rican; by 1967, that fraction became a majority at 60 percent. Newark's population declined by more than 110,000 people between 1940 and 1980 as the effect of suburbanization and the decline of the city's downtown took effect, As New Jersey whites experienced a job, housing, and consumer revolution, African Americans felt isolated, forgotten, and discriminated against. Newark suffered the disappearance of industrial jobs, severe housing and health services crises, and political animosity. In a decade when African Americans showed their anger, Newark's uprising in 1967 was among the most severe. Blacks in Newark made up 52 percent of the population, but had practically no representation in city government, on the police force, or among educators. Moreover, the Italian and Irish political machines that had controlled Newark for decades faltered.[2] Newark's decline was representative of all American cities.[3]

New Jersey's and Newark's taxation systems damaged the chances of inner-city residents. While New Jersey was fifth in the nation in per capita personal income, it ranked last in per capita expenditures. More than 62 percent of Newark's 15,104 acreage was tax exempt, representing in 1973 almost $80 million in lost revenue. The exempt properties were worth almost $800 million. Five hundred were public properties, including the airport and port. The Port Authority of New York and New Jersey paid annual lease fees of just $579,000 per year while reinvesting as much as $500 million as it upgraded to international status.[4]

Matters were equally bad in South Jersey. Beryl L. Satter's classic work on exploitation of black real estate dreams applies to Camden, as well as other cities in the state.[5] Howard Gillette Jr., writing about Camden, noted the city's rapid, downward transformation after World War II and observed how the development of lily-white suburbs around Camden, removal of factories and jobs to the city's margins, loss of tax revenue but an increase of inner-city taxation, were all causes for Camden's decline in the 1950s. As jobs left town and the black population replaced whites, Camden went from being a city that worked to an impoverished, dilapidated environment.[6]

Statewide, the black population of New Jersey continued to rise as the state drew more migrants from the South. The U.S. Census report for 1970 showed an in-migration of 56,634 blacks and an out-migration of 31,698, resulting in a net migration of nearly 25,000 people, significantly higher than neighboring New York City or Philadelphia. The state's black population rose from 514,000 in 1960 to 925,000 twenty years later.[7]

Interviewed later, these migrants told tales of struggle and some achievement. Eleven-year-old Doris Russell moved from North Carolina to Newark
in 1962. She was fascinated by the homes crowded with five or six families.
After graduation from high school, she married a paint mixer for Sherwin-
Williams, and gave birth to four children. Russell worked as a nurse's aide
in a hospital and did part-time typing and domestic work. N. Rebecca Taylor moved to Plainfield from South Carolina in her early twenties with her
husband. The descendant of former slaves who had bought their freedom,
Taylor graduated from Barber-Scotia College in North Carolina, then
worked for a Presbyterian church in James Island, South Carolina. She
married a fellow worker, Leslie Allen Taylor, who was a seminary student at
Lincoln College. The couple tired of racism in South Carolina and moved to
Plainfield in 1930 where he pastored the Bethel Presbyterian Church until
his death in 1952. Their two children graduated from college. The son
became director of a senior center in Brooklyn and the daughter, a Douglass College graduate, went on to earn a doctorate from the City University
of New York. After her husband's death, Taylor worked as a counselor to
delinquent children in New York City. Upon retirement she returned to be
near her friends and her husband's grave in Plainfield.[8]

Renford Glanville arrived in New Jersey at the age of nineteen from
Jamaica as a contract worker during World War II. He worked first at
Seabrook Farms in a warehouse in an integrated labor force lifting boxes of
asparagus ten hours a day for fifty cents per hour. On one occasion he and
fellow black workers tried to eat at a small diner only to be refused service.
Angered, his fellow workers jumped on the counter and smashed dishes.
When the restaurateur called Seabrook, he was told to serve the workers or
face a boycott. Glanville married a woman at a local Baptist church and
fathered a child with her. That union allowed him to return to the United
States after his contract expired. He continued to work at Seabrook for
another ten years before being laid off. He then toiled as a laborer for a gas
company in Vineland, quit for better pay and a union job commuting to
Delaware. After five years he became a fireman. Glanville built his own
home where he and his wife raised seven children, all but one of whom were

girls. One daughter graduated from Delaware State College and became a manager for International Telephone and Telegraph; a second daughter graduated from Lincoln College in Pennsylvania. Glanville's son also studied at Delaware State and became a certified public accountant.[9]

CHURCHES AND ACTIVIST ORGANIZATIONS

Churches remained of paramount importance to black New Jersey. The Metropolitan AME Zion Church of Jersey City expanded by purchasing a historic church built in 1847 . Within four years, the church had paid off a fifteen-year mortgage. Local churches banded together to battle racism and poverty, under the umbrella of an interracial and interdenominational organization called the Church of Christ United.[10]

The NAACP continued to work on racial discrimination outside of education. The organization urged a strengthening of the State Migrant Labor Law in 1966, to include seasonal workers. Most of the workers were black or Puerto Rican and had been systematically excluded from "virtually every piece of social legislation" enacted in the state over the previous four decades.[11] There was always work for the NAACP. Despite major cases in the past, swimming pools and beaches remained segregated. Black patrons in Atlantic City and Asbury Park in 1966 had to make do with gritty, poorly designed beaches. In Plainfield, residents complained for years about the inadequacy of pools in the largely black west end of town. Rather than build pools, the city government bussed blacks to nearby Rahway where they could swim in majority-black public pools. Gradually, the NAACP and CORE won battles to integrate public amusement parks and swimming pools, only to have such fun palaces close their doors as African American attendance rose.[12]

At the same time, the NAACP and New Jersey parents did not always agree on strategies or targets. In 1963, Englewood parents, descendants of household servants and groundskeepers who had served the local elite, were disgusted with conditions at the local 98 percent black Lincoln School. Traditional support did not emerge. The NAACP preferred to accentuate its southern strategy and not spend resources on northern schools. Thwarted, black parents made an uneasy alliance with white Democrats, who had moved into the town after construction of the George Washington Bridge in 1931. Radical leaders emerged, including the charismatic attorney Paul Zuber, who had conducted successful protests elsewhere, despite NAACP disapproval. Shirley Lacy was head of the Englewood CORE and attacked segregated schools and swimming pools in Englewood and nearby. To force their demands, Englewood's black parents staged a sit-in at the city hall, boycotted local stores with limited success, and jammed the phone lines of Governor Richard Hughes with protest calls. White parents largely rejected calls for integration. The eloquent Zuber demanded more, stating publicly that in the South bigots wore white sheets, but in the North they arrived in Brooks Brothers suits. His defiance attracted militants from New York City including Malcolm X and Milton Galamison. In July members of the Nation of Islam joined a picket line in Englewood. After months of picketing, the New Jersey commissioner of education ordered the Englewood School Board to desegregate in a clear victory for the militant approach.[13]

POLITICS

Each black political appointment became a "first." In 1966, Charles A. Matthews of Essex County became the first black to head a county government in New Jersey and possibly in the nation. He was a lifetime Democrat and mentioned as a possible successor to Hugh Addonizio as Mayor of Newark. Soon after, Westry Horne became the head of programs for minority and migrant workers for the state education department. His wife, Dorothy Horne was also appointed to a state educational position.[14] Being a first happened in business as well. Carolyn D. Martin of Princeton broke a long tradition of barring blacks from realty boards when she joined the Trenton and Mercer County Board of Realtors. Doing so was the culmination of an eleven-year lawsuit pressed by Martin and the NAACP. The successful suit cited the Fourteenth Amendment.[15]

What is noteworthy about these "firsts" is that they occurred during a period of somewhat liberalized racial relations. While much of the responses to President Johnson's Great Society and civil rights measures were negative, companies, universities, churches, and social organizations were gradually opening their doors to qualified blacks, something that was extremely rare during previous periods of racial discrimination such as the 1920s and 1930s. Certainly, racism in New Jersey existed in the 1960s, but crevices opened that allowed talented, experienced blacks to move from behind the veil into the general society. Such individual opportunities seldom differed from past methods, which had created niche positions but barely altered the impoverished lives of most New Jersey blacks. The 1960s marked the final transition of New Jersey blacks from the Republican to the Democratic Party. State black voters declined to support Barry Goldwater for the presidency in 1964, dedicated some of their ballots to Richard Nixon in 1968, but overall found the increasingly racially conservative Republicans unacceptable. The party also devoted very few resources to black New Jersey politics. The conservative black politician Clay Claiborne, a former Elk official, was unable to push a Republican agenda in the early 1970s because of a lack of party financial support. Nor did it help that young white Republicans formed groups such as the "Rat Finks," which distributed racist and anti-Semitic tracts.[16]

Good housing remained a significant problem for middle-class blacks. The parents of future U.S. Senator Cory Booker moved from Maryland to Bergen County in 1969. His father, Cary Booker, one of the top IBM salesmen in the nation, chose Harrington Park as their ideal family location. When looking for real estate, Cary and Carolyn Booker were repeatedly steered toward poorer black neighborhoods and told that better homes had just been sold. In league with the local Fair Housing Council, Booker's father set up a sting operation. First, Cary Booker put in an offer on a desirable home. After he was rebuffed, a white couple were welcomed as buyers. Cary and Marty Friedman, from the Fair Housing Council, confronted the agent about his duplicity and threatened a lawsuit. The agent punched Friedman and set a vicious dog on him. Cary Booker was able to subdue the animal while

Friedman and the agent traded blows. Despite the agent's defiance, the couple purchased the home. Carolyn Booker later worked for the council, which continues to defend black housing rights today.[17]

Younger, more radical and defiant activists formed new organizations that took cues from older activists. Ernie Thompson advised the fledgling Newark Coordinating Committee in its pursuits of improved civil rights. The local Congress of Racial Equality (CORE) in Newark, led by Robert Curvin, confronted unions and political leaders over segregated job selection for reconstruction of Barringer High School in Newark. The older high school, noted Curvin, had hidden Jim Crow features. For example, though no signs were apparent, black students understood they had to use a designated door to enter the school. Unions also declared they did not discriminate, but only 4 percent of Newark's majority black population were members. CORE and other civil rights groups picketed the rebuilding site. Ultimately they were not successful, but their actions demonstrated a new militancy in race relations.[18]

BLACK REBELLION

On July 12, 1967, black Newark residents rebelled. There had been earlier warnings: In April 1966, arsonists in Newark destroyed ten buildings, killing four children and injuring fifteen other people, in one of a series of suspicious fires over the previous five months.[19] Jersey City had experienced a wave of mini rebellions in early 1966, leading to the appointment of a black judge to serve in police courts.[20] Angry protesters in Atlantic City exhibited rats in parades past the homes of slumlords. The NAACP helped file suits against rapacious landlords.[21]

Lack of political power fed concerns about displacement. There was a controversial plan to uproot a Newark black community of 20,000 people to make room for a campus of the New Jersey College of Medicine and Dentistry: part of a plan to build a postindustrial economy in Newark that would include few blacks. Newark's industrial base had been declining for years, and, as Lizbeth Cohen and Kenneth Jackson have shown, sharp drops in individual and commercial property values were part of white flight to the suburbs. Unemployment among black men was widespread as were high rates of venereal disease, drug addiction, new cases of tuberculosis, and high infant mortality. Health problems present during the Depression were in fact worse because of widespread drug abuse and prostitution. Blacks who hoped to improve their lot through education were frustrated when Mayor Addonizio nominated James Callahan, a high school graduate, over Wilbur Parker, a respected black certified public accountant, to become Secretary to the Board of Education. Blacks already distrusted Addonizio, who the New Jersey Ku Klux Klan described as a dues-paying member. Radical black activists roused public unhappiness over the exclusion of African Americans from any positions of political power in a city that had the ninth highest concentration of black people in the nation.[22]

The trigger was the police beating of John Smith, a black cabdriver, after he was stopped for a minor traffic violation. As the police clubbed Smith, his fellow cabbies radioed about the incident. Smith's suffering was the last straw. CORE had called for investigations of police brutality for several years. Only 250 officers in the 1,400-member police force were black though African Americans made up almost 55 percent of the city's overall population.

Soon a large crowd gathered around Newark's Fourth Precinct police station where Smith was held, demanding information about Smith's condition. The next day an angry crowd pummeled the precinct with bricks, bottles, and Molotov cocktails. Armed riot police attempted to disperse the protesters, clubbing anyone with black skin. In response, blacks threw bricks and concrete blocks at the police before moving into downtown streets. The police arrested and beat poet and activist Leroi Jones (Amiri Baraka), then chained him to a wheelchair covered in blood at a hospital. Later Jones received a three-year prison term for rioting. He appealed the decision and it was reversed two years later.[23]

In the next five days, twenty-four blacks and two whites died in law enforcement maneuvers, from stray bullets and car accidents. More than 1,100 people were injured, 1,400 were arrested, and millions of dollars of

Figure 17. John William "J. W." Smith (1927–2002) was the Newark taxicab driver whose arrest and beating by Newark police sparked the 1967 Newark Rebellion. Newark Public Library, by permission of the *Newark Star-Ledger*.

Figure 18. The famed poet, playwright, and political activist Amiri Baraka (1934–2014) and his wife, Amina, with *Confirmation*, their 1983 collaborative anthology of African American female writers. Newark Public Library by permission of the *Newark Star-Ledger*.

damage was sustained to private and public buildings. Police and National Guardsmen, of whom only a fraction were black, battled looters and arsonists throughout the black-dominated Central Ward. Tanks became commonplace sights on Newark streets. Jeeps covered with barbed wire served as checkpoints in the middle of streets. Most participants later recalled that the law enforcement officers were blatantly racist and excessively violent as they fired guns indiscriminately at innocent people and destroyed black-owned property. Indeed, most of the National Guardsmen were from segregated towns, had never been to Newark before, and were anxious about their safety. After the death of one policeman from reported sniper fire, the police forced evacuation of a building and then riddled it with bullets. Community activists and black leaders convinced Governor Richard Hughes that the National Guard was exacerbating the troubles. He pulled the guardsmen from Newark on Monday, July 17. As the guardsmen left, one apparently shot to death a twelve-year-old African American boy who was emptying a garbage pail in front of his home. As the Newark police often used their own guns and ammunition rather than department-issued weapons, their contribution to the gunfire is unknown, but the state police and guardsmen tracked every shot. The number of their rounds came to an astonishing 2,904 and 10,414 respectively. As Brad Tuttle has concluded, such shooting went beyond the mission of securing the peace. Esteemed black educator Kenneth Clark observed the riot-torn streets and compared them to a war zone.[24]

Rebellions spilled into neighboring black communities, many of which suffered problems similar to those in Newark. Bad schools, collapsing urban infrastructure, and poorly designed housing projects with no recreational facilities indicated neglect and lack of funds. Unrest had already occurred in Jersey City, Paterson, and Elizabeth in 1964 and 1965. Jersey City and Elizabeth blacks nearly rose up again in June 1967 until the city government saturated their neighborhoods with heavily armed policemen. A grand jury criticized the police in Paterson for using goon tactics to suppress the demonstrations.[25]

Plainfield experienced the worst violence outside of Newark. The home to many commuters, it had few black residents before 1950, but over the next fifteen years, the city's population of 45,000 was nearly one-third black. As with Englewood to the north, Plainfield's black population divided into a middle class who lived in an East Side "golden ghetto," and the unskilled, unemployed, and underemployed who lived on the West Side. Promises of a swimming pool for blacks in 1966 lapsed into a plan involving a half-hour bus ride with a twenty-five-cent fare and no lunches, both of which caused strains for poorer families. Worse, the bus operated only three days during the week and not on weekends. Larger problems included de facto segregation in the schools giving higher educational tracks to whites. Blacks had much higher dropout rates. The NAACP had intervened over issues of schooling, housing, and employment but with limited success. Blacks had little political power with only two members of the eleven-person city common council, both of whom represented the prosperous East Side. As with Newark, frustrations and inequalities caused poorer blacks to rise up, in looting stores, smashing cars, and engaging in arson for over a week, despite the presence of heavily armed state troopers and militia. The peak of conflict occurred on July 17 when a policeman was killed amid widespread looting. Numerous arrests were made as white officials attempted to mediate the conflict. The state police searched homes of black residents without warrants, seeking stolen weapons. In 1967, eleven blacks were put on trial for rioting. In nearby New Brunswick, where no clearly defined ghetto existed, there were protests but little violence. Cranbury's high schools experienced racial tensions.[26]

In the immediate aftermath of the rebellion, three books encapsulated its events. Nathan Wright Jr., a minister and Black Power activist (albeit remaining a Republican), compiled important data on the causes of the riots. Wright and New Left activist Tom Hayden blamed the police and national guard for excessive violence. Ron Porambo, a veteran journalist, published a scorching first-person account.[27] In his thoughtful, fully researched discussion of Newark's ailments, published just after the urban rebellion, Wright identified key areas that sparked the uprising. He showed that in 1967 Newark had the highest crime rate, tuberculosis, syphilis, and gonorrhea, and highest maternal mortality levels in the nation. Worsening these problems were Newark's highest national proportionate urban tax rate, highest population density, highest proportion of land set aside for urban renewal, and highest daytime population turnover. Carefully examining census data, long before any other scholar did so, Wright demonstrated white flight from key parts of Newark, showed the overwhelming concentration of blacks, many with little urban experience, in downtown wards, known as the "rotten casket." Unlike earlier decades when men like George Cannon lived and worked in the city and helped build a vibrant black community, Wright found that African American leadership tended to move away from downtown Newark into somewhat integrated suburbs. Wright found downtown wards afflicted by despair with black and white poor locked in at the bottom and fighting each other in desperation.[28]

Subsequently there have been several significant interpretations of the rebellions. In a broader commentary on urban strife in the 1960s, Thomas

Sugrue has argued in his influential book on Detroit that only by looking at "the coincidence and mutual reinforcement of race, economics, and politics in a particular historical moment, the period between the 1940s and 1960s, set the stage for the fiscal, social and economic crisis that confront urban America today." The conditions in New Jersey's cities were remarkably similar.[29]

Lizbeth Cohen has argued that urban rebels focused on consumer goods by looting big department stores of appliances, television sets, children's toys, and baby necessities or by walking past the smashed windows of liquor stores to take what they desired. Over three-quarters of the 1,426 persons arrested were charged with crimes against property. Many were employed, stable members of the city's Central Ward. Demonstrating racial solidarity, rioters avoided black-owned businesses. Black rioters showed dissatisfaction with their roles as spectators not participants in the consumer revolution.[30]

Komozi Woodard and, later, Robert Curvin place the rebellion in the context of ongoing racial discrimination exacerbated by the Italian American political structure that controlled Newark. Woodard charts the rise of the black poet, playwright, and nationalist Amiri Baraka and the organization of the Committee for a Unified Newark (CFUN) as part of a national and international Black Power movement with links to black convention movements in the nineteenth century. Baraka's CFUN recruited talented college-educated youths not only from the surrounding suburbs like East Orange, Montclair, Hackensack, and Englewood but also from as far south as Burlington. At the same time, Baraka's statewide Congress of African People established branches of his movement as far south as Camden; and the New Jersey Black Assembly established branches in black communities throughout the state. Last but not least, the Black Arts Movement developed incubators for artists, directors, and writers throughout the state, encouraging talent including the award-winning Trenton playwright Ntozake Shange. Black Studies programs in New Jersey headquartered poets like Nikki Giovanni at Rutgers University. Baraka and CFUN revived the annual Crispus Attucks celebrations to connect the Revolutionary martyr with black nationalism. Woodard credits Baraka initially for successfully tying CFUN and the Black Arts Movement (which he founded with fellow poet Larry Neal) to the Modern Black Convention Movement. Baraka's organization of young blacks in Newark and the creation of legitimate political power led to the 1970 election of Kenneth Gibson as Mayor of Newark. Gibson was the second black mayor of a major American city, after Carl Stokes of Cleveland. Woodard contends that black nationalism was a necessary position for Newark's oppressed urban black population.[31]

Kevin Mumford contests Woodard by arguing that the riots demonstrated how blacks intended to take over such public spheres as neighborhoods, housing, and politics. He argues that Black Nationalists in particular harmed Newark's black citizens by rejecting civic traditions of sharing values with whites, a method as unfortunate as the evils of racism that plagued their lives before the riots.[32]

Mark Krasovic and Julia Rabig have recently deemphasized the actual riots. Newark's predicament was part of an ongoing debate and political implementation of President Lyndon Johnson's Great Society program. They also provide important insights into the construction of a narrative about the riots drawn from the presidential commission and its findings (Kerner Report), the New Jersey Gubernatorial Report and, significantly, the response by the Police Benevolent Association, which led to the creation of local militias and a massive increase in the weaponry owned by the police for use in disorders. Krasovic, importantly, concentrates on the interactions of political figures at the local, state, and federal levels with community leaders. Rabig contends that the rebellions produced "fixers" or Black Power advocates who could work pragmatically with African American residents and external white leadership.[33]

The National Advisory Commission on Urban Disorders cited a number of common traits among those arrested for rioting. Those detained were most likely to be young men between the ages of 15 and 24, locally born, raised and resident. Most had attended high school but did not graduate. Nearly 30 percent of those arrested were unemployed. Embittered, the young male rioters blamed not their lack of skills, ambition, or training, but racial discrimination for their conditions. The rioters were proud of their blackness and were hostile to whites, but also to middle-class African Americans. They were very aware of local, state and national politics, often taking part in civil rights actions, but they despaired of any real gains. Blacks who sought to calm the tumult had much more education, and held patriotic and optimistic views on Newark and the nation.[34]

Post Rebellion

In the aftermath of the Newark riots, Dr. Nathan Wright Jr., opened a four-day conference on Black Power attended by such groups as the Black Nationalists, NAACP, CORE, and the Student Nonviolent Coordinating Committee. The conference, attended by nearly 1,000 delegates from forty-two states, had large ambitions. It urged a "third force" of black men whose votes could swing between the Republican and Democratic Parties or even form their own party. Adam Clayton Powell Jr., was the first to enunciate this plan, though he did not attend the Newark conference. There were clashes between radicals and the Newark police. The most pressing idea to come out of the conference was a plan mandating a substantial amount of integration in public housing, an idea endorsed by the federal Department of Housing and Urban Development. Despite that moment of harmony, the speeches at the conference were generally angry and gloomy about American race relations. Nathan Wright Jr., tried to quell antireligious sentiment, but reporters were shocked to hear religion attacked as a hobble to black independence. Black was the preferred term of identification, while the word "negro" was out.[35]

Wright resigned from the pulpit after the conference, announcing that he was going full time into urban and educational work and had established a firm, the Empowerment Associates of Newark and New York. Wright was something of an anomaly among black activists, as he was a lifetime Republican.[36]

The American Civil Liberties Union (ACLU) and the National Lawyers Guild helped with the appeal of two young black men sentenced to life imprisonment for their alleged participation in a crowd-killing of two policemen in Plainfield in 1967. The two black men were convicted in a mass trial of eleven defendants in connection with a beating of another white policeman during the 1967 riots.[37] The ACLU, acting for the NAACP, also called upon law enforcement officers in New Jersey to destroy all secret intelligence files on demonstrators.[38]

Tougher forms of activism occurred among black New Jersey police when they joined their colleagues from across the nation in endorsing a protest against racist white policemen. Founded as the Council of Police Societies, the new group met in Atlantic City in the summer of 1969. Captain William Collette of Atlantic City argued that black cops were tired of working every-day with racist partners. While black officers had to work within rules, in order to be effective they also had to identify as black and to relate to the black community. The movement continued to exert pressure. Now known as the Bronze Shields, the organization of Newark cops placed a bias suit in 1973 against the police department for discriminatory testing. The tests used questions that were not job-related and placed emphasis on rote memoriza-tion and pencil-taking skills, rather than sound judgment and the ability to lead. The announcement indicated that the number of black and Hispanic cops in Newark had actually fallen from 250 in 1969 to 222 in 1973, with only 15 black and no Hispanic policemen holding a rank above patrolman.[39]

In a compromise reached months after the rebellion, the New Jersey College of Medicine and Dentistry agreed to build their new campus on a smaller tract and promised that blacks would find jobs in the construction of the buildings and, later, in the operation of the medical school. Fifty-four acres would be allocated immediately for new homes for all those who lost their homes in the construction of the new campus. The federal Secretary of Labor, Willard Wirtz, announced job programs for blacks in New Jersey.[40]

There were retaliations. Someone bombed the home of Tony Imperiale, a local political figure known for his racism and employment of a white vigi-lante group that patrolled Newark's white neighborhoods. Nine people said to be associated with the Black Panther Party were arrested for a drive-by machine-gun shooting of the Newark police station. The Panther head-quarters in Newark suffered an acid attack, police in plain clothes ganged

up and beat twenty Panthers in the local courthouse, and the Black Panthers in Jersey City complained of constant harassment by the police.
Police charged an extreme right-wing group with a bombing of the Jersey
City Panther headquarters. A grand jury indicted five white cops for van-
dalism of the Southern Leadership Council office in Newark.[41] However,
blacks lost in their first attempt to take over Newark from racist leadership
when three candidates for at-large positions in the city council lost in the
1968 elections.[42]

Two incidents a few years later indicate the festering violence in police
relations with the black community. New Jersey's shaky racial relations were
again roiled in May 1973 when Assata Shakur (JoAnne Deborah Byron
Chesimard), an activist and former member of the Black Panther Party who
joined the Black Liberation Army, was wounded in a shootout on the New
Jersey Turnpike. Shakur was traveling from New York City to Philadelphia
when New Jersey State Trooper Werner Foerster and his partner, Trooper
James Harper, pulled over Shakur's vehicle for a broken tail light. The trooper's inspection quickly escalated into a gunfight in which Foerster and the
driver of the car, Zayd Shakur, were killed and Assata Shakur and Harper
were wounded. Assata Shakur was already the focus of a nationwide FBI
hunt on suspicion in a series of killings and bank robberies from New York
to Tennessee. During the ensuing legal proceedings, Shakur's trial was
moved from Middlesex County, where the portion of the turnpike was
located, to Morris County, because more than 80 percent of Middlesex
residents polled believed that she was guilty. Because of the small black
population living in Morris County, Shakur sought to have the trial moved
to federal court. After Shakur became pregnant, the trial was suspended.
Meanwhile, she was also under indictment and in trial proceedings for
crimes in New York City. In a retrial for the turnpike killings in 1977, which
was reported widely around the world, Shakur was convicted on two counts
of murder and six assault charges. She was then remanded to prison, but
first had to undergo similar trials in New York City. Returned to New Jersey
for incarceration at the Clinton Correctional Facility for Women, she
escaped in 1979 aided by three visiting members of the Black Liberation

Army. After several years of hiding, she fled to Cuba and was granted political asylum. She has lived there ever since, referring to herself as a "twentieth-century-escaped slave." Despite normalized relations in 2015, Cuba has refused to extradite her to the United States. She remains a powerful cultural figure to militant blacks and whites.[43]

Equally controversial was the arrest and subsequent long-term incarceration of Rubin "Hurricane" Carter on charges of murder. Carter had been middleweight world champion just a few years before his arrest in 1966 on charges of the murder of a bartender. Convicted in 1967, Carter appealed and went through two more trials before he was released in 1985. Prosecutors declined to file further charges. Throughout the 1970s and early 1980s, Carter's case became synonymous for police injustice. Like Shakur, Carter attracted enormous cultural attention. Famed folksinger Bob Dylan wrote a song about him and actor Denzel Washington starred in a Hollywood film about his life in 1999. Carter's autobiography, *The Sixteenth Round*, published in 1975, remains in print.[44]

REBUILDING NEW JERSEY SOCIETY

Blacks in Camden formed an interracial group designed to help the city recover from urban decay and the flight of business to the suburbs. Richard Rhodes, a Vista Volunteer, started the Black People's Unity Movement. The organization devoted itself to helping people in need in practical ways such as home reconstruction, working with black contractors, and engaging black owners of small businesses in the movement.[45]

As Mark Krasovic has argued, black enterprises benefited from government grants in the aftermath of the riots. Black-owned research companies, such as Gourdine Systems, began to prosper. Dr. Meredith C. Gourdine, a graduate of Cornell University, received his PhD in Engineering Science from California Institute of Technology. He was a top aerospace engineer at Curtis-Wright Corporation before starting his own company, which employed more than 150 people in Livingston, New Jersey.[46] Similarly, a black-owned computer service in Newark received authorization from the

State of New Jersey to process local property tax rolls for towns and cities. Run by Leonard Prather, EDAPCO was the first black-owned computer service in the state.[47]

In addition, businesses began opening previously closed doors to black applicants. Banks in Passaic, under an agreement brokered by the U.S. Equal Opportunity Commission, accepted black applicants who lacked a high school diploma if the job did not reasonably require one. The banks created an "affirmative action" file of potential black applicants for use when openings occurred.[48]

ELECTING BLACK MAYORS

Electing a black mayor involved a major effort. Precedent existed in Jersey City, where Matthew G. Carter became the first black man to head a major New Jersey city in 1968. Kenneth Gibson was first mentioned as a potential mayoral candidate in Newark in 1966. He did very well in his first effort, forcing a runoff ballot against incumbent Hugh Addonizio. In a three-way race, Addonizio retained his mayoralty. Scandals, the Newark riots, and the conclusion by the Governor's Commission on Civil Disorders that Addonizio's office was rife with corruption, created solidarity among blacks and Puerto Ricans in support of Gibson for the election of 1970. The Black and Brown Convention, held in November 1969, urged a genuine black power via Gibson's election and sought national funding. A significant problem developed in explicit appeals to black and Puerto Rican voters, methods that might alienate sympathetic whites. The endorsement of the *Newark Evening News* helped Gibson.[49]

Newark's 1970 mayoral election resulted in a three-way runoff. Forty-three percent of voters supported Kenneth Gibson, but the continued presence of state assemblyman George Richardson in the race kept Gibson from attaining the required 50 percent. Gibson triumphed in the runoff shortly after, becoming Newark's first black mayor.[50] Building upon unity conferences and Kenneth Gibson's mayoral victory in Newark, black politicians began building alliances in the state assembly. George Richardson of

Newark, chairman of the newly formed six-member New Jersey Black Legislative Caucus, helped Mercer County Assemblyman S. Howard Woodson become assembly speaker and Newark Assemblyman Ronald Owens
ascended to assistant majority leader, the first time that two black men held
leadership posts.[51]

Gibson made some unorthodox moves as he took over the mayor's office,
such as the appointment of a seventeen-year-old high school honors student
to the unpaid Board of Education.[52] But Gibson was concerned about maintaining appearances. In addition to refusing bribes, Gibson complained of
being spied on and that his telephones were bugged by the Newark police
department. However, Robert Curvin, who was a participant in many of the
events of this period and has enormous credibility, argues that in the end
Gibson adapted to Newark's long-term patterns of corruption and patronage and paid less attention to African Americans than his supporters had
anticipated.[53]

Ravi K. Perry's careful analysis of the balancing act that black mayors
must perform is useful for understanding Kenneth Gibson's predicament.
As Perry notes, black voters supporting a first-time elected politician expect
wholesale transformation of society. One of Gibson's aides noted that Newark residents believed that the election meant jobs for everyone. Immediate
improvement of service and conditions in their neighborhoods, expectations that past black political figures did not face. Perry argues that those
expectations did not go away but continued into the 1990s. Accentuating the
problem was that black mayors often have to choose between trying to satisfy those goals and seeking reelection. Gibson, though representing a black
majority, clearly chose policies intended to help his reelection. Gibson also
headed a city deeply divided by anger and distrust. The 1967 rebellion and
subsequent repression was very recent. Newark was nearly a "hollow prize,"
a term that political scientists use to describe a city so bankrupt and bereft
of resources that no one could succeed as mayor.[54]

Certainly, radical activists pushed Gibson hard. By 1971, the *Pittsburgh
Courier* argued that Amiri Baraka had become a political kingmaker,
embroiled in educational and antipoverty programs as well as police rela-

tions. Baraka and Gibson soon clashed when the poet dismissed the mayor's efforts to recruit black policemen as being insufficient. Baraka argued that the community should control the police, not the reverse.[55] Baraka engaged in national politics as well, becoming an advisor to George McGovern's 1972 presidential campaign. Kenneth Gibson also endorsed McGovern's candidacy.[56] Baraka was a national literary force as one of the founders of the Black Arts Movement, a strongly nationalist genre that emphasized reverence to African culture, black self-governance, public interaction, and left-wing politics. Baraka hosted Black Arts conferences, established the Spirit House in Newark with his wife Amina (Sylvia Robinson), and introduced a black literary culture to Newark.[57]

Further challenges to Gibson came during a teachers' strike in 1971, which pitted the mayor's position against insurgent forces led by Baraka amidst lingering resentments gathered around Imperiale. Negotiations carried on over several months but proved futile. The strike ended only when students, anxious about graduation and chances for college admission, demanded a return to bargaining and an eventual settlement. At the same time, black and white teachers were for a time able to struggle together.[58]

Gibson was the first in a series of blacks elected to significant state offices in this era. Wynona Moore Lipman of Montclair was elected to the state senate in 1971 and served in office for twenty-seven years until her death in 1999. Born in Georgia in 1923, Moore graduated from Talladega College with a degree in French and received a master's degree in French Studies from Atlanta University. She taught at Morehouse College and earned her doctorate at Columbia University in 1952. She married Matthew Lipman, a white man, in Paris in 1952 at a time when such a union was illegal in Georgia; they divorced in 1974. Lipman championed causes for women, children, minorities, and small businesses. She pushed legislation for harsher punishments for adults patronizing child prostitutes and chaired committees battling AIDS and child abuse and neglect.[59]

More black mayors were elected in the next few years. William Hart became mayor of East Orange in 1970. Then there was a decade gap until Randy Primas was elected mayor of Camden in 1981 as was Everett C.

Lattimore in Plainfield. In 1984, James L. Usry won the top spot in Atlantic City and Douglas Palmer became mayor of Trenton in 1990.[60]

Gibson was easily reelected in 1974, triumphing over the right-wing candidate Imperiale. Over the next few years, enterprising, politically agile black leaders strived to work within the Gibson administration. What Julia Rabig has called fixers, these youthful organizers adapted Black Power to the treacherous world of Newark politics. Junius Williams enthusiastically embraced a position as director of the Model Cities Community Development Corporation to create better housing and more jobs. He survived until local politics and tightening federal funds ended his tenure. Gustav Heningburg, a Newark black activist, served as a go-between with progressive businessmen, community leaders, and radical blacks, including Baraka. Gibson survived succeeding elections until 1986, but he gradually alienated younger, more activist blacks. Even as Gibson's reputation among blacks suffered and, as Robert Curvin argues, splits with Baraka were inevitable, Black Power activists became institutionalized in the political process.[61]

Mount Laurel and the Push for Integrated Housing

Ordinary black citizens rose to extraordinary levels of activism in the next decade with long-term implications. Grassroots politics inspired court action to end discrimination. Battling segregation in housing required brave, persistent, and organized efforts. One of the most nationally famous drives for better housing occurred in 1969 when a group of lower income, primarily black residents of Mount Laurel, frustrated at their inability to find decent housing, cooperated with a local contractor to build thirty-six units of affordable housing for themselves and other low-income families in the region. Township officials immediately rejected the plan, claiming that it would violate zoning policies and land-use regulations that favored single-family dwellings. Local residents formed the Springdale Action Committee and joined forces with the NAACP and Camden Legal Services in 1971 to file suit, arguing that the township's policies were discriminatory on racial and income lines and in effect created racial segregation. The case went to the New Jersey Supreme Court, which ruled in a decision that became known as Mount Laurel I that municipalities had an obligation to enable lower-income housing with an emphasis on attaining economic equality. The decision provided a blueprint for solving housing litigation across the nation. Displeased with the decision, Mount Laurel officials stalled for time and rezoned three unacceptable properties while they appealed the case. In 1983, the New Jersey Supreme Court again heard arguments in the case and ordered in the decision known as Mount Laurel II that the township move quickly to implement plans. Sadly, local officials took until the year 2000 to complete a housing development that was 100 percent affordable. The development was named after Ethel R. Lawrence, a local black woman who was the lead plaintiff and organizer of long-term activism that resulted in the successful project.

In 1985 the New Jersey Legislature responded by passing the Fair Housing Act. Accepting the premise that there was a constitutional obligation for municipalities to foster some degree of affordable housing, this legislation created an administrative agency, the Council on Affordable Housing (COAH), to establish regulations setting the obligation of each municipality in terms of the number of units and how the obligation could be satisfied. The Mount Laurel decision and its aftermath continue to be controversial to the present. One issue is that most of the residents coming to New Jersey's Affordable Housing Management Services, which selects prospective clients, are now over 80 percent white, with few moving out from the inner city. As one scholar has noted, when local options allow municipalities to determine residency, outcomes are far from the goals set in the Mount Laurel decisions. One major problem is that an applicant needed to have a job before applying and that job had to be near the housing site. Employment opportunities, not housing, drove applicants' desires. As prices for the homes increased, the pool of potential buyers decreased and curtailed the number of black applicants. While the Mount Laurel decisions created some tangible improvements, subsequent improvement depended on examples based on the actions and determination of Ethel Lawrence. Further frustrating

progress were the obdurate attitudes of Republican administrations, especially during the recent tenure of Governor Chris Christie.[62]

New Jersey's State Supreme Court used economic arguments to attempt
leveling of school funds across the state. Because New Jersey has more than
600 school districts dependent on local tax funds to support education,
townships and cities, often with sizable black populations and low tax bases,
have schools with inadequate financial support. In Abbott v. Burke (1985)
and Robinson v. Cahill (1970), the State Supreme Court attempted to alleviate
inequality in New Jersey's school districts by mandating sufficient funds
across the state regardless of tax income. The state created "Abbott Districts"
that included major cities such as Newark, Camden, Jersey City, Trenton,
Paterson, and Elizabeth. The districts would receive higher state funding to
make up for inadequate tax bases. Pushed by the state branch of the NAACP,
Robinson v. Cahill became one of the most impactful national cases of the
late twentieth century. In New Jersey alone it spawned innumerable appeals
and retrials, with seven supreme court decisions regarding Robinson and
twenty-one about Abbott.[63]

BLACKS AT NEW JERSEY COLLEGES AND UNIVERSITIES

In the decades after the first black students' demonstrations, the presence of
African American students at New Jersey's colleges became more routine.
The Woodrow Wilson Foundation began awarding fellowships for gifted
students in honor of Martin Luther King, the slain civil rights leader. Princeton University, long a bastion of southern racial attitudes, made sweeping
reforms. Change occurred faster after Judge Bruce Wright spoke in town
about his experience in 1939. Robert Goheen, Princeton's president, heard
the speech and was aghast. Princeton University sped up the pace of integration.[64] In 1968 the number of blacks in Princeton's entering class rose
from twenty-eight the previous year to seventy-six. The same year, Elliott
Moorman from Newark became the president of the class of 1971. Princeton
appointed a committee to integrate materials on African American history

into the curriculum and promoted a black man, Carl A. Fields, to the post
of Assistant Dean of the College. In 1969, the school changed its election
rules to allow a black student to join the board of trustees And in 1971
Princeton created a cultural center for minority students. Nonetheless, four
Princeton football stars, dissatisfied with the pace of change, spoke out
against racism on the campus.[65]

The presence of Princeton's black faculty surged in the late 1980s. Dean
of the Faculty Ruth Simmons, a woman of color, initiated high-profile
recruitment of novelist Toni Morrison, historian Nell Irvin Painter, and phi-
losopher Cornel West. Morrison has made Princeton her home ever since.
Painter stayed in town until 2002 when she moved to Newark and became
key to the cultural renaissance there. West taught at Princeton from 1988 to
1994 and still teaches occasional courses there. Other leading and younger
black scholars arrived in the next years, soon making Princeton, a one-time
bastion of segregation, a leading center of African American culture.

But living in Princeton was not easy, even for the children of black faculty
members. Emily Raboteau recalled an early Halloween when she dressed as
Sojourner Truth and no one knew who she was. Raboteau's roman à clef is
dedicated to her father, Professor Albert Raboteau, an African American
scholar of religion who started teaching at Princeton in 1982. He later served
as dean of the faculty in the midst of a distinguished academic career that
ended with his retirement in 2016. Raboteau's novel describes a father who
integrates a department at Princeton while displaying all the traits, good
and bad, of his successful white colleagues. Deeply scholarly, an accomplished writer and teacher, the father figure is relentlessly careerist, often
neglecting family occasions for committee work and private study.[66]

Rutgers University in New Brunswick became radicalized in 1963 when
a recent black graduate, Don Harris, was arrested for taking part in a Student Non-Violent Coordinating Committee (SNCC) voter-registration drive
in Americus, Georgia. Harris penned a powerful note to the faculty and students at Rutgers from jail. The campus immediately rose in support of Harris. Stories about his plight ran daily in the student newspaper and more

than $3,000 in funds came from fraternities on campus. Eventually Harris was released, returned to speak at Rutgers, and continued his activism in the South. Rutgers University began admitting significant numbers of black and Spanish-speaking minority students between 1968 and 1972. One problem was the demand for a separate black wing of a dormitory, to be named after Paul Robeson, the famed actor and Rutgers graduate. There were unpleasant incidents of racial epithets and social distancing by white students, but blacks enrolled at Rutgers generally ignored them. Rutgers moved to introduce more black faculty. Dr. Samuel D. Proctor became a professor of education in 1969.[67]

Professor Clement Price of Rutgers-Newark emerged in the 1980s as a principal historian of black New Jersey. His 1980 book, *Freedom Not Far Distant: A Documentary History of Afro-Americans in New Jersey,* a compilation of essential documents with superb commentary, crystalized the narrative of black New Jersey history. Together with his close friends, historians Giles Wright and Larry Greene, Price formed the Marion Thompson Wright study group to recognize her achievements and energize study of New Jersey's African American past. Price became a leading public historian of Newark. In 1997 Rutgers-Newark established the Clement A. Price Institute on Ethnicity, Culture and the Modern Experience. Price later donated and gained national stature through President Barack Obama's appointment of him as vice-chair of the Advisory Council on Historic Preservation. He was also appointed as Newark City Historian in 2014 and as chairman of the 350th anniversary of Newark's founding in 1666. Price's connections to Lonnie Bunch, founding head of the National Museum of African American History and Culture, and Spencer Crew of the National Underground Railroad Center in Cincinnati and the Smithsonian Institution, resulted in Price's appointment to the Scholarly Advisory Committee to the Smithsonian Institution's National Museum of African American History and Culture.[68]

Figure 19. Larry A. Greene (1946–). Seton Hall history professor and leading scholar of black New Jersey. Courtesy of Seton Hall University Publicity Office.

Black New Jersey in the 1980s

Thirteen years after the Newark riots and a decade after Kenneth Gibson's election to the mayoralty, Newark's economic situation remained troubled. Douglas Massey and Nancy Denton's study of race and the making of an American underclass named Newark as second only to Chicago as the most segregated of the nation's cities in 1980. Blacks were four times as isolated in Newark in 1980 compared to 1930. Census data of neighboring New York City and Philadelphia also indicated nearly universal centralization of blacks in ghettos.[69] Petty and nasty violence occurred routinely. Three young men and an adult were arrested for beating the father of Newark's Mayor Gibson. Willie Gibson was on his way to the to wake of a friend when he was kicked to the ground. He regained his footing and fought off his attackers with a penknife.[70]

In the May elections of 1986, Sharpe James, a sixteen-year veteran city councilman, successfully challenged incumbent Mayor Gibson. James campaigned to increase the number of police officers, improve housing, and lower unemployment. Gibson shared these goals, but lacked public funds to do so. Despite the similarities in the platforms, James defeated Gibson decisively, netting over 55 percent of the popular vote. His victory could be attributed to his energy, style, and charisma and doubtless to voter fatigue with Mayor Gibson.[71]

Despite African American control over the mayor's office in Newark, local schools retained seemingly intractable problems, including limited tax revenue, decaying infrastructure patronage, corruption, and particularly an administration that kept Newark's schools in poor shape. As black and Hispanic students overwhelmed the classrooms, Newark's schools reached such a perilous condition in the early 1990s that the state of New Jersey took over management of the educational system. Only in 2017 did the state begin to return control of the schools to Newark city government. Construction of the New Jersey Performing Arts Center in 1997 marked the revival of Newark. Seen as a cultural symbol and reinvestment, the center beckoned people to return to the city.[72]

Incremental progress occurred in New Jersey's congressional representation. After failing to dislodge U.S. Congressman Peter Rodino in two elections, Donald M. Payne finally was elected to represent New Jersey's Tenth
Congressional District, covering portions of Essex, Hudson, and Union
Counties. Rodino had announced his retirement, easing the way for Payne's
election. Born in Newark in 1934, Payne received a bachelor's degree from
Seton Hall, worked for the YMCA, and rose to be its first black president in
1970. Elected to the Essex County Board of Chosen Freeholders in 1972, he
became its director in 1980. As congressman, he was chair of the Congressional Black Caucus, and worked in subcommittees on education, foreign
affairs, and world health. Payne headed a presidential humanitarian mission
to combat genocide in Rwanda and Sudan and worked toward a peace process in Ireland. His most prominent national role was as house manager for
the debate over using force in Iraq in 2004. He died in 2012 and was succeeded in office by his son, Donald M. Payne Jr.[73]

Other cities were unable to capitalize on major projects. Atlantic City's
revival via gambling casinos did not benefit African American residents.
Although noxious discrimination laws were banned, the architecture of the
new casinos turned a blank wall to the city itself. Parking garages and elevated walkways allowed patrons from the suburbs and beyond to avoid any
contact with the rough black neighborhoods. As Atlantic City faced a sharp
economic decline when pleasure seekers looked elsewhere for amusement,
older hotels, restaurants, and tourist shops closed and other ethnic groups
moved to the city's suburbs. African Americans, unable to gain loans or facing housing discrimination, were forced to remain in the rotting city
neighborhoods.[74]

Plans for Camden's revival were similar to those used in Newark and
Atlantic City. Emphasizing improvement of the waterfront area, Camden's
political leaders, all of them white, funded construction of an aquarium in
1992. It was initially successful, then faltered, and was renovated and
reopened in 2007. The aquarium also produced few new jobs, most of which
were filled by employees present in Camden only during daytime. Plans for
a minor-league baseball stadium and arena were initially unsuccessful due

to fiscal problems and concerns about an inability to compete with Philadelphia's sports complex just a few miles away. Ferry services to and from Philadelphia were partly successful but other schemes such as a barge-based light-and-sound show and a tram to transport people from Penn's Landing to Camden failed to move beyond blueprints. Later the city began to use monies from bridge and highway tolls to fund community-based projects such as the Camden Children's Garden, which opened at the entrance to the aquarium in 1999. Plus the waterfront backers were able to attract the *USS Jersey*, a retired naval ship, to serve as a popular museum in 2001. Added to that were private funds that made the baseball stadium possible in 2001 for use by an independent baseball team and by Rutgers-Camden University. The final piece of waterfront redevelopment was the transformation of the old RCA Victor factory to market-rate, often expensive housing.[75]

Waterfront redevelopment was not the answer to Camden's woes. The city could not compete with neighboring Philadelphia for tourism; often efforts created a tourist bubble in which specialized areas established to offer family entertainment ignored crime and poverty. Offering massive tax breaks to Sony to build an entertainment center further diluted city government revenue. Moreover, they created very few jobs. What Howard Gillette found most successful were community-based organizations such as BPUM and the CCCOP that worked to improve housing conditions and curb crime in Camden. While not always successful, such partnerships were more promising than the waterfront investment. Many were pessimistic that the political thinking in 2005 was sufficiently imaginative to solve the city's problems.[76]

Rural blacks in New Jersey remained mired in poverty. County planners in Cape May County in 1980 found that one of five black residents lived below the poverty line, three times the levels of their white neighbors. While much of Cape May prospered, blacks lived in dilapidated houses and projects. Lack of political representation hurt Cape May blacks' chances for improvement. Black veteran politicians were repeatedly passed over for vacant positions while the NAACP charged county freeholders with using subtle discrimination against black job applicants or in treatment of employees. Even the agricultural proletarian jobs of earlier eras were now out of reach for state blacks as immigrant labor replaced them.[77]

Blacks in New Jersey found government contracts hard to sustain. Government cutbacks after the end of the Cold War hit black-owned industries hard. New Jersey–based H. F. Henderson Industries, founded in 1954, manufactured defense electronics. In 1989 it was ranked number 37 in the national Black Enterprise list of the one hundred top black industrial companies, with $22.9 million in sales of which 70 percent was to the U.S. military. After cutbacks in the early 1990s, Henderson Industries fell to a rank of 80 in 1995 and by the following year was off the list entirely.[78]

Black workers were able to eke out new agreements on jobs. Under a consent decree accepted by two New Jersey Union locals, qualified black and Hispanic electrical workers were to get first chance at openings. Under the agreement, the unions were to notify minority workers every three months of openings and supply them with blank applications. If the returned applications were not processed within seven days, there were considered automatically approved. The unions agreed to admit any minority applicants with at least five years' experience who had lived in their area and had passed the journeyman's examination. Goals were established of 4 percent minority hiring the first year and 5, 6, 8, and 9 percent in succeeding years.[79]

Middle-class blacks were occasionally able to move out of the cities into the suburbs. Family networks enabled middle-class careers. New York University journalism professor Pamela Newkirk recalled her father Louis Newkirk's home in Englewood as a black treasure trove:

> There, amid antiques and splendor, he stockpiled images of black grace, brilliance and defiance that disrupted and buoyed. Here, a gilded-framed daguerreotype of an aristocratic African American boy; there a painting of Malcolm X in a flowing white robe. Bookcases brimmed with rare books filled with stories of black scientists, scholars, artists and dreamers who defied boundaries. Vintage posters, letters, and photographs summoned resilience and resolve.

Newkirk recalled auto excursions in Louis Newkirk's vintage Bentley over the George Washington Bridge to Harlem, the Schomburg Library, and the Tree of Life bookstore. Home was filled with cook-outs, reunions, weddings, basketball, badminton, chess, Ping-Pong, and jazz. Visitors included Dizzy Gillespie and the Isley Brothers. Future history professor Gretchen Sorin recalls her parents' decision to leave their home in the Clinton Hill district of Newark for Colonia because of her father's heart condition and in search of better schools. The town was not their first choice but other more prosperous communities convinced homeowners not to sell to the family. They did not leave the city behind completely and routinely ventured back for groceries, haircuts, and church services, though they later found a closer parish. The family also used Newark's train station for an annual trip to the South. Sorin fit in well with the white girls in Colonia and shared their clothing, hair styles, and enthusiasm for such black singing groups as New Jersey natives the Shirelles, who had achieved national fame with their hit songs. Generally, the teachers were color-blind; Sorin became the president of her school council. She enjoyed the racially mixed Episcopal Church where black and white teenagers held forth at fellowship meetings on such issues as premarital sex, race relations, the Vietnam War, drugs, and rock music. Sorin developed a secure identity as an African American. Racial exclusion only affected one major area of life: dating. White boys simply did not find her attractive, even as they adored such black singers as the Supremes and the Shirelles.[80]

Popular Culture and Social Mobility

The music that thrilled Gretchen Sorin and millions of other teenagers gave other young black New Jerseyans pathways to success. George Clinton, born in North Carolina, moved north in 1950. His father, a dockworker, found a home in Newark, while his mother lived in East Orange. Both parents' musical inclinations influenced him. Clinton's father was a churchgoer, but his mother loved rhythm and blues and played contemporary favorites such as B. B. King, Muddy Waters, and Wynonie Harris. Clinton regarded New

Jersey in the 1950s as a breeding ground for African American music. Family and community connections enabled this. Dionne Warwick, later a major pop star, lived next door to Clinton's mom. His cousin Ruth was close friends with the Shirelles. Clinton befriended Florence Birdsong, later of the Supremes. Ruth took young George routinely to Harlem's Apollo Theater where such doo-wop groups as the Chantels, Bobbettes, and the Bluebelles, who hailed from Trenton, entranced him. The lead singer of the Bluebelles later renamed herself Patti LaBelle and ascended to pop stardom. Clinton took pride in Clinton Avenue in Newark, named after New York State's first revolutionary governor. The avenue was lined with record stores and theaters that entranced young Clinton. He dropped out of school in his last year of senior high, preferring to study the works of Elvis Presley, the Isley Brothers, Jerry Lee Lewis, Little Richard, and other band leaders. To make ends meet some friends and he opened a barbershop. His first group, the Parliaments, sang doo-wop.

Following the trends, the Parliaments moved to Detroit to match the highly successful Motown Sound. Other connections developed and the Parliaments soon had a hit song. The group went on tour nationally, but New Jersey was always home. One of the key members of the band was innovative keyboardist Bernie Worrell, born in Long Branch and raised near Clinton in Plainfield. Later, Clinton and his band created a distinctive funk sound in the group known as Parliament-Funkadelic and became major pop figures in the 1980s and 1990s. During the last decade of the century, the hip-hop group The Fugees (Lauryn Hill, Wyclef Jean, and Pras Michel) formed in high school in South Orange and made world famous records before embarking on individual careers. Hill's 1998 award-winning smash hit album *The Miseducation of Lauryn Hill*, included a segment narrated by Ras Baraka, future mayor of Newark.[81]

Churches enabled female singers. The daughter of the leader of a famed gospel group from the American South named the Drinkard Singers, Cissy Houston matured to direct the choir at the New Hope Baptist Church in Newark. Later, Cissy Houston organized a pop group, the Sweet Inspirations, that featured her daughter Whitney, who rose to pop stardom in the

1980s and 1990s. The group provided backup singing for cousin Dionne Warwick, a major figure in American pop music. Singer-songwriter Regina Belle sang in the church choir in Englewood as a child and later graduated from Rutgers University.[82]

Singing gave other young blacks a start before they turned to education. Future historian James Oliver Horton often performed duets in high school with Dionne Warwick. Horton sang a solo at Carnegie Hall at the age of thirteen and sang briefly with the Count Basie Band. Given a chance at a recording contract after college, Horton chose instead to enroll in graduate school, a decision that set him on the path to become one of the nation's premier scholars of early American slavery and black freedom. Similarly, the five Thornton Sisters of Long Branch formed a singing group that toured extensively throughout the northeast and into the still-segregated south, always under the protective eye of their father. As they matured, each of the sisters entered college and eventually medical school, achieving medical and dental degrees and becoming prominent physicians. Yvonne, one of the sisters, chronicled the family story in a best-selling memoir, *The Ditchdigger's Daughters*, which was translated into nineteen languages and adapted into an award-winning film. Even those accomplishments plus her medical degree did not inure Yvonne from racism. Dedicated to her work, Yvonne commuted from her home in Teaneck into the metropolis only to find constant, irrational obstacles. Appointed to a prestigious professorship in New York City at one of the nation's leading hospitals, she suffered from job discrimination, sneers from her white male colleagues, and general discomfort in the position. Eventually she retreated to a lesser-known but prosperous practice in Morristown. Her family and her Jersey roots sustained her, even as she later found a better position in New York.[83]

Other women embraced rap, a musical form descended from the "dozens," an earlier black rhyming song style. Rap became globally popular in the 1990s. Dana Owens was born in Newark and raised in East Orange, and created a significant career in music and film.[84] Inspired by Malcolm X and Black Muslims, Dana Owens, though acknowledging that she loved her birth name, identified herself as Queen Latifah when she was just eight years old. Latifah's parents separated during her childhood and her mother had to move her children frequently. Despite impoverished abodes, Latifah's mother routinely took her daughter to Manhattan museums, the Bronx Zoo, and the Jersey Shore. Her father provided protection and support. School years included championship basketball teams, experiments with sex, work at a local Burger King, and support in a local rap scene. Family and church always remained paramount, even with the strains of her parents' divorce and the tragic death of her brother at twenty-four. The First Baptist Church of Nutley gave Latifah spiritual support.[85]

Outside of church, local networks of musicians emerged. Saxophone player Clarence Clemons played with pickup bands on the New Jersey shore before teaming up as lead saxophonist with future superstar Bruce Springsteen.[86] The Club Harlem in Atlantic City attracted top black acts and provided a welcome festive feeling for black New Jerseyans.[87]

An encounter with racism marked a coming of age for many young black male New Jerseyans. Ice-T, born in Newark and raised in Summit until his teens, experienced racism in childhood play when young whites allowed only their fellows to go inside a host's home after dark. African Americans, including the light-skinned future rapper, were sent home. After his father's death (his mother passed away earlier), Ice-T was sent to live with relatives in Los Angeles.[88]

New Jersey's black entertainment royalty today live isolated from urban problems. Alpine, New Jersey, regarded as the most expensive town in the United States, has few black residents, but those who reside there are very wealthy. Surprisingly, for a town that is 75 percent white, according to the latest U.S. census, Alpine has drawn a particularly large number of black stars—the *New York Times* described it as the home of hip-hop royalty. The comedian Chris Rock occasionally chews on this in his stand-up routines, once remarking: "There's like three, four black people in my neighborhood in Alpine. OK, it's me, [baseball player] Gary Sheffield, Mary J Blige, [basketball player] Patrick Ewing. Hall of famer, hall of famer, greatest R&B singer of our time, decent comedian." At the same time, black New Jersey performers and athletes cannot act too aloof from their supporters. In song, speech, and athletic feat, such celebrities are dependent upon ordinary blacks to buy music and athletic tickets and apparel.[89]

Sports

Athletic competition and performance became an even larger component in American society in the late twentieth century. Always a perceived avenue for mobility for the poor, despite the widely understood terrible odds of success, sports has attracted and enhanced the lives of a number of young black male New Jerseyans. Born in a troubled home in Orange and then blessed by a stern yet loving stepfather and by membership in a local Boys and Girls Club, Shaquille O'Neal became one the nation's leading basketball stars in the 1990s and early 2000s. O'Neal's dominance of his sport, his wide-ranging creativity and careful habits inculcated in him by parents and the local club made him a very wealthy man. He has now reinvested in Newark. Carl Lewis, a multiple Olympic gold medal winner, was born in Alabama but came as a teenager to Willingboro where he received expert coaching. Franco Harris, a leading football player of the 1970s and 1980s, was born in Fort Dix and educated in Mount Holly. Dennis Rodman, one of basketball's most ferocious rebounders and characters, came from a broken home in Trenton. His mother raised him, making ends meet with several part time jobs. Joetta Clark Diggs, born in East Orange in 1962, ran the 800- and 1,500-meter competitions for the United States in the 1988, 1992, 1996, and 2000 Olympic Games. She dominated the U.S. National Championships for eleven years. In 2000 her sister Hazel Clark, sister-in-law Jearl Miles-Clark, and their coach JJ became the first family to have three members of an Olympic sport. Her father, Principal Dr. Joe Clark was portrayed by Morgan Freeman in the popular movie "Lean on Me." Joetta Clark Diggs later became a prominent motivational speaker. There were a number of male and female Jersey athletes competing in the 2016 Olympics, including basketballer Kylie Irving, boxer Shakur Stevenson, hurdlers Jeff Porter and Ronnie Ash, wrestler Jordan Burroughs (a gold medal winner in 2012 and silver medalist in 2016), judo competitor Colton Brown, and female track stars Sydney McLaughlin, Ketur Orji, Nia Ali, Mariell Hall, Christina Epps, Ajee Wilson, and English Gardner.[90]

POLICE VIOLENCE AND RACIAL PROFILING IN THE 1990S

A tragic incident in Teaneck in April 1990 epitomized the shattered dreams of integration in New Jersey. A white police officer, Gary Spath, shot and killed a black teenager named Phillip Clinton Pannell. Spath believed that Pennell about to fire a gun at him when he shot the young man in the back. The killing bitterly divided Teaneck, a town that had always prided itself on its diversity and racial openness. Pannell's death revealed vast economic, educational, and social gulfs in the suburban town. The incident rapidly became politicized as the police united behind Spath and black teenagers trashed the main street in a protest. Soon, national black leaders Jesse Jackson, Al Sharpton, and Louis Farrakhan came to Teaneck and made highly critical, even incendiary remarks about Spath's alleged guilt.[91]

In 1998, a scandal erupted over police racial profiling on the New Jersey Turnpike. As the authors of a close study of the turnpike, America's most heavily traveled highway, have shown, authorities work strenuously to ensure that little outside a prescribed order happens on it. The turnpike is designed to be as straight as possible for its entire length. Motorists are forbidden to stop on it; rest stops are few and unattractive, serving only fast food and gas. Drivers must remain with a disabled vehicle until help comes from the police and licensed towers. Within such a controlled venue, suddenly state police began stopping black and Hispanic motorists on small pretexts to search their cars for drugs and weapons. On Sunday, February 28, 1999, the *Newark Star Ledger* published a lengthy interview with Colonel Carl Williams of the New Jersey State Police in which he talked about race and drugs: "Today . . . the drug problem is cocaine or marijuana. It is most likely a minority group that's involved with that." Williams condemned racial profiling, saying "As far as racial pro-filing is concerned, that is absolutely not right." However, he argued the illegal drug trade was ethnically balkanized: "If you're looking at the methamphetamine market, that

seems to be controlled by motorcycle gangs, which are basically predomi-
nantly white. If you're looking at heroin and stuff like that, your involvement
there is more or less Jamaicans." Hours later, Governor Christine Todd
Whitman fired Williams from his job as superintendent of the New Jersey
State Police because "his comments . . . are inconsistent with our efforts to
enhance public confidence in the State Police." Further outcry occurred
when police shot four men accused of speeding. A survey determined that
some 98 percent of all the drivers along the stretch of the turnpike were
going over the speed limit of 55 miles per hour, giving the police latitude to
stop virtually anybody. The survey found that while 13.5 percent of the
drivers on the stretch of highway were black, 46 percent of those halted by
the police over a forty-month period were black. "They were pulling over
blacks out of all proportion to the population of the turnpike," said Fred
Last, a public defender who helped design the survey. State documents further revealed that at least eight of every ten automobile searches carried out
by state troopers on the New Jersey Turnpike over most of the last decade
were conducted on vehicles driven by blacks and Hispanics. In the case of
the shooting of the three men, civil rights advocates quickly filed suit against
the state, which eventually settled by paying $13 million in damages and
dropping charges against 128 other people charged with crimes during profiling. After the 9/11 terrorist attacks on New York City and Washington,
D.C., some legal scholars argued that racial profiling had some merits, but
in the context of New Jersey's troubled racial history, that view seemed more
a justification for racial harassment than fighting crime.[92]

Mass Incarceration

One of the major issues for the new century is mass incarceration. In October 2012, there were just over 13,000 people incarcerated in New Jersey; the
state ranks thirty-ninth among fifty American states with an incarceration
rate of 298 per 100,000 persons. Nearly 55 percent of male prisoners were
black as were 44 percent of female prisoners . The next largest groups were
white, and female white prisoner percentages matched their black peers but

white male prisoners amounted to just under 26 percent.[93] Once they have completed their terms, New Jersey's ex-felons automatically have their voting rights restored, a basic tenet of American freedom lost upon their conviction of a crime. John E. Pinkard Sr.'s careful compilation and analysis of corrections department statistics indicate that in the year 2000, there were 2,720 felons released who had completed their terms and conditions of parole and were immediately eligible to vote. Another 12,612 were placed on parole following incarceration stemming from a felony conviction. That roughly 12,000 persons were somewhat free but unable to exercise the vote is a significant number in an era of political polarization and close margins of victory and loss in political races. New Jersey, as Pinkard points out, is actually more liberal than many American states in which a felony conviction mandates permanent loss of the vote.[94]

Pinkard's analysis indicates how heavily these losses bear upon African Americans, even those who have regained the vote. More than 55 percent of incarcerated men in New Jersey are black, despite being about 13 percent of the overall population. Black inmates were, unsurprisingly, poorer, less-educated, more likely to be unemployed, and impoverished. The number of people incarcerated in New Jersey has risen dramatically since 1980 and the start of the antidrug war. Most of the black inmates in New Jersey have been convicted of minor crimes of dealing or possessing drugs. At the same time, Pinkard finds, ex-felons are politically aware, believe in the power and utility of their vote, and feel that voting is responsible citizenship. Losing that right is a major loss of citizenship.[95]

Pinkard's work indicates the immense power that the state government has in enforcing racism. He begins his study with a personal anecdote in which he, a middle-class, educated black, was the victim of racial profiling. Two white policemen accosted him while driving because he seemingly fit the description of a criminal who had held up a nearby store. When Pinkard refused a police order, the officer held a gun next to his ear, cocked the trigger, and repeated the order. All this was done in public in a humiliating exercise. Pinkard's bad experience mirrors that of many other prosperous black men in New Jersey. Comedian Chris Rock, one of the wealthiest black men in New Jersey, has taken "selfies" of himself during the three times he was stopped by the police in New Jersey in a two-month period. Rock then posted the images of himself with a police car's flashing lights behind his car.

For poorer black men, racial profiling has more powerful implications. In her book *On the Run*, sociologist Alice Goffman portrays a horrifying situation in Philadelphia. Police and impoverished young blacks engage in a tragic dance in which officers of the law begin enmeshing African Americans in the penal system over minor drug charges even before children reach ten years of age. Goffman explicitly compares the constant police surveillance and black desperate need to hide to the world of enslaved fugitives. Young men anxious about past criminal records entrapping them in contemporary police searches are constantly on the run, fearful of getting health care at hospitals where police might arrest them, vigilant about avoiding social scenes or locales. Families learn to hide or deny knowledge of children's whereabouts. Every moment is governed by fear of police capture, creating a milieu as bad as slavery days. Recent data affirms these pessimistic findings. A report released in December 2015 showed that New Jersey blacks and other minorities face arrest at rates far higher than whites and that the state incarcerates twelve black men for every white man. Combined patterns of racial profiling and arrest percentages in New Jersey make Goffman's argument more prescient for New Jersey than Philadelphia's proximity to the state.[96]

Mass incarceration most profoundly affects black males; at the same time, it also affects families. As Matthew Desmond indicates, eviction from their homes deeply impaired the ability of black females, many of them single mothers, to achieve a stable life for themselves and their children. Desmond details how evictions, which have increased dramatically in the past few decades, disrupt families, push children around school districts several times each academic year, destroy dreams, promote depression, and are a key cause of early suicides. Evictions also damage the organic strength of a neighborhood and, by extension, a city.[97]

Crushed hopes destroyed even those with immense promise. Robert Peace emerged from Newark to enroll at Yale University, the product of his mother's extraordinary love and dedication, the massive emotional contributions of St. Benedict's School, and his own brilliance. Peace felt alienated from his affluent fellow students at Yale. When, at the first year reception they mistakenly assumed he was a member of the maintenance staff, he encouraged their error. In the dining hall, he sat near the door to talk daily with an older woman who checked student identification in preference to sitting with his classmates. A brilliant student who easily aced the hardest science courses, Peace acquired customers rather than friends by making frequent runs back to Newark to get supplies of marijuana, which he consumed and sold to his fellow students. After graduation, as his peers obtained prestigious jobs, Peace labored for months in the college cafeteria. After being fired from that job, he worked as a baggage handler at Newark Airport. Intent on regaining the several hundred thousand dollars he had made selling pot at Yale that later embezzled by a friend, Peace decided to invent a super-pot. He told few if any of his associates in Newark of his Yale degree. Local drug dealers, upset at the competition, had him shot to death. His mother had to take the morning off from her job at the hospital to attend his funeral. His father could not attend as he was incarcerated for life. Peace was thirty years old when he died.[98] Other young men encountered familiar travails, but succeeded by banding together. Facing police hostility, gang pressure, and threatening adolescent pitfalls, George Jenkins, Sampson Davis, and Rameck Hunt survived life in Newark by creating a pact to ensure mutual success. Eventually two became doctors and the third a dentist.[99]

Contrasting with Peace's tragically short life is the career of Cory Booker, who also attended top-ranked American universities. On May 9, 2006, Cory Booker won Newark's mayoralty with 72 percent of the popular vote, a total that indicated a clear mandate. Booker, though raised in an elite suburb, had plunged himself into Newark politics, working especially on crime in housing. He took his inspiration from community activists like his parents. He gained notoriety by setting up a tent city near a troubled housing project until the police offered greater protection for residents. Soon loyal, newly elected municipal council members joined him. Helping Booker's election was the withdrawal of Sharpe James, the incumbent, a few weeks before the ballot, allowing little time for opposition to coalesce. Opposition to Booker came from Newark's gangs. After Booker received a creditable threat that gang members might assassinate the mayor-elect, Newark's police put him under twenty-four-hour protection.[100]

The premise of Booker's election was that Newark and by extension Black New Jersey would enter a postracial era. That was not to be. Still his argument and its subsequent failure marks the close of a long period of hopes of integration. In the past half century black New Jerseyans have undergone the promise of integration, the transformation into Black Power and its sublimation into mainstream state and local politics. Just as African Americans in New Jersey have attained far more electoral power than ever before and the black middle class has stabilized, the same old problems continue. That dichotomy will be the subject of the concluding pages of this book.

CHAPTER 8

~

Present and Future

On January 8, 2014, Amiri Baraka, the legendary poet, playwright, and activist, died. Interim Newark Mayor Luis Quintana mourned Baraka, stating that he was "more than a poet, he was a leader in his own right." Quintana recalled Baraka's role in the 1969 Black and Puerto Rican convention, a landmark political meeting that resulted in the election of Ken Gibson, Newark's first black mayor. "We're going to remember him always for his contributions to Newark, New Jersey and America," Quintana said. "In this time of pain, the citizens of Newark and I are with him."[1] On November 5, 2014, Clement Price, the historian of black New Jersey, died after a stroke felled him six days earlier. Price, typically, had spoken on black history at the last of hundreds of public events that had marked his style as chronicler of Newark's African American history. Price had combined his academic career at Rutgers-Newark where he had published many influential books and articles and founded a center, with the world of public history. Price was an indefatigable promoter of Newark and its history and had become instrumental, along with his friends Lonnie Bunch and Spencer Crew, in the founding of what would become the wildly successful National Museum of African American History in Washington, D.C. Price's frequent coworker in black New Jersey history, Giles Wright, had passed away in 2009.[2]

On May 13, 2014, Amiri Baraka's son, Ras, was elected Mayor of Newark. Baraka did not receive support from many Democratic Party officials but won by campaigning against Cory Booker's reforms of the public school

Figure 20. Clement Alexander Price (1945–2014), the dean of New Jersey black history and the personification of the public historian. Newark Public Library by permission of the *Newark Star-Ledger*.

system. Baraka, experienced via his many years in the public schools as a teacher and administrator, showed a powerful ability to get out the vote. Matthew Hale, a political science professor at Seton Hall University, said even those who did not support Baraka now must make him their friend. "He has shown he can get the vote out," he said. "That's fundamental to politics in New Jersey and the big cities." Voters strongly approved of Baraka's

Figure 21. Giles R. Wright II (1935–2009) with his book *Afro-Americans in New Jersey*. Inaugural director of the Afro-American History Program at the New Jersey Historical Commission/Department of State, the first such post established in the United States, a leading historian of the Underground Railroad, and promoter of black New Jersey history in public schools. Newark Public Library, by permission of the *Newark Star-Ledger*.

longtime commitment and experience in Newark and rejected the telegenic
powers of Booker, the new U.S. Senator from New Jersey. One voter commented about Booker: "He was on Jay Leno . . . That's where you saw him. He
was on TV." Implicit within this criticism was the sense of class difference.
Hurting Booker, too, was the suspicion that he cared more about national
fame than about Newark's needs.[3]

To differentiate himself from Booker, Ras Baraka emphasized his community experience, making public education a primary focus. He was especially critical of charter school reforms initiated by Booker and partly paid
for by a challenge grant of $100 million by Facebook founder Mark Zucker-
berg. Booker, Zuckerberg, and Republican New Jersey Governor Chris
Christie planned to replace existing Newark schools taught by unionized
school teachers with nonunion charter schools. Zuckerberg's grant soon was
used to balance deals with the teachers' union. Their chosen superintendent,
Cami Anderson, failed to jibe with the parents of Newark's schoolchildren.
Parents and teachers viewed the highly regarded Anderson as an interloper
who lacked any understanding of local problems. Her resignation in the
summer of 2015 effectively ended the charter school reforms. With return
of control of Newark's schools to local authority, Baraka had a much freer
hand in running Newark's educational policies.[4]

Ras Baraka reformed the Newark police department. He drew upon a
harshly critical 2014 U.S. Department of Justice report that revealed that
75 percent of pedestrian stops cited by police had no justification and were
strongly tilted toward blacks. The report indicated excessive police reliance
upon force and patterns of theft of citizen's property by officers in narcotics,
gangs, and prisoner processing units. Overall, Ras Baraka's performance
appears to have been a sharp break from his predecessors. Newark has had
a black mayor since 1970. Gibson, James, and even Booker for a short term
were race-effacing managers more than leaders. Baraka combined manage-
rial excellence with a genuine commitment for reform and improvement for
the city. As Ravi Perry argues about Ohio black mayors, to be successful
Baraka and other Jersey magistrates must combine nationalism with themes
that embrace all Jersey citizens' needs. Ras Baraka has argued that Newark

and other Jersey cities need mayors "that will harness the power of small business, our universities, the promise of our seaport and our airport, to benefit the hundreds and thousands of us, a mayor that puts his city first, a mayor that never forgets how he got here. Yeah, we need a mayor that's radical."[5] Ras Baraka, Cory Booker, and other black New Jersey politicians planned methods for combating the Trump administration's retrograde policies on race. In a reference to the past, Baraka termed Trump's policies toward undocumented immigrants as modern-day slave catching.[6]

New Jersey blacks gained more and more political leaders. In the special election in October 2013 to replace recently deceased New Jersey Senator Frank Lautenberg, Cory Booker, the Democratic Mayor of Newark, easily defeated Steve Lonegan, the Republican candidate. Booker resigned as mayor to become the first black U.S. senator from New Jersey. He was reelected for a full term in the November 2014 elections. Recently, he has been mentioned as a 2020 presidential candidate.[7]

In 2017, black political leaders were spread across the state, three state senators and ten assemblymen.[8] There were in 2017 twenty-one black elected mayors. Lizette Parker was elected in 2014 as mayor of Teaneck, the first black female mayor of any municipality in Bergen County. Her untimely death at forty-four in 2016 was deeply mourned.[9]

Other examples of New Jersey's black female leaders include Mildred Scott, who was sworn in as sheriff of Middlesex County on January 1, 2011, having risen through the ranks from the police academy. She had constructed significant advances in the personnel structure of the Sheriff's Office, upgraded security for courthouses, added narcotics dogs, and added twenty-six sheriffs laid off from other counties, thereby reducing overtime and increasing community outreach. The American Diversity Council honored Scott in 2017 for her achievements.[10]

Sheila Y. Oliver of East Orange is a prominent member of the New Jersey State Assembly, serving as speaker for two terms from 2010 to 2014. She received a bachelor of arts degree from Lincoln University and was first elected to the assembly in 2003 and has retained her seat ever since. She is a member of numerous state committees including commerce and economic development, public schools, and transportation. On November 7, 2017, she was elected Lieutenant Governor of the state, to join Cory Booker as the highest elected black officials in New Jersey.[11]

Bonnie Watson Coleman served in the New Jersey General Assembly from 1998 to 2015, when she was elected as the first black female congressperson from New Jersey, representing the state's twelfth congressional district. The district includes portions of Mercer, Middlesex, Somerset, and Union Counties, and covers such research institutions as Princeton University, Rider College, the College of New Jersey, the Institute for Advanced Studies, and Bristol-Myers-Squibb and Johnson & Johnson. Born in Camden and educated at Thomas Edison Sate College, Coleman was director of the New Jersey Department of Transportation and in 2002 was elected as the first black female chair of the state Democratic Party. In Congress, she is on the Committee for Homeland Security and Oversight and Government Reform as well as founding the congressional caucus on black women and girls. She is a strong advocate for programs enabling criminal offenders to reenter society and find work.[12]

Black political figures are organizing at the municipal level. The New Jersey Black Mayors' Alliance for Social Justice, founded in 2014, includes twenty-one African Americans state mayors. In early 2017, the alliance issued a statement in response to the American president's plan to restrict immigration. The statement read: "Many Americans are the descendants of immigrants. Our faiths compel us to welcome strangers in need. We should welcome these refugees, mostly women, children and families who have already been extensively vetted through proper methods. It's our obligation to protect those individuals who have protected us, including military interpreters and overseas diplomats. We must also welcome back green-card holders, who are lawful U.S. permanent residents." The Alliance maintains the historic ties that black New Jerseyans have forged with the Democratic Party. As Barack Obama finished his distinguished presidency, the Alliance congratulated him for his conduct and accomplishments in office.[13]

New Jersey blacks have also consolidated their presence at state universities. Federal and state mandates have gradually increased the numbers of blacks at public and private New Jersey colleges and universities. By 2015, 7,655 black students were enrolled at institutions of higher education in the state, accounting for 13.4 percent of total enrollment. There were wide disparities. Among public colleges, one out of five students at Kean University in 2015 was African American; on the campuses of Rutgers, about one of twelve students was black. Princeton University enrolled ninety black students or just less than 7 percent of its total. At Bloomfield College, a much smaller institution, blacks made up more than 50 percent of the student population. Junior colleges skewed toward local attendance. Accordingly, more than 50 percent of students at Essex County Community College were black; Sussex County had fewer than 2 percent of its total. Overall, blacks were a decided presence at New Jersey colleges, but their representation was far less than their percentage of the state population. Black students also lagged behind whites in achievement of undergraduate and graduate degrees.[14]

Economically, blacks have more independence than ever. There are now over 11,000 black-owned businesses in the state. Among the listings are types familiar to earlier eras such as barbershops, funeral homes, beauty salons, restaurants, and taxi companies. But now black businesses include realtors, job training centers, internet companies, and banks and other financial services. Black people are now almost as equal to whites in homeownership around the state and have healthy percentages of college graduates. Black people are gaining staff positions at major New Jersey corporations and have internal lobbying groups that advertise openings, sponsor scholarships, and act as ombudsmen for employee concerns. At the same time, black executive presence at Fortune 500 companies remain rare. Ken Frazier, Chief Executive Officer at Merck, the seventy-second ranked company in America, is an exception.[15]

Yet major problems remain. In July 2016, after eight years of Barack Obama's presidency, the Pew Research Center issued a report indicating that racial equality was still a distant goal, rather than an accomplishment. Sadly, over 40 percent of black Americans believed that racial equality would never occur in the United States and that discrimination still existed in schools, housing, jobs, in elections, and in the court system. Another 40 percent believed that positive change might come but only 8 percent felt that equality had been accomplished. Among whites, 53 percent believed that more changes were necessary but many felt enough had already been done. The Pew survey buttressed a New Jersey report in 2015 that indicated that over half of black New Jerseyans felt that the police and court system treated them unfairly. Another report demonstrated in 2013 that blacks in New Jersey were three times as likely to be arrested for marijuana possession as were whites. Compounding these dismal report were more recent studies that stated that New Jersey schools and housing were increasingly segregated. The wealth gap between New Jersey schools was the highest of surrounding states. Income disparity had grown since 1990. The unemployment rates for young black men in Essex County tripled that of whites in the same age cohort; overall the rate for that age group was 15 percent in 2015. Worse, almost 35 percent of prison inmates were black males aged twenty-one to thirty. Sixty percent of inmates in New Jersey are black, more than five times their fraction of the state's population.[16]

New Jersey's population is more racially divided than ever, even as the state is slated to have a minority/majority population by 2030. In Paterson, the Passaic River marks boundaries between African American and Hispanic neighborhoods from whites.[17] Major national and local studies indicate that New Jersey's schools are more segregated than any southern state except Georgia and Texas.[18]

Jerseys' predominately black cities have had a divergent experience lately. Despite an improved central business district, Newark did not benefit from the economic recovery following the recession of 2008–2009. A *New York Times* report in 2016 cited Newark as the third most "distressed" city in America, behind Cleveland and Detroit. Thirty percent of Newark's adults had little education and nearly half of adults were unemployed. Its economic imbalance with the rest of the state continued, as the city's median income was 47 percent of New Jersey's overall wealth, the lowest of the major cities cited in the report. Employment rates were 3.1% better in 2016 than six years earlier but business startups were barely above zero.[19] The city's infrastructure continued to decay. In March 2016, city officials announced the presence of lead contamination in nearly half of the drinking water of local schools, requiring closure of drinking fountains and use of water coolers and plastic water bottles. Two months later the governor ordered tests for lead contamination in all New Jersey schools.[20] Recent signs are more positive. Newark's downtown is undergoing a renaissance and it was named one of the top ten American cities for artists. Mayor Ras Baraka hailed the reopening of the Hahne and Company Building as a luxury apartment dwelling in January 2017.[21]

What lessons about contemporary black New Jersey and its future may be drawn from three and a half centuries of history? Development of a solid middle class coming out of slavery, sharply increasing even during the Jim Crow Era, declining during the Great Depression, recovering somewhat after World War II, and asserting itself politically since then, has been a major achievement. Dips in its strengths during the Depression indicate its fragility. Recall that New Jersey blacks suffered under nearly two centuries of chattel bondage. Slavery's powerful impact remains, both socially and economically. Racism, slavery's ugly spawn, has remained constant and has hampered social integration as well as black nationalism after slavery. Over the centuries blacks and have received assistance from whites with "black hearts," including Quakers, abolitionists, members of the NAACP and Urban League, sympathetic jurists and politicians, and radicals from the 1960s and after. Mostly, New Jersey blacks have achieved equality themselves or pushed the white majority to live up to the promise of American ideals. As this book has demonstrated, black progress can be reversed. Neglect of black needs is a by-product of racism. For many New Jersey blacks, progress has always been an illusion, whether during slavery days or when living free and impoverished.

Now we live in an era of limited ideals and investment in human capital. Evil politicians have made racism socially acceptable. New Jersey blacks have faced such foes in the past and did not flinch from direct opposition to racism and injustice. History tells us that they will again. For all the glamour and inequality of contemporary American society, the efforts of New

Jersey blacks to lift themselves up remains the principal example for the future. This book is a history of Black New Jersey. History helps us to determine the future. Over the past 253 years, clear patterns have emerged. For two centuries New Jersey was a slave society, either by law or custom. Most whites viewed blacks as either enslaved or as unwelcome free people. Jim Crow was strong from the Civil War era to the 1960s and in some ways, to the present. So that history is bleak. At the same time, New Jersey blacks have struggled for their freedom the entire history, either individually or collectively. During slavery times such struggle was illegal by definition. After the era of gradual emancipation, blacks maintained freeholds, worked, had legal families and some civil rights. Bright moments occurred in the early Reconstruction Period, the late 1940s, and somewhat in the 1960s when state and local authorities strived to meet black needs and allot full citizenship.

As this book has demonstrated, New Jersey black people have often done the right things. Now there is a sizable black middle class, though without the accumulated, ancestral wealth held in the white middle classes. Black New Jerseyans possess more political power than ever before; at the same time, there is economic distress among many. Using its past and building on the present, black New Jersey citizens will combine electoral power with grassroots activism, a tactic that has succeeded in the past and can again. Because of the undeniable resurgence of white racism, Black New Jersey has no choice but to use the past to make the future better.[22]

Acknowledgments

Black New Jersey could not have been written without the assistance of extraordinary archivists at a number of institutions including the Alexander Library at Rutgers University–New Brunswick, the Newark Public Library, the New-Jersey Historical Society, the New-York Historical Society, New York Public Library (Forty-Second-Street Branch), the Schomburg Library, the New Jersey State Library, the Library Company of Philadelphia, the National Archives, and many smaller libraries. I am grateful to the New Jersey Historical Commission for a starter grant and book subvention as part of the 350th Anniversary of New Jersey Publication Project. Highly useful as well were supportive funds from the Colgate University Dean of Faculty and Faculty Research Council, the Africana Program at Colgate, and the George Dorland Langdon Jr., endowment. Colgate University also funded a number of terrific student workers who helped on the research for this book. They include Nicole Schroeder, Ann Canning, Warren Dennis, Tram and Chou Nyugen, and Karen Zhang.

Various historians enabled this book with information and criticism, often saving me from grievous errors. Helpful historians include Kate Clifford Larson, Barbara Dreyfus, Pamela Newkirk, Jonathan Sassi, Douglas Egerton, Carl and Linda Smith, Craig Wilder, Lois Horton, Manisha Sinha, Fergus Bordewich, and Clarence Taylor. James Amenasor of the New-Jersey Historical Society allowed me access to his invaluable collection of fugitive slave notices from 1784 to 1804. Komozi Woodard, Craig Wilder, and Nell

Painter read full drafts of the manuscript. I cannot thank Maxine Lurie enough for her selfless support and close readings of several versions of the manuscript. Any errors in the book are my responsibility.

This project started at Rutgers University Press under the editorship of Marlie Wasserman. After her retirement, Peter Mickulas has ably shepherded this book to press. I am grateful to him and to the copy editors.

My family, wife Yunxiang Gao, sons Graham Zhen Gao-Hodges and Russell Du Gao-Hodges, mother-in-law Du Xiuhwa, and sister Mary Buckley, now an historian in her own right, always provided love and support, providing meaning for life outside of this project.

This book is dedicated to four New Jersey black historians Marion Thompson Wright, Gilles Wright, Clement Price, and Larry Greene, without whose pioneering studies I could never have started this one.

Notes

INTRODUCTION

1. For population numbers see http://www.census.gov/prod/cen2010/briefs/c2010br -06.pdf; Mark Krasovic, *The Newark Frontier: Community Action in the Great Society* (Chicago: University of Chicago Press, 2015), 5.

2. Angus Kress Gillespie and Michael Aaron Rockland, *Looking for America on the New Jersey Turnpike* (New Brunswick, N.J.: Rutgers University Press, 1989); Marion Thompson Wright, "Racial Integration in the Public Schools of New Jersey," *The Journal of Negro Education* 23, no. 3 (Summer 1954), 282.

3. Isabel Wilkerson, "When Will the North Face Its Racism?" *New York Times*, January 10, 2015.

4. Marion Thompson Wright, *The Education of Negroes in New Jersey* (New York: Columbia University Press for Teachers College Press, 1941); Clement Alexander Price, *Freedom Not Far Distant: A Documentary History of Afro-Americans in New Jersey* (Newark: New Jersey Historical Society, 1980); Giles R. Wright, *Afro-Americans in New Jersey: A Short History* (Trenton: New Jersey Historical Commission, 1988); L. A. Greene, "A History of Afro-Americans in New Jersey," *Journal of the Rutgers University Library* 56, no. 1 (1994): 4–71.

5. James J. Gigantino II, *The Ragged Road to Abolition: Slavery and Freedom in New Jersey, 1775–1865* (Philadelphia: University of Pennsylvania Press, 2014), 240–242, 250–252; Greene, "A History," 4–5; Toni Morrison, *The Origin of Others* (Cambridge, Mass.: Harvard University Press, 2017).

6. Marion Thompson Wright, "The Quakers as Social Workers among Negroes in New Jersey from 1763 to 1804," *Bulletin of the Friends Historical Association* 30, no. 2 (Autumn 1941): 78–88.

7. Graham Russell Hodges, *Root & Branch: African Americans in New York and East Jersey, 1613–1863* (Chapel Hill: University of North Carolina Press, 1999);

Hodges, *Slavery and Freedom in the Rural North: African Americans in Monmouth County, New Jersey, 1660–1870* (Madison, Wis.: Madison House Publishers, 1997).

8. For an understanding of New Jersey as a cultural hearth but attached to urban regions see Liam Riordan, *Many Identities, One Nation: The Revolution and Its Legacy in the Mid-Atlantic* (Philadelphia: University of Pennsylvania Press, 2007); Randall H. Balmer, *A Perfect Babel of Confusion: Dutch Religion and English Culture in the Middle Colonies* (New York: Oxford University Press, 1989); Graham Russell Hodges, *Root & Branch*; Ned C. Landsman, *Crossroads of Empire: The Middle Colonies in British North America* (Baltimore: Johns Hopkins University Press, 2010); and for the modern period see Dennis E. Gale, *Greater New Jersey: Living in the Shadow of Gotham* (Philadelphia: University of Pennsylvania Press, 2006).

9. Wright, *Negro Education*; Clement Alexander Price, *Freedom Not Far Distant*; Giles R. Wright, *Afro-Americans in New Jersey*; L. A. Greene, "A History."

10. For list of black New Jersey federal office holders see http://www.blackpast.org and for the state level see http://www.njleg.state.nj.us/members/abcroster.asp.

11. See Gigantino, *Ragged Road to Abolition*, chapter 7 on the ACS.

12. Kenneth Jackson, *Crabgrass Frontiers: The Suburbanization of the United States* (New York: Oxford University Press, 1985), 274–275; Lizbeth Cohen, *A Consumers' Republic: The Politics of Mass Consumption in Postwar America* (New York: Knopf, 2003); Walter David Greason, *Suburban Erasure: How the Suburbs Ended the Civil Rights Movement in New Jersey* (Lanham, Md.: Fairleigh Dickinson University Press, 2013); Bryant Simon, *Boardwalk of Dreams: Atlantic City and the Fate of Urban America* (New York: Oxford University Press, 2004). For slavery's legacies see Douglas Blackmon, *Slavery by Another Name: The Re-Enslavement of Black Americans from the Civil War to World War II* (New York: Doubleday, 2008), and Michelle Alexander, *The New Jim Crow: Mass Incarceration in the Age of Colorblindness* (New York: New Press, 2010); Heather Ann Thompson, "Why Mass Incarceration Matters: Rethinking Crisis, Decline and Transformation in Postwar American History," *Journal of American History* (December 2010), 703–734.

13. Rebecca Solnit and Joshua Jelly-Schapiro, *Nonstop Metropolis: A New York City Atlas* (Oakland: University of California Press, 2016), 178–184; for Edwards, see Alex Potts and Tobias Wolford, *Melvin Edwards: Five Decades* (Dallas: Nasher Sculpture Center, 2015); for Ben F. Jones see https://cm-sites.icompendium.com/accounts/benfjones.net/bio.

14. See Hodges, *Slavery and Freedom*, and Gigantino, *The Ragged Road*, for contrasting views.

CHAPTER 1 — FROM INITIAL EURO-AFRICAN SETTLEMENT
TO THE PRE-REVOLUTION

1. Joyce Goodfriend, "Burghers and Blacks: The Evolution of a Slave Society at New Amsterdam," *New York History* 59 (1978): 125–144.

2. Peter O. Wacker, *Land and People: A Cultural Geography of Preindustrial New Jersey: Origins and Settlement Patterns* (New Brunswick, N.J.: Rutgers University Press, 1975), 123; Graham Russell Hodges, *Root and Branch: African Americans in New York and East Jersey, 1613–1863* (Chapel Hill: University of North Carolina Press, 1999), 9.

3. Ira Berlin, *Many Thousands Gone: The First Two Centuries of American Slavery* (Cambridge, Mass.: Harvard University Press, 1999), chapter 1; Wacker, *Land and People*, 203; Hodges, *Root and Branch*, 34–35.

4. The Grants and Concessions may be found in Clement Alexander Price, *Freedom Not Far Distant: A Documentary History of Afro-Americans in New Jersey* (Newark: New Jersey Historical Society, 1980), 6–9; Hodges, *Root and Branch*, 44; Trevor Burnard, *Planters, Merchants and Slaves: Plantation Societies in British America, 1650–1820* (Chicago: University of Chicago Press, 2015), 53–98.

5. Wacker, *Land and People*, 126–128, 246–252; Hodges, *Root and Branch*, 47; Maxine Lurie, "Colonial Period: The Complex and Contradictory Beginnings of a Mid-Atlantic Province," in *New Jersey: A History of the Garden State*, ed. Maxine Lurie and Richard Veit, (New Brunswick, N.J.: Rutgers University Press, 2012), 33–63. For New England see Wendy Warren, *New England Bound: Slavery and Colonization in Early America* (New York: Liveright, 2016).

6. For Anthony and New Sweden, see George Fishman, *The African American Struggle for Freedom and Equality: The Development of a People's Identity, New Jersey, 1624–1850* (New York: Garland, 1997), 12–15; Jean R. Soderlund, *Lenape Country: Delaware Valley Society before William Penn* (Philadelphia: University of Pennsylvania Press, 2015), 60–61, 112.

7. Jean R. Soderlund, *Quakers and Slavery: A Divided Spirit* (Princeton: Princeton University Press, 1985), 40–44; William Frost, "Why Quakers and Slavery, Why Not More Quakers," in *Quakers and Abolition*, ed. Brycchan Carey and Geoffrey Plank (Urbana: University of Illinois Press, 2014), 29–42. For Burlington, see Ernest Lyght, *Path of Freedom: The Black Presence in New Jersey's Burlington County, 1659–1900* (Cherry Hill, N.J.: E & E Publishing House, 1978), 1; for Camden County, see Jeffrey M. Dorwart, *Camden County, New Jersey: The Making of a Metropolitan Community, 1626–2000* (New Brunswick, N.J.: Rutgers University Press, 2001), 20, 29–30.

8. Jeffrey M. Dorwart, *Cape May, New Jersey: The Making of an American Resort Community* (New Brunswick, N.J.: Rutgers University Press, 1992), 15–18

9. Soderlund, *Lenape Country*, 182, 196–197.

10. Hodges, *Root and Branch*, 274: Wacker, *Land and People*, 190–191; Edgar J. McManus, *Black Bondage in the North* (Syracuse, N.Y.: Syracuse University Press, 1973), 212–213; Dorwart, *Cape May County*, 39–40

11. For law see Paul Axel-Lute, comp., "*The Law of Slavery in New Jersey* (Camden, N.J.: The New Jersey Digital Legal Library), A5, http://njlegallib.rutgers.edu /slavery/acts/. On early abolition see Manisha Sinha, *The Slave's Cause: A History of Abolition* (New Haven, Conn.: Yale University Press, 2016).

12. Fishman, *African American Struggle*, 44–46; Burnard, *Planters, Merchants and Slaves*, 60–68.

13. Price, *Freedom Not Far Distant*, 14–15: Marion Thompson Wright, "New Jersey Laws and the Negro," *Journal of Negro History* 28, no. 2 (1943), 163. For acts, see Axel-Lute, *Law of Slavery in New Jersey*, esp. A8 and A9 .

14. Wright, "New Jersey Laws," 166–167.

15. Price, *Freedom Not Far Distant*, 16–21; Hodges, *Root and Branch*, 53; Gary B. Nash and Jean R. Soderlund, *Freedom by Degrees: Emancipation in Pennsylvania and Its Aftermath* (New York: Oxford University Press, 1991), 13; Axel-Lute, *Law of Slavery*, A13.

16. Hodges, *Root and Branch*, 35, 86; Hodges, *Slavery and Freedom in the Rural North: African Americans in Monmouth County, New Jersey, 1660–1870* (Madison, Wis.: Madison House Publishers, 1997), 64–65; Anna Bustill Smith, "The Bustill Family," *Journal of Negro History* 10, no. 4 (1925), 638–644; Manisha Sinha, *The Slave's Cause: A History of Abolitionism* (New Haven, Conn.: Yale University Press, 2016), 269–270; Fishman, *African American Struggle*, 36. For Bergen County free blacks, see David Stephen Cohen, *The Ramapo Mountain People* (New Brunswick, N.J.: Rutgers University Press, 1974), 25–43.

17. Hodges, *Slavery and Freedom in the Rural North*, 61–64; Hodges, *Root and Branch*, 70–72; Fishman, *African American Struggle*, 58–60. For later gradual emancipation, see James J. Gigantino II, *The Ragged Road to Abolition: Slavery and Freedom in New Jersey, 1775–1865* (Philadelphia: University of Pennsylvania Press, 2014).

18. Lurie, "Colonial Period," 55.

19. Hodges, *Root and Branch*, 82–83; Hodges, *Slavery and Freedom in the Rural North*, 44–50; Fishman, *African American Struggle*, 35–38; on ironworkers and miners see L. A. Greene, "A History of Afro-Americans in New Jersey," *Journal of the Rutgers University Libraries* 56, no. 1 (1994), 7–8.

20. For numbers, see Wacker, *Land and People*, 201; Edmund Morgan, *American Slavery/American Freedom* (New York: W. W. Norton, 1975).

21. Price, *Freedom Not Far Distant*, 26–27; McManus, *Black Bondage*, 50.

22. Wacker, *Land and People*, 200–201.

23. Wacker, *Land and People*, 190

24. Wacker, *Land and People*, 189–191; Hodges, *Root and Branch*, 21–24.

25. Hodges, *Root and Branch*, 56–59.

26. Hodges, *Root and Branch*, 59, 63–64.

27. Hodges, *Slavery and Freedom*, 69–70; Hodges, *Root and Branch*, 85; Marion Thompson Wright, *The Education of Negroes in New Jersey* (New York: Teachers College Press, 1941), 9–12.

28. Jesse Bayker, Christopher Blakley, and Kendra Boyd, "His Name Was Will: Remembering Enslaved Individuals in Rutgers History," in *Scarlet and Black: Slavery and Dispossession in Rutgers History*, ed. Marisa J. Fuentes and Deborah Gray White, (New Brunswick: Rutgers University Press, 2016), 1:58–82.

29. Hodges, *Root and Branch*, 126–128; Leonard L. Bethel and Frederick A. Johnson, eds., *Plainfield's African-American from Northern Slavery to Church Freedom* (Lanham, Md.: United Press of America,1998), Introduction.

30. Hodges, *Root and Branch*, 127.

31. John Hepburn, *The American Defence of the Christian Golden Rule, or an essay to Prove the Unlawfulness of Making Slaves of Men. By Him Who Loves the Freedom and the Souls of All Men* (n.p. 1715) reprinted in Roger Bruns, ed., *Am I Not a Man and a Brother: The Antislavery Crusade of Revolutionary America* (New York: Chelsea House, 1977), 16–45. See also, Price, *Freedom Not Far Distant*, 10–13.

32. Marcus Rediker, *The Fearless Benjamin Lay: The Quaker Dwarf Who Became the First Revolutionary Abolitionist* (Boston: Beacon Press, 2017); David Waldstreicher, "The Origins of Antislavery in Pennsylvania," in *Antislavery and Abolition in Philadelphia: Emancipation and the Long Struggle for Racial Justice in the City of Brotherly Love*, ed. Richard Newman and James Mueller (Baton Rouge: Louisiana State University Press, 2011), 58.

33. Price, *Freedom Not Far Distant*, 21–26; Soderlund, *Quakers and Slavery*, 22; Wright, *Education of Negroes*, 19.

34. Hodges, *Root and Branch*, 125; Soderlund, *Quakers and Slavery*, 26–31; Marion Thompson Wright, "The Quakers as Social Workers Among Negroes in New Jersey from 1763 to 1804," *Bulletin of the Friends Historical Association* 30, no. 2 (1941), 79–88.

35. For a recent example, see Gigantino, *Ragged Road to Abolition*.

36. Sinha, *The Slave's Cause*, 1.

37. Fishman, *African American Struggle*, 47; Marion Thompson Wright, "New Jersey Laws," 161; Axel-Lute, *Law of Slavery*, A5.

38. Hodges, *Root and Branch*; Nash and Soderlund, *Freedom by Degrees*, 27; Hodges, *Slavery and Freedom in the Rural North*, 45 (for Cato).

39. For Stoffels, see *New-York Weekly Journal*, August 26, 1734. For Clause, see *New-York Gazette*, May 25, 1730, reprinted in Graham Russell Hodges and Alan Brown, eds., *"Pretends to be Free": Runaway Slave Advertisements from Colonial and Revolutionary New York and New Jersey* (New York: Garland, 1994), 7, 8, and 10. For others, see 22, 97.

40. *New-York Gazette*, May 1, 1749, in Hodges and Brown, *Pretends to be Free*, 30. For Cato, see *Pennsylvania Gazette*, April 15, 1756, in Hodges and Brown, *Pretends to be Free*, 58.

41. Hodges, *Slavery and Freedom in the Rural North*, 59.

42. Hodges, *Slavery and Freedom in the Rural North*, 60.

43. Fishman, *African American Struggle*, 65; Hodges, *Root and Branch*.

44. Hodges, *Root and Branch*, 90–91.

45. Hodges, *Root and Branch*, 134.

46. Hodges, *Root and Branch*, 89–90; Fishman, *African American Struggle*, 70–74; Manisha Sinha, *The Slave's Cause*, 1, 18.

47. Hodges, *Root and Branch*, 96–100; Fishman, *African American Struggle*, 74–75.

48. Hodges, *Root and Branch*, 134–136.

CHAPTER 2 — FROM REVOLUTION TO GRADUAL EMANCIPATION

1. For an extended discussion of this era, see Graham Russell Hodges, *Root and Branch: African Americans in New York and East Jersey, 1613–1863* (Chapel Hill: University of North Carolina Press, 1999), chapters 4, 5, and 6. See also George Fishman, *The African American Struggle for Freedom and Equality: The Development of a People's Identity, 1624–1850* (New York: Garland, 1997), chapters 4 and 5. For list of those departing from New Jersey, see "List of the Number, Names, and Owners of Negroes Carried off by the British from the several states in contravention of the Treaty of Paris, 9 August 1786," SDEA1001, Department of Defense, Adjutant General's Office/Revolutionary War, Numbered Manuscripts, ca 1776–1890s, New Jersey State Archives. For American Revolution as slave rebellion, see Steven Hahn, *The Political Worlds of Slavery and Freedom* (Cambridge, Mass.: Harvard University Press, 2009).

2. Jonathan D. Sassi, "Anthony Benezet as Intermediary between the Transatlantic and Provincial: New Jersey's Antislavery Campaign on the Eve of the American Revolution," in *The Atlantic World of Anthony Benezet (1713–1784): From French Reformation to North American Quaker Antislavery Activism*, eds. Marie-Jeanne Rossignol and Bertrand Van Ruymbeke, 129–146 (Leiden: Brill, 2016).

3. For Allinson and Livingston correspondence, see Hodges, *Root and Branch*, 143 and L. A. Greene, "A History of Afro-Americans in New Jersey," *Journal of the Rutgers University Libraries* 56, no. 1 (1994): 12.

4. S. Scott Rohrer, *Jacob Green's Revolution: Radical Religion in a Revolutionary Age* (University Park: Penn State University Press, 2014), 209–218; for similar comments by Reverend Nathan Niles, see Greene, "A History," 11; for Cooper, see Manisha Sinha, *The Slave's Cause: A History of Abolition* (New Haven, Conn.: Yale University Press, 2016), 35–39.

5. Hodges, *Slavery and Freedom*, 91.

6. Hodges, *Slavery and Freedom*, 91–92; Sinha, *Slave's Cause*, 51.

7. Hodges, *Slavery and Freedom*, 97–102: Hodges, *Root and Branch*, 152; Fishman, *African American Struggle*, 111.

8. For quotes, see Hodges, *Slavery and Freedom*, 93; Hodges, *Root and Branch*, 152.

9. Quote from Hodges, *Root and Branch*, 145.

10. James J. Gigantino II, *The Ragged Road to Abolition: Slavery and Freedom in New Jersey, 1775–1865* (Philadelphia: University of Pennsylvania Press, 2014), 36–40.

11. Fishman, *African American Struggle*, 104, 108.

12. Hodges, *Root and Branch*, 149–152, 275–277; Hodges, *Slavery and Freedom*, 105–106.

13. Hodges, *Root and Branch*, 158.

14. Hodges, *Root and Branch*, 155–156.

15. Hodges, *Root and Branch*, 157.

16. Hodges, *Root and Branch*, 160–161; Maya Jasanoff, *Liberty's Exiles: American Loyalists in the Revolutionary World* (New York: Knopf, 2011).

17. Hodges, *Root and Branch*, 141–142; Greene, "A History," 14; Fishman, *African American Struggle*, 111–112, 125–126; Axel-Lute, *Law of Slavery, An Act for Setting Free Peter Williams, a Negro, late the property of John Heard, September 1, 1784*, http://njlegallib.rutgers.edu/slavery/acts/A68.html; Judith Van Buskirk, *Standing in Their Own Light: African American Patriots in the American Revolution* (Norman: University of Oklahoma Press, 2017), 63, 73, 71, 88m, 100, 179, 182, 190, 213–216 (Sutphin), 254–258. For an example of colonial laws allowing enlistment of enslaved people with their master's consent 1764, see Axel-Lute, *Law of Slavery*, http://njlegallib.rutgers.edu/slavery/acts/A66.html.

18. Hodges, *Root and Branch*, 279; Giles Wright, *Afro-Americans in New Jersey: A Short History* (Trenton: New Jersey Historical Commission, 1988), 83; Jeffrey M. Dorwart, *Cape May County, New Jersey; The Making of an American Resort Community* (New Brunswick, N.J.: Rutgers University Press, 1992), 59–60; for white increase, see L. A. Greene, "A History," 19.

19. Hodges, *Root and Branch*, 162–163; Hodges, *Slavery and Freedom*, 113–114; Gigantino, *Ragged Road to Abolition*, 44, 46–53; Fishman, *Struggle for Freedom*, 133.

20. For an overview of these developments, see Graham Russell Gao Hodges, "New Jersey in the Early Republic," in *New Jersey: A History of the Garden State*, eds. Maxine Lurie and Richard Veit, 90–114 (New Brunswick, N.J.: Rutgers University Press, 2012).

21. Arthur Zilversmit, *The First Emancipation: The Abolition of Slavery in the North* (Chicago: University of Chicago Press, 1967), 152–154.

22. Fishman, *Struggle for Freedom*, 139–140.

23. Clement Alexander Price, *Freedom Not Far Distant: A Documentary History of Afro-Americans in New Jersey* (Newark: New Jersey Historical Society, 1980), 73–75; Hodges, *Slavery and Freedom*, 115; Hodges, *Root and Branch*, 167–168.

24. Hodges, *Slavery and Freedom*, 126, 128–129.

25. Fishman, *Struggle for Freedom*, 115–116, 145–147; Hodges, *Root and Branch*, 96.

26. For New York City, see Shane White, *Somewhat More Independent: The End of Slavery in New York City 1770–1810* (Athens: University of Georgia Press, 1991), 141–147; Gigantino, *Ragged Road to Abolition*, 82–83.

27. See for example, *Wood's New Jersey Gazette* (Newark), May 26, 1791; *Sentinel of Freedom* (Trenton), August 26, 1800; *New-Jersey Journal and Political Intelligencer*, July 25, 1787, and September 9, 1789 (blacksmiths).

28. *Sentinel of Freedom* (Trenton), March 2, 1802 (Will), May 18, 1802 (Jack), August 12, 1800 (Rob); *New-Jersey Journal*, June 23, 1801 (Pomp), April 16–June 11, 1805 (Peter).

29. Hodges, *Root and Branch*, 179–180; Gigantino, *Ragged Road to Abolition*, 83–84.

30. Hodges, *Root and Branch*, 167; Hodges, *Slavery and Freedom in the Rural North*, 115–116; Zilversmit, *First Emancipation*, 163; Gary B. Nash and Jean R. Soderlund, *Freedom by Degrees: Emancipation in Pennsylvania and Its Aftermath* (New York: Oxford University Press, 1991), 117.

31. Hodges, *Root and Branch*, 170; Zilversmit, *First Emancipation*, 185, 187–188.

32. Fishman, *Struggle for Freedom*, 130–131.

33. Newman, *The Transformation of American Abolitionism: Fighting Slavery in the Early Republic* (Chapel Hill: University of North Carolina Press, 2002), 31.

34. *Survey of Negro Life in New Jersey*, (Newark: Interracial Committee, New Jersey Department of Institutions and Agencies, 1932), 2:12, http://www.kean.edu/~NJHPP/proRef/greatMigr/pdf/greatMigrDoc2.pdf.

35. Nash and Soderlund, *Freedom by Degrees*, 135.

36. Axel-Lute, *Law of Slavery, An Act for the Establishment of Work-houses in the several counties of this state*, February 20, 1799, http://njlegallib.rutgers.edu/slavery/acts/A76.html, and *A Supplement to the Act. Intitled "An Act for the Punishment of Crimes,"* March 7, 1801, http://njlegallib.rutgers.edu/slavery/acts/A77.html.

37. Nash and Soderlund, *Freedom by Degrees*, 145–146.

38. Hodges, *Root and Branch*, 279; Peter O. Wacker, *Land and People: A Cultural Geography of Preindustrial New Jersey: Origins and Settlement Patterns* (New Brunswick, N.J.: Rutgers University Press, 1975), 194; Hodges, *Slavery and Freedom*, 130.

39. Edgar J. McManus, *Black Bondage in the North* (Syracuse, N.Y.: Syracuse University Press, 1973), 214.

40. Hodges, *Root and Branch*, 179–180; Hodges, *Slavery and Freedom*, 130.

41. *Sentinel of Freedom* (Trenton), December 3, 1799 (Cato); *Wood's New-Jersey Gazette*, August 7–28, 1786 (Gilbert).

42. Liam Riordan, *Many Identities, One Nation: The Revolution and Its Legacy in the Mid-Atlantic* (Philadelphia: University of Pennsylvania Press, 2007), 138–142; Graham Russell Hodges, ed., *Black Itinerants of the Gospel: The Narratives of George*

White and John Jea (Madison, Wis.: Madison House Publishers, 1993); Fishman, *African American Struggle*, 157–160.

43. Sibyl Moses, *African American Women Writers in New Jersey, 1836–2000* (New Brunswick: Rutgers University Press, 2003), 107–108; Jarena Lee, *The Life and Religious Experience of Jarena Lee, a Coloured Lady, Giving an Account of her Call to the Gospel* (Philadelphia, 2nd edition, 1849), http://www.umilta.net/jarena.html.

44. Marion M. Thompson Wright, *The Education of Negroes in New Jersey* (New York: Teachers College Press, 1941), 28–33, 38, 50–51; Sinha, *Slave's Cause*, 37–38.

45. Craig Steven Wilder, *Ebony and Ivy: Race, Slavery, and the Troubled History of America's Universities* (New York: Bloomsbury, 2013), 73–77, 122–123.

46. Fishman, *African American Struggle*, 152–153; Kenneth Marshall, *Manhood Enslaved: Bondmen in Eighteenth- and Early Nineteenth-Century New Jersey* (Rochester, N.Y.: University of Rochester Press, 2011), 97–98, 103–105, 122; Hodges, *Slavery and Freedom*, 123, 131; Joseph A. Grabas, *Owning New Jersey: Historic Tales of War, Property Disputes and the Pursuit of Happiness* (Charleston, S.C.: The History Press, 2014), 76–83.

47. Hodges, *Slavery and Freedom*, 131–132.

48. Gigantino coined the phrase that New Jersey blacks held in bondage became "slaves for a term."

49. For act, see Price, *Freedom Not Far Distant*, 79–83. For abandonment, Bergen County petition, and end of society, see Hodges, *Root and Branch*, 192; Zilversmit, *First Emancipation*, 192–195; Gigantino, *Ragged Road*, 108–121; for indentures, see Nash and Soderlund, *Freedom by Degrees*, 178–181.

CHAPTER 3 — SLAVERY, FREEDOM, AND STRUGGLE

1. Graham Russell Hodges, *Root and Branch: African Americans in New York and East Jersey, 1613–1863* (Chapel Hill: University of North Carolina Press, 1999), 228–229; Jeffrey M. Dorwart, *Cape May County, New Jersey: The Making of an American Resort Community* (New Brunswick: Rutgers University Press, 1992), 82–83.

2. Giles Wright, *Afro-Americans in New Jersey: A Short History* (Trenton: New Jersey Historical Commission, 1988), 82–86.

3. For a recent survey of the S.U.M. and Hamilton's decision, see Graham Russell Gao Hodges, "New Jersey in the Early Republic," in *New Jersey: A History of the Garden State*, eds. Maxine Lurie and Richard Veit (New Brunswick: Rutgers University Press, 2012), 90–114. For text of Hamilton's report, see http://www.constitution.org/ah/rpt_manufactures.htm, especially part 4.

4. For discussion of the rise of New Jersey's economy, see Michael Birkner, "New Jersey in the Jacksonian Era, 1820–1850," in *New Jersey: A History of the Garden State*, eds. Maxine Lurie and Richard Veit, 115–144 (New Brunswick: Rutgers University Press, 2012). For examples of artisan republicanism in New Jersey, see David

Roediger and Phillip S. Foner, *Our Own Time: A History of American Labor and the Working Day* (New York: Verso, 1989), 11; Brad R. Tuttle, *How Newark Became Newark: The Rise, Fall, and Rebirth of an American City* (Rivergate, N.J.: New Brunswick, 2011), 25–31; Peter O. Wacker, *Land and People: A Cultural Geography of Preindustrial New Jersey: Origins and Settlement Patterns* (New Brunswick, N.J.: Rutgers University Press, 1975), 200.

5. Spencer Crew, *Black Life in Secondary Cities: A Comparative Analysis of the Black Communities of Camden and Elizabeth, New Jersey* (New York: Garland, 1993), 14–15.

6. Crew, *Black Life in Secondary Cities*, 24–29; on Ishmael Locke, see Jeffrey Stewart, *The New Negro: The Life of Alain Locke* (New York: Oxford University Press, 2018), 16–17; Jack Washington, *In Search of a Community's Past: The Black Community in Trenton, New Jersey, 1860–1900* (Trenton: Africa World Press, 1990), 3–18.

7. Hodges, *Root and Branch*, 220.

8. Lucia McMahon and Deborah Shriver, eds., *To Read My Heart: The Journal of Rachel Van Dyke, 1810–1811* (Philadelphia: University of Pennsylvania Press, 2000), 35, 52–53, 92, 107–108, 135, 176, 220, 250–255; Dorwart, *Cape May County*, 83–84; Marisa J. Fuentes and Deborah Gray White, *Scarlet and Black: Slavery and Dispossession in Rutgers History* (New Brunswick: Rutgers University Press, 2016), 1:123; T. C. Upham, *Narrative of Phebe Ann Jacobs* (London: J. S. Stewart, 1850).

9. Kathryn Watterson, *I Hear My People Singing: Voices of African-American Princeton* (Princeton: Princeton University Press, 2017), 77–78. For a similar story of black fidelity and close contact with whites, see William J. Allinson, *Memoir of Quamino Buccau, A Pious Methodist* (Philadelphia: Henry Lonstreth, 1851).

10. Hodges, *Root and Branch*, 173–174, 221; Hodges, *Slavery and Freedom in the Rural North: African Americans in Monmouth County, New Jersey, 1660–1870* (Madison, Wis.: Madison House Publishers, 1997), 161, 163, 180, 206; Cohen, *The Ramapo Mountain People*, 43–50; Dorwart, *Cape May County*, 83.

11. Clement Alexander Price, *Freedom Not Far Distant: A Documentary History of Afro-Americans in New Jersey* (Newark: New Jersey Historical Society, 1980), 94; Hodges, *Root and Branch*, 215: George Fishman, *The African American Struggle for Freedom and Equality: The Development of a People's Identity, New Jersey, 1624–1850* (New York: Garland 1997), 182.

12. Price, *Freedom Not Far Distant*, 94–98; Marion Thompson Wright, *The Education of Negroes in New Jersey* (New York: Teachers College Press, 1941), 79–92.

13. Price, *Freedom Not Far Distant*, 104–113; Fishman, *African American Struggle*, 184–185.

14. Green quotes found in Price, *Freedom Not Far Distant*, 100–104; on the Assembly see L. A. Greene, "A History of Afro-Americans in New Jersey," *Journal of the Rutgers University Libraries* 56, no. 1 (1994): 22–23.

15. Fishman, *African American Struggle*, 186–187.

16. *Trenton True American*, September 17, 1825 as quoted in Marion Thompson Wright, "The Transition Years," *Journal of Negro History* 33, no. 2 (1948): 180.

17. James J. Gigantino, *The Ragged Road to Abolition: Slavery and Freedom in New Jersey, 1775–1865* (Philadelphia: University of Pennsylvania Press, 2014), chapter 7.

18. Graham Russell Hodges, ed., *Black Itinerants of the Gospel: The Narratives of John Jea and George White* (Madison, Wis.: Madison House, 1993); for Boen, see *Anecdotes and Memoirs of William Boen, a Coloured Man, Who Lived and Died Near Mount Holly, New Jersey. To which is Added, the Testimony of Friends of Mount Holly Monthly Meeting Concerning Him* (Philadelphia: Printed by J. Richards, 1834).

19. Washington, *In Search of a Community's Past*, 4–8; Spencer Crew, *Black Life in Secondary Cities: A Comparative Analysis of Black Communities of Camden and Elizabeth, N.J., 1860–1920* (New York: Garland, 1993), 16–20; Richard Allen, *The Life, Experience, and Gospel Labours of the Rt. Rev. Richard Allen. To Which is Annexed the Rise and Progress of the African Methodist Episcopal Church in the United States of America. Containing a Narrative of the Yellow Fever in the Year of Our Lord 1793: With an Address to the People of Colour in the United States* (Philadelphia: Martin and Boden, Printers, 1833); Hodges, *Root and Branch*, 217; for Burlington church, see Joseph H. Morgan, *Morgan's History of the New Jersey Conference of the A.M.E. Church from 1872–1887* (Camden: S. Chew, Printer, 1887), 64. For other black New Jersey ministers at this time, see Alexander W. Wayman, *Cyclopedia of African Methodism* (Baltimore: Methodist Episcopal Book Depository, 1882), 21, 22, 31, 32, 33, 42, 44, 45, 50, 57, 63, 67, and A. W. Wayman, *My Recollections African M. E. Ministers or Forty Years' Experience in the African Methodist Episcopal Church* (Philadelphia: A.M.W. Book Rooms, 1881).

20. Peter P. Hinks and Stephen Kantrowitz, eds., *All Men Free and Brethren: Essays on the History of African American Freemasonry* (Ithaca, N.Y.: Cornell University Press, 2013), 10, 22, 24, 59; Joseph H. Morgan, *History of Knights of Pythias State of New Jersey* (n.p., 1912).

21. For material in this paragraph, see Greene, "A History," 23–24.

22. Patrick Rael, *Black Identity and Black Protest in the Antebellum North* (Chapel Hill: University of North Carolina Press, 2002).

23. Hodges, *Root and Branch*, 219–220; Gary B. Nash and Graham Russell Gao Hodges, *Friends of Liberty: Thomas Jefferson, Tadeuz Kosciuszko and Agrippa Hull* (New York: Basic Books, 2008); Wright, *Education of Negroes*, 92–97.

24. Wright, *Education of Negroes*, 72–76.

25. Evelyn Blackmore Duck, "An Historical Sketch of a Racially Segregated School in New Jersey from 1886 to 1955" (PhD diss., Rutgers University, 1984), 28; Hodges, *Root and Branch*, 220; Thompson, *Education of Negroes*, 109–112.

26. Wright, *Education of Negroes*, 133–139; Davison M. Douglas, *Jim Crow Moves North: The Battle over Northern School Segregation, 1865–1954* (New York: Cambridge University Press, 2005), 38–39, 44–45; Carter Woodson, *The Education of the Negro Prior to 1861*, 2nd ed. (New York: Arno Press, 1969), 310.

27. Davison, *Jim Crow Moves North*, 54–57.

28. Hodges, *Root and Branch*, 221–222.

29. Kenneth E. Marshall, *Manhood Enslaved: Bondmen in Eighteenth- and Early Nineteenth-Century New Jersey* (Rochester, N.Y.: University of Rochester Press, 2011), 114–115.

30. Marshall, *Manhood Enslaved*, 120–122.

31. Meaders, *Kidnappers in Philadelphia*, 37–39, 235. There are ample other cases of kidnappers in this collection but I limit my references to those directly involving New Jersey people. For Egg Harbor incident and removal, see Price, *Freedom Not Far Distant*, 76, 85–86. For sale to Easttown, see Nash and Soderlund, *Freedom by Degrees*, 121–122.

32. Eric Foner, *Gateway to Freedom: The Hidden History of the Underground Railroad* (New York: W. W. Norton, 2015); Graham Russell Gao Hodges, *David Ruggles: A Radical Black Abolitionist and the Underground Railroad in New York City* (Chapel Hill: University of North Carolina Press, 2010); David G. Smith, *On the Edge of Freedom: The Fugitive Slave Issue in South Central Pennsylvania, 1820–1870* (New York: Fordham University Press, 2012); Fergus Bordewich, *Bound for Canaan: The Epic Story of the Underground Railroad, America's First Civil Rights Movement* (New York: Amistad, 2005).

33. Child, *Life of Isaac Hopper*, 62, 77, 123, 163–167: Daniel Meaders, ed., *Kidnappers in Philadelphia: Isaac Hopper's Tales of Oppression, 1789–1843* (New York: Garland Publishing, 1994), 37, 334, 347, 366.

34. Child, *Life of Isaac Hopper*, 190–192.

35. Meaders, *Kidnappers in Philadelphia*, 223–228, 325–328.

36. Price, *Freedom Not Far Distant*, 122–123.

37. Greene, "A History," 27.

38. Leonard Black, *The Life and Suffering of Leonard Black, A Fugitive From Slavery, Written by Himself* (New Bedford, Mass.: Press of Benjamin Lindsey, 1847).

39. Morgan, *Morgan's History*, 25–26.

40. William Frost, "Why Quakers and Slavery? Why Not More Quakers?," in *Quakers and Abolition*, eds. Brycchan Carey and Geoffrey Plank, 29–42 (Urbana: University of Illinois Press), 2014).

41. For quotes and the most recent discussion of these sordid incidents within the context of an emerging American capitalism, see Calvin Schermerhorn, *The Business of Slavery and the Rise of American Capitalism* (New Haven, Conn.: Yale University Press, 2015), 69–80.

42. Gigantino, *Ragged Road to Abolition*, 159–161.

43. Gigantino, *Ragged Road to Abolition*, 168; Foner, *Gateway to Freedom*, 106; Richard Bell, "'Thence to Patty Cannon's' Gender, Family, and the Reverse Underground Railroad," *Slavery and Abolition* 37, no. 4 (2016): 661–679; Carol Wilson, *Freedom at Risk: The Kidnapping of Free Blacks in America, 1780–1865* (Lexington: University Press of Kentucky, 1994),19–37, 52; *Trenton State Gazette*, December 27, 1850; *Pennsylvania Freeman*, January 9, 1851.

44. Congressional Globe, 31st Congress, 1st Session, App. 311 (February 21, 1850), as quoted in Alfred I. Brophy, *University, Court, and Slave: Pro-Slavery Thought in Southern Colleges and Courts and the Coming of the Civil War* (New York: Oxford University Press, 2016), 164.

45. "Thomas Clement Oliver interview, Toronto, Ontario, July 31, 1895, in Wilbur Siebert, *The Underground Railroad from Slavery to Freedom* (New York: MacMillan, 1898), 123–125; New Jersey Writers Project, Works Project Administration, Bulletin 9, "The Underground Railroad in New Jersey"; Emma Trusty, *The Underground Railroad, Ties That Bind: A History of the Underground Railroad in Southern New Jersey from 1770 to 1861* (Philadelphia: Amed Literary, 1999); Giles R. Wright, *New Jersey's Underground Railroad: Steal Away, Steal Away to Freedom* (Trenton: New Jersey Historical Commission, 2002); Giles Wright, *Afro-American New Jersey: A Short History* (Trenton: New Jersey Historical Commission, 1988), 39–40; Richard E. Newman, *The Transformation of American Abolitionism: Fighting Slavery in the Early Republic* (Chapel Hill; University of North Carolina Press, 2002), 69; William J. Switala, *Underground Railroad in New York and New Jersey* (Mechanicsburg, N.Y.: Stackpole Books, 2006), 43–71; Eric Foner, *Gateway to Freedom: The Hidden History of the Underground Railroad* (New York: W. W. Norton, 2015), 106; Don Papson and Tom Calarco, *Secret Lives of the Underground Railroad to New York City: Sidney Howard Gay, Louis Napoleon, and the Record of Fugitives* (Jefferson, N.C.: McFarland, 2015), 57, 121, 139, 164, 169, 212, 222. On 1818 law, see Edgar J. McManus, *Black Bondage in the North* (Syracuse: Syracuse University Press, 1973) 183; Dennis Rizzo, *Parallel Communities: The Underground Railroad in South Jersey* (Charleston, S.C.: The History Press, 2008); for letter "John Brown to Willis Augustus Hodges," October 28, 1848, see Heritage Auctions catalog, April 5, 2016; Dorwart, *Cape May County*, 83–84; for Colemantown, see Philly.com, June 16, 2017. For Raritan Bay Union, see Marie Marmo Mullaney, "Feminism, Utopianism and Domesticity: The Career of Rebecca Buffum Spring, 1811–1911," in *A New Jersey Anthology*, ed. Maxine N. Lurie, 161–186 (Newark: New Jersey Historical Society, 1994), and Raritan Bay Union and Eagleswood Military Academy Collection, 1809–1973, New Jersey Historical Society.

46. For biographical detail on the Still family, see Ernest Lyght, *Path of Freedom: The Black Presence in New Jersey's Burlington County, 1659–1900* (Cherry Hill, N.J.:

E and E Publishing House, 1978), 48–58; see also Greene, " A History," 29, and [Peter Still] *The Kidnapped and the Ransomed: The Narrative of Peter and Vina Still after forty years of slavery* (Syracuse, N.Y.: William T. Hamilton, 1856), 282–299; William Still, *The Underground Railroad* (Philadelphia: Porter and Coates, 1872).

47. Stanley Harrold, *Border War: Fighting Over Slavery before the Civil War* (Chapel Hill: University of North Carolina Press, 2010), 57, 98, 108–110; Gigantino, *Ragged Road to Abolition*, 218.

48. H. Robert Baker, *Prigg v. Pennsylvania: Slavery, the Supreme Court, and the Ambivalent Constitution* (Lawrence: University of Kansas Press, 2012), 96–97; Gigantino, *Ragged Road to Abolition*, 219–222.

49. Gigantino, *Ragged Road to Abolition*, 216–219; Dennis Rizzo, *Parallel Communities: The Underground Railroad in New Jersey* (Charleston, S.C.: The History Press, 2008), 77.

50. William Steward and Rev. Theophilus G. Steward, *Gouldtown: A Very Remarkable Settlement of Ancient Date* (Philadelphia: J. B. Lippincott, 1913), 144–152.

51. Reverend Theophilus Gould, *The Memoirs of Mrs. Rebecca Steward, containing a full sketch of her life, with various selections from her writings and letters* (Philadelphia: Publication Department of the AME Church, 1877).

52. Steward and Steward, *Gouldtown*, 113–118.

53. Still, *Underground Railroad*, 702–706.

54. Greene, "A History," 24; for comment on humbugs, see "New Jersey State Anti-Slavery Society Record Book," New Jersey Historical Society, as quoted in Price, *Freedom Not Far Distant*, 114–115; Arthur Zilversmit, *The First Emancipation: The Abolition of Slavery in the North* (Chicago: University of Chicago Press, 1967), 217–218; for "the colored people," see Marion Thompson Wright, "Negro Suffrage in New Jersey, 1776–1875: The Transition Years," *Journal of Negro History* 33 no. 2 (1948): 177–183; Reinhardt O. Johnson, *The Liberty Party, 1840–1848: Antislavery, Third-Party Politics in the United States* (Baton Rouge: Louisiana State University Press, 2009), 160–163; Daniel R. Ernst, "Legal Positivism, Abolitionist Litigation, and the New Jersey Slave Case of 1845," *Law and History Review*, 4: 2 (Autumn, 1986), 337–365.

55. "Essex County Anti-Slavery Society Minutes," 1839, Manuscript Collections, New-Jersey Historical Society, 187, Weld and Grimke, two of the most important abolitionists, lived in Bellevue, Perth Amboy, and Englewood. Robert H. Abzug *Passionate Liberator: Theodore Dwight Weld and the Dilemma of Reform* (New York: Oxford University Press, 1980).

56. Wright, "Negro Suffrage," 183.

57. Zilversmit, *First Emancipation*, 220–222.

58. (New York) *Weekly Sun*, May 31, 1845. I am grateful to Shane White for this reference.

59. "An Address from the Coloured Convention, Assembled at Trenton, on the 21st and 22nd Days of August 1849," and *North Star*, February 8, 1850, both in Price, *Freedom Not Far Distant*, 118–121. See also Wright, "Negro Suffrage," 186–198; Greene, "A History," 26. For full proceedings, see Philip S. Foner and George E. Walker, eds., *Proceedings of the Black State Conventions, 1840–1865* (Philadelphia: Temple University Press, 1980), 2:3–6.

60. Purvis Carter, "The Negro in Periodical Literature, Part III," *Journal of Negro History* (July 1967): 92–102.

61. Sarah H. Bradford, *Scenes in the Life of Harriet Tubman* (Auburn, N.Y.: W. J. Moses, 1869) 20–21; Greene, "A History," 27; Rizzo, *Parallel Communities*.

62. Still, *Underground Railroad*, 203–204, 619.

63. William Gillette, *Jersey Blue: Civil War Politics in New Jersey, 1854–1865* (New Brunswick: Rutgers University Press, 1995), 49.

64. For Judas quote, see *Belvidere Intelligencer*, printed in the *National Anti-Slavery Standard*, August 22, 1857, and collected in Samuel J. May, *The Fugitive Slave Law and its Victims* (New York: Printed by the American Anti-Slavery Society, 1861), 77, 81.

65. Gigantino, *Ragged Road*; Hodges, *Slavery and Freedom in the Rural North*; Hodges, *Root and Branch*.

66. Wilson J. Moses, *The Golden Age of Black Nationalism, 1850–1925*, rev. ed. (New York: Oxford University Press, 1988), and Patrick Rael, *Black Identity and Protest in the Antebellum North* (Chapel Hill: University of North Carolina Press, 2002).

CHAPTER 4 — THE CIVIL WAR AND RECONSTRUCTION TO WORLD WAR I

1. For population data, see U.S. Department of Census, 1870–1900. For determinations, see Hugh Davis, *"We Will Be Satisfied with Nothing Less": The African American Struggle for Equal Rights in the North during Reconstruction* (Ithaca, N.Y.: Cornell University Press, 2011), xiii. For the South, see Steven Hahn, *A Nation Under Our Feet: Black Political Struggles in the Rural South from Slavery to Reconstruction* (Cambridge, Mass.: Harvard University Press, 2003).

2. For the classic argument about these ties, see Philip S. Foner, *Business and Slavery: The New York Merchants and the Irrepressible Conflict* (Chapel Hill: University of North Carolina Press, 1941), updated by Edward E. Baptist, *The Half Has Never Been Told: Slavery and the Making of American Capitalism* (New York: Basic Books, 2014). For Philadelphia, see William Dusinberre, *Civil War Issues in Philadelphia, 1856–1865* (Philadelphia: University of Pennsylvania Press, 1965);

Matthew Gallman, *Mastering Wartime: A Social History of Philadelphia during the Civil War* (New York: Cambridge University Press, 1990).

3. Susan E. Hirsch, *Roots of the American Working Class: The Industrialization of Crafts in Newark, 1800–1860* (Philadelphia: University of Pennsylvania Press, 1978), xix; Richard F. Miller, ed., *States at War* (Hanover: University of New Hampshire Press, 2015), 4:562–565.

4. Brad R. Tuttle, *How Newark Became Newark: The Rise, Fall and Rebirth of an American City* (New Brunswick, N.J.: Rivergate Books, 2011), 39–45.

5. Cheryl C. Turkington, *Setting Up Our Own City: The Black Community in Morristown: An Oral History Project* (Morristown, N.J.: Joint Free Library of Morristown and Morris Townships, 1992), 4–5; Miller, *States at War*, 4:638.

6. Clement Alexander Price, *Freedom Not Far Distant: A Documentary History of African Americans in New Jersey* (Newark: New Jersey Historical Society, 1980), 123–124; Tuttle, *How Newark Became Newark*, 46–48; Miller, *States at War*, 4:650.

7. A. P. Smith, "A Black Man's Talk to the President," *National Anti-Slavery Standard*, September 6, 1862, reprinted in Price, *Freedom Not Far Distant*, 126–129.

8. "As absurd as it was fanatical," Eric Foner, *The Fiery Trial: Abraham Lincoln and Slavery* (New York: W. W. Norton, 2010); "miserable crusade," see Tuttle, *How Newark Became Newark*, 51–53; William L. Jackson, *New Jerseyans in the Civil War: For Union and Liberty* (New Brunswick, N.J.: Rutgers University Press, 2000), 51; Marion Thompson Wright, "Intensified Battles for Emancipation and the Rights of Citizenship," *Journal of Negro History* 33, no. 2 (1948): 198; Maurice Tandler, "The Political Front in Civil War New Jersey," in *A New Jersey Anthology*, ed. Maxine N. Lurie, 209–223 (Newark: New Jersey Historical Society, 1994).

9. Jackson, *New Jerseyans in the Civil War*, 52.

10. Jackson, *New Jerseyans in the Civil War*, 146–147; Douglas Egerton, *Thunder at the Gates: The Three Black Regiments That Changed America* (New York: Bloomsbury, 2016); Miller, *States at War*, 4:650–655, 677.

11. Miller, *States at War*, 4:749, using Giles R. Wright, *Afro-Americans in New Jersey* (Trenton, 1986), and Joseph Bilby, *"Freedom to All": New Jersey's African-American Civil War Soldiers* (Hightstown, N.J.: Longstreet House, 2011).

12. Price, *Freedom Not Far Distant*, 125–129; Tuttle, *How Newark Became Newark*, 58. For descendants of the Creoles, see David Steven Cohen, *The Ramapo Mountain People* (New Brunswick, N.J.: Rutgers University Press, 1974), 58.

13. Jackson, *New Jerseyans in the Civil War*, 148–149.

14. L. D. Sims to Marcus L. Ward, June 11, 1863, as quoted in Price, *Freedom Not Far Distant*, 125–126; on Ward, see Miller, *States at War*, 4:779–780.

15. Wallace Trusty Pension Record, *National Archives*, Stack 18W3, Row 19, Compartment 14, Shelf C; David M. Trusty, *National Archives*, Stack Area 17W4, Row 2, Compartment 9, Shelf 2. Samuel J. Trusty, *National Archives*, Stack Area 17W4, Row

3, Compartment 10, Shelf 2. See also Spencer Trusty, *National Archives*, Stack Area, Row 5, Compartment 21, Shelf B; James Trusty, *National Archives*, Stack Area 17W4, Row 3, Compartment 19, Shelf 5.

16. James Crawford, *National Archives*, Stack Area 17W4, Row 16, Compartment 21, Shelf 1; Charles H. Harris, *National Archives*, Stack Area 16E4, Row 8, Compartment 7, Shelf 1; John Coy, *National Archives*, Stack Area 18E3, Row 1, Compartment 25, Shelf 5; Charles Finnaman, *National Archives*, Stack Area 7W1, Row 6, Compartment 1, Shelf 4.

17. New Jersey Home for Disabled Soldiers, Case Files, 1866–1920, *New Jersey State Archives*, Trenton, Reel 2, Box 2 (Cromwell, Amman, Jackson); Reel 34 (Huff)

18. "Newark Directories, 1869–1887," Newark Public Library.

19. Hugh Davis, *We Will Be Satisfied*, 17.

20. *Proceedings Held in the City of Syracuse, NY, October 4–7, 1864, with a Bill of Wrongs and Rights, Addressed to the American People* (Boston: Published by John Rock and George Ruffin, 1864).

21. Davis, *We Will Be Satisfied*, 18–26.

22. Philip S. Foner and George E. Walker, eds., *Proceedings of the Black State Conventions, 1840–1865* (Philadelphia: Temple University Press, 1980), 2:7–15; Wright, "Intensified Battles," 119–120.

23. Miller, *States at War*, 4:723.

24. Davis, *We Will Be Satisfied*, 34–35.

25. Wright, "Intensified Battles," 202–205; Marion Thompson Wright, "New Jersey Laws and the Negro" *Journal of Negro History* 28, no. 2 (1943), 156–199; *New York Age*, May 19, 1934. For Whipper's speech, see Price, *Freedom Not Far Distant*, 138–142; L. A. Greene, "A History of Afro-Americans in New Jersey," *Journal of the Rutgers University Libraries* 56, no. 1 (1994): 33.

26. Louis B. Moore, "Response the Reconstruction: Change and Continuity in New Jersey Politics, 1866–1874" (PhD diss., Rutgers University, 1999), 133–182; Michael Birkner, Donald Linky, and Peter Mickulas, eds., *The Governors of New Jersey: Biographical Essays*, 2nd ed. (New Brunswick, N.J.: Rutgers University Press, 2014), 196, 199.

27. Davis, *We Will Be Satisfied*, 137–139; for an excellent study of Hays and his decision, see Rayford W. Logan, *The Negro Life in American Life and History: The Nadir, 1877–1901* (New York: Dial Press, 1954), 23–48.

28. For Washington quote and discussion, see Logan, *Negro Life*, 41–44, 73–81, 276–292.

29. On Washington, see Louis Harlan, *Booker T. Washington* (New York: Oxford University Press, 1983), and August Meier, *Negro Thought in America, 1880–1915 Racial Ideologies in the Age of Booker T. Washington* (Ann Arbor: University of Michigan Press, 1963).

30. Wright, *Afro-Americans in New Jersey*, 44–46; Nelson Johnson, *The Northside: African Americans and the Creation of Atlantic City* (Medford, N.J.: Plexus, 2010), 34–35.

31. Daniel M. Johnson and Rex R. Campbell, *Black Migration in America: A Social Demographic History* (Durham, N.C.: Duke University Press, 1981), 59.

32. Francis Tyson, "The Negro Migrant in the North," in *Negro Migration in 1916–1917*, ed. R. H. Leavell et al., 115–155 (Washington, D.C.: Government Printing Office, 1919), 115.

33. Spencer Crew, *Black Life in Secondary Cities: A Comparative Analysis of the Black Communities of Camden and Elizabeth, New Jersey* (New York: Garland, 1993), 40–43.

34. L. A. Greene, "A History of Afro-Americans in New Jersey," *Journal of the Rutgers University Libraries* 56, no. 1 (1994): 39–40; Price, *Freedom Not Far Distant*, 135.

35. Crew, *Black Life*, 52–55.

36. For quote see *Christian Recorder*, June 16, 1866: Clement Richardson, ed., *National Cyclopedia of the Colored Race* (Montgomery, Ala.: National Publishing Company, 1919), 221, 442.

37. Greene, "A History," 43–44; Johnson, *Northside*, 5–64, 79–81, 92–103; Charles E. Funnell, "Newport of the Nouveaux Bourgeois," in *A New Jersey Anthology*, ed. Maxine N. Lurie, 223–266 (Newark: New Jersey Historical Society, 1994).

38. Cindy Hahamovitch, *The Fruits of Their Labor: Atlantic Coast Farm Workers and the Making of Migrant Poverty, 1870–1945* (Chapel Hill: University of North Carolina Press, 1997), 14–25; On Italians and whiteness in this period, see Michael Frye Jacobson, *Whiteness of a Different Color: European Immigrants and the Alchemy of Race* (Cambridge, Mass.: Harvard University Press, 1998), 56–62.

39. *Souvenir program. Dr. Booker T. Washington's tour of New Jersey. September 7th, 8th, 9th, 10th, 1914. With a few facts about the state of New Jersey, Morristown, Montclair, Paterson, Newark, Princeton, Burlington, Bridgeton, Gouldtown, Ocean City, Cape May, Salem, the Oranges. Tour committee: James N. Vandervall, chairman; W. P. Burrell, executive secretary. Compiled by W. P. Burrell.* (n.p. 1914), New York Public Library Digital collection, 2–5; Harlan, *Booker T. Washington*, 2 vols. (New York: Oxford University Press, 1973, 1983), 2:163.

40. *Souvenir Program*, 33–34; Cheryl C. Turkington, *Setting Up Our Own City*, 33.

41. *Souvenir Program*, 34–36; *Baltimore Afro-American*, September 13, 1913, September 19, 1914 (speech); *Afro-American Ledger* (Baltimore), September 19, 1914. For more on the black YM and YWCAs and their impact on culture in Montclair, See Hettie V. Williams, " The Garden of Opportunity: Black Women Intellectuals and the Struggle for Equality in New Jersey, 1912–1949" (Ph.D. diss., Drew University, 2017), chap. 2.

42. *Souvenir Program*, 37–40.

43. *Souvenir Program*, 36–45; Jeffrey M. Dorwart, *Cape May County, New Jersey: The Making of an American Resort Community* (New Brunswick: Rutgers University Press, 1992), 173.

44. William J. Simmons, *Men of Mark: Eminent, Progressive and Rising* (Cleveland, Ohio: Geo. M. Rewell, 1887).

45. *New York Age*, May 7, 1908; *Afro-American Ledger* (Baltimore), February 20, 1909.

46. *Afro-American Ledger* (Baltimore), January 12, April 6, 1906, July 27, 1907 (Eggleston); February 8, 1909 (Lyman-Wheaton), May 8, 1909 (ministers).

47. *New York Age*, April 26, 1906, May 4, 1907.

48. *New York Age*, May 10, 1906 (rotation); others include May 17, 1906, April 26, 1906 (Simmons).

49. *New York Age*, February 14, 1907.

50. Amanda Smith, *An Autobiography: The Story of the Lord's Dealings with Mrs. Amanda Smith, the Colored Evangelist: Containing an Account of Her Life Work of Faith, and Her Travels in America, England, Ireland, Scotland, India, and Africa as an Independent Missionary* (Chicago: Meyer and Brother Publishers, 1893); Richard R. Wright Jr. *Centennial Encyclopaedia of the African Methodist Episcopal Church. Containing Principally the Biographies of the Men and Women, both Ministers and Laymen, Whose Labors During a Hundred Years, Helped Make the A. M. E. Church What It Is; Also Short Historical Sketches of Annual Conferences, Educational Institutions, General Departments, Missionary Societies of the A. M. E. Church, and General Information about African Methodism and the Christian Church in General; Being a Literary Contribution to the Celebration of the One Hundredth Anniversary of the Formation of the African Methodist Episcopal Church Denomination by Richard Allen and others, at Philadelphia, Penna., in 1816* (Philadelphia: Book Concern of the A.M.E. Church, 1916).

51. Gloria H. Dickinson and J. Maurice Hicks, "Florence Spearing Randolph," in Joan N. Burstyn, ed., *Past and Promise: Lives of New Jersey Women*, 185–186 (Syracuse University Press 1996); Betty Livingston Adams, *Black Women's Christian Activism: Seeking Social Justice in a Northern Suburb* (New York: NYU Press, 2016), 4–23.

52. *New York Age*, May 24 and 31, July 5, 1906; Dennis C. Dickerson, "Charles H. Trusty: Black Presbyterian Minister and Denominational Leader," *American Presbyterians* 67, no. 4 (1989): 283–296.

53. *New York Age*, February 28, 1931.

54. Robeson Jr., *The Undiscovered Paul Robeson;* Watterson, *I Hear My People Singing: Voices of African-American Princeton* (Princeton: Princeton University

Press, 2017), 259–260; on Locke, see Jeffrey C. Stewart, *The New Negro: The Life of Alaine Locke* (New York: Oxford University Press, 2018), 108.

55. Arthur R. Ashe Jr., *A Hard Road to Glory: Glory: A History of the African-American Athlete, 1619–1918* (New York: Amistad, 1988), 100–101.

56. Robeson, *Undiscovered Paul Robeson*, 20–36.

57. Horace Mann Bond, *Education for Freedom: A History of Lincoln University, Pennsylvania* (Princeton: Princeton University Press, 1976), 323–327; for Ashby, see *New York Times,* May 19, 1991, and his book, *Tales Without Hate* (Newark: Newark Preservation and Landmarks Committee, 1980).

58. Jack Washington, *The Quest for Equality: Trenton's Black Community, 1890–1965* (Trenton, N.J.: Africa World Press, 1993), 207.

59. *New York Age,* May 3, 1906.

60. *Baltimore Afro-American, National Edition,* May 8, 1926.

61. *New York Age,* January 2, 1913.

62. *New York Age,* March 5 and 14, 1927; Arthur Ashe, *Hard Road to Glory,* 49.

63. *New York Age,* January 1, 1949.

64. *Pittsburgh Courier,* September 15, 1928.

65. *New York Age,* March 23, 1905, March 21, 1907 (YMCA), April 4, 1907.

66. Dennis Clark Dickerson, "George E. Cannon: Black Churchman, Physician and Republican Politician," *Journal of Presbyterian History* 51, no. 4 (1973): 411–432.

67. Dickerson, "George E. Cannon," 414–415.

68. Dickerson, "George E. Cannon," 418–420.

69. *Baltimore Afro-American, National Edition,* June 8, 1925; *New York Age,* January 26, 1924, May 4, 1925. On film and theater, see http://archive.is/Id67l#selection-289.0-305.9.

70. Dickerson, "George E. Cannon," 421–422.

71. Carol R. Byerly, *Fever of War: The Influenza Epidemic in the U.S. Army during World War I* (New York: New York University Press, 2005), 30.

72. *Baltimore Afro-American, National Edition,* September 29, 1917.

73. *Baltimore Afro-American, National Edition,* December 12, 1920; for a brief summary of Hague, see Barbara G. Salmore, *New Jersey Politics and Government,* 4th ed. (New Brunswick, N.J.: Rutgers University Press, 2013), 34–37.

74. *Afro-American Ledger* (Baltimore), February 17, 1917.

75. Dickerson, "George E. Cannon," 424–428.

76. *New York Age,* April 15, May 13, 1922, July 28, 1923.

77. *New York Amsterdam News,* April 4 and 8, 1925; W.E.B. Du Bois to Genevieve Cannon, April 10, 1925, Du Bois Papers, Special Collections and University Archives, University of Massachusetts Amherst Libraries, MS 312; Dickerson, "George E. Cannon," 430.

78. Dickerson, "George E. Cannon," 431–432.

79. George E. Cannon Papers, Schomburg Center of New York Public Library; Henry Louis Gates and Evelyn Higginbotham, eds., *African American Lives* (New York: Oxford University Press, 2004), 134–135.

80. V. P. Franklin and Bettye Collier-Thomas, "'For the Race in General and Black Women in Particular': The Civil Rights Activities of African American Women's Organizations, 1915–50," in *Their Sisters in the Struggle: African American Women in the Civil Rights-Black Power Movement*, 23–27 (New York: New York University Press, 2001).

81. Felice D. Gordon, *After Winning: The Legacy of the New Jersey Suffragists, 1920–1947* (New Brunswick, N.J.: Rutgers University Press, 1986), 25–26, 79, 90; *Afro-American Ledger* (Baltimore), April 17, 1915; *Pittsburgh Courier*, February 23, 1928; *New York Age*, August 10, 1929.

82. Greene, "A History," 43.

83. Douglas, *Jim Crow Moves North*, 130–136.

84. *Afro-American Ledger* (Baltimore), October 13, 1906.

85. *Afro-American Ledger* (Baltimore), June 20, August 1, 1903, October 5, 1910; *New York Age*, November 7, 1912, August 9, 1919 (redcaps), June 21, 1919 (AFL).

86. Greene, "A History," 43.

87. *Afro-American Ledger* (Baltimore), March 25 and 30, 1903 (social work and society); for collapse, see *New York Age*, October 5, 1905.

88. James M. DiClercio and Barry J. Pavelec, *The Jersey Game: The History of Modern Baseball from Its Birth to the Big Leagues in the Garden State* (New Brunswick, N.J.: Rutgers University Press, 1991), 135–137; Washington, *Quest for Equality*, 8–10.

89. *Pittsburgh Courier*, May 18, 1940, https://en.wikipedia.org/wiki/Joe_Jeanette.

90. Leonard L. Bethel and Frederick A. Johnson, eds., *Plainfield's African-Americans from Northern Slavery to Church Freedom* (Lanham, Md.: University Press of America, 1998), 21–43.

91. Wright, *Afro-Americans in New Jersey*, 62.

92. *Afro-American Ledger* (Baltimore), January 20, 1912.

93. *Afro-American Ledger* (Baltimore), July 16, August 27, September 24, 1904, August 7, 1909, March 19, 1909, August 13, September 6, 1913.

94. *Afro-American Ledger* (Baltimore), September 24, October 1, November 26, 1910.

95. David E. Goldberg, *The Retreats of Reconstruction: Race, Leisure, and the Politics of Segregation at the New Jersey Shore* (New York: Fordham University Press, 2016), esp. 59–67.

96. Martin Paulsson, *The Social Anxieties of Progressive Reform: Atlantic City, 1854–1920* (New York: New York University Press, 1994), 33–40, 147; Goldberg, *Retreats of Reconstruction*; Dorwart, *Cape May County*, 172; *New York Age*, August 2,

1906 (Jim Crow); *Pittsburgh Courier*, July 27, 1912; *Afro-American Ledger*, March 15, 1913; *New York Age*, August 12, 1912, January 22, 1913, February 27, 1913 (druggist), March 20, 1909 (Brown), April 17, 1909 (Easter).

97. For Easter, see *Afro-American Ledger* (Baltimore), April 9, 1904. See also *Afro-American Ledger*, June 11, 1904, July 23 and 30, August 13, 1910: Bryant Simon, *Boardwalk of Dreams: Atlantic City and the Fate of Urban America* (New York: Oxford University Press, 2004), 33–40.

98. *New York Age*, October 5, 1905, February, 1, 1906.

99. *Afro-American Ledger* (Baltimore), November 25, 1909; *Baltimore Afro-American, National Edition*, June 20, 1925.

100. *New York Age*, March 7, 1912, April 15, 1916; *Baltimore Afro-American National Edition*, April 1, 1916.

101. *Afro-American Ledger* (Baltimore), October 13, 1912, February 22, March 15, 1913.

102. *New York Age*, September 26, 1905; *New York Amsterdam News*, May 29, 1923.

103. *Afro-American Ledger* (Baltimore), December 4, 1904, January 5, 1905, March 5, 1905, March 5, 1910 (movie).

104. *New York Age*, May 11, 1905, September 6, 1906; *Pittsburgh Courier*, September 3, 1910, September 16, December 16, 1911, January 20, April 12, 1912; *Baltimore Afro-American*, August 30, 1913.

105. *Baltimore Afro-American, National Edition*, July 26, 1918.

106. Davis, *We Will Be Satisfied*, 75.

107. Douglas, *Jim Crow Moves North*, 63; Greene, "A History," 37–38.

108. Douglas, *Jim Crow Moves North*, 76, 101, 105–112; Johnson, *Northside*, 133–135.

109. Greene, "A History," 36; for text of decision, see Price, *Freedom Not Far Distant*, 143–150.

110. August Meier and Elliott M. Rudwick, "Early Boycotts of Segregated Schools: The East Orange, New Jersey Experience, 1899–1906," *History of Education Quarterly* 7, no. 1 (1967): 22–35; Douglas, *Jim Crow Moves North*, 70–76.

111. *New York Age*, November 30, 1906.

112. Douglas, *Jim Crow Moves North*, 155–156, 159, 162 (quote), 166, 175.

113. Wright, "New Jersey Laws," 190–195; Joseph L. Bustard, "The Development of Racially Integrated Public Schools, *Journal of Negro Education* 21, no. 3 (1952): 275–285. Greene, "A History," 36.

114. Evelyn Blackmore Duck, "An Historical Study of a Racially Segregated School in New Jersey, 1886 to 1955" (PhD diss., Rutgers University, 1984), 75–88; *New York Age*, May 1, 1948 (Driscoll).

115. Wright, "New Jersey Laws," 191; *Afro-American Ledger* (Baltimore), June 28, 1902, April 22, 1910 (colleges); *Baltimore Afro-American*, February 13, 1914.

116. *Afro-American Ledger* (Baltimore), February 18, March 13, 1915, January 22, April 29, 1916; *Baltimore Afro-American National Edition*, April 29, 1916.

117. Stefan M. Bradley, "The Southern-Most Ivy: Princeton University from Jim Crow Admissions to Anti-Apartheid Protests, 1794–1969," *American Studies* 51, no. 3/4 (2010): 109–130; Watterson, *I Hear My People Singing*, 25–29.

118. *Afro-American Ledger* (Baltimore), January 17, 1903; G. F. Richings, *Evidence of Progress Among the Colored People* (Philadelphia: George Ferguson, 1900), 333.

119. Greene, "A History," 38–39; Price, *Freedom Not Far Distant*, 155–167.

120. *New York Age*, January 18, 1905.

121. *Baltimore Afro-American*, September 13, October 3, 1913; *New York Age*, November 14, 1912, July 24, 1913; *Afro-American Ledger*, October 4 and 18, 1913; Mabel O. Jones, *Negro Building: Black Americans in the World of Fairs and Museums* (Berkeley: University of California Press, 2012), 148–149; David W. Blight, *Race and Reunion: The Civil War in American Memory* (Cambridge, Mass.: Harvard University Press, 2001).

122. *Souvenir Program*, 31–32.

123. *New York Age*, May 2, 1925, February 7, 1931; *Frederick Douglass Building and Loan Association Passbook*, author's collection.

124. *Pittsburgh Courier*, February 23, 1924. For later meeting, see *New York Age*, February 6, 1927.

125. *Baltimore Afro-American, National Edition*, August 24, 1919.

126. *Baltimore Afro-American, National Edition*, February 21, 1925.

127. *New York Age*, September 17 and 24, 1908, October 31, 1912, December 21, 1911; *Afro-American Ledger* (Baltimore), July 22, 1911.

128. *Souvenir Program of Dr. Booker T. Washington's Tour of New Jersey, September 7th, 8th, 9th, 10th, 1914*, comp. W. P. Burrell (n.p., 1914); For Fortune quote see *Baltimore Afro-American*, July 25, September 12, 1914; *Afro-American Ledger*, September 12, 1914. For previous visits, see *New York Age*, March 12, 1908, and *Pittsburgh Courier*, May 13, 1911.

129. *New York Age*, January 18, 1906 (Fortune), January 24, 1907 (Trenton); Emma Lou Thornbrough, "The National Afro-American League, 1887–1908," *Journal of Southern History* 27, no. 4 (1961): 494–512.

130. *Afro-American Ledger* (Baltimore), December 23, 1905; *New York Age*, September 19, 1907 (Orange), February 14, 1914 (Washington), July 15, 1906 (Camden).

131. *Afro-American Ledger* (Baltimore), May 7, 1910.

132. *New York Age*, April 28, 1928.

133. *New York Age*, February 22, 1906, July 3 and 24, 1915. The Alpha Institute, founded in 1911 in Cranford, followed the Bordentown method. See *Pittsburgh Courier*, June 28, 1912, and *Afro-American Ledger* (Baltimore), June 29, 1912; *Baltimore Afro-American*, June 27, 1914.

134. Kenneth M. Hamilton, *Booker T. Washington in American Memory* (Urbana: University of Illinois Press, 2017), 98, 131, 133, 134, 144.

135. For quotes, see Susan D. Carle, *Defining the Struggle: National Organizing for Social Justice, 1880–1915* (New York: Oxford University Press, 2013), 218.

136. Kellogg, *NAACP*, 9–67; Patricia Sullivan, *Lift Every Voice: The NAACP and Making of the Civil Rights Movement* (New York: New Press, 2009); Washington, *Quest for Equality*, 28–31; Price, *Freedom Not Far Distant*, 192; Greene, "A History," 42. On Newark, see Williams, "The Garden of Opportunity," 45.

137. Charles Flint Kellogg, *NAACP*, 123.

138. *New York Age*, May 8, 1913. For the rise of Jim Crow in the federal government, see Eric Yellin, *Racism in the Nation's Service: Government Workers and the Color Line in Woodrow Wilson's America* (Chapel Hill: University of North Carolina Press, 2013), and Nicholas Patler, *Jim Crow and the Wilson Administration: Protesting Federal Segregation in the Early Twentieth Century* (Boulder: University of Colorado Press, 2004). For NAACP and Wilson, see Kellogg, *NAACP*, 155–182.

139. Yellin, *Racism in the Nation's Service*, 3–5, 16–20, 41–42, 67–71, 134, 147, 194.

140. Washington, *Quest for Equality*, 13.

141. *Afro-American Ledger* (Baltimore), September 25, 1915.

142. *New York Age*, July 25, 1907 (dentist), February 13, 1908 (Eclectic), January 15, 1916 (railroad); *Baltimore Afro-American*, January 24, 1914 (railroad).

143. *Afro-American Ledger* (Baltimore), April 14, 1917.

144. *Afro-American Ledger* (Baltimore), September 16, 1911.

145. Washington, *Quest for Equality*, 31–38; "History and Membership of American Legion Post," #152, typescript, Newark Public Library. The lodge was renamed Guyton-Callahan to honor Archie Callahan, a Newark soldier killed in the 1941 bombing of Pearl Harbor.

146. Sherrie Mershon and Steven Schlossman, *Foxholes and Color Lines: Desegregating the U.S. Armed Forces* (Baltimore: Johns Hopkins University Press, 1998), 8–12.

147. *New York Age*, August 10, 17, and 24, 1918.

148. *Pittsburgh Courier*, September 17, 1938.

149. *Baltimore Afro-American, National Edition*, March 1, 1918.

150. W.E.B. Du Bois, *The Souls of Black Folk: Essays and Sketches* (Chicago: S. S. McClure, 1903), 4.

CHAPTER 5 — BLACK NEW JERSEY BATTLES JIM CROW

1. Jones, Johnson, and James transcripts, The Krueger-Scott African American Oral History Collection, Newark Public Library, Newark, New Jersey. All quoted in Williams, "The Garden of Opportunity," 74–77. For population data, see Wright, *Afro-Americans in New Jersey*, appendix 1.

2. Brad R. Tuttle, *How Newark Became Newark: The Rise and Fall and Rebirth of an American City* (New Brunswick: Rivergate Books, 2011), 105; Count Basie and Albert Murray, *Good Morning Blues: The Autobiography of Count Basie* (New York: Random House, 1985), 24–49; Clement A. Price, "The Beleaguered City as Promised Land: Blacks in Newark, 1917–1947," in *A New Jersey Anthology*, ed. Maxine N. Lurie, 433–462 (Newark: New Jersey Historical Society, 1994).

3. L. A. Greene, "A History of Afro-Americans in New Jersey," *Journal of the Rutgers University Libraries* 56, no. 1 (1994): 45; Price, "Beleaguered City," 444–445.

4. Ira De A. Reid, "The Negro Population of Elizabeth, New Jersey: A Survey of its Economic and Social Condition," unpaginated typescript report (New York: The National Urban League for the Elizabeth Interracial Committee, 1930).

5. Reid, "Negro Population of Elizabeth."

6. Reid, "Negro Population of Elizabeth."

7. Reid, "Negro Population of Elizabeth."

8. Reid, "Negro Population of Elizabeth."

9. *New York Age*, November 30, 1917, March 5, 1921.

10. *New York Age*, March 5, April 9, May 21, 1921.

11. *New York Age*, September 24, 1921, September 25, 1926: *New York Amsterdam News,* March 28, July 4, 1923.

12. *Pittsburgh Courier*, July 10, 1924, September 13, 1924; *Baltimore Afro-American, National Edition*, August 15, 1924; *New York Age*, August 16, 1924.

13. *New York Age*, December 19, 1927, January 4 and March 24, 1928, March 8, 1930. On women see Adams, *Black Women's Christian Activism*, 70.

14. *New York Age*, July 23, 1922.

15. *New York Age*, November 21 and December 15, 1928; *Pittsburgh Courier*, January 5, 1929.

16. *Pittsburgh Courier*, September 8, 1928; *New York Amsterdam News*, April 29, 1925.

17. *Baltimore Afro-American, National Edition,* July 11 and 18, 1925; *New York Age*, July 16, 1925, July 7, 1928.

18. *Pittsburgh Courier*, September 15 and 29, October 13, 1928.

19. *Baltimore Afro-American, National Edition*, August 4 and 11, 1924.

20. *Baltimore Afro-American, National Edition,* May 23, 1924.

21. *New York Age*, March 11, 1921, June 27, 1925, January 27, 1927; *Baltimore Afro-American, National Edition*, May 16, 1925.

22. *New York Age*, May 15, 1926.

23. *Pittsburgh Courier*, June 6, November 16, 1929.

24. *Pittsburgh Courier*, March 8, 1930; *New York Age*, August 13, 1929.

25. *New York Age*, October 22, 1927; *Pittsburgh Courier*, July 4, 1931, July 9 and October 8, 1938.

26. *New York Age*, April 27, September 6, 1919; Price, "Beleaguered City," 447.

27. *New York Age*, May 2, 1931.

28. *Pittsburgh Courier*, May 7, November 1, 14, and 28, 1931, August 27, October 1, 1932; *New York Age*, March 14, 1931; W.E.B. Du Bois speech denouncing David Baird, September 2, 1931, Du Bois Papers, Special Collections and University Archives, University of Massachusetts Amherst Libraries.

29. *New York Age*, March 7, 1931.

30. *New York Age*, October 10, 1931.

31. *New York Age*, July 28, 1932.

32. For the trend nationally, see Leah Wright Rigueur, *The Loneliness of the Black Republican* (Princeton: Princeton University Press, 2015), 17, 24.

33. *New York Age*, May 3, 1933.

34. *Pittsburgh Courier*, July 30, 1938.

35. *Pittsburgh Courier*, November 3, 1923 (bootleggers), August 31, 1929, April 9, 1938; *Baltimore Afro-American, National Edition*, August 29, 1924 (black and tans). See also *Pittsburgh Courier*, July 23, 1938, for an instance in which white girls pleaded with police not to arrest them so they could mother their mixed race babies.

36. *New York Age*, March 12, 1927.

37. Greene, "A History," 45.

38. *New York Age*, February 26, March 19, 1921, March 29, 1924.

39. *Pittsburgh Courier*, June 28, 1924; John T. Cumbler, *Social History of Economic Decline: Business, Politics, and Work in Trenton* (New Brunswick: Rutgers University Press, 1989), 151.

40. *New York Age*, June 30, 1934; *Pittsburgh Courier*, September 10, 1938.

41. *New York Age*, May 18, 1929, May 17, 1930.

42. *New York Age*, June 17, 1933.

43. *Pittsburgh Courier*, August 8, 1937.

44. *Pittsburgh Courier*, August 13, 1929; *New York Age*, July 13, 1929.

45. Lizbeth Cohen, *A Consumer's Republic: The Politics of Mass Consumption in Postwar America* (New York: Knopf, 2003), 175–177.

46. *Pittsburgh Courier*, July 9, August 20 and 26, October 15, 1938.

47. *Pittsburgh Courier*, February 4, 1939.

48. Davison M. Douglas, *Jim Crow Moves North: The Battle Over Northern School Segregation, 1865–1954* (New York: Cambridge University Press, 2005), 175–178; Cumbler, *Social History of Economic Decline*, 151.

49. *New York Age*, March 19, 1921; for Alexander's life, see his obituary in the *New York Times*, February 6, 1953.

50. Douglas, *Jim Crow Moves North*, 179, 182–183, 188.

51. *New York Age*, May 31, 1924.

52. *New York Amsterdam News*, June 20, 1923.

53. *Baltimore Afro-American, National Edition*, May 16, 1925.

54. *New York Age*, February 26, 1921, July 1, October 14, 1922; March 23 and 31, 1923; on the NAACP's overall strategy on school desegregation, see Mark V. Tushnet, *The NAACP's Legal Strategy against Segregated Education* (Chapel Hill: University of North Carolina Press, 1987).

55. "Toms River Case, 1927," in *Papers of the NAACP*, The Campaign for Educational Equality, Legal Department and Central Office Records, 1913–1940 (Frederick, Md.: University Publications of America, 1986), series A, part 3, reels, 12–13, boxes 91–92; *Pittsburgh Courier*, March 17, 1927; *New York Age*, March 19, 26, April 2, 1927; Patricia Sullivan, *Lift Every Voice and Sing: The NAACP and the Making of the Civil Rights Movement* (New York: New Press, 2009), 129–130.

56. "Atlantic City Case, 1928," *Papers of the NAACP*, box D-44.

57. Douglas, *Jim Crow Moves North*, 196–201.

58. Thomas J. Segrue, *Sweet Land of Liberty: The Forgotten Civil Rights Movement in the North* (New York: Random House, 2008), 176–179; Douglas, *Jim Crow Moves North*, 206; *New York Age*, October 28, 1933, April 28, 1934; *Pittsburgh Courier*, September 10, October 8, 1936.

59. *Baltimore Afro-American, National Edition*, January 24, 1925; *New York Age*, September 30, 1922; *New York Age*, January 24, 1925; Price, "Beleaguered City," 447.

60. *New York Age*, April 11, 1926, October 6, 1928; *Pittsburgh Courier*, August 4, 1928.

61. *New York Age*, February 16, 1924.

62. *New York Age*, June 27, 1931, July 14, 1934. See also *Pittsburgh Courier*, July 25, 1936, for a subsequent meeting at Bordentown.

63. *New York Age*, August 19, 1922.

64. *New York Age*, May 1 and 8, 1926.

65. *New York Age*, March 22, December 20,1930.

66. *Baltimore Afro-American, National Edition*, July 25, 1925.

67. *New York Age*, June 27, 1925. For other riots, see *Pittsburgh Courier*, February 1, 1936.

68. *Baltimore Afro-American, National Edition*, April 24, 1926.

69. *Pittsburgh Courier*, January 13, November 3, 1923.

70. *Pittsburgh Courier*, March 15, 1930; *New York Age*, March 3, 1934.

71. *Baltimore Afro-American, National Edition*, August 1, 1925.

72. *Baltimore Afro-American, National Edition*, September 16, 1921.

73. *Afro-American Ledger* (Baltimore), March 17, 1917.

74. *New York Age*, March 15, 1926.

75. *New York Age*, July 6, 1905, November 7, 1907. Two years later the church, now rebuilt and restored, celebrated its one hundredth anniversary with a love feast, a sermon, and singing by the famous Epworth league in the afternoon and evening. The celebration lasted for two weeks.

76. *Pittsburgh Courier*, June 21, 1930.

77. Charles H. Wesley, *History of the Improved Benevolent and Protective Order of Elks of the World 1898 to 1954* (Washington: Association for the Study of Negro Life and History, 1954).

78. Wesley, *History*, 39, 126, 132, 149, 148, 442. For Jim Crow in Atlantic City during this period, see Bryant Simon, *Boardwalk of Dreams: Atlantic City and the Fate of Urban America* (New York: Oxford University Press, 2004), 35–44; for social capital, see Theda Skocpol, Ariane Liazos, and Marshall Ganz, *What a Mighty Power We Can Be: African American Fraternal Groups and the Struggle for Racial Equality* (Princeton: Princeton University Press, 2006), 223.

79. *Baltimore Afro-American, National Edition*, August 4, 1919.

80. *Baltimore Afro-American, National Edition*, September 21, 1921; *New York Amsterdam News*, May 16, 1923. For a good summary of Harding's failures, see Richard B. Sherman, "The Harding Administration and the Negro: An Opportunity Lost," *Journal of Negro History* 49, no. 3 (1964): 151–168.

81. Kenneth T. Jackson, *The Ku Klux Klan in the City, 1915–1930* (New York: Oxford University Press, 1967), 178–179; Thomas R. Pegram, *One Hundred Percent American: The Rebirth and Decline of the Ku Klux Klan in the 1920s* (Lanham, Md.: Ivan Dee, 2011), 59, 177; Kelly J. Baker, *The Gospel According to the Klan: The KKK's Appeal to Protestant America, 1915–1930* (Lawrence: University Press of Kansas, 2011), 165–167, 184.

82. *Baltimore Afro-American, National Edition*, April 11, 1921.

83. *Baltimore Afro-American, National Edition*, August 10, 1921, April 4, 1921 (Howard singers), April 4, 1925 (Lincoln singers), June 20, 1924 (Field Club), May 16, 1924 (bathrooms), January 16, 1925 (traffic cop), January 23, 1926 (Sunshine Charity Club).

84. *Baltimore Afro-American, National Edition*, August 21, 1915, December 28, 1923, August 8, 1924; *New York Age*, April 28, 1928, February 7, 1930, September 19, 1931; *Pittsburgh Courier*, March 28, 1936, May 28, 1938, January 28, 1939. For the NAACP's initial reluctance to act against the film, see Charles Flint Kellogg, *NAACP: A History of the National Association for the Advancement of Colored People* (Baltimore: Johns Hopkins University Press, 1967), 140–146. For general black reaction to the film, see Ibram X. Kendi, *Stamped from the Beginning: The Definitive History of Racist Ideas in America* (New York: Nation Books, 2016), 304.

85. *Pittsburgh Courier*, September 27, November 24, 1923; *New York Age*, May 22, 1922; *New York Amsterdam News*, September 9, 1923.

86. *New York Amsterdam News*, December 13 and 20, 1922.

87. *New York Age*, September 10, 1921, June 4, 1924.

88. *Pittsburgh Courier*, August 23, 1924.

89. *Baltimore Afro-American, National Edition*, November 23, 1923, May 16, 1924, October 30, 1924, June 20 and 24, 1925; *New York Age*, November 15, 1924; *New York Amsterdam News*, June 17, 1925.

90. *New York Age*, July 17, 1926.

91. *New York Age*, September 4 and 18, 1926.

92. *Baltimore Afro-American, National Edition*, August 25, 1925.

93. *New York Age*, August 17, September 14, 1929.

94. *New York Age*, September 8, 1928 (Asbury Park), November 2, 1929 (Williamson).

95. *New York Age*, April 1, May 13, 1933.

96. Greene, "A History," 46; Prince, "The Beleaguered City," 441.

97. For quotes see Helen Jackson Lee, *Nigger in the Window* (Garden City, N.Y.: Doubleday, 1978), 148: Cumbler, *Social History of Economic Decline*, 152–153

98. Mary Pool, *Segregated Origins of Social Security: African Americans and the Welfare State* (Chapel Hill: University of North Carolina Press, 2006), 18–20, 69.

99. *Survey of Negro Life in New Jersey*, 3 vols. (Trenton: New Jersey Conference of Social Work 1932), https://catalog.hathitrust.org/Record/000339540.

100. Greene, "A History," 48.

101. *Baltimore Afro-American, National Edition*, April 11, 1924.

102. *New York Age*, March 17, 1923.

103. *New York Age*, April 28, 1928; Price, "Beleaguered City," 450.

104. *New York Age*, June 2, 1934.

105. *Pittsburgh Courier*, October 8, 1936.

106. *Pittsburgh Courier*, July 3, 1937 (quote); Pool, *Segregated Origins*, 18.

107. Greene, "A History," 49.

108. For quote see *New York Age*, January 24, 1931. For church numbers see Works Progress Administration, *The Negro Church in New Jersey* (Hackensack, N.J.: 1938), 47, as quoted in Williams, "The Garden of Opportunity," 81.

109. *Pittsburgh Courier*, April 3, May 1, 1937.

110. *New York Age*, July 30, 1932, August 6, 1932.

111. Howard Gillette Jr., *Camden After the Fall: Decline and Renewal in a Post-Industrial City* (Philadelphia: University of Pennsylvania Press, 2005), 17–39; Daniel Sidorick, *Condensed Capitalism: Campbell Soup and the Pursuit of Cheap Production in the Twentieth Century* (Ithaca, N.Y.: Cornell University Press, 2009).

112. *Pittsburgh Courier*, March 15, 1930.

113. Pool, *Segregated Origins*, 186.

114. Beatrice A. Myers and Ira De A. Reid, "The Toll of Tuberculosis Among Negroes in New Jersey," *Opportunity* 10 (1932): 279–282, reprinted in Clement Alexander Price, ed., *Freedom Not Far Distant: A Documentary History of Afro-Americans in New Jersey* (Newark: New Jersey Historical Society, 1980), 217–224.

115. *Negroes on the Road: A Survey of the Transient Negro in New Jersey* (Trenton: State of New Jersey Emergency Relief Commission, 1935).

116. Cindy Hahamovitch, *The Fruits of Their Labor: Atlantic Coast Farmworkers and the Making of Migrant Poverty, 1870–1945* (Chapel Hill: University of North Carolina Press, 1997), 131–140. For attacks and reactions, see *Pittsburgh Courier*, August 19 and 26, September 13, 1939.

117. Hahamovitch, *Fruits of their Labor*, 140–150; Andrew Urban, "Digging Up the Backyard: Seabrook Farms and the Importance of Critical Local History," *New Jersey Studies* 3, no. 2 (2017); Charles H. Harrison, *Growing a Global Village: Making History at Seabrook Farms* (New York: Holmes and Meier, 2003), 40–41.

118. Walter D. Greason, *The Path to Freedom: Black Families in New Jersey* (Charleston, S.C.: The History Press, 2010).

119. Kathryn Watterson, *I Hear My People Singing: Voices of African American Princeton* (Princeton: Princeton University Press, 2017), 120–123.

120. Martha Jo Black and Chuck Schoffner, *Joe Black: More Than a Dodger* (Chicago: Academy Chicago Publishers, 2015), 28–30.

121. *Pittsburgh Courier*, September 22, 1928; Price, "The Beleaguered City," 440.

122. Moses, *African American Women Writers in New Jersey*, 82–83; Watterson, *I Hear My People Singing*, 15.

123. Sanford Bell Powell, *Colored American Biography Mile Post Register* (Newark, N.J.: John M. Stoute, printer, 1939), 8–10.

124. G. F. Richings, *Evidence of Progress among Colored People* (Philadelphia: George F. Ferguson, 1902), 333, 343, 423; Nelson Johnson, *Northside: African Americans and the Creation of Atlantic City* (Medford: Plexus Publishing, 2010), 117–124; Wright, *Afro-Americans in New Jersey*, 60–62; *New York Age*, July 30, 1949, September 6, 1906 (jeweler); *Pittsburgh Courier*, May 5, 1951, January 5, 1952 (Walker); Juliet E. K. Walker, *The History of Black Business in America: Capitalism, Race, Entrepreneurship* (New York: Macmillan Reference, 1998), 210; David E. Goldberg, *The Retreats of Reconstruction: Race, Leisure, and the Politics of Segregation at the New Jersey Shore, 1865–1920* (New York: Fordham University Press, 2016).

125. *Baltimore Afro-American, National Edition*, August 1, 1925; *New York Age*, April 5, 1924.

126. A. A. Phillips, "The Negro Physician in North Jersey and the Early History of the North Jersey Medical Society" (unpublished manuscript, n.d.)

127. *New York Age*, February 11, 1933. On Wiggins, see Williams, "Garden of Opportunity," 65–66. For an extended list of black "firsts" in Newark, see http://knowingnewark.npl.org/the-list-of-firsts-african-americans-who-pioneered-the-way/.

128. Sanford Bell Powell, *Colored American Biography*, 8.

129. Janet Sims-Wood, *Dorothy Porter Wesley at Howard University: Building a Legacy of Black History* (Charleston, S.C.: History Press, 2014), http://www.blackpast .org/aah/dorothy-porter-wesley-1905-1995.

130. This paragraph and others about Wright are drawn from the most complete study of her in *Pedagogies of Resistance: Women Educator Activists, 1880–1960*, eds. Margaret Smith Crocco, Petra Munro, and Kathleen Weiler (New York: Teachers College Press, 1999), 61–75. Theodore Brunson, founder of the Jersey City Afro-American Historical Society Museum, was born in 1925. See his obituary in *New Jersey.com*, July 28, 2012.

131. *New York Age*, September 15, 1923.

132. Quotes and information from Michael J. Birkner, "From Hackensack to the White House: The Triumph and Travail of E. Frederic Morrow," *New Jersey Studies* (Summer 2017): 78–117.

133. *New York Age*, March 10, 1928, April 24, 1933; E. Frederic Morrow, *Way Down South Up North* (Philadelphia: United Church Press, 1973), 13–15, 24–26; John H. Morrow earned a PhD from the University of Pennsylvania before embarking on a fruitful career as an academic and diplomat. See John H. Morrow, *First American Ambassador to Guinea* (New Brunswick, N.J.: Rutgers University Press, 1967); *New York Age*, June 18, 1931. For Randolph, see *Pittsburgh Courier*, August 30, 1923; *New York Age*, March 17, 1923.

134. W.E.B. Du Bois to New Jersey State Federation of Colored Women's Clubs, September 1, 14, 1925; W.E.B. Du Bois to Bordentown YMCA, March 17, 1926; W.E.B. Du Bois to New Jersey State Normal School, February 3, 6, 1928; Intergroup Bureau of Social Education to W.E.B. Du Bois, October 25, 1928; Monmouth County Emancipation Celebration, January 1, 1931, in Du Bois Papers, Special Collections and University Archives, University of Massachusetts Amherst Libraries.

135. *New York Age*, March 18, 1933; *New York Amsterdam News*, May 23, 1923; *New York Age*, May 17, 1930; Pete McDaniel, *Uneven Lies: The Heroic Story of African-Americans in Golf* (Greenwich, Conn.: American Golfer, 2000), 6–62; on Shippen, see Calvin H. Sinnette, *Forbidden Fairways: African Americans and the Game of Golf* (Chelsea MI.: Sleeping Bear Press, 1998), 15–25: for Montclair YWCA, see Williams, "Garden of Opportunity," 121.

136. *New York Age*, February 11, 1933.

137. James M. DiClercio and Barry J. Pavelic, *The Jersey Game: The History of Baseball from its Birth to the Big Leagues in the Garden State* (New Brunswick: Rutgers University Press, 1991), 143–145; *New York Age*, March 18, May 3, 1924.

138. DiClercio and Pavelic, *Jersey Game*, 146–149, 153–156; Alfred M. Martin and Alfred T. Martin, *The Negro Leagues in New Jersey* (Jefferson, N.C.: McFarland, 2008), 6–7, 106–133; Brad R. Tuttle, *How Newark Became Newark: The Rise, Fall and Rebirth of an American City* (New Brunswick, N.J.: Rivergate, 2011), 151; Monte

Irvin, *Nice Guys Finish First* (New York: Carroll and Graf, 1996), 39–51: James A. Riley, *The Biographical Encyclopedia of the Negro Baseball Leagues* (New York: Carroll and Graf, 1994), 509–509, 580–581; Bob Luke, *The Most Famous Woman in Baseball: Effa Manley and the Negro Leagues* (Washington, D.C.: Potomac Books, 2011), 48, 61, 72, 98.

139. Barbara J. Kukla, *Swing City: Newark Night Life, 1925–50* (Philadelphia: Temple University Press, 1991); Cissy Houston, *How Sweet the Sound: My Life with God and the Gospel* (New York: Bantam Doubleday, 1998), 38–39.

140. *Pittsburgh Courier*, March 19, 1938.

141. *New York Age*, February 18, 1933.

142. *New York Age*, March 11, 1933, January 13, 1934; Sullivan, *Lift Every Voice and Sing*, 125.

143. *New York Age*, July 8, 1933.

144. *Pittsburgh Courier*, April 30, 1931.

145. *Pittsburgh Courier*, July 14, September 13, October 4, 1930, June 18, July 30, August 27, 1938.

146. *Pittsburgh Courier*, February 13, 1932.

147. *New York Age*, February 26, 1927.

148. *Pittsburgh Courier*, May 14, 1931.

149. *Pittsburgh Courier*, March 6, 1930, March 15, 1937; *New York Age*, May 6, June 3, October 7, 1933, December 8, 1934.

150. *Pittsburgh Courier*, December 19, 1936.

151. *Pittsburgh Courier*, January 15, October 1, 1938; *New Jersey.com*, April 14, 2014, on Savage-Jennings.

152. *Pittsburgh Courier*, March 5 and 19, 1938.

153. *Pittsburgh Courier*, March 5, 1938.

154. *Pittsburgh Courier*, November 26, December 17, 1938, February 18, 1939; Greene, "A History," 46.

155. *Pittsburgh Courier*, September 30, November 8, 1937.

156. *Pittsburgh Courier*, June 18, July 9, 1931.

157. *Baltimore Afro-American, National Edition*, November 14, 1925; *New York Age*, November 14, 1925.

158. *Pittsburgh Courier*, March 22, 1930; Pegram, *One Hundred Percent American*, 63; Baker, *Gospel According the Klan*, 132–133.

159. *Pittsburgh Courier*, June 13, 1936, July 9, 1938.

160. *Baltimore Afro-American, National Edition*, April 7, 1925: *New York Age*, November 7, 1925.

161. Fred Jerome and Rodger Taylor, *Einstein on Race and Racism* (New Brunswick: Rutgers University Press, 2007); Kathryn Watterson, *I Hear My People Singing*, 57.

CHAPTER 6 — WORLD WAR II AND ITS AFTERMATH

1. For an extensive account of Du Bois's comments on Japanese and Chinese conflicts, see Yunxiang Gao, "W. E. B. and Shirley Graham Du Bois in Maoist China," *Du Bois Review: Social Science Research on Race* 10, no. 1 (2013): 59–85; for double V strategy in New Jersey, see L. A. Greene, "A History of Afro-Americans in New Jersey," *Journal of the Rutgers University Libraries* 56, no. 1 (1994): 49–59.

2. [The Commission on Urban Colored Population], *The New Jersey Negro in World War II, contributions and activities* (Trenton: n.p., 1945).

3. *Pittsburgh Courier*, August 22, December 12, 1942; *New York Age*, January 20, 1945.

4. James Baldwin, *Notes of a Native Son* (Boston: Beacon Press, 1955), 109–110.

5. U.S. Bureau of the Census, 1940, 1950; Daniel M. Johnson, *Black Migration in America: A Social Demographic History* (Durham, N.C.: Duke University Press, 1981), 131; Wright, *Afro-Americans in New Jersey,* appendix 1.

6. Lizbeth Cohen, *A Consumer's Republic: The Politics of Mass Consumption in Postwar America* (New York: Knopf, 2003); Kenneth T. Jackson, *Crabgrass Frontier: The Suburbanization of the United States* (New York: Oxford University Press, 1985), 141, 284, 302, 322; Robert Curvin, *Inside Newark: Decline, Rebellion, and the Search for Transformation* (New Brunswick, N.J.: Rutgers University Press, 2014), 9, 21–31, 40–42. On Weequahic, see Sherry B. Ortner, *New Jersey Dreaming: Capital, Class and the Class of '58* (Durham, N.C.: Duke University Press, 2003).

7. *Pittsburgh Courier*, February 26, May 21 and 28, June 11, September 9, October 1, 8, and 29, November 5, 1938.

8. For quote on Bordentown see *Pittsburgh Courier*, January 21, 1939;for other quotes see for other quotes see Douglas, *Jim Crow Moves North*, 229.

9. Greene, "A History," 58–59; Clement A. Price, "The Beleaguered City as Promised Land: Blacks in Newark, 1917–1947," in *A New Jersey Anthology*, ed. Maxine N. Lurie, 433–462 (Newark: New Jersey Historical Society, 1994).

10. Quoted in Douglas, *Jim Crow Moves North*, 235.

11. Phyllis Palmer, *Living as Equals: How Three White Communities Struggled to Make Interracial Connections During the Civil Rights Era* (Nashville: Vanderbilt University Press, 2008); interview with Lois Horton, April 10, 2017.

12. Linda B. Forgosh, *Louis Bamberger: Department Store Innovator and Philanthropist* (Waltham, Mass.: Brandeis University Press, 2016), 51.

13. *New York Age*, November 14, 1953 (radio station); *Pittsburgh Courier*, June 4, 1949 (Cook).

14. *Pittsburgh Courier*, September 30, 1939 (Pleasantville).

15. Thomas J. Sugrue, *Sweet Land of Liberty: The Forgotten Struggle for Civil Rights in the North* (New York: Random House, 2008), 169.

16. *New York Age*, March 25, 1944.

17. *New York Age*, October 2, 1943; https://en.wikipedia.org/wiki/Hedgepeth_and _Williams v. Board_of_Education; Sugrue, *Sweet Land of Liberty*, 177.

18. Ernest Thompson and Mindy Thompson, *Homeboy Came to Orange: A Story of People's Power* (Newark, N.J.: Bridgebuilder Press, 1976); Maggie Thompson, *From One to Ninety-one: The Life of Maggie Thompson* (Amherst: Levellers Press for the University of Orange Bridgebuilder Press, 2011); Mindy Thompson, *The National Negro Labor Council: A History* (unpublished manuscript, Rutgers University, Alexander Library, New Brunswick, N. J., 1978).

19. Ernest Thompson Papers, Alexander Library, Rutgers University, Box 2, Folders 5, 11.

20. Douglas, *Jim Crow Moves North*, 224; Christopher Parker, "War and African American Citizenship, 1865–1965: The Role of Military Service," in *The Oxford Handbook of African American Citizenship, 1865–Present*, eds. Henry Louis Gates Jr., et al., 425–463 (New York: Oxford University Press, 2012).

21. *Pittsburgh Courier*, December 15, 1951, August 16, 1952.

22. *New York Age*, May 5, 1945.

23. See http://www.state.nj.us/lps/dcr/happy_bday_lad.html.

24. Cohen, *Consumer's Republic*, 168–171, 242–244, 271: Jackson, *Crabgrass Frontiers*, 155; Ira Katznelson, *When Affirmative Action Was White: An Untold History of Racial Inequality in Twentieth-Century America* (New York: W. W. Norton, 2005), 140.

25. *New York Age,* November 24, 1945, May 25, 1946; *Pittsburgh Courier*, May 25, July 22, 1946.

26. *Pittsburgh Courier*, September 28, 1939 (Bullock); *New York Age*, February 5, April 29, 1944 (Wilhemsteen).

27. *Pittsburgh Courier*, December 4 and 23, 1939 (Buchanan), January 5, 1952 (Lark). See also the case of Gus Davidson in *Pittsburgh Courier*, May 12, June 2, 1951.

28. Patricia Sullivan, *Lift Every Voice: The NAACP and the Making of the Civil Rights Movement* (New York: New Press, 2009), 297.

29. For Klan events, see *Pittsburgh Courier*, August 19 and 26, December 23, 1939, February 24, 1940, March 11, 1944, October 19 and 26, 1946; *New York Age*, June 19, 1948. See also John Whiteclay Chambers 3rd, *Cranbury: A New Jersey Town from the Colonial Era to the Present* (New Brunswick: Rivergate Books, 2012), 136–138.

30. Clarence Taylor, *Knocking at Our Own Door: Milton A. Galamison and the Struggle to Integrate New York City Schools* (New York: Columbia University Press, 1997), 28–32; *Pittsburgh Courier*, July 29, 1939; *New York Age*, June 21, 1947 (Baptists), April 13, June 1, 1940 (Methodists).

31. Robert A. Hill, ed., *The FBI's RACON: Racial Conditions in the United States during World War II* (Boston: Northeastern University Press, 1995), 166–168, 457–458, 462, 470, 475, 521, 529, 652.

32. Sugrue, *Sweet Land of Liberty*, 177.

33. Sugrue, *Sweet Land of Liberty*, 178–179; Douglas, *Jim Crow Moves North*, 241–246, 259; Robin M. Williams Jr., and Margaret W. Ryan, eds., *Schools in Transition: Community Experiences in Desegregation* (Chapel Hill: University of North Carolina Press, 1954), 120–153; Wright, "New Jersey Leads," 408; *New York Age*, December 22 and 24, 1945, October 12, 1946 (Trenton), January 26, 1946 (employment); *Pittsburgh Courier*, February 28, 1948 (achievements).

34. Wright, "New Jersey Leads," 405; *New York Age*, November 13, 1948.

35. "Closter B. Current, Department of Branches, New Jersey to NAACP Public Relations Department, April 10, 1947, New Jersey Schools, File C, NAACP Papers, Manuscript Division, Library of Congress, Washington, D.C.

36. "A Survey of the Public School System in the State of New Jersey, Made under the direction of the New Jersey State Conference of NAACP Branches," May 1947, NAACP Papers, Library of Congress; *New York Age*, May 3, 1943. For comment, see *Pittsburgh Courier*, February 15, 1947.

37. Lovejoy was a nineteenth-century abolitionist killed by a mob wanting to suppress his antislavery journalism. For the impact of the 1947 constitution, see John B. Wefing, "Conclusion: New Jersey's 1947 Constitution and the Creation of a Modern State Supreme Court," in *Courting Justice: Ten New Jersey Cases that Shook the Nation*, ed. Paul L. Tractenberg, 235–255 (New Brunswick, N.J.: Rutgers University Press, 2013). All the cases covered in this book are useful for our subject. For award, see Charles H. Wesley, *History of the Improved Benevolent and Protective Order of Elks of the World 1898–1954* (Washington, D.C.: Association for the Study of Negro Life and History, Inc., 1954), 363–369. The Elks also sponsored and operated a farm commemorating John Brown. See Wesley, *History*, 380–382.

38. Marion Thompson Wright, "A Dramatic Historical Event," *Journal of Negro History* 33, no. 2 (1948) 177–223; Joseph L. Bustard, "The Development of Racially Integrated Public Schools," *Journal of Negro Education* 21, no. 3 (1952): 275–285. See also *New York Age*, May 8, 1948, and *Pittsburgh Courier*, November 15, 1947 (voters). For Driscoll, see Michael Birkner, Donald Linky, and Peter Mickulas, eds., *The Governors of New Jersey: Biographical Essays*, rev. ed. (New Brunswick, N.J.: Rutgers University Press, 2014), 281–288.

39. Watterson, *I Hear My People Singing*, 76–80.

40. Watterson, *I Hear My People Singing*, 82–83.

41. NAACP Statement on Camden School Case, August 25, 1948, NAACP Papers, Library of Congress; *Pittsburgh Courier*, January 19 (Lucas), October 11, 1952 (teachers).

42. *New York Age*, February 14, March 6, 1948; *Pittsburgh Courier*, October 15, 1949 (destiny); *Pittsburgh Courier*, February 14, 1948 (army).

43. *New York Age*, March 16 and 23, 1946; *Pittsburgh Courier*, March 16, 1946 (YWCA); *Pittsburgh Courier*, March 30, 1946; *New York Age*, May 8, 1948 (YMCA).

44. *New York Age*, February 8, May 4, August 30, October 26, 1946; May 8 and 15, 1948; *Pittsburgh Courier*, May 4, 1946.

45. *New York Age*, February 22, 1947 (artists); *New York Age*, July 5, 1947 (opera); *Pittsburgh Courier*, October 4, 1947 (Rotary), February 12, 1949 (cartoon).

46. Martha Biondi, *To Stand and Fight: The Struggle for Civil Rights in Postwar New York City* (Cambridge, Mass.: Harvard University Press, 2003), 83–85; Thomas J. Sugrue, *Sweet Land of Liberty*, 154–161; Greene, "A History," 54; *New York Age*, July 19, August 9 and 23, 1947, February 14, 21, and 28, June 20, 1948; *Pittsburgh Courier*, August 23, 1947.

47. *New York Age*, August 20, 1947.

48. *New York Age*, January 15 and 22, August 13 and 27, 1949; *Pittsburgh Courier*, September 6, 1947 (commentator), March 26, 1949 (vote), April 16, 1949 (governor's signature), February 3, 1951.

49. *Pittsburgh Courier*, June 15, 1957, February 12, 1966.

50. *Pittsburgh Courier*, April 26, May 17, 1941, December 2, 1944, January 22, 1949 (Orange); *New York Age*, November 20, December 11, 1948 (Spencer).

51. Cohen, *A Consumer's Republic*, 227; Wright, "New Jersey Leads," 401–417.

52. *New York Age*, December 18 and 25, 1948, January 8, 1949; *Pittsburgh Courier*, January 1, 1949 (Cleveland).

53. Cohen, *Consumer's Republic*, 286–289; Robert J. Gordon, *The Rise and Fall of American Growth: The U.S. Standard of Living since the Civil War* (Princeton: Princeton University Press, 2016), 379–408, 419–433; Cumbler, *Social History of Economic Decline*, 156–158.

54. New York Age, *October 26, 1949, April 29, October 28, 1950.*

55. Cathy D. Knepper, *Jersey Justice: The Case of the Trenton Six* (New Brunswick, N.J.: Rutgers University Press, 2011); *New York Age*, January 8 and 15, April 2, 1949, January 10, February 28, 1953, April 7, 1951 (Baker); *Pittsburgh Courier*, January 13, March 5, 1949.

56. For Hill, see *New York Age*, April 14, 1945; for Howell, see *New York Age*, June 17, 1944; *New York Age*, April 14, 1947 (Randolph), April 3, 1948 (Johnson); for Morrow, see E. Frederic Morrow, *Black Man in the White House* (Philadelphia: Coward, McCann, 1963), and *Forty Years a Guinea Pig: A Black Man's View from the Top* (New York: Pilgrim Press, 1980); Robert Frederick Durk, *The Eisenhower Administration and Black Civil Rights* (Knoxville: University of Tennessee Press, 1984), 70, 79–87; Michael J. Birkner, "From Hackensack to the White House: The Triumph and Travail of E. Frederic Morrow," *New Jersey History* (Summer 2017): 78–117.

57. Leah Wright Rigueur, *The Loneliness of the Black Republican* (Princeton: Princeton University Press, 2015), 35–36; Joshua Farrington, *Black Republicans and the Transformation of the GOP* (Philadelphia: University of Pennsylvania Press, 2016).

58. Rigueur, *Loneliness of the Black Republican*, 31–35; Farrington, *Black Republicans*, 45–47, 71–73, 76.

59. *Pittsburgh Courier*, April 2, 1966.

60. http://www.njwomenshistory.org/discover/biographies/madline-worthy-williams/. Very little is known about Hill, including his origins, death, and place of burial.

61. Priscilla B. Anderson, *The History and Contribution of Black Americans to the Development of Willingboro, Burlington, New Jersey* (Trenton: New Jersey Historical Commission, 1985); https://en.wikipedia.org/wiki/Willingboro_Township,_New_Jersey#cite_note-Anderson-26; "Report of Prospects Now on Record," Lett Papers, 1958, Newark Public Library. The Lett Papers contain voluminous exchanges between the Levitts and Lett.

62. *Pittsburgh Courier*, September 19 and 21, October 21, 1942; Cindy Hahamovitch, *The Fruits of Their Labor: Atlantic Coast Farmworkers and the Making of Migrant Poverty* (Chapel Hill: University of North Carolina Press, 1997), 187–193.

63. Watterson, *I Hear My People Singing*, 159–188.

64. *Pittsburgh Courier*, January 24, 1957, February 5, 1966 (Jack and Jill).

65. *Pittsburgh Courier*, March 31, 1951; *Pittsburgh Courier*, November 19 and 28, 1949 (bar exam); *New York Age*, March 24, 1945 (Priest); *Pittsburgh Courier*, January 26, 1946 (McConnell); December 18, 1954 (Parker); Mich Kachun, *First Martyr of Liberty: Crispus Attucks in American Memory* (New York: Oxford University Press, 2017), 145.

66. *Pittsburgh Courier*, May 29, 1950; *New York Age* August 17, 1946. For Rickey, see Wesley, *History*, 288–389.

67. Juliet E. K. Walker, *The History of Black Business in America: Capitalism, Race, Entrepreneurship* (New York: Macmillan Reference, 1998), 251.

68. *Pittsburgh Courier*, December 14, 1957.

69. *Pittsburgh Courier*, November 5, 1945 (Murchison), February 12, 1949 (Hatchett).

70. Watterson, *I Hear My People Singing*, 110; Simeon Moss, "The Persistence of Slavery and Involuntary Servitude in a Free State (1685–1866)," *Journal of Negro History* 35 (1950): 289–310; Sibyl E. Moses, *African American Women Writers in New Jersey, 1836–2000* (New Brunswick, N.J.: Rutgers University Press, 2003), 219–220; *Pittsburgh Courier*, July 30, 1955 (Davis).

71. Barbara Kukla with Delores Collins Benjamin, *Sounds of Music: The Delores Collins Benjamin Story* (Newark, N.J.: Swing City Press, 2007); Carl J. (Tiny Prince) Papers, Newark Public Library. Brinson lived until 2015, see http://obits.nj.com/obituaries/starledger/obituary.aspx?pid=175556889.

72. Nelson Johnson, *The Northside: African Americans and the Creation of Atlantic City* (Medford, N.J.: Plexus, 2010), 159–163, 227–228.

73. Barbara J. Kukla's several books on local musicians featured glee clubs, gospel singers and groups, pop stars, and dancers. Kukla, a white woman from northern Jersey and a longtime columnist at the *Newark Star-Ledger,* spent years studying, writing, and participating in Newark's rich sacred and secular cultures. Her book *Defying the Odds* highlights many of city's black female physicians, churchgoers and leaders, philanthropists, athletes, singers, and politicians with an appendix of dozens of mini-biographies of Newark's storied women. Barbara J. Kukla, *Defying the Odds: Triumphant Black Women of Newark* (Newark, N.J.: Swing City Press, 2003); Barbara J. Kukla, *Newark Inside My Soul: A Fifty-Year Memoir* (Newark, N.J.: Swing City Press, 2012).

74. Amiri Baraka, *The Autobiography of Leroi Jones* (New York: Freundlich Books, 1984), 13–18, 31, 34–35.

75. *Pittsburgh Courier,* November 29, 1947, January 8, 1949, February 23, 1957 (Vaughan); Elaine M. Hayes, *Queen of Bebop: The Musical Lives of Sarah Vaughan* (New York: Ecco Press, 2017), 20–30.

76. *New York Age,* January 22, 1949; *New York Times,* April 10, 1990. Nona Hendryx of the Bluebelles and later Labelle grew up in a Trenton home where music was a constant presence. See Gillian G. Gaar, *She's a Rebel: The History of Women in Rock & Roll* (Seattle: Seal Press, 1992), 53.

77. *Pittsburgh Courier,* January 29, 1940, February 3, April 13, May 1 (boxing), August 19 (Club Harlem), 1939, June 15 (Basie), June 24 (Paradise Club), 1940, July 12 and 25, August 1, September 5, October 3 and 10, 1942; *New York Age,* August 15, 1953 (AME); *Pittsburgh Courier,* September 29, 1951, December 1, 1951, January 26, 1952 (Walker), January 28, 1952; *New York Age,* October 5 and 26, 1946 (nurses), July 5, 1952 (fraternities), September 24, 1945, September 21, 1946 (Roosevelt); *Pittsburgh Courier,* July 17 and 31, 1948 (real estate), August 21, 1949 (Club Harlem).

78. *Pittsburgh Courier,* November 6, 1949.

79. *New York Age,* March 22, April 12, 1947; *Pittsburgh Courier,* March 22, 1947 (sorority).

80. *Pittsburgh Courier,* July 23, 1948, August 12, September 6, 1952. See also the Atlantic City meeting of the National Order of Negro Undertakers, *Pittsburgh Courier,* August 17 and 24, 1946, for condemnation of southern mobs. See *Pittsburgh Courier,* January 15, 1949; for bowling convention see *Pittsburgh Courier* March 5, 1949.

81. *Pittsburgh Courier,* August 20 and 27, September 3, 1955.

82. *Pittsburgh Courier,* September 3, 1955; Morrow, *Black Man in the White House,* 243–244.

83. *Pittsburgh Courier,* October 2, 1954.

84. *Pittsburgh Courier,* June 25, July 2, 1955.

85. New Jersey State Federation of Colored Women's Clubs, *37th Annual Convention Program,* July 16, 1952, and *Proceedings of the New Jersey Peace, Trade and Jobs*

Conference, Galilee Baptist Church, Newark, May 15, 1954, with associated letters, in Du Bois Papers, Special Collections and University Archives, University of Massachusetts Amherst Libraries; for NAACP conference, see *Pittsburgh Courier*, July 2, 1955.

86. *Pittsburgh Courier*, October 30, 1954.

87. *Pittsburgh Courier*, January 22, 1955.

88. *Pittsburgh Courier*, May 28, June 4, 1955.

89. *Pittsburgh Courier*, November 19, 1966.

90. *Pittsburgh Courier*, March 10 and 31, 1956.

91. *Pittsburgh Courier*, May 28, 1955.

92. Wright, *The Education of Negroes in New Jersey* (Columbia University Press for Teachers College, 1941). Wright's important articles include, among many others, "Educational Programs for the Improvement of Race Relations: Negro Advancement Organizations," *The Journal of Negro Education* 13, no. 3 (1944): 349–360; "Racial Integration in the Public Schools in New Jersey," *The Journal of Negro Education* 23, no. 3 (1954): 282–289; "The Quakers as Social Workers Among the Negroes in New Jersey from 1763–1804," *Bulletin of Friends Historical Association* 30, no. 2 (1941): 79–88; "Extending Civil Rights in New Jersey Through the Division Against Discrimination," *The Journal of Negro History* 38, no. 1 (1953): 91–107; "New Jersey Leads in the Struggle for Educational Integration," *The Journal of Educational Sociology* 26, no. 9 (1953): 401–417; and "A Period of Transition, 1804–1865," *The Journal of Negro History* 28, no. 2 (1943): 176–189.

CHAPTER 7 — THE 1960S–2014

1. For a good account of the 1964 convention, see Nelson Johnson, *The Northside: African Americans and the Making of Atlantic City* (Medford, N.J.: Plexus, 2010), 211–219.

2. Robert Curvin, *Inside Newark: Decline, Rebellion and the Search for Transformation* (New Brunswick: Rutgers University Press, 2014), 66–70.

3. Brad R. Tuttle, *How Newark Became Newark: The Rise, Fall, and Rebirth of an American City* (New Brunswick: Rivergate, 2011), 5–11; *Report of the National Advisory Commission on Civil Disorders* (Kerner Report), (Washington, D.C.: Government Printing Office, 1968), 30–38;

4. *Pittsburgh Courier*, March 17, 1973.

5. Beryl Satter, *Family Properties: Race, Real Estate, and the Exploitation of Black Urban America* (New York: Metropolitan Books, 2009).

6. Howard Gillette Jr., *Camden After the Fall: Decline and Renewal in a Post-Industrial City* (Philadelphia: University of Pennsylvania Press, 2005), 32–61.

7. Daniel M. Johnson, *Black Migration in America: A Social Demographic History* (Durham, N.C.: Duke University Press, 1981), 161; Wright, *Afro-Americans in New Jersey*, appendix 1.

8. Giles R. Wright, *Arrival and Settlement in a New Place* (Trenton: New Jersey Historical Commission, 1986), 15–16, 47; Giles R. Wright, *Looking Back: Eleven Life Histories* (Trenton: New Jersey Historical Commission, 1986), 58–62.

9. Wright, *Looking Back,*18–24.

10. *Pittsburgh Courier,* May 27, 1967, January 23 and 30, February 13, 1971.

11. *Pittsburgh Courier,* January 8, 1966.

12. Thomas J. Sugrue, *Sweet Land of Liberty: The Forgotten Struggle for Civil Rights in the North* (New York: Random House, 2008), 155.

13. Sugrue, *Sweet Land of Liberty,* 455–456.

14. *Pittsburgh Courier,* January 1, May 14, 1966.

15. *Pittsburgh Courier,* February 4, 1966. For similar instances of "firsts," see *Pittsburgh Courier,* April 26, May 3 and 17, 1969, January 24, 1970.

16. Joshua D. Farrington, *Black Republicans and the Transformation of the GOP* (Philadelphia: University of Pennsylvania Press, 2016), 119–122, 143–145, 161–162, 176, 199–201.

17. Cory Booker, *United: Thoughts on Finding Common Ground and Advancing the Common Good* (New York: Ballantine Books, 2016), 7–22.

18. Curvin, *Inside Newark,* 72–75; Julia Rabig, *The Fixers: Devolution, Development and Civil Society in Newark, 1960–1990* (Chicago: University of Chicago Press, 2016), 25, 37.

19. *Pittsburgh Courier,* April 23, 1966.

20. *Pittsburgh Courier,* July 16, 1966.

21. *Pittsburgh Courier,* December 31, 1967.

22. Komozi Woodard, *A Nation Within a Nation: Amiri Baraka (LeRoi Jones and Black Power Politics)* (Chapel Hill: University of North Carolina Press, 1999), 32, 75–78; *Newark Star-Ledger,* July 13, 1967; *Pittsburgh Courier,* July 5, 1968 (Ku Klux Klan); Tom Hayden, *Rebellion in Newark: Official Violence and Ghetto Response* (New York: Vintage Books, 1967), 10; Curvin, *Inside Newark,* 101–114.

23. Woodard, *Nation Within a Nation,* 80–81; Kevin Mumford, *Newark: A History of Race, Rights and Riots in America* (New York: New York University Press, 2007), 98, 125–140; Tuttle, *How Newark Became Newark,* 142–170; *Newark Star-Ledger,* July 14 and 15, 1967; *Pittsburgh Courier,* January 13, 1968, January 4, March 29, June 25, 1969, (Jones/Baraka). Baraka was then accused of receiving a stolen duplicating machine. He was ordered to stand trial on that accusation

24. Mumford, *Newark,* 146–148; Tuttle, *How Newark Became Newark,* 160–162, 164–166, 169; Clark, quoted in Mitchell Duneier, *Ghetto: The Invention of a Place: The History of an Idea* (New York: Hill and Wang, 2016), 125.

25. Kerner Report, 38–41; *Pittsburgh Courier,* November 9 and 16, 1968 (Paterson).

26. Kerner Report, 40–47, 401; for trials, see *Pittsburgh Courier,* September 21, 1968; John Whiteclay Chambers 3rd, *Cranbury: A New Jersey Town from the*

Colonial Era to the Present (New Brunswick, N.J.: Rivergate Books, 2012), 159–162.

27. Ron Porambo, *No Cause for Indictment: An Autopsy of Newark* (New York: Holt, Rinehart and Winston, 1971); Nathan Wright Jr., *Ready to Riot* (New York: Holt, Rinehart and Winston, 1967); Tom Hayden, *Rebellion in Newark: Official Violence and Ghetto Response* (New York: Vintage Books, 1967). For an excellent discussion of Wright and Hayden, see Mark Krasovic, *The Newark Frontier: Community Action in the Great Society* (Chicago: University of Chicago Press, 2015), 228–243.

28. Wright, *Ready to Riot*, 2–3, 7–9, 23, 51, 60–62, 140–141.

29. Thomas J. Sugrue, *The Origins of the Urban Crisis: Race and Inequality in Postwar Detroit* (Princeton: Princeton University Press, 1996).

30. Lizbeth Cohen, *A Consumer's Republic: The Politics of Mass Consumption in Postwar America* (New York: Knopf, 2003), 375–379.

31. Woodard, *Nation Within a Nation*, 2–5; Komozi Woodard, "It's Nation Time in NewArk: Amiri Baraka and the Black Power Experiments in Newark, New Jersey," in *Freedom North: Black Freedom Struggles Outside the South, 1940–1980*, eds. Jeanne F. Theoharis and Komozi Woodard, 287–312 (New York: Palgrave Macmillan, 2003); Daniel Matlin, "'Lift Up Yr Self!,' Reinterpreting Amiri Baraka (LeRoi Jones), Black Power, and the Uplift Tradition," *Journal of American History* 93, no. 1 (2006): 91–116; *Pittsburgh Courier*, July 5, 1968; Curvin, *Inside Newark*, 111–115; Rabig, *Fixers*, 4–10. On Attucks, see Mitch Kachun, *First Martyr of Liberty: Crispus Attucks in American Memory* (New York: Oxford University Press, 2017), 166–168.

32. Mumford, *Newark*, 6.

33. Krasovic, *Newark Frontier*, 7–10, 35, 279–291; Rabig, *Fixers*, 3–8.

34. Kerner Report, 73–76.

35. *Pittsburgh Courier*, July 29, August 5, 1967; Krasovic, *Newark Frontier*, 232–237.

36. *Pittsburgh Courier*, April 19, 1969; *New York Times*, February 24, 2005 (obituary).

37. *Pittsburgh Courier*, July 26, August 9, 1969.

38. *Pittsburgh Courier*, August 16, 1969, May 9, 1970.

39. *Pittsburgh Courier*, June 25, 1969, January 6, 1973.

40. *Pittsburgh Courier*, March 16, April 20, 1968.

41. *Pittsburgh Courier*, September 7, December 21 and 28, 1968, February 7, 1970.

42. *Pittsburgh Courier*, November 23, 1968, August 23, 1969, April 4, 1970.

43. For a full balanced account, see https://en.wikipedia.org/wiki/Assata_Shakur.

44. Ruben "Hurricane" Carter, *The Sixteenth Round* (New York: Viking Press, 1975); Paul B. Wice, *Rubin "Hurricane" Carter and the American Justice System* (New Brunswick, N.J.: Rutgers University Press, 2000).

45. *Pittsburgh Courier*, April 4, 1970.

46. *Pittsburgh Courier*, August 16, 1969.

47. *Pittsburgh Courier*, April 4, 1970.

48. *Pittsburgh Courier*, August 2, 1969.

49. *Pittsburgh Courier*, April 16, 1966, December 6, 13, and 27, 1969, January 24, 1970, March 28, May 16, 1970.

50. *Pittsburgh Courier*, May 23, July 11, 1970.

51. *Pittsburgh Courier*, January 1, 1972; Curvin, *Inside Newark*, 129, 135, 160–164.

52. *Pittsburgh Courier*, July 10, 1971.

53. *Pittsburgh Courier*, July 10, 1971.

54. Ravi K. Perry, *Black Mayors, White Majorities: The Balancing Act of Racial Politics* (Lincoln: University of Nebraska Press, 2013), introduction.

55. *Pittsburgh Courier*, July 24, 1971.

56. *Pittsburgh Courier*, July 1, 1972.

57. James Smethurst, *The Black Arts Movement: Literary Nationalism in the 1960s and 1970s* (Chapel Hill: University of North Carolina Press, 2005); Michael Simanga, *Amiri Baraka and the Congress of African People: History and Memory* (New York: Palgrave Macmillan, 2015).

58. Steve Golin, *The Newark Teachers' Strikes: Hope on the Line* (New Brunswick, N.J.: Rutgers University Press, 2002); Curvin, *Inside Newark*, 166–170.

59. *New York Times*, May 12, 1999: Barbara J. Kukla, *Defying the Odds: Triumphant Black Women of Newark* (West Orange, N.J.: Swing City Press, 2005), 135–156.

60. http://blackdemographics.com/culture/black-politics/black-mayors/.

61. *Pittsburgh Courier*, May 24, 1974; Junius Williams, *Unfinished Agenda: Urban Politics in the Era of Black Power* (Berkeley, CA: North Atlantic Books, 2014); Curvin, *Inside Newark*, 177–183; Rabig, *Fixers*, 89–93, 101–113.

62. Douglas S. Massey, et al., *Climbing Mount Laurel: The Struggle for Affordable Housing and Social Mobility in an American Suburb* (Princeton: Princeton University Press, 2013); Richard C. Holmes, "Southern Burlington NAACP v. Township of Mount Laurel (1975): Establishing a Right to Affordable Housing Throughout the State by Confronting the Inequality Demon," in *Courting Justice: Ten New Jersey Cases that Shook the Nation*, ed. Paul Tractenberg, 45–77 (New Brunswick, N.J.: Rutgers University Press, 2013); Gillette, *Camden After the Fall*, 175–187.

63. Paul L. Tractenberg, "New Jersey's School Funding Litigation, Robinson v. Cahill and Abbott v. Burke," *Courting Justice: Ten New Jersey Cases that Shook the Nation*, ed. Paul L. Tractenberg, 195–233 (New Brunswick, N.J.: Rutgers University Press, 2013).

64. Watterson, *I Hear My People Singing*, 112.

65. *Pittsburgh Courier*, May 4, 11, and 18, June 29, 1968, April 5, 1969 (Princeton), October 19, 1968 (King), January 11, 1969 (football), July 8, 1969 (trustee); *New Pittsburgh Courier*, September 27, 1971.

66. Emily Raboteau, *The Professor's Daughter, A Novel* (New York: Henry Holt, 2005).

67. Michael Moffat, *Coming of Age in New Jersey: College and American Culture* (New Brunswick, N.J.: Rutgers University Press, 1989), 143–155; *Pittsburgh Courier*, March 14, 1970. On Harris, see Paul G. E. Clemens, *Rutgers Since 1945: A History of the State University of New Jersey* (New Brunswick, N.J.: Rutgers University Press, 2015), 168–171.

68. Clement A. Price, *Freedom Not Far Distant: A Documentary History of Afro-Americans in New Jersey* (Newark: New Jersey Historical Society, 1980). For a summary of Price's life and career, see https://en.wikipedia.org/wiki/Clement_Alexander _Price. For Bunch, see https://en.wikipedia.org/wiki/Lonnie_Bunch; on Crew, see https://robinsonprofessors.gmu.edu/about/spencer-crew/.

69. Douglas S. Massey and Nancy A. Denton, *American Apartheid: Segregation and the Making of an Underclass* (Cambridge, Mass.: Harvard University Press, 1993), 48, 71, 77.

70. *Pittsburgh Courier*, April 10, 1971.

71. Tuttle, *How Newark Became Newark*, 221; Andra Gillespie, *The New Black Politician: Cory Booker, Newark, and Post-Racial America* (New York: New York University Press, 2012), 48–49; Sharpe James, *Political Prisoner: A Memoir* (Newark, N.J.: Nutany, 2013); Curvin, *Inside Newark*, 180–184.

72. Jean Ayon, *Ghetto Schooling: A Political Economy of Urban Educational Reform* (New York: Teachers College Press, 1997).

73. *New York Times*, March 6, 2012, https://www.govtrack.us/congress/members /NJ/10.

74. Bryant Simon, *Boardwalk of Dreams: Atlantic City and the Fate of Urban America* (New York: Oxford University Press, 2004), 83–132.

75. Gillette, *Camden After the Fall*, 140–143.

76. Gillette, *Camden After the Fall*, 244–250.

77. Jeffrey M. Dorwart, *Cape May County: The Making of an American Resort Community* (New Brunswick, N.J.: Rutgers University Press, 1992), 261–262.

78. Juliet E. K. Walker, *The History of Black Business in America: Capitalism, Race, Entrepreneurship* (New York: Macmillan Reference, 1998), 289.

79. *Pittsburgh Courier*, August 12, 1972.

80. Gretchen Sullivan Sorin, "'Respectable People': Growing up Black in the New Jersey Suburbs," *Teenage New Jersey, 1941–1975*, ed. Kathryn Grover, 37–49 (Newark: New Jersey Historical Society, 1997); Pamela Newkirk, "Ode to Black Fathers," June 2016, author's collection.

81. George Clinton with Ben Greenman, *Brothas Be, Yo Like George: Ain't that Funkin' Kinda Hard on You* (New York: Atria Books, 2014), 5–55; on Worrell, see his obituary in the *New York Times*, June 22, 2016; for Fugees, see Cameron Lazerine and Devin Lazerine, *Rap-Up: The Ultimate Guide to Hip-Hop and R&B* (New York: Grand Central, 2008), and Chris Nickson, *Lauryn Hill: She's Got That Thing* (New York: St. Martin's, 1999); Wyclef Jean with Anthony Bozza, *Purpose: An Immigrant's Story* (New York: It Books, 2012); https://www.youtube.com/watch?v=zJ-gI7Pz2_M.

82. Gillian A. Gaar, *She's a Rebel: A History of Women in Rock and Roll* (Seattle: Seal Press, 1992), 339; Cissy Houston, *How Sweet the Sound: My Life with God and Gospel* (New York: Bantam Doubleday, 1998), and *Remembering Whitney: My Story of Love, Loss, and the Night the Music Stopped* (New York: HarperCollins, 2013); Dionne Warwick, *My Life As I See It* (New York: Atria Books, 2010); for Regina Belle, see *Ebony Magazine*, June 1990.

83. For Horton, see Lois Horton (widow) email to author, April 10, 2017; Yvonne S. Thornton, *The Ditchdigger's Daughters: A Black Family's Astonishing Success Story* (New York: Birch Lane Books, 1995), and *Something to Prove: A Daughter's Journey to Fulfill a Father's Legacy* (New York: Kaplan Publishing, 2010).

84. Gaar, *She's a Rebel*, 422.

85. Queen Latifah with Karen Hunter, *Ladies First: Revelations of a Strong Woman* (New York: William Morrow, 1999), 15–16, 47–56, 90–92, 100.

86. Clarence Clemons and Don Reo, *Big Man: Real Life and Tall Tales* (New York: Grand Central Publishing, 2009), 26–28, 33–34, 46–48.

87. *Pittsburgh Courier*, July 8, 1967.

88. Ice-T, *A Memoir of Gangster Life and Redemption: From South Central to Hollywood* (New York: Ballantine Books, 2011), 4–7.

89. *Manchester Guardian*, September 11, 2009.

90. Shaquille O'Neal, *Shaq Uncut: My Story* (New York: Grand Central Publishing, 2011); Carl Lewis, *Inside Track: Autobiography of Carl Lewis* (New York: Simon and Schuster, 2013); Donald Kowet, *Franco Harris* (New York: Coward and McCann, 1977); Dennis Rodman and Tim Keowne, *Bad As I Want to Be* (New York: Delacorte, 1996); https://en.wikipedia.org/wiki/Joetta_Clark_Diggs; http://www.joettasports andbeyond.com/about/team/.https://patch.com/new-jersey/woodbridge/meet-20 -olympians-new-jersey; *NJ.com*, July 15, 2016.

91. Mike Kelly, *Color Lines: The Troubled Dreams of Racial Harmony in an American Town* (New York: William Morrow, 1995).

92. Angus Kress Gillespie and Michael Aaron Rockland, *Looking for America on the New Jersey Turnpike* (New Brunswick: Rutgers University Press, 1989); Paul Heaton, "Understanding the Effects of Antiprofiling Policies," *Journal of Law and Economics* 53, no. 1 (2010): 29–64; Williams's quotes from Samuel R. Gross and Katherine Y. Barnes, "Road Work: Racial Profiling and Drug Interdiction on the Highway,"

Michigan Law Review 101, no. 3 (2002): 651–754. For surveys and settlement, see *New York Times*, May 10, 1998, November 24, 2000, February 3, 2001.

93. For incarceration rates, see http://en.wikipedia.org/wiki/List_of_U.S._states _by_incarceration_rate. For percentages, see Marie Van Nostrand, *New Jersey Jail Population Analysis: Identifying Opportunities to Safely and Responsibly Reduce the Jail Population* (St. Petersburg, Fla.: Luminosity, 2013); https://www.drugpolicy.org /sites/default/files/New_Jersey_Jail_Population_Analysis_March_2013.pdf.

94. John E. Pinkard, Sr., *African American Felon Disenfranchisement: Case Studies in Modern Racism and Political Exclusion* (El Paso, TX: Scholarly Publishing, 2013), 77–79.

95. Pinkard, *African American Felon Disenfranchisement*, 85–90.

96. Pinkard, *African American Felon Disenfranchisement*, 22. For Rock's "selfies," see http://www.usmagazine.com/celebrity-news/news/chris-rock-takes-selfies -when-pulled-over-by-police-photos-201524; Alice Goffman, *On the Run: Fugitive Life in an American City* (Chicago: University of Chicago Press, 2014). I am aware of the harsh criticisms this book has received, but do not believe their comments about her data collection and possible criminal collaboration disprove the fundamental tenets of the book. For recent data, see *NewJersey.com*, June 27, 2016.

97. Matthew Desmond, *Evicted: Poverty and Profit in the American City* (New York: Crown, 2016).

98. Jeff Hobbs, *The Short and Tragic Death of Robert Peace: Brilliant Young Man Who Left Newark for the Ivy League* (New York: Scribners, 2014).

99. Sampson Davis, George Jenkins, and Rameck Hunt, *The Pact: Three Young Men Make a Promise and Fulfill a Dream* (New York: Riverhead Books, 2002).

100. *Newark Star-Ledger*, May 10, 2006; *New York Times*, June 6, 2006. See also Gillespie, *New Black Politician*, 193, and Jonathan L. Wharton, *A Post-Racial Change Is Gonna Come: Newark, Cory Booker, and the Transformation of Urban America* (New York: Palgrave Macmillan, 2013), 42–65, esp. 45; Booker, *United*, 86.

CHAPTER 8 — PRESENT AND FUTURE

1. *Newark Star-Ledger*, January 9, 2014; Jelani Cobb, "Cory Booker Never Spoke for Newark Like Amiri Baraka Did," *New Republic*, January 21, 2014.

2. *Newark Star-Ledger*, November 8, 2014; *New York Times*, November 8, 2014.

3. *Newark Star-Ledger*, May 14 and 19, 2014.

4. Dale Rusakoff, *The Prize: Who's in Charge of America's Schools?* (New York: Houghton Mifflin, 2015); Robert Curvin, *Inside Newark: Decline, Rebellion and the Search for Transformation* (New Brunswick: Rutgers University Press, 2014), 262–265.

5. Ravi Perry, *Black Mayors, White Majorities* (Lincoln: University of Nebraska Press, 2014), introduction.

6. *New York Times*, March 30, 2016; *Newark Star-Ledger*, October 2, 2016; *WNYC*, January 9, 2017; for black mayors as managers, see Cornel West, *Race Matters* (Boston: Beacon Books, 1993), 59.

7. *Newark Star-Ledger*, October 17 and 30, 2013, May 4, 2014.

8. http://www.njcommunityresources.info/njlegislators.html.

9. *New Jersey.com*, April 25, 2016.

10. http://www.middlesexcountynj.gov/Government/ElectedOfficials/Pages /Sheriff-Scott.aspx.

11. http://www.njleg.state.nj.us/members/bio.asp?Leg=242; *New York Times*, November 8, 2017.

12. https://watsoncoleman.house.gov; https://en.wikipedia.org/wiki/New_Jersey %27s_12th_congressional_district.

13. https://www.facebook.com/blackmayorsallianceinnj/.

14. http://www.state.nj.us/highereducation/statistics/.

15. https://www.supportblackowned.com/states/nj; U.S. Census Bureau, 2000–2015 American Community Survey posted by New Jersey Black Chamber of Commerce, 2017; http://www.merck.com/about/leadership/home.html; https://www.blackentrepreneurprofile.com/fortune-500-ceos/.

16. Pew Research Center, *On Views of Race and Inequality, Blacks and Whites Are Worlds Apart*, June 27, 2016; *New York Times*, February 10, 2010, June 30, 2016; *New Jersey.com*, June 4, 2013, May 24, 2015; Greg Flaxman, et al., "A Status Quo of Segregation: Racial and Economic Imbalance in New Jersey Schools, 1989–2010," Civil Rights Project Series on Segregation in East Coast Schools, no. 4 (Los Angeles: UCLA, 2013); Kendra Bischoff and Sean F. Reardon, *Residential Segregation by Income, 1970–2009* (New York: Russell Sage Foundation, 2013).

17. *NewJersey.com*, June 27, 2016.

18. UCLA Civil Rights Project, quoted on *Wordpress.com*, May 23, 2015; Richard D. Kahlenberg, Halley Potter, and Kimberly Quick, "Why Private School Vouchers Could Exacerbate School Segregation," tcf.org, December 19, 2016, https:// tcf.org/content/commentary/private-school-vouchers-exacerbate-school -segregation/; *New York Times*, February 18, 2010.

19. *New York Times*, February 25, March 31, May 2, 2016.

20. *Vice*, March 9, 2016.

21. *NewJersey.com*, January 24, June 9, 2017.

22. Michael Dawson, "African American Politics from the Civil Rights to the Present," in *The Oxford Handbook of African American Citizenship, 1865–Present*, ed. Henry Louis Gates, et al., 492–518 (New York: Oxford University Press, 2012); Peniel E. Joseph, ed., *Neighborhood Rebels: Black Power at the Local Level* (New York: Palgrave Macmillan, 2010).

Index

Unless otherwise noted, all geographic references are to New Jersey.

About the Author

GRAHAM RUSSELL GAO HODGES is the George Dorland Langdon Jr., Professor of History and Africana Studies at Colgate University. He is the author or editor of seventeen books including *Root and Branch: African Americans in New York and East Jersey, 1613–1863*, and *Slavery and Freedom in the Rural North: African Americans in Monmouth County, New Jersey, 1665–1865*.